SO-BDN-265

"Fascinating and timely." —Tracy Kidder

"A fine example of literary and psychological investigation. . . .
It wrenches the heart. Yet it is neither maudlin nor excessive.
It is affectionate but dispassionate, and it reaches its
conclusions calmly."
—Jonathan Yardley, *New York Times Book Review* (front page)

"A deeply compassionate double portrait of the artist in
creation and in crisis. An extraordinary achievement."
—Mel Gussow, *Newsday*

"Leggett has told us more about the tragedy of American
Success than a dozen novelists could."
—Frederick Exley

"A riveting, utterly engrossing psychological probe."
—*Publishers Weekly*

"If, as Jimmy Walker once said, no woman was ever ruined by
a book, men have nonetheless been killed by them. . . . In
these two case histories of obsession and ruin, Leggett reveals
much about ambition, vanity, and the self-destructiveness that
often accompany literary success in America.
This is a compelling book."
—Peter S. Prescott, *Newsweek*

"John Leggett has written the literary biography of Ross
Lockridge and Tom Heggen, and of our age as well."
—Jerome Klinkowitz, *Chicago Tribune*

"A powerful and engrossing picture."
—Francis Steegmuller

"A distinguished literary event."
—Robert Downing, *Denver Post*

"For writers and aspiring writers (and how many of us are not in the latter category?), this book is indispensable reading. . . . No one who has had anything to do with the literary life in America—or, for that matter, with the pursuit of achievement in America—can fail to hear the relevant echoes. The book, quite apart from its fascinating narrative, its Rashomon quality of detection, has as much to say about the nature and quality of ourselves as about the two protagonists."
—Robert Kirsch, *Los Angeles Times*

ROSS
AND TOM

Books by John Leggett

NOVELS   *Wilder Stone*
           The Gloucester Branch
           Who Took the Gold Away

BIOGRAPHY   Ross and Tom

ROSS
AND TOM

Two American Tragedies

by JOHN LEGGETT

DA CAPO PRESS

Copyright © 1974 by John Leggett

All rights reserved. No part of this publication may be reproduced, stored in a retrieval system, or transmitted, in any form or by any means, electronic, mechanical, photocopying, recording, or otherwise, without the prior written permission of the publisher. Printed in the United States of America.

A CIP catalog record for this book is available from the Library of Congress.
ISBN 0-306-80992-3

First Da Capo Press Edition 2000

Published by Da Capo Press
A Member of the Perseus Books Group
http://www.dacapopress.com

1 2 3 4 5 6 7 8 9 10——04 03 02 01 00

TO NAN TALESE

Author's Note

I am a novelist and I believe that forceful biography employs all the techniques of the novel; those of setting, narrative, characterization and subjectivity. I believe in the biographer's right, within a limit, to portray his subject's reaction to experience, and the limit is truth, insofar as that can be determined from evidence.

I have spent seven years collecting and assessing the evidence for this book and wherever I have failed my subjects it is not for lack of seeking the truth about them.

Their own books provide a great deal. Each is written out of its author's whole consciousness, so that *Raintree County* is a revelation of Ross Lockridge's restless spirit and his vision of America, just as *Mister Roberts* is Tom Heggen's own consuming conflict and the tragicomedy which was his conception of the world.

Their unpublished writing—letters, notes and stories—as well as public and official records provide more. But the greatest source of information about them has been those who knew them best. I am particularly grateful to members of the Lockridge and Heggen families; to Laurence, Anne, Francis and Betty Wylie, Warren Tryon, Richard Scowcroft, John McCaffery, Carol Brandt, Malcolm and Ruth Correll, and Curtis Lamorey for their recollections of Ross Lockridge; to Carol Lynn Yellin, Wallace Stegner, Budd Schulberg, Helen Parker, Joshua Logan, the late Leland Hayward, Max Shulman, Charles Roberts, Victor Cohn, Vera Lawrence Harper, Peter and Barbara Cary, James Awe, Alfred Jones and Robert Litman for their recollections of Tom Heggen;

7

and to my former colleagues at Houghton Mifflin for their recollections of publishing both writers.

I am further indebted to Budd Schulberg's *The Four Seasons of Success* (Doubleday), to Houghton Mifflin Company for permission to quote from *Raintree County*, and to the Christopher Morley Knothole Collection in the Bryant Library, Roslyn, New York, for permission to quote from Christopher Morley's letter about *Raintree County*.

ROSS AND TOM

I

Taking my life is inconceivable to me. I shall lose it soon enough. To abandon even one of my allotted minutes might be to miss some important or funny thing, perhaps even the point.

Also—and there is a connection—I am ambitious. I have been bred to "getting ahead," to the belief that if I fall behind, shame and starvation will catch me, but if I achieve some thing I will be looked after, admired and loved in perpetuity. Long ago I accepted these as the rules of the game. I only quarrel with them when the score is running against me.

Sometime during World War II I decided to have my achievement as a writer. It took me five years and a fat swatch of rejection slips to find out how hard that was and, in frustration, to take a job with a book publisher.

Thus it was in Houghton Mifflin's warren overlooking Boston Common that I learned about a dark side of achievement—how, a few years earlier, two young novelists, just my age and no more promising in background, had been published so successfully that their first books made them rich and famous. Then, at the peak of their acclaim, they died.

The first, Ross Lockridge, took his own life, locking his new garage doors behind his new Kaiser and asphyxiating himself. The second, Thomas Heggen, drowned in his bathwater—an accident, it was claimed, but it was the accident of a desperate man.

Tom and Ross were similar in that neither had any previous notoriety and they came from obscure, middle-class, Midwest backgrounds. Yet as men they could not have been more different.

Ross was an oak of prudence and industry. He rarely drank and he never smoked. He excelled at everything he did. He had married his hometown sweetheart, was proudly faithful to her and produced four fine children. After a sampling of success on both coasts he had gone home to the Indiana of his parents and childhood friends.

Tom Heggen had a taste for low life. He had been divorced, had no children and shared bachelor quarters in New York with an ex-actor and screenwriter, Dorothy Parker's estranged husband, Alan Campbell. Tom was a drinker and a pill addict. He turned up regularly at the fashionable restaurant "21," usually bringing along a new girl, a dancer or an actress.

After the success of their first novels, neither Ross nor Tom had been able to start a new book. At the time of their deaths neither had written anything in months.

What had happened to them? There were grumblings that some villainy of Houghton Mifflin's had done Ross Lockridge in, that in publishing his huge novel, Raintree County, the firm had exploited him, somehow threatened both his income and his privacy. (There had been a quarrel and Ross had made unpleasant accusations.)

Could it have been fatigue—had the two novelists written themselves out, found they had nothing more to say? Or was it disappointment: had the finished book—or in Heggen's case the dramatic version of Mister Roberts which was then playing on Broadway—fallen short of some original notion of perfection? There are always spoilers. Raintree County's first reviews had called it a masterpiece and compared its author to Thomas Wolfe, but these were followed by some contemptuous ones, and there had been a denouncement by a Jesuit priest which struck at Ross's own self-doubts.

Still, none of these sounded as likely an explanation as that of the bitch-goddess herself—the writer spoiled by success, his need to write smothered in a surfeit of reward. Clearly there is something disillusioning in attainment. Many writers (such as J. D. Salinger and James Gould Cozzens, among others) drift into unproductivity after a big, popular success, just as the very productive ones such as Henry James are often those who pursue, yet never quite attain, an enthusiastic public embrace.

There is still another area for conjecture. Suppose that Tom Heggen's and Ross Lockridge's final act was not one of surrender at all, but defiance. Perhaps success had brought them to some promontory from which they could see the whole of their path and from there they had made this appalling comment about it. What could so disillusion them about that view? I needed to know. If they were rejecting their own incentives, they were, so far as I knew, rejecting mine.

Searching for an entryway to their spirits, I drew a professional comparison. Lockridge was a Vesuvius. When he was at work, twenty or thirty pages spewed from his typewriter each day, some on their way to the wastebasket, others to be revised, endlessly before they were satisfactory, but always expanding. Progress toward a desired shape was by laying on more material.

Heggen was the reverse, a distiller. The molding was a prelude to writing and was done in his head. He would sit by the hour, staring out a window, so that a passerby would think him daydreaming. But then he would turn to his typewriter and strike a flawless passage, each word and inflection so precisely chosen there was no need for revision.

But in spite of this difference in the way they worked, Ross and Tom appeared to be equally single-minded about writing, each compelled to it with a force that dwarfed the other elements of his life. Thus the common experience preceding their deaths, of wanting to write again and not being able to, is significant. The being able to—the energy—is the essential part of incentive and I had the impression they had lost that, knew they had lost it and knew that without it they were useless men.

What is a writer's incentive? That he has a gift for expression in words can be taken for granted; but I suspect that gift doesn't contribute half so much to motivation as social failure. I know that my own feelings of inadequacy and shyness were first routed when, in the third grade, my piece on tadpoles appeared in the school paper, and I suspect that only a man who doubts the persuasiveness of his tongue and fists would sit alone dirtying good paper when he could be in company.

Wanting to write fiction has even more elaborate roots and these reach not just into a writer's present reveries but back into his childhood. When he is read to, when he is sick and is brought an adventure book with his medicine, a child gets a first set of furnishings for his dream world. When he graduates to adult novels his debt to fiction is increased by a more utilitarian, though still romantic, vision of himself and a way to behave. If he chooses wisely and is lucky in the library he can find dream enough to sustain him for a lifetime.

But the path of a writer is too lonely and discouraging for any kind of propulsion but the hugest. In an essay on Willa Cather, Leon Edel notes that for her novel about an ambitious opera singer, *The Song of the Lark*, she chose the epigraph "It was a wondrous lovely storm that drove me," and that this was not only appropriate for Thea, the heroine, but for the author.

"It was a wondrous, lovely storm that drove Willa Cather," he says, "and what she cared for above all was the storm. With success achieved . . . she felt depressed. She didn't know what to do with success; or rather, she seems to have experienced a despair altogether out of proportion to the actual circumstances of her achievement . . . Success, by the very testimony of the tales she wrote, created for Willa Cather a deep despair and even a wish for death . . ."

Willa Cather's experience of depression in achievement makes a striking parallel with Ross's and Tom's. And I cannot find a better description for the kind of force a novelist wants to contain than "the wondrous lovely storm." It is vague, yet so evocative of the emotion and energy that can bring forth a significant book—

wondrous in its mysterious origin and awesome power, lovely because it is not terrifying at all, but blissful, as though it is love itself.

When I first looked into Tom Heggen's and Ross Lockridge's lives, seeking some clues to their deaths, I found myself in barren country. Neither had the nature for casual confessions nor the kind of apprenticeships which called for public self-examinations. An even bigger difficulty lay with those who had known them best. They suffered from having been present at, yet unable to prevent, a tragedy. Understandably the families were wary of talking about the darker, human parts of the natures and experiences of the two writers.

Still, inconsequential, even irrelevant details about them intrigued me. Instead of flagging, my interest grew. Occasionally I felt I might be guilty of dancing on their graves, a jig for my own compensating survival. But what most absorbed me was self-discovery.

Ross, Tom and I grew up to the same music, worshiping the same idols, suffering from the same inhibitions. It was remarkably easy for me to slip into their adolescent skins. As an adult and a writer, I could recognize in those highs of self-certainty, in those plunging lows of self-doubt, my own emotional weather. Finally, in each of their natures—one black, reckless; the other a marching band of virtues—I saw two halves of my own.

As I write, Tom's father is still alive, as are his sisters and his former wife. So too, Ross's wife and four children survive him. Today both men are as esteemed by and as dear to their families as when they lived, so at the outset I am caught between my obligations to the living and to the dead. But in the end it is truth I'm after and for that I must depend on my own interpretations and my own conscience. Thus this book is an unauthorized biography, and its views are my own.

ROSS

II

Although I would have preferred that Houghton Mifflin Company publish rather than hire me, it was not my choice and I was glad enough to be there in 1950 starting an apprenticeship.

The firm had the crust and pride of a distinguished Boston family and I felt like a parvenu marrying into it. The boss was Henry Laughlin, a Pittsburgh steel Laughlin, with a handsome, bright-pink face, a foam of white hair and a gruff kindliness that made him the consummate paterfamilias. Publishing Winston Churchill was his pride but printing was his joy and there was no question as to which of Houghton's three divisions he loved most.

At a sign of trouble from the Riverside Press he was off like a fire chief, heading his black Jaguar across the Charles. On the scene he would huddle with the foreman and then, to the pressmen's delight, crawl right into the jaws of the huge flat-bed press to see the problem for himself.

He kept a stable at his house in Concord and on a wintry morning his horse fell and rolled on him, breaking Henry's hip and leaving him in the freezing woods. It was half a day before they found H.A.L., but no horse could keep him from the company party he had planned nor from greeting us at the door. On crutches, a metal pin in his hip, he welcomed us as he always did, calling each of us, each of our wives, by first name and making us feel there was some kind of blood relationship among us all.

The blood was blue and had its obligations. We were not, of course, immune to familial jealousies and resentments, but they were decently clothed. We were gentlemen. Ours was a business, but the business was books and that made a difference. Our purpose was to make money, but not at the expense of principles. There was no need.

The firm's headquarters was a brownstone building which overlooked the Common from 2 Park Street. A lacy, iron cage rose and descended through its six floors with seemly languor, bearing members of educational and trade departments on their errands. While the educational department was ten times more profitable, we of trade, dealing with fiction and nonfiction, felt so superior that we scarcely spoke to our opposite numbers. We felt that texts, in their utilitarian purpose and predictable market, were not really books at all.

The trade department's head, Lovell Thompson, was the gentlest, most bemused Bostonian ever to put his trust in the power of reason. Feet crossed on his pile of correspondence, he was ever ready to speculate about readers and books.

Paul Brooks was editor-in-chief. He was a preoccupied, Lincolnesque man, an outdoorsman and devoted naturalist. His voice was deeply resonant and, heard approaching in the halls, it was the sound of thunder at a picnic.

Over Paul's desk hung a drawing of an Indian and a frontiersman in a fierce embrace, each choking the other. It was titled "The Author-Publisher Relationship," suggesting this was the lair of a whimsical man. It was not. Sitting at the corner of that desk a journeyman could learn some cold common sense about publishing and authors, and some charity too, but one did not linger. There was urgency here. In Paul's dark, penetrating eyes there was a constant awareness of his responsibility, surely the gravest and most vulnerable, of deciding which books to include on the list.

Dorothy Hillyer was managing editor and true queen of the third floor or, as the stationery described it, "the editorial rooms."

She was a huge woman with a fair, delicate face and a beguiling Beacon Hill voice, precise as Mozart, yet cajoling and rather flirtatious.

My own feelings about Dorothy were mixed. Aware of her influence and as subject as the other men to her spell, I was always trying to please her, even after a peek in the files disclosed it was her distaste for my novel that had jettisoned it.

Laurette Murdoch, a tentative but no less appealing gentlewoman, was a copy editor who, each Thursday, offered us a one-dollar lunch. The site was her spacious studio, three rickety flights above a Chinese laundry at the top of Pinckney Street. Laurette's guest list was select but drawn from each of the three publishing functions: editorial, production/design, and promotion. Sitting around her table, flushed with wine and shoptalk, I grasped one essential truth about the business, that for all its technicalities it was an intensely human performance.

While the editorial people predominated, they were quiet about guiding theory, except for the one which holds that excellence, while no assurance of success, is usually an ingredient. Clearly, whether a book is good, or even salable, is subjective and I guessed that the matter of choosing which to pass up and which to publish was too sensitive for interdepartment conversation.

I had the impression that the choosing was an emotional act, rarely done without agony, and it usually led to progressive doubts and anxieties. The topic was surely skirted at the lunches and yet the process was plain enough.

The first readers, moody girls with untidy hair, waded away the weeks in the dismal swamp of submissions, but when one did pluck out a manuscript she would come into Laurette's radiant with infatuation, even as she paled at the sight of the course it must run before being given a Houghton imprint.

The grayer, more skeptical heads had memories of other seasons which stretched into our past like a regimental history, each marked with its victories and defeats. Here and there were monuments, but anonymous cemeteries reached like cornfields for the horizon.

Houghton did well with fiction and we published a great deal
of it. Novels accounted for nearly half the list and each season we
offered a variety. There was usually one dependable performer, an
Anya Seton or a Lloyd Douglas. If we were lucky there was a
critic's darling, a James Agee or a Carson McCullers, and there
were always debuts, young men and women being readied for first
publication and, just possibly, a career.

The job of the whole group, the younger members particularly, was to bring along the new writers, to make them a con-
stituency. Success was a contagion most likely to begin within the
house, a personal enthusiasm that sprang like joy and affection
between two or three of us. So we were alert to fresh winds, eager
to have an opinion and to give odds on the chances; we were quick
with approval, but private, even conspiratorial, with doubts.

Dorothy Hillyer was articulate and decisive about new fiction.
She was easily moved herself and had a feeling for the public heart.
She was so sure of her instincts that the men deferred to her. She
could be wrong about a new novelist, of course, but whatever the
result of her hunches they lost none of their Delphic authority, and
Paul Brooks, who was far more at home with nonfiction, depended
on her judgments. It was a Jack Spratt relationship.

Among publishers, Houghton was unique in not delegating
editorial authority. Paul Brooks was alone at the top of the pyra-
mid and although he acted on the judgments a manuscript collected on its way to him, Paul alone decided.

At Laurette's the designers and production people made up a
second guild and we could defer to it, fondling a new book, riffling
its newly cut pages, sniffing at the mint freshness of ink and glue,
each of us an art critic and typographer as we examined jacket and
title page. But printing failed to hold our attention for long.

By all odds, the favorite subject of the group was the final
publishing function of selling. The salesmen were our proselytes
and they came home from their travels to be sprinkled with our
enthusiasm for the new list and, incidentally, to bring us news of
the last.

As we lingered over our coffee cups, shading our eyes from the bath of afternoon light (there was always some trouble with the huge windowshade meant to diffuse it), we were hypnotized by travelers' tales of what became of our books, how they fared out there in the real world of the market.

I remember how appalled we were to learn that some bookstore owners were massively indifferent to what our Radcliffe girls thought enlightening; they had made their selections with the taste of a specific customer in mind, one for each copy.

Our failures were buried in a common grave as quickly as decency permitted and we did not linger over requiems, but our hearts would bound again like jackrabbits at a success story, one of our own, or one drifting in from New York, some fresh commotion at Knopf or Harper's.

We probed the antecedents of the season's winners looking for the explanation, some thumbrule to guide us, attributing it to a piece of preposterous publicity luck, a clever advertising campaign, an attractive dust jacket or perhaps the harvesttime of an author's career. But answers were maddeningly elusive and in the end a book's popularity had to be written off to a particular, and probably temporary, thirst of the public.

Talk of best sellers inevitably led to gossip and conjecture about our own authors and particularly to our mysterious, double-doored legend of Ross Lockridge and Tom Heggen. When their names were mentioned there was always a pause in the merriment, as though a cloud had passed across the great slant of glass overhead. It was the recurring feeling that their deaths might in fact be laid to our avidness for success and our manipulating of such promotional machinery as had just been entrusted to me.

I brought this melancholy curiosity about Ross Lockridge back to my office one afternoon and fetched his publicity folder out of my file. On top, an editorial from the *Washington Post* puzzled over the irony of Lockridge's suicide, noting that although *Raintree County* had set off a moral controversy and some critics had scored its length and diffuseness, critics had been almost unanimous in their praise of the book's passionate, lyric vision of America. It was as important a debut as any in recent years and it had made Lockridge rich and famous. What more could he ask?

The *Post's* editorial pointed out that a major theme of the book was its repudiation of materialism and affirmation of faith in the American dream and destiny. How, the *Post's* editorialist asked, had Lockridge himself lost that hope and optimism?

I unfolded the *Raintree County* reviews. They were of a prominence and profusion that is no longer seen. Although it was a first novel by an unknown author the critical community had joined to celebrate the book's publication. With the *Life* excerpts, the huge MGM prize and the Book-of-the-Month selection it had become an institution even before publication day, shimmering on high ground beyond the reach of detractors.

James Hilton had opened his review on the cover of the *New York Herald Tribune* book section by suggesting that *Raintree County's* impact on America would be similar to that of Sinclair Lewis's *Main Street*, since both books had appeared at the close of a great war to offer America a self-portrait, towering in victory and prosperity over a shattered world.

The Sunday *New York Times* added its laurel wreath, describing *Raintree County* as a work of art, enormously complex and with a cosmic, brooding purpose. Even the skeptical critics agreed that Lockridge had fashioned a triumphant hero: John Wesley Shawnessy was outsize, yet touchingly human.

I could recall that in 1948, the year *Raintree County* was published, I had carried it along on my honeymoon, and that Shawnessy had won me very early in the book with his feelings toward women. He was desirous, yet sensibly shy of the creatures. He carried such a burden of conscience about them that his reason was sometimes impaired. He could not believe so attractive a girl as Nell Gaither loved him.

The character Shawnessy is a dreamer rather than a doer. He leaves the making of fortunes and careers to others and yet he is driven by ambition. As teacher and poet he must influence everybody, and this scorning of the game and still wanting to prevail was, I found, just as sympathetic a conflict as his sexual one.

Shawnessy's wish and rationale about fame are openly borrowed from Hawthorne's tale *The Great Stone Face*, which tells of a small boy named Ernest who lives in a valley dominated by a cliff shaped like a human face. The legend is that a child from this valley will become the greatest and noblest person of his time, and in manhood his face will resemble that of the Great Stone Face.

Throughout Ernest's lifetime, men leave the valley to become successful and return, hoping to find they have fulfilled the prophecy. The rich merchant, the illustrious commander, the eminent statesman are all disappointed—and so is Ernest, until a poet, seeing the sunset shining on his face, cries, "Behold! Behold! Ernest is himself the likeness of The Great Stone Face!"

The boyish Johnny Shawnessy calls it the most wonderful story ever told and only the modesty of the maturing one keeps him from announcing his candidacy for the Ernest role.

So far Shawnessy is an exceptional fellow, but flesh. However, there is more. His young manhood unfolds to reveal parallels with the young nation as it plunges toward Civil War, is shattered by it and survives in a new, more cynical consciousness. Clearly Shawnessy has become the Republic itself in eruption and change.

Nor is that all of him. In his mystical, philosophical quest for life's meaning, continually seeking his lost Eden and in the end finding it, he is apparently Mankind.

As if this were not enough grand design, Lockridge tells Shawnessy's story by a clock similar to the one Joyce used for *Ulysses*. It starts at dawn on July 4, 1892, when Shawnessy is fifty-three, and moves through the hours and celebrations of that Independence Day, then spins back erratically into Shawnessy's past, assembling it like a vast jigsaw puzzle, the climactic pieces withheld until last.

In reading the book I had been wholly caught up in the story of Shawnessy the exuberant boy, recognizing the honesty of the portrait and the skill with which Lockridge had built his Raintree

County, a patch of Indiana so vivid it had to be authentic and yet so bustling with sharp-eyed, sharp-tongued boys and provocative girls it was far more desirable than any Eden I had imagined.

But then I lost Shawnessy in transition, in those toils of conscience which deliver him from Nell Gaither, his river nymph and true love, into that sinister marriage with Susanna Drake and the South. It is the moment when Shawnessy becomes more man than boy, and more symbol than individual.

His New Orleans honeymoon, his loss of wife and child, his campaigning with the Union Army—Chickamauga, Chattanooga, the capture of Atlanta and the March to the Sea—his postwar wanderings and his baffling relationship with the actress Laura Golden made a vast, impressive structure into which the real Shawnessy had disappeared. I laid the creeping indifference I felt to shortcomings of my own.

Shawnessy's return, in maturity, to Raintree County restored him to life. There were three women: a good, if intimidated wife, an attractive feminist, and an enchanting daughter. Even better, there was the devilish Prof. Jerusalem Webster Stiles, the other side of the Shawnessy coin and the perfect Shawnessy foil. In the Socratic dialogues between the two, Lockridge was wrapping up his story and, he hoped, the human experience.

Turning the last of the 1066 pages I was staggered at what Lockridge had set out to do. Far from home, groping toward a first novel of my own, I could scarcely believe it. He was my own age. Where did he get the brass and courage, to say nothing of the knowledge, for so heroic an undertaking?

Now, a few years later, I had joined Lockridge's publisher and I still knew little about him. The Book-of-the-Month Club bulletin which announced *Raintree County* told club members he was a native of Bloomington, Indiana, the seat of Indiana University, and was the son of an authority on local history. He had been outstanding as both scholar and athlete and he had married his high school sweetheart. This was Vernice Baker, a girl described as "lovely, rather than pretty, with very fair hair, very fair skin and a completely tranquil disposition." She had typed the final manuscript and at the same time kept peace among their four small children.

At Houghton, the people who had known Lockridge best recalled his exuberance. He was of medium size, with curly, dark-brown hair and a striking handsomeness, but the unusual thing about him was his energy. It glowed and crackled. It was very much a part of his attractiveness and, at the same time, was wearying. They found it exhausting to be with him for more than a few minutes.

He had an accountant's eye for the small change, even after his book had made him rich. And yet he was still naïve. Although he had spent a year in Paris as a student, done graduate work at Harvard and lived in Boston for several years, he gave the impression of someone fresh from Indiana.

Although he had often talked of doing so, Ross had never brought his wife to meet his friends at Houghton Mifflin. Not one had ever met her and after Ross's death Vernice was notably cool to them, letting the firm know she felt it had, in its own interest, brought pressures to bear on Ross and these had contributed to his suicide.

During the next fifteen years, in which I published some novels of my own and moved to New York to work at Harper's, I asked anyone who might know for news of the Lockridge family and learned that Vernice continued her strong, custodial feelings about her husband. Obviously a private sort of person, she was bringing up her children with great care and an awareness of their father's accomplishment. The two older boys were taking on the Lockridge pattern of academic brilliance and an interest in writing.

When I met Vernice it was January 1967. We had agreed to meet for dinner at the Student Union on the Indiana University campus. Her children were grown now, all away and busy with writing and teaching careers of their own. She had married again, but only recently. Her husband was Russell Noyes, a professor of English at Indiana under whom Ross had studied.

Cautiously, with an emotion clearly painful, Vernice told me that her first glimpse of Ross had been at a meeting of the

Epworth League, the youth organization of the Methodist Church. Most of the sanctioned fraternizing between Bloomington's boys and girls took place at these sessions and although there was some praying they were not at all grave.

She had known his name from headlines in their high school paper, The Optimist: "Ross Lockridge Heads Honor Roll," "Ross Lockridge Elected Class President," always telling about some new honor for him. So she was surprised to find him this slight, dark-haired boy with blue-gray eyes that shone in joy.

After one Epworth meeting, at which Ross, as secretary, wrote hilarious minutes, he asked her to come along on a search for a forest fire reported in Brown County. Malcolm Correll, his closest friend, drove and joined with Ross in telling stories about "F" Sharp, their violin teacher, one picking up the narrative as the other choked on his laughter.

They did not find the fire but Vernice was not disappointed, for on the way home Ross sat beside her in the back seat and recited the whole of "The Raven."

This was not much to go on but it was enough for Vernice, though only a junior, to come to Ross's graduation exercises. He was valedictorian and had barely begun the address when a freight train was heard approaching. It was an infinite one. Car after car thumped across the tracks just outside the gymnasium, drowning him out, but Ross did not even consider surrender. He continued to speak, smiling and gesturing as though he could be heard perfectly, right into the teeth of the thunderstorm which broke the moment the train had passed. Seeing him under attack from both the Monon Railroad and the heavens themselves, Vernice decided he was dauntless.

Ross was the youngest, by a decade, of a family fervently loyal to Indiana University. His father, mother, brother and sister were graduates. It was as natural as breathing that he should follow them, but in entering college, Ross was lost to Vernice. He was immediately caught up in campus life, on the run from fraternity to class to field house to armory. He seemed to belong to everything, and Vernice realized he was moving in many directions, all away from the path of their adolescence and surely into the path of other girls. She felt that Ross, with his good looks, would have his pick of them.

The following year she entered the university herself but beaus and dates were not on her program. She had to have a job to pay her thirty-five-dollar-a-term tuition and rarely had enough on hand for more than a five-dollar installment to the bursar. There was little play and no luxury in her life.

While Vernice lacked the leisure and clothes other coeds enjoyed, she made good friends among them and was habitually optimistic. Even though she did not see him, she still thought about Ross—the exuberance in his voice, the way he carried his head slightly forward, as though he were really going places, the shy modesty which never quite contained the belief he could do anything.

She was sure that college would bring them together again, but then in the spring of her freshman year she learned that Ross had won a scholarship and was going away to the Sorbonne in France.

In the midst of her despair, a friend urged her to come along to an Epworth meeting, one which was to plan the Rivervale Retreat. This was a week-long holiday at the church camp, famous for its romantic possibilities, and one of the vacation joys she felt denied. She weighed the idea of begging off, but then agreed to go.

Ross was at the meeting and when she congratulated him on his French year, he sat beside her. When she told him she could not go to Rivervale because of her job, he suggested she come for the weekend. She agreed.

That weekend she discovered that during the week Ross had taken an interest in Mary Eloise Humphrey, a girl from Bloomfield whose lustrous red hair swung in long braids down her back by day, and by night made a coronet for her handsome head.

Later, Ross had his own turn with jealousy over the track

team's star half-miler, Charlie Hornbostel, but he continued to ask Vernice for dates and he found that the more they were together the more he disliked being apart.

By summer's end he had fallen in love with her with all the seriousness of a first time and of a boy who always had been shy of girls. Still, his seriousness did not outweigh the uncertainty and adventure of the year ahead, not enough for a promise—and none was made, except that they would write each other often.

III

On the morning of September 14, 1933, father, mother and son stood on the platform of the Monon railroad station in Bloomington awaiting the train that would start Ross on his long journey to Paris. Frank Lockridge paced nervously, pausing to peer up the track, still not reconciled to his son's French leave. Elsie stood calmly beside her youngest, looking up admiringly as she asked if he had packed his heavy socks and reminding him to write immediately for whatever he lacked.

Although Ross nodded and tried to reassure her, he had become oddly and acutely joyless about the trip. He was sweltering in his new pepper-and-salt suit and felt weak as a baby. Voices had a faraway sound and his stomach was on a vertiginous course of its own.

A sleepless night had followed his last date with Vernice. She might have been here too but it was the peak of the bookstore's registration business and she was conscientious about her job. Moreover, the older Lockridges were faintly chilly about Vernice. She was wholesome as milk and it was impossible to dislike her, but hard times had made a cautious, rather than imaginative, girl of her and somehow they were disappointed that Ross had chosen her.

Bloomington was as free of snobbery as a small American town can be and Elsie the last to invoke any but democratic

31

judgments. Nevertheless, Hugh Baker, Vernice's father, had been a letter carrier. The Depression had cost him a subsequent job with a Bloomington loan company and after some idle years in which his daughters supported him, he became paymaster at the W.P.A.

Elsie hoped that Ross would choose someone with a more intellectual background, perhaps one of those girls who were always hurrying along faculty row clutching a violin case, someone more like herself.

If Ross's unexpected, last-minute misgivings about leaving Bloomington were in part lovesickness, they were equally an anticipation of homesickness. He was going to miss the whole town, university and way of life here just as poignantly as he was going to miss his mother. At this moment he shared his father's view of the place and wondered what had ever possessed him to leave.

But when the train arrived he managed to boost his valise up onto the platform and climb after it, to blow a kiss and wave until mother and father drew from sight. Sitting by the window, watching the outskirts of Bloomington change into fields and woods which had already taken on a strange and foreign look, his misery was complete. When the quaking of his bowels and the swooning of his head would permit he thought of ways to return home on the next train.

Ross's setting out on this painful exile was due, at least in part, to his admiration for a fraternity brother who had been off on the University of Delaware's junior-year-abroad program.

In his freshman year, Ross had pledged Phi Gamma Delta, as his father and brother had before him. He put in the customary five-month novitiate, waxing the house floors, polishing its windows, memorizing doggerel, submitting to the paddling of upperclassmen and assurances he was "the lowest thing in the world—lower than whaleshit." Ross took the hazing with a legacy's forbearance but he was struck by a freckled, red-headed graduate member who had the audacity to deplore these traditional persecutions. This was Larry Wylie, the younger son of his father's dear friend, Reverend Will Wylie. Larry had a warm, interested voice and a bemused manner. He was four years older than Ross and wise in the ways of the world, and when Ross learned that Larry was putting in a first year as an instructor, he signed up for his course, Introductory French.

It was the beginning of a durable friendship between them. Ross was a bright, responsive student not just of language but of Larry's sense of humor and ranging ambition. Larry told Ross that he was staying on at I.U. only long enough to get his master's degree. He was not going to be satisfied with what was offered here until he had a further look at the alternatives. His year of study in France had given him some perspective on Bloomington and made him aware of its double standard.

There were two kinds of accomplishment recognized in Indiana. There was the outside kind of a Wendell Willkie or a Hoagy Carmichael, and the inside kind, intended for home consumption, the kind, they agreed, with which their fathers were content. Loyalty was implicit in an insider's behavior. "Why would anyone roam," he asks, "when there is Indiana?" And his reward is honor that equals, possibly surpasses, that of the outsider.

This was especially true of the university, where faculty identified with Indiana were as admired and sought after by new students as those with reputations negotiable on any campus, and doubtless on their way to Columbia or Berkeley. But the two roads were separate; if you took one you were unlikely ever to walk the other.

So it was specifically an emulation of Larry Wylie's venturing that had packed Ross off on this train, but in a larger sense it was a response to the hopes of his dynamic mother.

Elsie Shockley Lockridge had such keen blue eyes, such good humor and incandescent vitality, that it never occurred to Ross she was not beautiful. She believed in the power of the human spirit, her own and others', to change the course of rivers and to move mountains and she wanted to see that spirit trained and thriving in her children.

Ross was more than a decade younger than his brothers, Bruce and Shockley, and seven years younger than his sister, Louise, so that he felt a certain remove from his family. He was its adored baby but still he had to prove his right to membership. The Lockridge household itself was plain, for Elsie thought "homemaking" a waste of good time. She scorned *things*, thought acquisitive people fools and associated money in any quantity with greed, but Ross's father went her one better in a careless improvidence that brought Elsie a regular anxiousness about the rent. It was she who sharpened her pencil and made a budget that took the anguish out of the week before payday. If her house had a piano and some books it was furnished. She kept it clean, saw that the children were properly dressed, provided simple, nourishing meals at regular hours and that was the end of it.

But when the family gathered there was noise. New plans, new ideas were always being proposed and the atmosphere was one of expectancy and accomplishment—both were Lockridge habits.

Elsie Lockridge's main concern for her children was with the school and whether its teachers could pace her children's capacity to learn. It was typical that during some trying years in Oklahoma, she had turned her despair over the Shawnee school to a constructive countermeasure. With a kit of Montessori teaching materials she had put her children to work matching its colored skeins and filling its cutouts into the holes of a plaque. The introduction to spatial logic worked so well that she invited neighbors to join and so started a primary school whose techniques were the most advanced of the day. She was forever transforming her own thoughts into some performance for her children's benefit.

As a result, Ross's brothers had thrived and developed a family style of eagerness. They were always edging forward on their chairs, ready to spring at any challenge to their knowledge. This was less true of Louise, who would sit back as her mother did and admire the performance of her brothers and father. But the boys debated, teased each other, ran off spelling bees and argued about American history. They quoted, actually declaimed, poetry to each other, held their own in adult conversation and seemed never to run out of enthusiasm.

Bruce had been the eldest and most favored. It was assumed that he would make some wonderful, intellectual mark for himself and Elsie had hoped that like her father and grandfather, both amateur poets, he would write. In the spring of 1919, just as he was graduating from high school and making plans to enter Indiana University, Bruce took a group of boys to an outing at a nearby lake. While swimming, one of the boys got beyond his depth and Bruce, going after him, was drowned.

Ross, who was only five, escaped the full impact of Bruce's death but understood that he had gone, never to return, that his possessions had become talismans, and he viewed with awe Bruce's empty bed and his chair drawn back against the wall.

It was his mother, of course, who suffered most grievously. Elsie had had her share of disappointments. The man she most admired was her father and in dying he had left her with a feeling she had failed him. Also, her husband had spent so much of his life in trying and discarding careers that she had a further sense of waste in her marriage.

But as in past crises, Elsie turned to Christian Science for the courage and grace to accept the loss of her first child. Gradually she transferred her hopes for Bruce to Shockley, who was in fact no less promising, and ultimately to her youngest.

As little Ross grew he found that he shared his brothers' dark handsomeness and capacity to excel. In the early grades of school he bore home report cards that showed him "admirable" in reading, language, spelling, penmanship and physical education, while in drawing and geography he was merely "excellent."

So it was an awareness of what his mother expected of him that kept Ross aboard that eastbound train, and as it swept him toward New York, calmed his innards, restored his trust in survival and lent his thoughts a certain "forward tendency."

When the Delaware Foreign Study Group #11 first assembled in the ballroom of the Hotel New Yorker, Prof. George Brinton of the University of Delaware, its grave, white-haired director, welcomed them. He offered a caution about necessary documents and procedures for embarkation and congratulations on the opportunity for them and for their country which lay in the year ahead.

Dorothy Littlefield, assistant director of the group, plied among them distributing tags for their lapels and doing her best for the alone. One boy, from the University of Pennsylvania, was blind and his special limitation led Ross to relinquish anxiousness over his own misgivings.

He found himself among thirty-three girls, mostly from Eastern colleges, Sweet Briar, Mount Holyoke, Vassar and Wellesley predominating, and only nine boys, four of them from Dartmouth. They were superior students and looked it but a few of the girls were well dressed, their felt hats raked over an eye, and there was a garnishing of furs and flowers. Ross, who had never seen such costly modishness, was wary of it.

But Ross himself was fully conscious of his slim, curly-haired good looks, his blue-gray eyes which shone with a direct good nature and his Hoosier smile, which could thaw the most glacial social iceberg. He undertook his gregarious role at once, offering around his purposeful handshake and befriending in particular Sydney Roseman, the blind boy.

While he stood talking to Huntington Harrison and Walter Pruden, two of the Dartmouth boys, Ross sensed a "rush-night" situation. He was being looked over. As each identified himself by home town and family custom Ross gave both these new friends the impression his father was a well-known history professor at the University of Indiana.

This was a stretching of the truth. Ross's father, Ross Franklin Lockridge, or Frank as Ross's mother called him, was a five-foot-six, powerfully built barrel of a man. He had published a number of books, notably short biographies of historical figures that were of particular interest to schoolchildren, but he earned his living as a book salesman and had only a remote connection with the university. Nevertheless he was known and in fact celebrated throughout the state as a historian. The history he dealt in was Indiana's and he had a Barnum-like flair for it.

During the winter months he made the rounds of Indiana's men's clubs to speak about the state's great past. At the first warming of the weather he would gather family, friends and a few members of the historical society on the semicircle of benches in his yard. He was an able storyteller and standing in a bonfire's flickering light he would tell about the Miami Indians who had given their name to his home county and of Little Turtle, their chief and "the greatest Indian of all time."

Listening, little Ross could see the braves moving through the maple grove beyond, and when he was ready for bed his father would come up to his small second-story bedroom, sit on the foot of his cot and tell how as a boy he had swum, skated, trapped and dreamed along the Eel River shores where Little Turtle had fought with such bravery and counseled so wisely. Together they planned trips of their own and in July father and son would set off for a week's camping, pitching their tent on that same Eel River bank.

Also in midsummer, Frank Lockridge climaxed the year's performances with a three-week trip strung to Indiana's historical sites. He advertised in the cities along his route of march, announcing the date and program of events. A company of thirty or more Bloomingtonians would come along, sleeping in tents and gathering around picnic tables for meals. It was the kind of work Frank Lockridge enjoyed, among people he liked, and they respected him for it.

Ross not only admired his father but had acquired his promotional zeal. An evangelical best-foot-forwardism was stock in trade for a local historian and touting Frank's accomplishments had become a habit shared in by the whole family.

Yet here, clear of his father, Ross could see him in a more candid light than ever before. From bits of family reminiscence he could piece together his diverse career and recognize it as a long search for work he could endure.

Before going off to college, Ross's father had taught in a country school and had always thought of himself as a teacher. After graduating from I.U. he had taught at and then become principal at the Peru, Indiana, high school, but he had disliked it and then, nearly thirty, had gone back to the university for a law degree.

Next he had put in some years as public defender at Shawnee,

Oklahoma, and a few more as constitutional reformer in Indianapolis. When World War II came along he was too old for
military service but he had spent those years in the personnel office
of the Wayne Knitting Mills at Fort Wayne, and he was forty-five
before he found a job, with World Book Company, he liked well
enough to keep.

Despite the surging energy and vision which had pointed
toward some grandly designed, widely recognized career, Frank
Lockridge lacked the persistence for it. He was a dreamer. He had
the patience of a butterfly for fine print and the usual grind. He
was always torn between making his way and a distaste for the
game itself. For all his popularity on the platform circuit, among
the real dons he so much admired, he was a dilettante.

Ross could even sense that within the innocent deceptions
about his father, in which his mother so diligently collaborated, lay
disappointment. From New York, and the threshold of this adventure which was to be wholly his own, Ross had some newly
competitive feelings toward his father and just a suspicion of his
own superiority.

That same afternoon the Delaware group embarked on S.S.
Scythia for the ten-day journey to England, which, for Ross, was a
revelation. Although booze and bootleggers had made some inroads
at the Phi Gam house, and Franklin Roosevelt was just repealing
the Volstead Act, teetotalism was the norm in Bloomington. Its
Y.P.B., Young People's Branch of the Women's Christian Tem-
perance Union, was as socially active as the Epworth League and
Ross's notion of a party was not only that it be alcohol-free, but
also that it be given in the name of abstinence. Ross's mother
tolerated alcohol to the degree she did poisonous snakes. She
allowed none in the house and Ross had never tasted it.

So Ross instinctively avoided the Scythia's bar and he was
surprised to find the girls joining the noisy crowd there, climbing
onto the stools for a chat with the cheery steward.

When Marion Monaco, a quiet, dark-haired girl from New
Jersey, decided on an afterdinner drink and ordered knowledgeably
from among the liqueurs, he asked her about it. She explained that

her family was Italian and she had grown up with wine at table. Having a drink before, during and after a meal seemed only natural to her.

When innocent-looking Wendy Watkeys assured him she liked whiskey, Ross not only doubted her, he bet her the price of a Scotch and soda and watched, with the concentration of a boy who has just flung a lighted firecracker through the church door, while she casually tossed it off.

Although he drank nothing himself, Ross was as exuberant as the bar's best customers. Later that evening he introduced Wendy to the Indiana Hop, a polkalike dance step. It was the rage of I.U.'s fraternity row, he told her, as they lunged menacingly about *Scythia*'s tipsy deck like a pair of kangaroos.

Already there was some pairing off. The girls were so much in the majority, all of them seemingly eager for attention, that Ross's opportunities for shipboard romance were plentiful. But as he wandered *Scythia*'s decks, pausing at different steamer chairs to ask each girl about her college, where she lived and, as the weather improved, to play whirlwind games of Ping-Pong, he showed no preference.

Whatever vulnerableness he was feeling was shored up on the fourth day at sea by finding the purser was holding a packet of mail for him. There were letters from his mother, father, Larry Wylie and, the one he wanted most, Vernice.

While Ross seemed indifferent to the flirting and love making that now began to take place around him he was not. Beneath his air of amused tolerance lay a singular innocence and what he saw both dismayed and fascinated him.

On the first calm night he had wandered back to steerage and watched some young Irishmen and their girls dancing to an accordion on deck and swapping partners for what looked to him an orgiastic intermission. Then, as they revealed themselves, the Delaware girls presented an even more dramatic contrast to Bloomington behavior. They not only laughed at the boys' risqué jokes but replied with a share of their own.

By night they paired off where they could and sought the

ship's dark corners for necking, playing hide-and-seek with a steward who followed them about, switching on the lights as they turned them off. Some stayed up the whole night at their pleasures and watched the sun as it rose from the rim of the sea. The girls, Ross found, were as wanton as the boys.

But what shocked Ross most was his roommate's plan to seduce one of the loveliest girls. When asked to find another berth for the night, Ross agreed but kept an eye on events. He observed that during the dance in First Class, his roommate was lacing his courage with plenty of drink, topping off a procession of whiskey sours and Tom Collinses with champagne.

At midnight, returning to his borrowed bunk, Ross tried the door of his own cabin, found it locked, and presumed the act was in progress, but the door opened and a courtly steward appeared to say, "Your roommate is sick, sir. There's a lady with him."

Although Ross could not explain the steward's presence, he assumed the man's explanation was Cunard tact and went on to bed, believing his roommate had triumphed. But in the morning, Ross found him wan and wretched. "It was the champagne," he told Ross. "If I hadn't drunk the damned champagne everything would have gone all right."

It seems he had brought the girl into his stateroom without difficulty, but it was immediately evident she was to be his nurse rather than lover. While he threw up copiously, she held and aimed his head.

On the last night at sea, however, Ross's roommate remounted his campaign. This time he was more moderate with the whiskey, avoided the champagne altogether and, in the morning, proclaimed his victory. Ross was astounded and as he and his roommate rode up to London on the train, he questioned him closely, wanting to know how he had managed it and whether he believed most of the Delaware girls were sexually experienced, if theirs was a particularly fast crowd or typical of Eastern colleges, until the roommate, who could not believe Ross's naïveté, grew exasperated with him.

The Delawares assembled for London sightseeing in a pub and

as the glasses were brimmed and passed over the bar, the boys made fun of Ross's now-famous abstinence. He did not take to the bumpkin role; his skin was far too thin for ribbing and when one of the girls joined in the laughter, daring him, he took his first drink. It was a lager and he liked it well enough to have a second before boarding the bus.

At Westminster Abbey, Ross made straight for the Poets' Corner trailing five less certain companions who watched him pause before Chaucer's marker with a look of exaltation on his face, a pilgrim at last before his goal.

His audience was further impressed to see Ross move from Chaucer's monument to Ben Jonson's, Hardy's and Scott's and finally the lone American, Longfellow's, offering each poet a tribute of his own lines.

He was showing off his knowledge and recall of English literature but the performance was also a conditioned reflex to a historic place. Here among the worn stones, the celebrated names, the murmuring of guides, Ross could not avoid the vision of his father pointing to the trampled grass underfoot and announcing, "Upon this very ground where you are now standing . . ." and then retelling the story of Morgan's Raid or the siege of Fort Sackville.

When Ross had turned sixteen his father had taken him on as apprentice, allowed him to type out his manuscripts and taught him to memorize historical passages for recital, and he had soon become indispensable to the caravan. He had driven the old truck with its load of tents and cooking equipment from site to site and had grown skillful at changing and patching its threadbare tires. He had learned how to set up camp and contrive an amphitheater and to take part in the recitals themselves. In his eighteenth summer, that of the Washington bicentennial, he had taken the Patrick Henry role, reciting the "If this be treason . . ." speech.

When Ross was a young boy, his father had rewarded him for some feat of memory by a trip to Lincoln City and while they motored the hundred miles from Bloomington, Frank Lockridge explained it was where Abe Lincoln had lived when he was Ross's age, where the man who was to be the nation's sixteenth president had split his fence rails, borrowed his books, walked to school and grown into a man.

Then, as they stood at the graveside of Nancy Hanks Lincoln, his father had asked him to say the Gettysburg Address and he did so in a clear voice. In the silence which followed, Ross could believe for an instant that Abe himself had joined them and, as his father intended, Ross had had a feeling of being spliced to the past, just as he uncoiled toward the future.

Here in the echoing Abbey, Ross heard his father's voice within his own.

After only a day's pause in London, the group proceeded to Paris by Channel steamer and train, arriving at ten o'clock on a beautiful late-September evening. As the bus scuttled along the famous boulevards, Ross and the others had a first glimpse of Parisians enjoying their city, strolling, talking, crowding the tables of the lighted street cafés, and as they passed the landmarks— Concorde, Invalides, Eiffel Tower—they could no longer contain their excitement and they called out to one another like school-children.

One by one they were dropped off with their "French families," for the most part homes of widows who had agreed to supplement waning incomes by boarding students. The girls in particular were apprehensive as they were delivered to forbidding ancient doorways throughout the Latin Quarter. Nor were they much heartened by the false encouragement shouted from the safety of the bus.

Ross was paired with Cloise Crane, one of the Dartmouth boys, and they were billeted chez Pernot on the Rue Soufflot, the street running from the Panthéon down to the Luxembourg Gardens.

With Crane, Ross would share a single fourth-floor room which in grander days had been servant quarters. There were two beds, two desks and a wood-burning stove, which provided the only heat. Though wood would be brought to them when it grew colder, they would build their own fire each morning. They would dine, of course, with the family, which consisted of Mme. Pernot, her sister and her son, Felix.

Ross liked Mme. Pernot at once. For a widow, well past her prime, she was a lively woman, instantly rechristening the boys to her liking. "Cloise," she decided, was better as "Jacques," and since "Rosse" meant an old nag in French, thus a sort of insult, she preferred his middle name. "Franklin," she thought, had not just an American, but an auspicious, a presidential, ring. Thenceforth he was "Franc" to her, and she astonished and delighted him by her enthusiasms.

Ross described Mme. Pernot's table in an early letter home, reassuring his mother that he was getting plenty to eat now he had made the necessary adaptations:

> I came to France with a long training in polite table manners, pre-pared to spend a year of small bites and slow movements. The first meal I was nearly stabbed to death; the second I was nearly choked; the third I was hardly able to defend a place at the table to say nothing of eating. The French eat much; the French eat fast; the French eat skillfully. Madame's son, Felix, is large and hungry. Madame is old and apparently feeble, but age has only quickened and subtilized the incredibly swift jab of her short, sure fork.
>
> I could hear a thousand ancestral Lockridges, who had never failed their meat and potatoes, shouting for vengeance. There was too much good old rich tradition behind me to allow me to resign feebly to the challenge of these foreigners. The slumbering abilities translated to me by my forefathers began to develop wonderfully under the stimulus of this new environment. I uncovered miracles of swiftness that I never thought to possess; I soon accustomed my-self to the weapons of the French. I quickly learned to parry Felix with remarkable dexterity. My knife glitters like lightning around the table.
>
> The hardest thing to overcome was the habit my mother has ingrained into me, never to have both hands above the table. The French never put their hands below the table. It's actually impolite, probably a carry-over from the feudal period when the noblemen used to stab each other in the stomach during the course of a meal.

At any rate I am now an awesome character in the household, the family having at length learned the natural superiority of a Lockridge in these matters. It's true that we eat a long time, but the reason for this is to be found in the division of a French meal in courses, so that scarcely ever does one eat more than one thing at a time. A second reason is the fact that one simply eats more in France.

The evening meal usually goes along like this; the soup is in our bowls when we arrive. We toss this off with large spoons, exercising care only when someone at the table has a new suit. The family then waits feverishly for the second course, moistening its eyebrows and humming nervously. Madame enters with the second course, a salad perhaps. A glitter of forks, a champing of teeth—and the salad is gone. We aren't even breathing hard as yet. Madame then enters with a dish of meat, swimming in a toothsome sauce. We then murder the meat in short order. By this time the old girl, Auntie, across the table is tiring a bit and breathing pretty hard. Madame seems to eat very easily. She probably gets her share before she brings it in. It then reduces to a struggle between Jack, Felix and me for the remainder of the meat and some vegetables that are usually sitting around here and there on the table. Add to this that the French talk all the time they're eating, and you have some idea of our table.

At 14 Rue de la Glacière, the three-story stone house which was Delaware headquarters, Ross learned that the first five weeks would be a shakedown and testing of their knowledge of French grammar and their background in French literature and history. With only two years of the language, Ross was the least prepared of all. The others had had at least one additional year of history or literature. Nevertheless, he was a disciplined, confident student and he set to work enthusiastically.

Elsie Lockridge had taught Ross how to concentrate and use the clock as pacer. In grade school he would arrive at his friend Malcolm Correll's for the evening, saying, "O.K. We'll study from seven-thirty to eight-thirty, and *then* we'll play." Only at the end of an hour's forbearance would he take time out for fun. If there was a test next day he had a system to review for it. His self-discipline was a rock and to the awed Malcolm he seemed on top of every assignment.

His academic style was exuberant abundance: his papers were twice the required length, bursting with excesses of information and language, and his teachers, used to perfunctory work, gratefully rewarded him with the As and A+s that became his trademark.

His classmates accepted Ross's front-running as another manifestation of his likable exuberance and few resented it, while for Ross it was no more than natural. On the rare occasions when he did turn up in second place, pique drove him to greater effort, and next time he would be first again.

At the Sorbonne each day, except Sunday, began with an 8:30 lecture at the Dotation Carnegie on Boulevard St. Germain, from which he would hurry to Rue de la Glacière to spend the balance of the morning in grammar and dissertation classes. Early afternoon was free for study, but lectures, one in literature and another in history, resumed at 5:30.

In addition a dissertation was required every Friday, one demanding much supplementary reading, and Ross always found himself typing it up with an eye on the clock, allowing a final half-hour to put in the accents and then, manuscript tucked under an arm, sprinting to the Rue de la Glacière to make the deadline.

The results of the first examination, held at the end of two weeks, put Ross tenth in the group as a whole, and first among the boys. He now set out after the girls and during the weeks that remained before the final used every available moment for supplementary study, managing eight hours of it on regular class days and fourteen to sixteen on the Sunday and the day of congé preceding the examination.

The examination itself lasted nine hours and covered not only language but history and literature from the seventeenth century to the present. During the morning session he wrote so steadily and furiously that he attracted the attention of his neighbors and, as he reported to Larry Wylie, "since they were on honor, a very socialistic attitude developed in the matter of answering questions. My paper was as well-thumbed as a pack of fraternity cards . . . In the afternoon, I pulled off to a table by myself, not to have to breathe the tobacco-tainted breath of a lot of ignorant girls who had clustered around me, like vultures on a piece of carrion."

He was quick to qualify his irritation with his countrywomen, deciding that they were, on average, the finest he'd ever seen but that their morale had simply cracked under the burden of work.

To Ross's disappointment—for he believed he had landed "awfully near the top"—the results of this examination were not published. He questioned Professor Brinton, who would reveal only that he had done "very, very well." In any case he knew he had come *un bon bout de chemin pour attraper les jeunes filles* and "made by a mile" the *groupe supérieur*. In this lofty order, one which Larry Wylie had not attained, Ross would take no more grammar but instead a course in modern theater with twice-weekly visits to the Opéra Comique, Odéon, Mogador or Vieux Colombier.

Now, at the beginning of November, the Delawares began their formal studies in the *Cours de Civilisation* at the Sorbonne and Ross elected *Histoire de l'Art, Histoire Générale* and *Littérature Contemporaine* (1800–present). He would have liked more literature, the courses offered in *Moyen Age* and *Classicisme*, but was limited to three in all, and not wanting to forgo the history, decided to audit the others. He wrote Larry Wylie that "from now on, the work will be a game of pleasure."

The fall of 1933 was an uneasy time for France. The Third Republic had lost faith in its own parliamentary system and was under attack from both the left, where the Third Internationale argued for a dictatorship of the proletariat, and the right, where monarchists and totalitarians preferred the German example, the political success of young Adolf Hitler.

An unfavorable exchange discouraged American tourists but the Delaware administration had managed to change a block of dollars into francs at the old rate, eighteen, instead of the current twelve, and the students had the benefit. Paris life seemed both normal and enjoyable to them and as representatives of F.D.R.'s hopeful New Deal America, toward which many French were looking enviously, they felt welcome everywhere.

Ross was discovering that he had a good ear and a deft tongue and he liked to try them as he made his rounds of the Quarter and occasional forays into other parts of Paris. Reading about Les Halles in Zola, he went off one November evening to explore them for himself. He peered into their great iron sheds and sniffed the "peculiar odor formed of a thousand different essences of meat and vegetables, old and new." He wrote his family:

> I had walked some time before I noticed a number of dim figures littered like dead men along the sidewalks, and against the walls of the buildings. These were human beings, not dead but sleeping, on a night so cold that despite three of my sweaters and an overcoat on my back, I was forced to walk briskly to keep from chilling.
>
> Yes, these were actually people, poor people from the country I suppose, waiting for the Halles to open in the morning, miserables too poor to buy lodging for the night. I've never had such a stunning impression of wretched poverty. In the filth of the sidewalks, among the decomposing debris of the great market, breathing the impure odors of the district, these people lay in their filthy rags, covered with paper, sacks, straw, and even boards.
>
> There were hundreds, like so many corpses left unburied in the streets after a great plague, some lying in groups, wadded, crossed and tumbled together in disgusting confusion; some poor fellows, who probably had B.O., lying in a big box, half buried in the straw, so that only a hand and a foot emerged.
>
> In one street I ran into a fellow that hadn't yet retired for the night, but who was evidently arranging his quarters because he was carrying an arm-full of straw. As he approached me I saw he was going to stop and say something to me, probably, as I thought, some beggarly plea or some vulgar sentiment. Instead, he said something very pathetic and even lyrical. I don't know whether he took me for one of the fellowship in my old gray overcoat or not, but as he passed me, he said very distinctly in a deep, powerful voice: "*Mon cher, c'est comme la mort à la tombée de la nuit,*" which translated literally means, "My friend, it's like death at the fall of night."

Each day Ross not only sounded more Gallic but was beginning to look it. He bought a beret and wore it so constantly that it acquired the patina of grease and stains so admired in the Latin Quarter. It gave an unusual shape to his hair, clumped in front where it protruded, wavy where confined over the crown. He added a second Sorbonne badge, the long muffler slung carelessly about the throat, its tails flapping in the crisp fall winds as he hurried to class.

At Thanksgiving there was a group party at a restaurant called Le Plat d'Argent, complete with *dindon roti* and plentiful wine. Speeches were followed by patriotic and college songs and Ross, for the first time in his life, got drunk. He astounded the prim Miss Littlefield by asking for a kiss and then suggested to Wendy Watkeys they go on together afterward.

Jack Parsons, Wendy's regular beau, was a huge, black-haired fellow from Rollins, who had already pegged Ross for a know-it-all and disliked him. Ross and Parsons scuffled in the street over Wendy and the outcome was disputed, but Ross bundled into a taxi with others and the last he recalled with clarity was a girl passenger doing a striptease and Sydney Roseman, the blind student, protesting it as a discriminatory act.

After these unaccustomed excesses Ross was hung over and visibly remorseful. Typically, his expiation was neither confession nor penance, but a rationalizing. In a long letter home he gave a whimsical, bowdlerized account of the party and concluded by reassuring his mother that, "Fortunately, wine is harmless."

"The French say that France is the first among nations and champagne the first among drinks," he wrote. "There can't be any doubt about the second part of that statement. A more heady, sparkling, lovely beverage couldn't be imagined. You probably begin to think me a drunkard, but one can drink any amount of red wine without getting tipsy. Besides, all the French drink wine anyway, and it would be deuced impolite not to drink with them. Even grandmother Shockley drinks grape juice and wine is just excited grape juice."

Ross's mother had no cause for alarm. His Thanksgiving binge left him immune as ever to Paris temptations. He had neither the desire nor the money for them.

Across from headquarters stood the Brasserie de la Glacière, a source of excellent Alsatian beer, and here fellow students Lamorey, Harrison, Ford and Mitchell mustered regularly after class to exchange information about their social and love life. Harrison, for example, had preempted Alison Dunne, a stunning blonde from San Francisco, and together they had met some of the Paris *Tribune* people and been included in their parties.

Although the Dartmouth boys were on full pension they were flush enough to take their girls out for restaurant meals and a taste of night life. Ross, so well schooled in frugality, could keep within the Delaware "allocation" of ten dollars a month spending money but not without seeing the others as different: they were *jeunesse dorée* and a threat to his purse. Thus, while he was welcome enough, he shunned the council at the Brasserie.

Of all Ross's new acquaintances only one, Curt Lamorey, had the makings of a friend. They had come to like one another on an Armistice Day visit to the battlefield at Verdun. Walking along the banks of the Meuse where the German offensive had been stopped in the bloodiest fighting, they discovered a shared revulsion for warfare.

Curt was a Dartmouth boy but he was from Barre, Vermont, and Ross sensed a kinship in their being small-towners whose families had made a sacrifice to send them to France. But what endeared Curt to him even more than empty pockets was his being a big, placid fellow and a good listener. He brought out Ross's playfulness.

The tavern of Demoy's brewery was a way station between Rue de la Glacière and Rue Soufflot and Ross and Curt often stopped there for a beer on their way home. One night Ross capped an account of his cross-country feats for I.U. with a bet he could outrun the bus. So, with Curt riding the back platform and running up to urge on the driver, Ross sprinted through the winding Left Bank streets to a narrow victory at Rue Soufflot.

With the approach of Christmas holidays Ross and Curt planned a trip to Italy. They saved prudently, wrote home for a few extra dollars and found they were entitled to student reductions on already inexpensive third-class rail travel. They bought round-trip tickets to Naples which permitted them stopovers along the way and this left them fifteen dollars apiece, about a dollar a day, for meals, accommodations and sightseeing. It was barebones, even for the times, but in traveling by night, getting what sleep they could on the train, they hoped to economize on hotel expenses and make do.

Italy in midwinter was not the balmy land they had hoped for. They found snow in Torino and Ross's case of tourist-feet was aggravated by chilblains. Arriving in Rome at daybreak he could scarcely squeeze his puffy toes back into his shoes and walking was agony. But he was stoical about every privation and indignant only when he suspected a hotelkeeper was trying to cheat them. For five days they dutifully tramped the galleries, cathedrals and ruins.

Ross acted as guide. He had prepared himself as though for an exam, boning up on Roman history and mythology, and yet he was not much moved by the sight of old buildings and old masters. He showed neither surprise nor wonder, but rather a satisfaction in finding these celebrated works of man much as he had expected them.

Curt was a good companion and they had a fine time together. Visiting the Forum, Ross could not resist the opportunity to perform for an English-speaking tour, and with Curt as a dead Caesar, he delivered Antony's funeral speech. In Pompeii they laughed over the lascivious frescoes of the lupanar and in Capri at the Blue Grotto they stripped off their clothes for an early-morning plunge in the luminous and, for December, tolerable water.

Ross had not felt so close to another human since leaving home and indeed found Curt so much a brother that as they talked away the cold nights in train compartments, he was forever challenging him over who had greater knowledge of the *Cours de Civilisation*. When Curt conceded him an easy victory in literature, Ross turned to Curt's specialty, history, and bested him there as well.

Ross offered Curt some candid glimpses of himself and his ambition, saying that he had always thought of himself as a writer and was going to write. He would write poetry, of course, and he promised that someday he would write a big, a really big, novel.

He made no secret of his need to win at everything. At one predawn moment while the train paused at a small station, both of them weary and kept awake only by the cold, Ross was proudly remembering how well he had scored highest on a particular test.

This made Curt recall how Ross habitually emerged from a test pleading, "I'm sure I didn't do well on that. I just went blank on the second question . . ." and then came up with the top mark. Until this moment Curt had thought that such remarks were simple modesty but now he grasped that Ross was goaded by a specter of failure, that he was ever-anxious, rather than secure, about his scholarship. It was a telling insight.

When they talked about the Delaware girls and their love affairs, Curt suggested to Ross that almost anyone might be his for the asking and wondered who appealed to him. Ross mentioned Huldah Smith, a handsome, well-groomed Vassar girl from Boston. Huldah was quiet, an appreciative listener, and he liked that. She reminded him of Vernice.

Producing his photograph of Vernice, Ross said it did her less than justice. She was an authentic American Venus, sprung from the rich Indiana earth. To describe her adequately was beyond his powers but she was more desirable in every way than these tobacco-burners from the East. There was a healthy abundance about her, not just of physical beauty but of wholesomeness, affection, and constancy—those qualities which seemed in ever-shorter supply the farther one got from Indiana.

Ross did not need Curt to tell him that the girls still had a hopeful eye on him. They liked his perceptiveness and his gaiety. They liked his freshness, the way a swallow of beer or wine would set him off on some extravagant story or demonstration, and they were touched at how the slightest excess in the wine and women prescription always being urged on him resulted in such exquisite remorse.

Back in Paris, he did lower his guard. It was the season for dances and get-togethers of all sorts and Ross offered himself first to one, then another of the girls. He applied himself to the job with remarkable exuberance, Indiana Hopping to waltzes, foxtrots and tangos alike, and astonishing Parisians with his *espèce de saut*.

When he decided that Ruth Jackson, a girl from Winnetka, had the most interesting mind of the lot, he took to spending afternoons with her, walking the Quarter's narrow streets, nursing a beer for an hour, while they talked of books they were reading and plays they were seeing.

Ross guessed his relation with Ruth was platonic but when he found Walt Pruden actively courting her, he made competitive demands. They would see her on alternate nights, and it nettled Ross that he no longer had her to himself.

Nevertheless, Ross was too single-minded for flirtation; there was no room in his emotional budget for the demands most girls would inevitably put upon him. The girl who most appealed to him, as he had told Curt Lamorey, was Huldah Smith, although Huldah had some reservations about Ross. She felt he was good-humored, rather than witty or clever. She let him know that his grimy beret, loose tie and coat a-flap in the breeze were a bit too "slap-happy" for her precise taste and that occasionally he was unintentionally rude.

Nevertheless, Huldah was receptive. She confessed her awe of Ross's mastery of the French language, complete with the latest Parisian argot and, like the other girls, she was captivated by his vitality. They often double-dated—with her roommate, Josephine Powe, and Curt Lamorey—and soon Ross began to focus his interest on Huldah.

On the morning of February 17 she was among the first to hear how he had taken part in the Stavisky riots of the night before and nearly been trampled by the crowd. On a Saturday afternoon they would meet at a café for a glass of beer and then go to the American Club for the free tea-dancing. Still, Ross found it hard to cross that gulf between the form and the actuality of courtship.

The armor which had kept him wary of girls until this nineteenth year of life had been cast by his mother. Elsie had taught him out of her own sexual experience which, thanks to a lusty husband and the painful deliveries of her children, had been distasteful. Ross had brought along his original baggage of motherly inhibitions: the belief that sex was both sinful and dangerous, that it left a young man vulnerable to every kind of predator, to unworthy girls, to unwanted children and unmentionable diseases.

Bolstering Elsie's injunction was his own wish to be true to Vernice. He had made her no promises and yet absence was working a powerful magic on his heart. His letters were growing fonder with every exchange.

But with the coming of Paris's famous springtime, Ross's determined innocence was besieged. After the shock and disillusionment of his first few weeks with the Delawares' *jeunesse dorée* he had grown tolerant. He admitted that Hunt Harrison's taking a party of Delaware girls to the Sphinx, the brothel-cabaret near Invalides, had been harmless after all, that Cloise Crane's immersions in the free-flowing wine were his own affair and even accepted that some of the prettiest girls did go off to hotel-room trysts to return lightheartedly and, far from coming to harm, they seemed, like the Parisians around them, to thrive on casual love-making.

The city had done its work. As Ross wrote Larry Wylie, it had been "a renaissance for this poor little provincial from the United States, this lank, wide-eyed D'Artagnan who had never been away from home before."

Ross had become not only generous toward behavior that had shocked him in September, but fascinated with it. He was always talking about concupiscent carryings-on, laughing about them, describing them with a Rabelaisian relish and he admitted he was quite willing to part with his own virginity.

And he did lose it—to a girl from a prestigious Eastern woman's college who took him to her room one night and there resolutely seduced him. The experience left Ross with a bad taste and the conviction that a Bloomington morality, for him at least, was far more plausible than the Parisian.

Even though it withheld a joyful love affair, the spring of 1934 brought Ross a buoyant experience. When Mme. Pernot told Ross that her family now required his room, he welcomed the news. He was glad enough to part with Crane, who moved in with Harrison and Lamorey, while the headquarters found him a single room nearby on Rue d'Ulm.

It was here, on an early-April evening, that Ross had a sort of vision, a moment of inspiration and prophecy. He had been sitting at his desk typing his thesis, the culmination of a year's reading in the French novel, when it struck him that he had, already planted in his heart and mind, the seed of a novel that could be as revealing of America as *Eugénie Grandet* was of Balzac's France.

Staring out at the thicket of chimney pots he recalled his childhood visits to his sprightly grandmother, Emma Rhoton Shockley. From the time he was seven his mother would pack him along on these hundred-mile journeys to Straughn. There he would sit quietly in the parlor of the old house while the old woman entertained them with ancient family doings, her father-in-law's experiences as a country doctor and her late husband's adventures as a Henry County schoolteacher and occasional writer.

While she talked Ross was allowed to thumb the family albums and read his grandfather's herb cures and his poetry, written in his own fading yet still sure hand, and his newspaper articles, some signed with the pseudonym Seth Twiggs.

Now, a dozen years later and half a world removed, Ross recalled it all, mixing it with homesickness, a recollecting of camping with his father and a painfully sweet longing for all the sights and smells of the land where he had grown up. In the midst of this reverie he realized that his mother's family and rural Indiana were the materials with which he could build a, perhaps *the*, Great American Novel.

It seemed as if the wraiths of his forebears, who had clung to this world only in his grandmother's memory and who had vanished with her, were reappearing and he sensed his own power to summon them back from oblivion.

He had never doubted his "gift." There had been a gravity in his grandmother's voice as she retold the legend of the family's bar sinister, explaining that the Shockley bent for letters was no accident: it was their shame and glory to be the illegitimate but no less fortunate descendants of that illustrious Scot Thomas Carlyle. While Elsie dismissed her mother's claim as fanciful and wholly unsubstantiated, Ross clung to it. He liked to think he had inherited genius and was a *chosen seed*.

In his seventh year, while in the third grade, he had spent a rainy afternoon rummaging in the attic and had come across a box of stories his brother Shockley had written when he was Ross's age. They were romances, more like Elsie's fairy stories than Frank's frontier yarns, and Ross devoured them. At bedtime he carried them off to his room to reread them under his blanket by flashlight.

His own first story, "The Dragon with the Fiery Tongue," written soon after, was an imitation of Shockley's tales and when his mother approved, Ross knew that he had settled the matter of purpose for all time. He was going to write. It would be his life work. He would write a great and good book.

In high school he wrote more romantic stories around heroic knights and brave Union soldiers, all readily acceptable to the school's *Reflector*, and as a matter of course fiction prizes went to him. Then the discovery in the library at home of Brander Matthews's *Study of Versification* turned him to poetry. He tried his hand at every sort of poem. He wrote them on drowsing in assembly, in praise of pioneers, on the glories of poetry itself, and laid elaborate plans for a Great Elegy.

Now Paris and its perspective had given Ross another grand scheme to file away beside it. While he loved this kind of daydream with its mapping of future construction, there was no idleness about it. He was certain the day of ground-breaking would come and he could scarcely wait. But in these last few weeks before the final examinations, France demanded his full attention.

On the last day of June the students from some twenty nations who had been enrolled in the *Cours de Civilisation* filed into the amphitheater that was the Sorbonne's main lecture hall for the awarding of certificates. The student who rose to accept the top honor, leading scholar among all the *étudiants étrangers*, was Ross Lockridge, Jr.

He had surpassed his own ambitions, outstripping the Americans and then the whole field. But then, instead of basking in his accomplishment or giving some thought to extending and exploiting it, he simply smacked the dust from his hands and turned his back on it.

The majority of the Delawares had an eye on the political clouds and guessed this might be a last chance to see the France they had been studying about all winter, and besides there was widespread reluctance to put an end to this glorious year just as its loveliest season was coming in. Hunt Harrison was making up a party to visit the valley of the Loire and the Breton coast while others were off to the mountains.

But Ross had only one thought in mind—going home.

IV

One of the lines reeling Ross back to Bloomington was the news, in a letter from Malcolm Correll, that Vernice was seeing a good deal of Charlie Hornbostel. He felt his presence was urgently needed on that scene. With Ruth Jackson's help, he visited the Galeries Lafayette, selected some Vol de Nuit perfume —one bottle for Vernice, one for his mother—and bade Paris an abrupt farewell.

But returning on the *Mauretania* with those Delawares obliged to come home for summer jobs, Ross had a distracting experience. On the trip over, Marion Monaco had seemed something of a misfit among the fair, snub-nosed Anglo-Saxon beauties. Her pronounced nose, olive skin and long, dark hair now seemed classic to him. He felt she had acquired a particular serenity and dignity during the year in Paris and he was strongly drawn to her. He shared her reflective moods and walked the deck with her constantly, talking, listening, nodding. The others, recognizing a "rush," left them alone.

Ross's heart had finally been reached by one of the Delaware girls and when the *Mauretania* docked in New York, saying goodbye to Marion and in that act closing the door on the whole extraordinary experience of these eight months was unexpectedly painful. But he did close it. His progress toward Bloomington was unswerving and his homecoming victorious. France had been won and, oddly, already forgotten.

Although his friends looked in vain for cosmopolitan refinements in his accent and nature, one change was noticeable. Where the old Ross had run in every sort of race without commitment to any, the new one was engaged. He had no more time for experiment or indecision.

It was particularly true of his heart. By a timely return he had nosed out the competition for Vernice and he was so resolute about having her that both his father and his mother surrendered without a skirmish. Ross's triangular Phi Gam pin appeared on Vernice's handsome bosom, warning off further encroachments.

To Curt Lamorey, now back at Dartmouth but presumably still worried about Ross's asceticism, he sent reassurances. Vernice was all he had described and now unquestionably his. He shed a crocodile tear for "poor old Hornbostel." In March, as the maple grove bordering the campfire site in the Lockridge yard swelled with buds, Ross and Vernice announced their engagement.

He could read his immediate future clearly enough. Enlightening freshmen was a livelihood and graduation would put it within grasp. He had completed requirements for a bachelor's degree by midyear and in the spring enrolled in the first of the graduate courses that would bring him a master's degree in English and ensure an academic career.

In June 1935 he graduated from Indiana "With High Distinction," his grade average the highest of any student in the university's history. He was elected to Phi Beta Kappa and chosen first alternate for a Rhodes scholarship. When the Rhodes committee regretted it had not found a place for him, Vernice wept. She could not conceive of an honors committee so foolish as to pass him over. But Ross seemed scarcely disappointed, as though he had something else on his mind—which he did.

Behind the traditional smile and loping academic stride, Ross was fitting out for a literary expedition. He was not yet sure of its nature or its route but he was narrowing choice and trying out skills. Poetry was a strong current. He preferred the romantics, the grander the better. Byron fascinated him. Among Americans he was drawn to Whitman and Benét, and he had no use for the cynical moderns so much in vogue, T. S. Eliot in particular.

When Prof. Alexander Judson proposed to the members of his class in Elizabethan literature that they try their hand at Spenserian meter, he was unprepared for Ross's response, half a dozen stanzas, original in concept yet so faultless an imitation of *The Faerie Queene* that the class had to be persuaded—grudgingly— they were not Spenser's own.

Elsie, now in her fifties, had resumed her university education where she had left it to marry a quarter century earlier, and was now pursuing her M.A. in psychology. She had a job in the departmental office and Ross absorbed his mother's enthusiasm for her subject, read the books she brought home and appropriated the insights and the passwords of the order.

Just as with poetry, Ross had a specific application in mind. He thought the Freudian point of view with its new understanding of man's behavior was obligatory for anyone who now set out to write something significant.

Joyce had already made that plain. Reading *Portrait of the Artist as a Young Man* and *Ulysses*, Ross found in the fresh, stunning, poetic language, in the classical allusion and erudition and above all in the exploration of the subconscious, his literary home.

During the spring of his graduation year he took a job in the English department and, since the department was changing quarters, his work involved staggering upstairs with filing cabinets and cases of books. When he felt ill from this he decided he was rundown or at worst suffering some transitory summer ailment and prescribed for himself vigorous workouts in the gymnasium.

This was just the wrong treatment for a real illness. Frank Lockridge's brother-in-law, Robert Peters, was a physician in Indianapolis and his rather dazzled admiration for all the Lockridges made him a regular visitor in Bloomington. When he learned his nephew wasn't feeling well and noticed his peeling hands, he suspected Ross had had scarlatina, a mild form of scarlet fever. Examination not only confirmed it but convinced him the strenuous exercise while suffering from the disease had damaged Ross's heart. Dr. Peters promptly ordered him to bed.

Ross stayed, protesting, for a few days but then, feeling better and sure of recovery, arose. He was no sooner back at the English office than he collapsed. This time Elsie put him firmly back to bed and kept him there for three months.

Although it was Elsie Lockridge who cared for Ross—indeed, she quit her job at the psychology office and abandoned her graduate program within a few academic inches of attainment in order to look after him—Ross gave some of the credit for his recovery to Vernice. He was most responsive to her nursing, he wrote Curt Lamorey, slyly assuring him that illness had not enfeebled his desire.

Actually his recovery took the eight months following his graduation and each afternoon Vernice appeared to bring him the news and gossip of the campus and to talk about their future. Ross shared many confidences with her. He told how his Uncle Bob Peters, with no children of his own, had offered to put him through medical school and ultimately take him into his own practice, but that he had refused. He told her about his friend Larry Wylie, who had gone off to Brown for graduate work, and how he hoped to get just such a scholarship that would take them east.

He spoke in general terms of his writing plans, how he hoped to write important plays, poems and novels, all before he was thirty. But it was not in Ross's nature to discuss the writing itself. Talking about it was a jinx. It let cold air into the incubator. A man's writing was a truly private matter, between him and God.

A full academic year of idleness was frustrating and yet fortunate since it gave Ross time for reflection and planning his first work. He decided it should be the novel about his mother's family, the Shockleys, which had first occurred to him in Paris the previous spring, one that drew on the stories overheard in his grandmother's house at Straughn.

For central figures he chose his mother and her two brothers, Ernest and Frank. He would open with their childhood in the rural Indiana of 1895 with its one-room schools and Fourth-of-July celebrations and bring them to maturity in the industrialized present of the 1930s. It would be a big novel about the great change that had taken place in American life in the twentieth century.

Another bedside visitor was Ross's former writing teacher, John Robert Moore, a man toward whom he had mixed feelings. Professor Moore was one of the few people Ross admired who recognized his talent yet withheld a full measure of praise. He was often critical of Ross's effusiveness and in freshman year he had read some of it aloud, making the class laugh at the festoons of self-conscious adjectives.

Ross did not seem offended by this and often had dropped in at Moore's house, which was on his way home. On one of these visits Ross admitted that Jonathan Swift's precise, economical concept of style was admirable but it had no effect on his own leaning toward full orchestration.

Moore was not only a teacher of writing but a coach of the chess team and now he proposed that since Ross faced a long siege in bed it was time for him to learn chess and agreed to give him lessons.

Six months later, with Ross's confinement ending, Moore declared him one of the best players in the state and put him on the team he was taking to Indianapolis to engage the champion Bishops. He pitted Ross against an eccentric player known for his "Indiana Haymaker," an extravagant opener in which he surrendered not only the gambit pawn but half his pieces. Moore explained that in the resulting chaos this fellow was often able to free his queen for a checkmate and advised Ross to stick with cautious, conventional play.

Ross promised the coach a victory, then parried the "Haymaker" with an equally dramatic maneuver of his own and, with the game scarcely underway, he was checkmated and went down to cataclysmic defeat.

The match itself was saved by other, less spectacular players but as they left the hall it was Ross who trotted beside Moore, defending the subtlety of his strategy and insisting that it should, by all rights, have won the game. Moore thought he was joking but Ross was in earnest. Turning defeat into some kind of victory was the only experience acceptable to him.

With health restored, Ross took on a full academic load and proved a popular instructor. He was actor enough to bask in the attention of a class and to respond to it with wit and erudition. The new, self-propelled Ross was less available for his father's historical projects but he did offer occasional help, especially when there was a specific reward. In 1937 he agreed to write a pageant which would celebrate the history of New Harmony, the former Utopian community in the southwest corner of the state. He would be paid fifty dollars for it and this, rather than the possibility of acclaim, attracted him.

Although he had never written for the stage or, aside from a Phi Gamma Delta song, set words to music, Ross had not the slightest doubt he could produce a satisfactory script within a few days. He refreshed his memory of New Harmony, the rise and fall of Robert Owen's nineteenth-century social experiment, which was essentially a dispensing with "the trinity of evils"—unreasonable religion, ownership of property and marriage, which "robs a woman of all her rights."

For a suitable tone, Ross dipped into The Tempest, and then set out with the confidence of a Ben Jonson. Calling for a narrator, choral singing, dancing, a ball scene with an onstage orchestra, a cast of two hundred twenty-five characters in period costumes, he dashed off, in a dauntless assault on his typewriter, sixteen scenes of blank verse.

In spite of his grandiloquent approach, Ross became intrigued with Owen's plight, recognized it was inevitable that a few lazy rascals would prey on the virtuous and so collapse his grand dream. But Ross could no more admit to Owen's failure than imagine his own in writing a pageant about him and so he fashioned a happy ending around recognition that men rise to truth only by slow degrees and "the great past still pours its giant strength into the present and our very life is fashioned from the dreams of other days."

To dramatize this rosy view of disappointment Ross recalled

how a packet of exotic seeds was sent back to the colony by one disheartened Owenite and when these were scattered they sprang up as the trees of golden rain which stood today in New Harmony dooryards, each June bursting into bloom and showering the earth with their yellow petals.

Wherever possible Ross had assigned roles to surviving great- and great-great-grandchildren of the Owenites and when these and several hundred additional actors, musicians and technicians were assembled for rehearsal, the confusion brought the director to despair and Ross to sense the possibility of a flop. With a mounting sense of kinship with Owen, Ross washed his hands of *A Pageant of New Harmony*. He would attend no more rehearsals, he declared, nor the performance itself.

Reading a newspaper announcement of it, Vernice was surprised to learn that Ross was the author. She was puzzled by his explanation that it was of such small consequence to him he had not bothered to mention it, but she accepted as the order of things that Ross did not talk about what he was writing.

He had no objection to Vernice's attending the performance and she went along with Elsie and Frank Lockridge to New Harmony. It was well received that night; indeed, it was to be revived in five subsequent years but Ross was unmoved by Vernice's assurances, saying he would like to use the fifty dollars he had been paid for it to buy it back.

Ross and Vernice knew in the spring of 1937 that they wanted to be married that summer but in April they watched the logical site, the Methodist Church, burn down and in May Ross had a recurrence of illness.

At the end of June he put an end to indecision by traveling to Indianapolis and asking his Uncle Bob Peters if he was well enough to marry at all. Ross was examined and assured he was. Ross and Vernice set their wedding date in two weeks' time, even though this worked some hardship on Vernice's older sister, Clona. As family seamstress, Clona had agreed to supply the bride's wedding and traveling dress as well as a dress for their mother.

Dressmaking was completed in the final hour and Ross and

Vernice were married on a hot, sticky July 11 at the Christian Church. Economy had been agreed upon and the guests were invited by telephone. The ceremony was austere, without attendants. Bride and groom walked up the aisle alone to take their vows before Reverend Moore. Afterward, the Baker family, Lockridges from all over and "the gang," Ross's and Vernice's friends, gathered at the white-clapboard Lockridge house on South High Street for an outdoor ice-cream-and-cake reception.

Their honeymoon took Ross and Vernice to a cottage on Lake Manitou for a week and to the Shockley house in Straughn for another. Then, returning to Bloomington, they rented a new log cabin at 612 South Park Street. Although it had been built as a modern novelty the cabin was as spartan as a frontier original. On winter mornings Ross would stick a finger out from under the blankets to try the temperature and with a cry of "41!" he would leap out to stoke up the one stove in the kitchen.

The following summer, 1938, Ross at last got down to work on his novel. He wrote several chapters and was so disappointed with them he put them aside. He decided that his forebears were too remote to hold his interest and that the form he had chosen was unsuitable. But Ross chose to see this thwarting as progress and in the fall he set out cheerfully on an entirely new project.

He felt he expressed himself best in poetry and settled on an epic poem that would deal with events of his own lifetime—1914 to the present. The subject matter would be immediate and the medium more exciting. He anticipated the work would be vast in compass and grandly adventurous in design.

But he had no sooner replenished his optimism and made ready to start when there were new obligations. One of the cabin's hardships was the creosote smell of the logs. It permeated food and clothing and made Ross refer to Vernice and himself as "The Creosote Kids." Vernice, who felt she could put up with anything, could not understand why the smell grew ever more nauseating—until March, when she found she was pregnant.

Ross's first child, a son, was born on November 28, 1938, and in choosing a name it was hard to decide whether to honor his father or mother, but Ross and Vernice settled on Ernest, for that had good associations all around. Although he had spelled it Earnest, this was Elsie's brother's name. It was also that of the modest, fortunate hero of *The Great Stone Face.*

Ross had planned to take fatherhood in stride but it made more demands than he had anticipated. Then his teaching, the writing of his master's thesis and preparing for his orals took what was left of his time.

But in 1939, with his degree in hand, he received a scholarship which allowed him to drop the instructorship, to do some independent study in Greek and philology and to begin serious work on the narrative poem, which he had titled *The Dream of the Flesh of Iron.* He was beginning to recognize its shadowy outline as the mine of the subconscious, a labyrinth of memory and illusion from which he could make excursions into real experience.

During this time of conception and planning Ross became so absorbed with the workings of his own subconscious that he kept a tablet at his bedside and waking from one of his frequent, elaborate dreams he would turn on the light and set it down in shorthand. He urged Vernice to help by waking him, as well as herself, from her own dreams so as to record them before they escaped her. Though hers were rare and far simpler, she dutifully complied.

From this collection Ross was evolving a basic dream situation which would be the recurring pattern of *The Dream of the Flesh of Iron. The Dream's* narrator and central figure, The Dreamer, is attracted to The Beautiful One, a woman who suffers the tyranny of a third figure, a lustful, predatory man known as The Rival or The Enemy. The Dreamer's role is passive. Sometimes he watches, sometimes he shares The Beautiful One's painful experience, but he is invariably disillusioned and corrupted by it.

Ross was aware that he was drawing the classic Oedipal phenomenon from his dreams but he saw it as a universal one, the common form of the "basic, instinctive drives in our passional and aspirational life."

Convinced that triumphant ends did not flow from timid beginnings, Ross drew a bold plan and while Freudianism was surely a page, it was only one of many. Style preoccupied him. He was finding it easier to compose in formal, rhymed stanzas of iambic pentameter but he intended free verse for the final form.

Technique fascinated him. When he and Vernice saw the Cinema Club's screening of D. W. Griffith's *Intolerance*, Ross recognized immediate parallels to *The Dream of the Flesh of Iron*. His master plan was of a multistoried structure and he was busy, as Griffith was, on several levels simultaneously. He seized on the director's use of transitional dissolves, deciding it was just the device to get him from his subconscious world into the realistic one where he hoped to unfold his social theme.

This was essentially a condemnation of modern society. In episodes titled "The Mill," "The Boss," "The Accident," and "The Strike," The Dreamer recognizes and becomes victim of the sickness of the age, materialism. There would be a similar indictment of the times for its revolution and mindless war. In incidents of espionage, a sinking submarine and the clash of armies, Ross planned to show the same progressive malignancy leading society to collapse.

While some of the episodes turned out satisfactorily Ross, who had never been at home with political ideas, found progress slow. His enthusiasm was undiminished but the time he had set aside for *The Dream* was running out and so he applied to Harvard and Yale for a scholarship with which to complete his work for a Ph.D. In the same mail he learned he was welcome at both universities and, knowing that Larry Wylie was in Boston, Harvard was an easy choice.

At the end of the summer of 1940 Ross, Vernice and Ernest, two months shy of his second birthday, set out for Massachusetts. They found an apartment at 18D Shaler Lane in Cambridge, and at Harvard Ross signed up for two philosophy courses and Hyder Rollins's course in Elizabethan poetry and decided on Walt Whitman as the subject for his thesis.

But even as he resumed a full program of study he was giving most of his time—nine-tenths by his own estimate—to *The Dream*, which was still growing in reach. On its grandest level *The*

Dream's stage had become the universe; its time was eternity and its story that of evolution. In this cosmic application of *The Dream*, Ross cast The Dreamer in the role of a suffering Everyman who pursues life's meaning.

Meaning, he finds, is there, entrusted to The Beautiful One. She is all women and she is "oneness sought," which was to say beauty, truth, goodness and freedom. But she perpetually eludes him and so the object, pursuit without attainment—the meaning in the conflict itself—becomes clear to him.

Finally, a villainous civilization is punished by ruin, such that "A hundred stories webbed of stone and steel were crumbling, but with no exploding sound. I watched the rotten carcass shake and reel, enormously collapsing to the ground . . ." At the poem's end a new structure is arising from the rubble. The Dreamer's prescience tells him that whatever its improvements over the old, it will be no more satisfying to him. He is dying anyway and must move on. So, having played his part in the eternal struggle he reenters the elemental lake to become one again with its ooze.

With the approach of the Christmas holidays, Ross took a few days to assess what he had already written. He had four hundred typewritten pages making up a partial draft of the poem, its unfinished sections filled in with prose. But a reading of the typescript left him queasy. The three protean characters continually led him into melodrama and he was not sure of his protagonist. Playing his alternating roles of "beloved ego," spectator and Everyman had cost The Dreamer something in recognition and sympathy. Nor was Ross pleased with the doom-filled mood so uncharacteristic of his own.

In any case he thought it time for a professional opinion. Recalling that Louise Wylie, a Bloomington friend and their occasional babysitter, worked at Houghton Mifflin Company in Boston, he asked her if the firm would be interested in publishing a long poem. Louise, who worked in Houghton's college department, could not say, but she agreed to submit the manuscript and did so on February 1, 1941.

Houghton's reader reported that *The Dream of the Flesh of*

Iron was "an immensely long narrative poem divided into short lyrics, interspersed with frequent prose passages of exposition. This is all about War and the Machine, human depravity and human aspiration, pretty well tangled up together and expressed through symbols that aren't very fresh."

Houghton Mifflin's reaction bruised Ross's pride and, with what he was to describe as "a characteristic, grandiose decision," he shelved the manuscript. But self-certainty was undamaged. He concluded that *The Dream* was sound enough, simply not commercial, and he cast off his depression.

He decided that he had been working a field that was too literary and thus too limited in appeal. What he wanted to do now was write a book that would *sell*. With that in mind he looked for a new concept.

He prescribed for himself a course in contemporary fiction which would clarify for him the nature of "the American theme," and be a warm-up for the popular novel he felt sure he could produce.

Although Thomas Wolfe had died three years earlier, his posthumous novels *The Web and the Rock* and *You Can't Go Home Again* had brought him to the peak of his fame. Ross felt a particular kinship with Wolfe for they shared a gift of prolixity. Long ago, at his father's urging, Ross had taken a stenographic course and gone on to win a state championship in speed typing. Ever since, whether he was writing a letter, lecture notes or fiction, he had addressed his typewriter with a great burst of energy. His fingers flew at the keys. The carriage surged back and forth to a regular ringing of its bell. He could plan, compose and phrase while the pages flew from the roller. If, as Bernard De Voto had suggested, Wolfe's outpouring of words was "like lava from a volcano," Ross's was the spouting of a geyser.

While Ross thought much of Wolfe's work was undisciplined he read him carefully now, noting how successful he had been in turning his own youthful experience directly into fiction.

In *The Magic Mountain* Ross studied the way Thomas Mann

had drawn a portrait of "the disintegrating and warring European culture." It was an accomplishment he thought comparable to Plato's mirroring of Greek civilization in *The Republic* and it suggested to him that a reflection of American culture would be a central purpose of his own book.

But what impressed Ross most was revisiting James Joyce. He admired the portrayal of "subliminal areas of human behavior" in *Ulysses* and was so envious of the novel's overall plan, the single, synoptic day, he felt he could borrow it without being imitative, in fact could use it for breaking new fictional ground.

With these fresh ideas of scope, Ross unearthed the Indiana-at-the-turn-of-the-century novel he had abandoned two years earlier and saw some possibilities in it. His absence made him recognize this territory as his own; here he could maneuver with authority.

For his new superstructure he modified the Joycean single day to a series of days "existing like palimpsests on older days." In moving thus backward in time he could salvage the devices he had discovered in *Intolerance* and, more recently, in Orson Welles's *Citizen Kane*. In the "imbedded flashback" and the "poetic dissolve from Day to Flashback," he saw his way to using some of the dream techniques of *The Dream of the Flesh of Iron* and to blend actual history with the fictional experience of his characters, those modeled on his mother and her brothers.

The old friend and counselor of Ross's undergraduate years, Larry Wylie, had been teaching at Simmons, a women's college, in Boston and now, in the spring of 1941, with another decision to make, Ross turned to him. He confided to Larry that he was giving so little attention to his studies that Harvard had reproved him with a B+. He wanted a less demanding schedule and he wanted some income, enough to support wife and child, and, above all, the time to write. He was quite willing to forgo his Ph.D. until he got this novel out of his system.

Larry agreed to talk to Wylie Sypher of the Simmons humanities department about an opening for the following year. When he interviewed Ross, Sypher was favorably impressed and offered him an instructorship. The salary would be barely two thousand dollars a year but it would be enough, Ross thought, to live and to write, and he accepted.

When the opportunity came to swap their quarters in Cambridge for Don Smalley's house in Bloomington over the summer, Ross leaped at it. With Vernice and Ernest he hurried home, determined to finish a big piece of the novel during his vacation.

During that summer in Bloomington he worked at breathing life into the body of a novel he had despaired of, and by fall he felt he had done it.

Returning to Boston in September, he found an inexpensive three-room apartment for his family. It was number 19, on the fourth floor of the brick walk-up at 46 Mountfort Street, not far from Kenmore Square. Opposite the bedroom an alley opened onto the main-line tracks of the New Haven railroad and their nights were rent by the sounds of heavy freight on the move. The groaning locomotives seemed to explode as they passed beneath their windows but the Lockridges soon grew accustomed to the din and learned to sleep through it. The location was fine for Ross; it was a short walk from Simmons, and Larry Wylie lived nearby on Brookline Avenue.

Afternoons and evenings, the Mountfort Street apartment was the scene of single-minded activity. Ross set up his typewriter in the bedroom and he was always there, absorbed, clattering away at the machine while Vernice looked after young Ernest and prepared their simple meals.

They rarely went out. Vernice seemed shy and awkward to Ross's associates and in fact she did not enjoy the dinner-party exchange. Her punishment was that little kindness was spent on her. One story had it that Ross, hoping to cultivate her taste for Proust, read aloud to Vernice from *Remembrance of Things Past*, and swiftly put her to sleep.

Ross and Vernice kept up a friendship and a semblance of social life with only one couple, Larry Wylie and his wife. Larry had married one of his students, Anne Stiles, an appealing irrepressible Michigan girl. The Lockridges liked her and when she called one day to say she had four tickets to the ballet, they could not resist her invitation. It was a rare event for the Lockridges to set out for an evening's entertainment and the first experience of all four with the ballet.

At intermission the Wylies were surprised to find Ross passing judgment like an old balletomane, his comments salted with such knowledgeable terms as *pas de deux* and *entrechat*. When Larry asked, Ross was perfectly willing to admit he had taken a book on ballet from the library and, with Vernice, spent the afternoon "boning up."

When the Wylies visited the Lockridges they could not get over the austerities practiced at 46 Mountfort Street. The place was pathetically bleak, books and clothing stored in makeshift boxes, piles of papers everywhere. When they came for supper it was likely to be canned beans and franks, the result of Ross's prudent marketing.

On Ross's first day at Simmons, Larry had taken him to meet some of his colleagues, telling him he thought he would enjoy his own closest friend here, a history professor named Warren S. Tryon.

Tryon, known as Steve, was an attractively cynical fellow several years older than Ross and they hit it off at once. Steve called forth Ross's skill at ridicule and Ross played to him, kept him laughing at academic pretentiousness as displayed among the Simmons faculty.

While at first the three met together, it was soon just Ross and Steve who sought each other after class. Sometimes they settled into a bar on Brookline Avenue, a few blocks from the campus, and nursed a beer through the better part of an afternoon, heads together, sharing opinions and revealing themselves. Within a few months, Larry had yielded to Ross his own close friendship with Steve Tryon.

Ross, who had led Steve to believe he was the son of a highly regarded professor at Indiana, gradually permitted a glimpse of his ambivalent feelings toward his father, indicating that he saw through pretense to the undistinguished man within. With a family and life of his own now, he resented his father's domination, the continuing tribute of awe and obligation he required, making Steve wonder if this was the real source of Ross's sport with their colleagues.

When Ross was making a new friend he was often quick to portray himself as a virile fellow and with Steve Tryon particularly he indicated this, bragging a bit about the powerful physical relationship he enjoyed with Vernice.

His humor at these barroom conferences ran to the bawdy. But Ross's determined worldliness was no cloak for the wholesome Hoosier within. When he talked of Paris and its scandalous ways he made it clear they had not rubbed off on him. Actual moral irregularities upset him and he was a wholly faithful husband.

Steve Tryon admired the dynamic, confident Larry Wylie as thoroughly as Ross did. Both recognized that under his easy manner was a man of rare intelligence and deep conviction. Far from having excluded him, they felt abandoned by Larry.

There was some basis for this and it lay with the developing war. Each day the nation grew closer to full participation; the papers were full of convoys and torpedoings in the Atlantic, and young men in uniform hurried through Kenmore Square. Ross professed a new patriotism, saw himself a quick study of the hero's role, and he and Steve often spoke of volunteering for one service or another.

But Larry Wylie's abhorrence for the war was growing deeper and he promised that when the time came he would not go, but become a conscientious objector.

On the afternoon of December 7, hearing the news of the fall of Pearl Harbor, Ross called Steve to say he was going to enlist and suggested they go together to the recruiting office. Steve thought that impetuous and in the end Ross did too, allowing his friend to persuade him that with a wife, an infant son, and a second child due in early summer, it would be wiser to await a draft call.

But as Larry Wylie had promised, he acted out his conscience, going to work as a volunteer janitor at Children's Hospital and, ultimately, leaving Boston to study with the Quakers at Haverford.

Ross was dismayed at his old friend's behavior. Added to their difference about the war was an even more fundamental one—about the way to live. Along with his conviction about acting out his conscience, Larry believed in getting some pleasure out of life. Ross had no time for that. An evening with friends and enjoyment of a good meal or a play were luxuries he was only too glad to sacrifice for his book. Although Ross and Larry Wylie had shared so much in the past, their paths were diverging.

In the spring of 1942 Ross suggested to Steve Tryon they team-teach a course that would combine their fields of history and literature and give a general picture of the social and economic issues of nineteenth-century America. Masking their enthusiasm with superciliousness, they nicknamed it Whiskey Sour 10, vowed to keep it entertaining and to not swamp "our girls" with detail.

Ross proposed to give them a sense "of entering into the course (intercourse)"—making a specific girl responsible for a book, others for intelligent questions. One student, in a class hour, was to report on main concepts, limiting herself to five or ten minutes, while other members of the panel were to ask questions with the free participation of the class and the two instructors.

The advantages, he pointed out, were that the girls would get contact with primary sources, that there would always be something to discuss and that the girls would do a lot of work while the instructors would do none.

In choosing suitable texts, Ross discovered that Steve had a book of his own in mind. He had talked with Houghton Mifflin about writing a history of its predecessor, Ticknor and Fields. This led Ross to confess he too was at work on a book—a novel. Then, at a subsequent session, Ross guardedly produced a section of his work-in-progress and read it aloud. To Ross's satisfaction, Steve liked it enormously.

Encouraged, Ross let Steve read more. The passages were mostly short, poetic ones and Steve continued to approve of them. Ross had been parched for praise and this of Tryon's, with the weight of his few years' seniority, now became the strongest cord of their friendship.

Ross had had close friends before—Malcolm Correll, Larry Wylie, Curt Lamorey. He had always matched himself against them in various ways and seized on each with a startling intimacy and self-exposure, but none of these earlier friendships was quite so intense as this with Steve Tryon. It was because of a present need that had directly to do with the book he was writing.

Ross was wary of all reaction to his work. Years ago, studying Melville's life in high school, he had persuaded himself that public opinion was blundering, as likely as not to ignore true worth and to idolize fatuousness, and that a writer was best off ignoring it altogether. He was equally suspicious of individuals for he realized that uninformed opinion was worthless and informed it was a two-edged knife. And yet he had been alone on this book for over a year. It was as though he had set off at night and after feeling his way in the wilderness for hundreds of days he had yet to see the light. He was desperate for some assurance that he was not lost.

Steve Tryon sensed how vulnerable Ross was, how easily and deeply he could be offended by criticism and how he flourished on admiration. He also realized Ross had given him a privilege, that even Vernice knew next to nothing of what he was writing about.

As for Ross, the possibility of sowing some jealousy between them did not bother him. The book was a professional matter.

For the summer of 1942, the first of the war and of their Simmons years, Ross and Vernice returned to his parents' home in Bloomington. It was here, on July 1, that a second son was born and named Larry Shockley. The Larry, "Not Lawrence, but just Larry," Ross insisted, was for Larry Wylie and the Shockley, of course, honored his mother's family.

During the summer Ross wrote to Steve with some advice for his work. "I hope you can start writing your book soon," he encouraged him. "The hardest thing of all is getting started. Sometimes you just have to pitch in and submerge. Get it going even if it goes badly. After a while things will straighten out. One can always revise."

But with a friend as close as Steve, Ross could not resist the competitive tweak—an expansiveness about his own productivity and, incidentally, the Lockridge spread. "I have had a heck of a good summer. Right now I am typing down in my office, which is a space of cleared ground under three enormous maples in our South Field. I do all my work and reading down there, except when the heat drives me in. Now and then I strike off for a long walk down the road and over the hills, sometimes hiking as much as four miles."

Actually Ross was anxious to get back to Boston. Bloomington and life with his parents had never seemed more restrictive. Used to balancing a dozen undertakings at once, Frank Lockridge could not understand his son's preoccupation with only one, and Ross had hurt him by resisting all efforts to enlist him in his projects. So, in early September, Ross hurried his family back to 46 Mountfort Street, looking forward to long evenings of uninterrupted work.

Over the five Simmons years, their life varied little. It was grueling and yet precisely what Ross and Vernice wanted. No promise of an easier or more luxurious one could have lured them from it, nor was their happiness in it entirely promissory.

For all his cynicism about Simmons and the scant time and energy he gave it, Ross enjoyed teaching there. Whiskey Sour 10 had become a favorite of the students and so had he. The girls sensed his naïveté and thought him remarkably uninformed about the real world. Ross encouraged a legend about himself that he had not read a newspaper in seven years. Some of his more earnest students deplored his readiness to clown for an audience. Still, he was the most popular of their instructors and they believed that inside the show-off was a serious and learned man.

Although getting along on their two thousand dollars was always a problem, Ross was proud of his poverty and welcomed Steve Tryon's cautious offer to pass on some of his boys' outgrown clothing and toys which his wife, Rachel, had assembled.

In the spring of 1943, Ross knew that the most economical summer would be a return to Bloomington and yet he dreaded it. His father had appealed for help with a book about the Wabash River and Ross had turned him down firmly, wanting to establish, once and for all, his independence of the Bloomington workshop.

Steve Tryon had told Ross about his summers at Rockport, a village at the easternmost point of Cape Ann. Once a major source of structural granite it was now an unspoiled summer colony popular with writers and painters.

Ross asked Steve to keep an eye out for an inexpensive place that might house the Lockridges for the summer and Steve located one in Pigeon Cove. It was a slim, white-painted building known as the Cleaves' barn, perched on the side of Pigeon Hill. The first floor contained a large room with a Franklin stove and a rough dining table; the rest was divided by matchboard partitions into kitchen, bathroom and bedrooms. Some narrow stairs led to an overhead loft which would make an ideal workroom. From its narrow, arched windows there was a glimpse, across the abandoned cow yard and a thicket of wisteria, of blue Atlantic.

The rent was two hundred dollars for the season and Ross, confident he could ease the pinch by subletting the Mountfort Street apartment to a graduate student, agreed to take it.

As soon as Simmons was out, Ross, Vernice, Ernest and Larry moved into the Cleaves' barn and a period that was to be joyful and productive. The rocky public beach with access to the clear, cold sea was an easy stroll, and the sparsely settled countryside was ideal for afternoon walks. In the early summer there were blueberries to be picked and later the fruit trees of their orchard ripened with Bartlett pears and apples, from which Vernice would put up enough preserves to last the winter.

The Tryons were prepared to look after them. Steve's property, acquired some years earlier from the Rockport Granite Company, included a rocky wharf with a giant stone bollard, where barges had loaded the great blocks for shipment down the coast, and here in "The Cove" the Tryons entertained at picnics. Neighbors and friends gathered around the grill to munch hamburgers and to look out, over the lobster boats and the roost of cormorants on Gull Rock, at the sea.

But just as in Boston, the Lockridges were not a gregarious couple and it took some urging to get them down from Pigeon Hill. With children to care for it was always difficult for Vernice to get away and when she did turn up at a gathering she tended, unlike Ross, to be shy.

Edith Hellman, a Simmons Spanish instructor whom Ross knew and liked, was often on hand at The Cove, as was her husband, Ben. There was also an Armenian émigré couple, the Arsenians, who summered nearby and who took an immediate interest in the Lockridges.

Aaron Arsenian operated the valet service at the Hotel Manger in Boston, and his wife, Josephine, was a handsome, vital woman with a taste for the arts and creative people. Born and educated in Constantinople, she spoke fluent French and she jabbered away with Ross, admiring his accent, discussing Turgenev, whom she esteemed, and Paris, which Ross told her he loved and hoped to revisit.

Although she had intended no flirtation, Josephine Arsenian caught some dark looks from Vernice. Judging by the usual run of Rockport visitors she guessed that Ross, with his brilliance and good looks, would be giving his stay-at-home wife some grounds for jealousy this summer—but she had misjudged her man. Ross had come to write.

Rachel Tryon did not share her husband's liking for Ross. She thought him insensitive toward his wife and she was particularly annoyed with him one evening when both couples went to the movies in Gloucester.

Passing through the theater lobby, Ross was discovered by a cluster of Simmons girls and as he enjoyed the round of girlish adulations he made no attempt at introducing Vernice and the Tryons but kept them in awkward suspension. Rachel felt this was an unforgivable breach of manners and the baring of an unnatural egoism.

As the season wore on, Rachel Tryon was further irked that Ross showed so little gratitude for their efforts in locating the Cleaves' barn for him at a reasonable rent. She decided that Ross, with his easy recourse to a parental haven in Bloomington, tended to overplay his need. She and her friends were used to being short of money, yet tried not to make a general burden of it.

But if Rachel Tryon was cooling toward Ross, it had no apparent effect on Steve. Each afternoon, as Ross finished his day's work in the loft, Steve waited for him on the grassy slope below and the two men would stroll off together along Drumlin Road.

Neither wives nor children were invited on these outings. The walks took them along the narrowing, rutted lane of granite grout to wind for a mile and a half through sweet-smelling pine and blueberry scrub before it opened into one of the abandoned quarries that are carved, like great amphitheaters, into Cape Ann's green flanks.

Although they carried bathing trunks in case they had to share the quarry, they generally had it to themselves and simply stripped and climbed down along the huge granite steps shelving into the agreeably warm water. While Steve paddled near the shore, Ross would strike out for the bottomless center of the pool and, floating there, gaze up at the awesome, pine-crested wall which plunged without a toehold into black depths.

After their swim the two friends would dry themselves in the sun and talk about books and writing. Then Ross would produce his pocket chess set and they would play until the long shadow of the ridge reached them.

Ross spoke authoritatively about the game, recalling strategies from his tournament experience and he won consistently. Only once did Steve Tryon see his chance for a checkmate and press on to victory but Ross was not amused. He was angry and, as they walked home, remote and silent.

In the loft on Pigeon Hill, Ross's book was going well. Stacked on his worktable lay the nearly two thousand pages of manuscript which, for a year and a half, had been streaming from his typewriter.

In the early phases he had often felt adrift in a sea of his own words, his meaning lost, his ideas shifting like sandbars in the tide of the week's work. Yet recently he had a clarity of vision and a control over the unwieldy manuscript and it often seemed to him that within it a structure, rather like the bones of a living creature, was forming. He was struck by the notion that the work was acquiring a mind and a destiny of its own and guiding him.

On an evening toward the end of summer, while Vernice was busy at jelly making in the kitchen, Ross, a new radiance in his face, burst upon her to report an important discovery. Much of what he had done so far was all right. The characters, insofar as they went, were good ones and the structure and techniques were working perfectly. What he had done wrong was to come too far forward in time. He was off by a generation, for his best material lay in the Civil War days of his grandfather. Not his grandfather's children, but John Wesley Shockley himself would be the main character and his coming-of-age-and-understanding would dominate the book.

It was the first time Ross had admitted her to any details of what he was writing, and Vernice was jubilant and as certain as he that at last he was on the main road to his goal.

And a veil had been lifted from his eyes. He could see everything now, possibilities which had stood before him all along but he had failed to recognize. All that he had yearned to do with a book he saw within his grasp. He felt certain he could "express the American myth—give shape to the lasting 'heroic' qualities of the American people." He would build on two existing myths—the Oriental one of Eden-and-the-Fall-of-Man and the American one of greatness-discovered-at-home.

He felt he could "write the American republic," much as Plato had done, showing the interrelation of his individuals with their state. And he would describe the spirit of nineteenth-century American life with all the "dogmas" on which its Democratic Faith is founded, the dualism between its materialism and idealism, its religious and political rites, its sexual characteristics; and, above all, he would tell a story which would so blend the philosophic, poetic, realistic and comic that it would be the first real representation of the American culture in fiction.

As he began again it seemed to Ross that everything he had seen and felt and done came crowding into the crucible of revision.

Without the slightest regret he drew a line through the top page of his towering first draft and, turning it over, began to rewrite his novel from the start.

Discarding the framework of telescoping days he returned to the plan of a "single, synoptic day." He chose the "Glorious Fourth of July, 1892." The holiday provided patriotic feeling and pageantry while the year, that of the national election, gave him a chance for political speculation.

From that day he would retrace, through a sequence of flashbacks, his now-mature hero's lifetime to reveal its true nature, as well as that of the spiritual and political history of the republic.

When college opened Ross was fully underway and reluctant to quit the loft in Pigeon Cove, so they stayed on into October. Ernest was enrolled in the local kindergarten and Ross commuted to Boston on the train carrying, on each inbound trip, a couple of jars of Vernice's apple jelly.

Late that fall, with his family settled again at Mountfort Street, Ross recalled that little was known of his grandfather Shockley's early marriage, but that there was some mystery about it and that a single child had resulted. He saw here the opportunity to bring in the issue that had divided the nation in war.

He knew about John Shockley's second marriage at first hand, from Emma Shockley herself. Here was the plateau on which his grandfather had consolidated his experiences and been able to write and to be of some influence in his community. For the early years Ross had his own powerful recollections of Indiana boyhood, which he thought could be transposed to his grandfather.

Ross browsed the secondhand bookshops of Boston and Cambridge, buying Civil War books he found on the bargain tables. When he had digested whatever was useful he often presented them to Steve Tryon, inscribed with a scholarly flourish and the hope they would be of value.

As drafts of scenes fell from his typewriter he jotted immediate reactions to them in the margins, clipped them and put them away, "like raw wines . . . to ripen," and pressed on with more of his harvest. While making some changes in a "dream sequence," the idea of a professor who would befriend and guide his hero first occurred to Ross. He began to see this character as the opposite, the dark, cynical side, of John Wesley Shockley. He was given the same initials in the name, Jerusalem Webster Stiles.

Then, with 1944 scarcely begun, Ross received a sobering notice from his draft board. His long-deferred number had come up and he was ordered to appear for an examination of physical fitness in mid-February.

He was still torn about military service. A prompting toward heroism was balanced by absorption in his book and belief in its importance. Also there was the practical problem of his family and its fragile livelihood. This was poignantly emphasized by the date of his physical examination: it coincided with the expected arrival of another child.

There was no assurance that Ross's dependents, now almost four, or his occupation would weigh toward his deferment. Most of his friends were teachers of a similar age with generous counts of children and they had already been called.

Vernice was more apprehensive about Ross's ordeal than her own. Ross was sure he would be inducted and told her that she must return to Bloomington with the children and stay with his parents for the duration of the war.

On February 16, 1944, the day Ross reported for his physical examination, Vernice was in the hospital giving birth to a girl, Jeanne Marie.

Meanwhile, at the induction center, an Army doctor was compiling Ross's bill of health. He found him satisfactory on all counts but then hesitated over a slight irregularity of his heartbeat. He asked about the long convalescence from scarlatina and called in another doctor. After the two had consulted, Ross was told he would not be detained further. He was 4-F, physically unqualified for service.

Ross was deflated. Some vestigial patriotism had finally been denied. He felt left out of an adventure in which other men were taking part, but Vernice received the news with relief.

All in the same day, unflustered by the birth of a first daughter and his deliverance from the Army, Ross got back to work. By the end of spring semester, when they returned to Pigeon Hill and the Cleaves' barn, he had completed most of the research and by the end of July he had finished a first draft of his flashback episodes, some fifty of them, which were to constitute three-quarters of the book; he had also accomplished the rough-hewing of his central figure—John Wesley Shockley.

Now Ross turned to The Day itself and began to write the passages that would show its progress and lead into the flashbacks. Also Ross felt in comfortable command of his characters. While each had required a model, the fictional counterpart had taken on a life of his own and now had to be cut free of the original.

His hero was surely strong enough to stand on his own and Ross changed his last name from Shockley to Shawnessy. Also, he changed his grandmother's maiden name from Rhoton to Root. He thought the scene, Henry County, might also benefit from disguise. He began to juggle words, trying them for sound and associations, and in recalling a snatch of A Pageant of New Harmony, he remembered the raintree. The thought started a string of associations. He particularly liked the raintree's Oriental origin, for it underlined his hope of blending the Oriental Eden myth with a newer, American one in the life story of his hero. "Raintree" County pleased him.

He took up a pencil and began to sketch a map of it that resembled but varied from the real Henry County. Straughn be- became Strawland, later Waycross. New Castle became Freehaven. A lake grew in the center which he gave the meaningful name Lake Paradise, and he looped a river toward it, spelling, rather vaguely, his hero's name—Johnny.

As this second summer at Pigeon Hill drew to a close he was so sure of his progress that his thoughts returned to publication. He talked about it to Steve Tryon, telling him more about the nature of his book, permitting him glimpses of scenes and saying he was leaning toward a New York house.

Steve cautioned against this in favor of a Boston one, pointing out the advantage of having an editor within walking distance.

Although Steve offered to open the way for him at Houghton Mifflin, Ross had the feeling that, lately, the man's enthusiasm for the book had cooled.

On a trip to the village during this same August, Ross recognized an acquaintance from graduate school days at Harvard. It was Richard Scowcroft, an intense, intelligent yet self-effacing fellow, and Ross was interested to learn he was here in Rockport completing a novel. It was his first, *Children of the Covenant*, and Houghton Mifflin was going to publish it.

Ross admitted to Dick Scowcroft that he too was winding up a first novel. He told him that although he had great confidence in the book, in view of its length it might be difficult to place with a commercial publisher and he asked advice about an agent.

Scowcroft thought that if a writer had access to a publisher, an agent was not essential and he volunteered to help at Houghton Mifflin. Ross said that his friend Tryon had already agreed to do the same.

Returning to Boston in that fall of 1944, Ross kept up his pace. He forged ahead on The Day passages while he was fresh in the morning, and in the afternoon he went back to revise and polish the book from its beginning.

Ross worked in the "bedroom-study," sharing it with one or more of the children while they slept or, more often, played around him. Once, while he was out of the room, one of them did put a page of the first flashback into a wastebasket and it was emptied before the loss was discovered. Ross could never recapture the phrasing of the original and spoke of it painfully as the one "lost chord" of his book.

When Larry was a year old he climbed onto a pile of manuscript and urinated triumphantly upon it. His father not only forgave him but in due course commended him for "the only advanced critical faculty in the family." For the most part, children underfoot did not bother Ross. He had a deaf ear where they were concerned and could concentrate even while immersed in noise— provided it was *good-humored* noise.

In October Ross was ready for Vernice to begin the fair copy of the manuscript. Hers was to be a stenographic ordeal of eighteen months. Each night, when the children were put to bed, Ross would give her an episode for final copying and Vernice would carry it into the front room, where she had set up her own typewriter, and go to work.

As yet he had revealed nothing to her but the general plan of the book so that Vernice discovered its characters and story as she typed. Ross was delighted to find her anticipating each day's installment as though following a serialization. He asked her not to read beyond what she was copying and when he heard her machine pause for a suspiciously long period he would call out, "No fair, Honey. Stop reading the manuscript." Whereupon Vernice would resume typing, obediently curbing her curiosity.

She was soon convinced that the main character, while modeled on John Wesley Shockley, was Ross himself as a young man, and she took exception, very close to mutiny at her keyboard, at his interest in one female character. She was certain the girl would be as recognizable to her friends as to herself. Though neither she nor Ross had seen her since school days, she was still jealous.

It was a serious moment, involving as it did the welfare of book and marriage, but Ross handled it with characteristic firmness. It was his right as author, he explained, to write the book as he saw fit and proposed that if the copying gave her pain he would spare her. He felt sure one of the Simmons girls would oblige.

It was Vernice's last objection to the text.

In early May 1945, with the German surrender indicating the war was all but over, Ross hoped to repeat the pattern of his two previous summers. Learning the Cleaves' barn had been sold, he asked Steve Tryon to find him another place in Rockport, perhaps a roomier one than the barn, and closer to town. Ross said he would be willing to go two hundred and fifty dollars for the season.

Nothing did turn up in Rockport, but Ross learned of an available house in South Byfield, a town not far from Cape Ann that promised little in swimming or social stimulus but a seclusion fit for a novelist with work to do.

Ross took it—and in mid-June all five Lockridges moved to South Byfield, where they had to adjust to the mosquitoes, a temperamental water pump and the stillness. "Everything out here is so goddam peaceful," Ross reported to Steve Tryon. "Sweet Byfield! loveliest village of the plain. Where human beings go quietly insane."

In thanking the Tryons for another batch of clothes, Ross noted that they had been of great help in outfitting Ernest and that Vernice, who had "been meaning to write Rachel and thank her for everything," had been somewhat overwhelmed by the summer's demands. He had a final, wistful thought for past seasons. "One of the things we're really going to miss . . . will be the wonderful evenings when you and Rachel came up to visit us on the hill."

But they were soon making the best of it and by mid-July he announced to Steve that "The Great Work" was proceeding at a terrific pace—"1200 copied pages of incandescent prose at this reading."

Returning to Boston and to Simmons in the fall of 1945, Ross felt truly on the homestretch. All the major architecture was complete and only some final details remained to be worked out. Ross estimated that between them, he and Vernice would have the manuscript complete and on its way to a publisher before the birth of a fourth child, due in midwinter.

But, understandably, the tidying stage dragged on and "the stork won the derby," as Ross observed in announcing to Steve Tryon the arrival, on February 21, of "Ross Franklin Lockridge. Tertius (et ultimus, I trust)."

Back from the hospital, Vernice fed and bedded down her four children and resumed typing where she had left off. Then, one night in April, Ross heard her typewriter pause and was about to reprimand her for the relapse when it occurred to him that "something much more august and momentous had occurred." Going into the front room he found her weeping over the last page of the manuscript. Vernice had typed the final line.

Believing her tears welled not from relief at having finished her task but the emotional impact of that final page, Ross resolved never to change a word of it.

The manuscript stood at six hundred thousand words, far more than in the published *Gone with the Wind* and roughly equal to the word count of the three colossi of American fiction, *Anthony Adverse* and the *Studs Lonigan* and *U.S.A.* trilogies. He affixed a working title, *The Riddle of Raintree County*, to the two-thousand-page manuscript, divided it into five volumes —each the size of a conventional manuscript—and enclosed them in five spring binders. He was ready to offer it for publication.

Although he had received an inquiry from Gorham Munson at Prentice-Hall and knew that his cousin, Mary Jane Ward, would arrange an introduction to her publisher, Random House, Steve Tryon's advice, supported by Dick Scowcroft's, pointed to Houghton Mifflin for a first submission.

Ross had given Steve a copy of the early part of the revised manuscript to read and he had not only kept it for several weeks but then confessed he had not had time to read it all. As though this were not enough indifference, instead of the customary praise Steve had reacted with the whimsical judgment that from what he had read it was either a masterpiece or nonsense.

Although Ross was nettled by such capriciousness, Steve had redeemed himself somewhat by stirring up Houghton's interest in seeing the manuscript. A letter from the publisher arrived on April 9, asking about it and suggesting Ross forgo the interview he had proposed as a prelude to submission until the editors had read the novel.

Thus, on April 24, 1945, Ross carried the five volumes of *The Riddle of Raintree County* to the Houghton Mifflin offices at 2 Park Street, left them with a receptionist and went home to wait.

His first bulletin came from Steve Tryon and was disquieting. After the lapse of two weeks, Steve had phoned an inquiry to his friend Ferris Greenslet, emeritus editor-in-chief, then followed it up with a visit. Greenslet told Tryon that when he had called about the Lockridge manuscript, a new member of the editorial staff had been in his office and he had asked this young man to have a look at the novel and tell him something about it in the morning.

This report was respectful. Indeed, the reader confessed to "being a little stunned" by the author's ambitiousness and thought the book might "draw a small but passionate following," but he took particular exception to the fifth volume, the coda or dream section, which was imitative of Joyce; he didn't think the book would sell well and was doubtful about publication. His recommendation was for someone else to have a look at it.

Interpreting this as bad news, Steve Tryon pointed out to Ferris Greenslet that he had persuaded Ross to offer his book to Houghton in the face of other advice and the author's own preference for a New York house. He repeated his own opinion, that *The Riddle of Raintree County* was either a masterpiece or nonsense, but in either case it would be a mistake to turn his friend's book down without further consideration.

Greenslet assured Tryon it would have that. He would have a look at it himself and then turn it over to Dorothy Hillyer, who he felt would have a particular feeling for this sort of fiction.

On hearing a full account of Steve's efforts on *The Riddle of Raintree County's* behalf, Ross was not nearly so pleased as Steve imagined. He saw him as exploiting his role of mediator at both ends—indicating to Houghton that but for his own good offices the manuscript would have gone elsewhere, and to Ross that if it were not for his having such a good friend at court *The Riddle of Raintree County* would have been turned away at the door.

As a hedge against further disappointments at Houghton Mifflin, Ross unearthed the Prentice-Hall inquiry and mailed Gorham Munson a copy of the manuscript. Then, on May 10, he fired off a letter to Dorothy Hillyer which began, "Mr. Tryon, who seems to be a self-appointed ambassador between me and Houghton Mifflin," and is surely "a very charming person and a very good and devoted friend of mine, has a way of overplaying his hand."

Of Tryon's opinion that *The Riddle of Raintree County* is "either one of the great books of our time or a pile of nonsense," he assured her that it was most certainly not the latter and that Tryon was unqualified to make an assessment, having "had time so far to read hastily only one-fifth of the book." In any case, as the author, he felt the book quite able to stand on its own merits.

Nonetheless, he could not resist a little salesmanship of his own. An intelligent editor, he pointed out, "will see the essential clarity and beauty of the design and the essential novelty of the book—and a touch of imagination should lead that editor to see that its novelty and size—the very qualities which Tryon feels scared about," will sell it to the critics—it's a critic's book—and in turn to a huge public. "It will be talked about, written about, and read, read, read!"

What he was looking for, he confessed, was an editor who would provide "the same conviction and backing . . . that Wolfe got from Perkins . . . not that *Raintree County* is a huge chaos crying for the knife. It's as solid as a rock. But it does need cutting, sharpening, rearranging . . . *Bref*, what I want is a chance to liberate the classic that is in it."

He added a further admonition about the publishing opportunity at hand, pointing out his own inclination toward Random House, where "my cousin, Mary Jane Ward, who would do anything for me, has just published *The Snake Pit*, a B. of the M.C. choice" and noting that he had "heard Houghton Mifflin is timid and conservative about taking and pushing a work that doesn't conform to some easily recognizable and saleable genre." He had been told that "my book and I are cut out for certain New York publishers who have, it is said, more dash and dare and might go mad about a big, ambitious, 'different,' first novel like this one."

In closing, he reassured her that "no one has yet received a copy of the MS but you . . ." Nevertheless, he would want the one at Houghton Mifflin returned in three weeks' time, when, with school out, he would be "off on my adventures."

Ross's bold advice did not go unheeded at 2 Park Street, where *The Riddle of Raintree County* was making the rounds from Greenslet to Dorothy Hillyer and other editors, acquiring some snubs for its prolixity, diffuseness and derivativeness but increasing admiration for its scope and vigor.

The members of Houghton's editorial department wrote unusually long reports on it. They were critical of the dream section, but respectful. They found much to admire and each was more effusive than the last. One five-page report concluded, "After much consideration, now for, now against, I finally vote to publish. Whether R. C. is a great American novel or not is beside the point; we need more of this kind of courageous stab at it, and I would be willing to gamble."

Another reader, in full awareness of the hazards, described it as "a work of genius." The next argued that point but admitted, "I have pretty well made up my mind that Lockridge is the man from Mars." The last man surrendered completely, finding *The Riddle of Raintree County* "the novel Walt Whitman might have written." It had "Stephen Benét's sweep of American history, Sinclair Lewis's debunking strain, the symbolism of Hawthorne . . . While some will find the satire harsh, the nature writing too lush, the symbolism overpowering—when all is said, there remains a work whose boldness takes your breath and throughout whose great length, your interest is held fast."

During these days toward the end of May and of the academic year, Ross had some indications from Mrs. Hillyer that Houghton was getting interested in *The Riddle of Raintree County.* Since he had no telephone at home and did not like the idea of these tense, perhaps disappointing, conversations being overheard in the English department office, he kept in touch with her from the telephone booth in the ground-floor lobby.

On an early June morning, Ross called Mrs. Hillyer to ask if Houghton Mifflin had reached a decision and she replied that it had. They wished to publish *The Riddle of Raintree County,* subject of course to certain revisions and cutting, particularly in the fifth volume, the dream section. But they foresaw no real difficulties there. The main thing, she wanted Ross to know, was that a great wave of enthusiasm for his book had swept Houghton

Mifflin's editorial department. She felt it was going to be an immensely successful book, and as an indication of house confidence, they were offering him herewith an advance of thirty-five hundred dollars.

Emerging from the booth, Ross started down the corridor and in passing the door of the Romance languages department, caught sight of Edith Hellman, his colleague and Rockport friend. Dancing in, he threw his arms around her crying, "Edith, they say it's terrific! And I know it *is!*"

He hurried on to his waiting class, one of the last of the year but there was no question of teaching the girls today. He could only share his great news with them and dash on with it to Vernice, and then telegraph it home to Bloomington.

Although Ross was apprehensive at what he would find behind Houghton Mifflin's stone façade at 2 Park Street, Dorothy Hillyer's welcome reassured him. She was obviously an intelligent and sophisticated person. He learned that she had been married to the poet Robert Hillyer. But there was nothing in the least forbidding about her. She was warm and womanly and she still bubbled with enthusiasm about his book. It was as though she had been awaiting it for a long time.

She took him on to meet Dale Warren, Craig Wylie and the other editors, each of whom had praise for his book and a deference that would suit a gladiator on his way to the victory celebration.

Ross was surprised to find Paul Brooks a young man, not much older than himself. He had only recently returned from service with the Office of War Information but he was fully in command of the department as Ferris Greenslet's successor as editor-in-chief. Brooks, he realized, was not an effusive man, but there was a rocklike authority and sincerity about him which Ross liked and trusted.

Dorothy Hillyer then led Ross up to the third floor to meet Lovell Thompson, head of the trade department and the firm's vice-president. Thompson explained that he would oversee *The Riddle of Raintree County's* design, manufacture and advertising and Ross was taken by his subtle, countryman's humor.

He recalled that Larry Wylie's wife, Anne, had been Thompson's secretary and now he was pleased to find that Martha Stiles, Anne's sister and also a Simmons graduate, had replaced her. He was overwhelmed by all these clearly good people and their enthusiasm for him and his book.

As he left, Ross confessed to Dorothy Hillyer that in entering the building there had been some question if he wouldn't be better off at a New York house. Prentice-Hall had responded quickly and favorably to the manuscript he had sent them. But there was no question now. He had been won by the men and women here and was happy to be published by Houghton Mifflin.

He agreed to do some thinking about cutting and revision, made an appointment to return on July 2 for an editorial conference and left 2 Park Street on a comber of euphoria.

The advance of thirty-five hundred dollars, almost double his yearly salary, convinced him that he had passed from the vast company of the wistful into the select fellowship of literary professionals. He was in a position to make the decision he had dreamed of for the eleven years since his graduation from college—to quit teaching. He would certainly not return to Simmons. For the next few months he would give all his energy to revising *The Riddle of Raintree County* and then get on to whatever was next in his writing career.

When he announced all this news to Steve Tryon his friend had some words of caution. A writer's life, he pointed out, was always a precarious one and until he had a firm, negotiable reputation, it was a good idea for him to keep his academic anchor in place. What was the point in quitting Simmons now?

Ross disagreed. His book was going to be so big the critics could not ignore it. He had complete faith in its success and in his own as a writer. Tingling with all the gratifying, role-reversing sensations of a sweepstakes winner, he headed for the office of President Bancroft Beatley and the exquisite pleasure of resigning.

That night he wrote Larry Wylie at Haverford about the happy outcome of his five-year labor. "It promises to be the longest novel ever published in one piece by an American . . .," he told him and he could not resist the one-upman's impulse, fattening Houghton's confidence in him to "$5000 in advance royalties." Ross went on:

> With that, I finally did my long postponed but all the sweeter act of kissing the unsightly pile of Simmons College farewell. It was a wonderful place to have been, and my whole attitude toward it is sweetley elegiac. Mr. Beatley graciously granted me a leave of absence, which we both knew was just an academic gesture. I verbally applied the toe of my shoe to Wylie Sypher's pants, and showed the whole world of teaching a swiftly receding view of my derriere.
>
> We hope to get the thing out by Xmas, at which time I will expedite to you your own personally autographed gift copy, a small token of my great personal esteem and admiration for both of you. By the way it is no exaggeration to say, Larry, that this book would never have appeared in this form except for your influence—always good—in my life. Largely because of you I went to France and acquired that all-important cosmopolitan point-of-view, and because of you I got my five-year sinecure at Simmons, just when I needed a position of that kind to make the book and a family possible at the same time.

Since there was no need for his family to delay summer plans while Ross awaited his editorial conference, Vernice agreed to go to Bloomington at once, settle the children with the senior Lockridges and look for a suitable home of their own.

When Vernice arrived in Bloomington in early June, expecting to be overwhelmed with questions about Ross's publication, she was surprised to find that his telegram had never arrived. Thus it was she who brought home the glorious news about *The Riddle of Raintree County*.

Frank proudly notified the third author of the family, Mary Jane Ward Quayle, in Elgin, Illinois, who replied at once, rejoicing with him in this further proof of family virtuosity and offering to provide a comment on the book if Houghton wanted one.

Learning of Mrs. Quayle's offer from his father, Ross sent it along to Dorothy Hillyer, explaining that although he had not asked her help, his cousin Mary Jane Ward had offered it. She was the author and, he confided, an alumna of *The Snake Pit*.

Aside from Mary Jane Ward, Ross knew only one published novelist, Dick Scowcroft. Established now by the appearance of *Children of the Covenant*, Scowcroft knew the literary game, Houghton Mifflin's in particular. So Ross telephoned him to say he was joining the Houghton list and to suggest they have dinner together.

When he turned up at Scowcroft's in Cambridge, Ross felt very much the fraternity pledge in a first interview with a chapter member. He hoped to learn the dos and don'ts and also to display his own credentials favorably. But he found Scowcroft already impressed with him. Checking up with Dorothy Hillyer Dick had learned that Houghton was indeed taking the Lockridge book, that she and others were enthusiastic and that it "smells of money."

Assuring Ross he was in good hands and had every reason to celebrate, Scowcroft produced a bottle of bourbon and filled two glasses. Even now, at thirty-one, Ross was unaccustomed to hard liquor and disliked its taste, but he knew an initiation ceremony when he saw one and drank along with his host.

Ross described his book with a kind of scholarly remove, as though it were someone else's work which he was presenting to a roomful of Simmons girls. "One of the really exciting things about this novel . . . ," he would begin and go on to tell about some feature he felt was unique.

With Scowcroft nodding encouragement and Ross deciding they were fellow craftsmen, sharing discoveries about their trade, he went on ever more warmly about his accomplishment. There was nothing haphazard about it, he explained. He had planned it all carefully. For example, he had prepared himself, before beginning to write, by reading dozens of novels and calculating the essentials of a major theme.

Even though Dick told him that theirs was a fine publisher in every way, Ross was anxious about Houghton's capacity for promoting the book and told him that after all he had put into the writing of *The Riddle of Raintree County*, he would be a fool not to put an equal amount of energy into its promotion—not simply leaving that up to them.

Dick Scowcroft's willingness to listen and his knowledgeable assurances made him a fine audience and Ross could not be sure if it was more the whiskey or Dick's receptiveness that had loosened his tongue.

Whichever, as they drank their way to the bottom of the bottle, Ross was ever more revealing of himself. He knew that some writers had sexual problems, but he had none. He felt homosexuality was abhorrent and he dismissed the idea there was an element of it in male friendship.

He spoke of his Paris days and told how he had lost his virginity there to an Eastern college girl, but he quickly assured Dick he had no inclination to promiscuousness for he had married a wonderful girl who became more so, in every way, with the years.

He had no personal difficulties. He had not been bothered by poverty or the necessity to teach. Life had been joyous; it was now and the prospects were infinitely so.

They finished the bottle before they made their way down into Harvard Square for a sandwich, and in parting, Ross was exalted. Dick Scowcroft had not only accepted him into the fellowship of novelists, but acknowledged his candidacy as an officer.

On June 20, a few days before his editorial conference, Ross received a telegram which read, "Just heard about the book from Larry and have talked to HM about my doing a possible article on you for *Life*. Hope we can discuss it further. Will you call?" It was signed by Larry Wylie's older brother, Francis, or commonly "Jeff," Wylie. He was the *Time* and *Life* correspondent in Boston and he gave the telephone number of his office in the Statler Building.

Ross recognized this as the knocking of a rare publicity opportunity and a sign of the good fortune which lay ahead. He did not believe in luck. Luck was a lazy man's explanation of talent and hard work. But he suspected that with the finishing of his book he had passed into a world where happy, marvelous events were a matter of course—and he was counting on them.

That same afternoon, Ross was at Jeff Wylie's desk, recalling that they had met at a Phi Gam reunion, that Jeff had been a classmate and fraternity brother of Shockley's as well as a friend of Vernice's older sister, Clona.

With these good Indiana cords secured, Ross told Jeff Wylie that he had drawn on family recollections and their own Indiana for his big book. He admitted that while no one in his right mind would set out to write "The Great American Novel," *The Riddle of Raintree County* was conceived on so vast a scale that it was going to be regarded as just that.

He explained his book's radical techniques, told Johnny Shawnessy's story and of how it was equally the story of America's progress from the innocence of the old republic, through "the great sleepwalk of the Civil War," into the bloody beginnings of modern industrial warfare.

But he had transcended the merely historical, Ross explained. His scene of Raintree County was the mythical America, just as John Wesley Shawnessy was the mythical American; it was important to recognize that, since man lives in a world of myth. He does so since that is the only world in which he can live, and indeed the only world where life is. The book embraced a philosophy of ideas as daring as Plato's. In short, it was the American *Republic*.

Jeff Wylie was a good listener and Ross now suggested four schemes whereby *Life* could exploit *The Riddle of Raintree County*. An article on "The Glorious Fourth" could use his dramatization of it to celebrate the traditional holiday and all its institutions, the speeches, the races, the distinguished visitors, the parades. Another piece could be done on motion picture possibilities. The book was full of cinematic techniques and would lend itself to the panoramic photography which was *Life*'s specialty. A third was an article on him and the artistic process of his novel's growth. He thought he might be persuaded to sit for such a portrait.

Finally, he saw an article in exploring Raintree County's real-life model, Henry County, Indiana, and the prototypes from which he had made his characters. A family album would yield pictures of grandfather Shockley, his wife, Emma, and his daughter, Elsie, as a young girl.

When Ross described the Indiana possibilities, Jeff told him he would be in Bloomington on vacation next month, and with Ross there too, they might go over the ground together. They agreed to do so and meanwhile Jeff promised to propose all of Ross's ideas to his editors in New York.

Ross was confident of his persuasive power. There was a science to it, naturally, and subtlety was not the essential instrument. As in Indian wrestling, a little leverage made all the difference. So he left Jeff Wylie with the thought that their fellow Hoosier and fellow alumnus Harlan Logan was editor of *Look* and thus he had "a hot wire open" to a principal competitor—still, his preference was strong for *Life*.

Preparing himself for his editorial conference on July 2, Ross could see no purpose in cutting the book simply to reduce its size. In any case it would fall into the giant category and it seemed wise to make a virtue of that. Incidentally, he decided that "The Riddle" with its suggestion of a mystery story, and thus of superficiality, should be dropped from the title. But he was troubled by what to do about the dream section. Although he had acknowledged Houghton's reservations about it, he still thought it was the book's supreme stylistic feat.

It compared favorably with Joyce's *Walpurgisnacht*, he told Dorothy Hillyer, "less verbally pedantic and clinically sexual than Mr. Bloom's circean trance, the woven dream of Raintree County is more poetic, dramatic, atmospheric and readable . . . it goes beyond *Ulysses*, blending the collective experience of humanity with the private and American experience of Mr. Shawnessy."

From the beginnings, not only of the book, but his own as a creative artist, he told her, "the problem of the use of dreams and the 'unconscious' life in literary form has been a preoccupation. It began, not as might be imagined with reading of Joyce . . . but straight from the source—Freud. I read Freud at seventeen and kept on reading and studying him from that time forward. I reject Freudeanism as a life-philosophy, but consider that it has brought new materials of an incomparable richness to the exposition of human personality."

The dream section, he pleaded, "is intended as a dessert after the main banquet. It is the epilogue of A *Midsummer Night's Dream*. The dramatic action is in a sense over but the play is not over and the little enchanted people come and murmur their incantations over the sleepers."

But, in first indication of a malleable side, Ross did consider Dorothy Hillyer's patient counsel that the dream section was a device which had served him as a springboard for the novel but now should be absorbed, if not eliminated. He conceded that it was "too long—out of all proportion to the rest of the book" and that it was "more difficult to read." However, he could not resist pointing out that his purpose here was "the opposite of Joyce's." Where Joyce, with his "natural antipathy to aquacity," attempted to make the simple obscure, "my whole intention is to make the obscure simple. There are more *ideas* in fifty pages of *Raintree County* than in the whole of *Ulysses*, but *Raintree County* is much more readable. I want the same principle to apply to the Dream Section. I want it to be a delightful reader-experience, as I think all the highest art should give delight and pleasure and be a kind of godlike and enchanting game. On careful reconsideration, I feel the Dream Section might be cut by half—not divided by an axe, but compressed."

Ross was given a list of suggestions for revision. Among them was a query about the long Elsie section with its admiring view of her father. It seemed irrelevant to the narrative and interfered with its progress. A question was raised about Edith Vaughn, the actress of Shawnessy's sojourn in the city. She was felt to be unconvincing because she was symbol made to look like character. Finally, it was proposed that the Evalina Brown episode obscured Shawnessy's relationship during The Day with his wife, Emma.

Ross accepted his editors' suggestions with an unexpected humility and indicated he would add them to an equally imposing list of his own. He was now anxious to be home in Bloomington and to get to work. Dorothy Hillyer, who had recognized and respected Ross's intransigence over some of his book's vulnerable aspects and had warned Paul Brooks of her doubts they could persuade him to much cutting and revision, was overjoyed at Ross's willingness and enthusiasm for the job.

Just as he was leaving for Bloomington, Ross heard from Jeff Wylie that he had had a reaction from New York and read him Lillian Rixey's memorandum. It went: "Your Bloomington author sounds good—particularly the idea of re-enacting novel with real Bloomingtonians, pegged on what happens there on July 4th. Sounds like a combination of Whitman and Joyce . . ."

So Ross started for home with the feeling that a destiny as abundant as he had imagined it over the years of waiting now lay before him.

V

Traveling west Ross recognized this journey as an ascent to a first summit and savored each of its satisfactions. Throughout the spring months with their uncertainties and exasperations, there had been no question in his mind of returning to South Byfield or Cape Ann. The Atlantic breezes, so alluring in previous summers, had lost their appeal, just as Indiana's August discomforts were forgotten. This was the journey he had been awaiting for six years. He was going home—victorious.

In the rack overhead lay the manuscript copy of the novel which he now felt to be alive and bursting with the richest possibilities. His friends at Houghton had left no doubt about it. The book was going to bring him success to match the dream which had been coming into ever sharper focus since childhood. Moreover, these exquisite, anticipatory joys were compounded by finding himself one with his own hero. He was beginning to live the very triumph he had created in fiction.

Homecoming was at the core of it. All Ross's own yearning for literary ascendancy was implicit in the young John Shawnessy, who identifies with "that other gifted child of nature, Willie Shakespeare . . . ," and imagines himself dreaming kindred dreams of "how one day he would go to the city and tup the most exciting woman and make much gold and come back at last to Stratford-on-Avon and buy the finest house in town . . ."

Ross had made homecoming the very essence of his novel through the myth of the Great Stone Face, with its prophecy of a man who, though he travel far in search of glory, must return home to be recognized.

But there was an even more primary fulfillment in homecoming than that of ambition. It was the blood compulsion of it and Ross was experiencing this with an increasing poignance the closer he drew to Bloomington. It was the emotion he described in John Shawnessy's heart.

Shawnessy, summoned from the city by a telegram that begins "come home . . ." and awakens his concern for his mother, entrains for Indiana. Just as Ross found no joy in travel for its own sake, so Shawnessy is repelled by the ugly, industrial right-of-way. "These miles of iron roadways, these planless cities, these stations, depots, roundhouses, warehouses, grain elevators, factories, were the gray huge swollen river of American time. Like a gulf of bitter waters he had to drink it down before he could come home . . ."

But through the journey he comes "to understand as never before the isolation and uniqueness of other human beings. Each one he knew was going on a private voyage across time, approaching or departing from the terminals of birth, marriage, death, from the cities of joy and sorrow; and each, whether he knew it or not, carried in his pocket a crumpled telegram telling him to come back home."

When he arrived in Bloomington on the glorious Fourth, Ross had not been home in four years, not since the summer of 1942, and the reunion with his mother, father and sister as well as that with his wife and children was joyous.

Vernice had told Frank and Elsie only that Houghton had agreed to publish Ross's book and now he was able to tell about the events of the last weeks, of the publisher's assurances that both popular acclaim and literary distinction were in store for *Raintree County*, that he had, in his first book, written no ordinary novel, but a masterpiece—a work that was going to take its place alongside the monuments of American fiction.

One of the book clubs was pretty certain to choose it and a

magazine to serialize it. In fact, *Life* was already planning an article and he told of Jeff Wylie's involvement, his impending arrival in Bloomington and their proposed journey to Henry County.

Ross was feeling cocky and he did not hide it from old acquaintances as he wandered around Bloomington. He was delighted to tell John Robert Moore, his scourge from composition class and chess team, that his Boston publisher was content with his style, in fact had assured him that his book would stand secure on both popular and literary ground. Like all great literature it was going to sell and it was going to endure.

Steve Tryon had just received a Guggenheim fellowship for his history of the publisher Ticknor and Fields and was taking the following year off to write it. Ross wrote, advising him, "The important thing is to have a book—substantial and saleable. I am perfectly sure that when your book goes in to H.M., if you plan to let them 'have the refusal,' it will get a very careful reading from the big shots—and I may be in a position by that time to help it even more."

Coming, as it did, from a young man who just a few months earlier Steve had been helping through the doors at 2 Park Street, it was a patronizing offer, hardly sweetened by the promise of a complimentary copy of *Raintree County*, "For your interest in my book and the generous—and helpful—things you said about that part of it which you saw . . ."

Jeff Wylie had arrived in Bloomington on vacation, bringing word that his editors had cooled on the idea of a Bloomington Independence Day celebration. A telegram from them foresaw no more than a "short news story angled on fantastic length novel so guess we unwant lengthy Bloomington background suggest you holding on to it for future cover possibilities."

But Ross was not discouraged in the least. He bustled ahead with plans for their trip to Henry County and wrote to Lovell Thompson as though the *Life* article, a year hence, was a sure thing. He was worried about the schedule, he said. The Book-of-the-Month Club would need time to act, and so it was important to base a publication timetable around *Life's* use of *Raintree County* material the next Fourth of July and to provide the book clubs with galleys early in the year. This meant he must complete his revisions within two months, ten weeks at the outside.

He was concerned about publicity too and confided his theory of it. "Like Walt Whitman I believe in 'spending for big returns,' especially when the spending is in energy and faith rather than money. It always seemed to me that the best publicity is free publicity or—still better—publicity that someone else pays for."

Houghton Mifflin's publicity director was Diggory Venn, a lively ex-newspaperman, and Ross wrote him a long letter calculated to leave him in no doubt about this author's expectations. As a result of his own groundwork with Jeff Wylie, the *Time* and *Life* editors in New York were well informed about *Raintree County* and their interest was deep. It only remained for Venn to cultivate this.

He interpreted Jeff's telegram from Rockefeller Plaza in the rosiest light, as instructions to gather material for a future cover story and a request for immediate news. Ross warned Venn against playing his book as a freak. Still, mention of it now, giving *Time* a scoop on it, so to speak, months before publication, "would alert the whole world to the existence of such a book, and everyone, including *Time*, would then be on the watch for its appearance."

His novel's newsworthiness, Ross explained, was its size, the amount of work that went into it and, of course, "the general impression that Houghton Mifflin is sitting on something hot." He was more explicit. "Now, while it would be inaccurate to say the work is a million words long (it is actually more than 600,000 in present MS form—about the length of *Anthony Adverse*), the vague but impressive statement might be made that it is over 2000 pages in MS or that it is in five huge MS volumes, both perfectly truthful observations, committing no one to anything. But then I leave the subtleties of the problem up to you."

Henry County lies along Route 40, the National Road, some twenty-five miles east of Indianapolis. From Bloomington it is nearly a hundred miles to the northeast, and on the morning of

July 13, Ross assembled his expedition. He was at the wheel of the family car, sharing the front seat with Ernest and his mother, who would act as guide. In the back seat were Vernice, Jeff Wylie and his wife, Betty.

They arrived in New Castle, Henry County's seat, in time for lunch, and afterward Ross led a walking tour which circled the Victorian courthouse with its statue of blindfolded justice and ended in an inspection of the museum. This had been a school and Ross explained it was his model for Professor Stiles's Pedee Academy. Indeed, he had taken the whole town and its features for Raintree County's center, renaming it Freehaven.

Leaving town they paused at the old home place, which Elsie explained had been the Shockley farm, her father's boyhood home, and although there was no longer a trace of it, there had been a tiny town here, no more than a post office really, known as Danwebster.

She led the party over a barbed-wire fence, around a hog-wallow and, with increasing dismay, through a jungle of underbrush to what had been a well-kept family graveyard. Only a few head-stones were standing and these Ross crouched to read. He decided to take one along, lugged it back to the fence, heaved it over and was astonished to see the stone shatter on the ground. "Judgment for sacrilege," he announced and proceeded toward the car.

They stopped at Straughn, the village on the National Road which was *Raintree County*'s Waycross. Here Elsie pointed out the Shockley house with its sundial and garden house. It too had passed from family hands but was still fresh in her recollection. This was the house where she had been married in 1902, where she had brought Ross as a child to visit his grandmother and where Ross and Vernice had spent part of their honeymoon in 1937. It was also the house in which Ross had settled his mature John Shawnessy with his wife, Esther, and their three children.

On his return from Henry County, Ross realized his revisions were going slowly and he was anxious about meeting the deadline he had set himself. The children seemed more unruly in Bloomington and his mother less tolerant of them than he had expected.

The small household with its three generations in orbit was at odds with his need for uninterrupted hours of work. Although he now had the first part of his advance in hand and Vernice had been scouting for a place to rent, there was not a modest house to be had in all Bloomington.

Thus, in mid-July, Ross wrote Larry Wylie, who was summering at the Stiles's family enclave in Manistee, Michigan, far up Lake Michigan's eastern shore. He described himself as being "independent and completely unapologetic for the first time in my life," yet never "so completely behind the eight-ball in my effort to achieve the leisure and peace of mind necessary to finish the book properly." He explained:

> The trouble is that we cannot get away to ourselves. The children are too much for the old folks, and the old folks are too much for us, and we are desperate to get away somewhere. But the housing shortage in Bloomington is absolutely tight—you wouldn't believe how tight unless you had prospected the place as I have. Meanwhile, time is running out, and ten weeks from now I am supposed to present at HM this huge book with my final corrections and revisions—no small task.
>
> It occurred to me that, although it's dreadfully late to inquire, there might be a way of getting a place something like yours on Lake Michigan for about two or three months. I would pay $250.00 or $300.00 for such a place for the "season" provided that we would be reasonably close to the necessities of life. I'd love to see you all and have a really good talk. It seems to me years since I've had really good talks. I've been a strangely preoccupied—perhaps almost obsessed—personality for about five years while I built the quaint perspectives of Raintree County. In a way I never really lived in Boston but all the time in the legendary landscape of my book.

To Ross's relief, he heard from Larry Wylie that a cottage near the Stiles's place in Manistee would be available in August. The rental was twenty-five dollars a week from August 10 to September 15, and since the cottage could be kept somewhat warm and he was not certain he could finish his revisions by the end of the summer season, Ross was to have the option of staying on into the fall at forty dollars a month.

Having made these arrangements by telephone, he wrote Larry Wylie on July 21:

Good Old Larry! I am reminded of one of the old copybook maxims:

> Remember well and bear in mind
> A constant friend is hard to find
> And when you find one that is true
> Change not the old one for the new.

We are eternally indebted to you for your pains. It seems too good to be true. We certainly don't expect a palace and these days just four walls and a location on a lake seem paradisial. The rent seems to me remarkably reasonable for the times. The really nice thing about it all is that we'll be in easy visiting distance of you kids. Let's have a *Réunion des Anciens Elèves du Groupe Delaware!* Our best to Ann and the petit bonhomme. A bientôt!"

Ross went shopping for a secondhand car and chose a ravaged 1940 Hudson, which he felt was painfully overpriced but, given that the automotive shortage was as acute as the housing shortage, it was still the most economical way to transport family and trappings to Michigan.

As Ross's stay at South High Street drew to a close, his father grew nostalgic, recalling the good times they had had together when Ross was Ernest's age and he felt they owed his grandson a camping trip to Miami County. Ross agreed. It meant an interruption of work but it was the perfect act of conciliation on which to leave.

The trip itself was short. Ernest was too young to enjoy its privations and Ross was soon bored with camp life, brightening only while photographing this countryside he had taken for *Raintree County*.

Then, just before leaving Bloomington, Ross wrote Paul

Brooks about the manuscript. "You will be pleased to know that the long dream section will disappear in its entirety and in its place will be a very short section (relatively speaking)—not over 15 pages printed." This would be an entirely new coda, not made up from the dream section but "completely revisualized." He admitted his editors were right about Volume V. It was too tricky and he suggested to Paul Brooks that he omit it if the manuscript were given out for readings.

Early in August family belongings were collected, a paper bag often as not serving as a suitcase, and stowed in the car. Places were found for Vernice and the four children while Ross climbed behind the wheel. He started the Hudson's wheezing engine and waved to his mother, father and sister and they chugged off, looking like a family of migrant workers pursuing a rumor there were jobs in the next county.

Manistee, four hundred miles to the north, had been a busy lumbering town but now it suffered from the loss of its timber. Its large houses, built when the sawmills sang out across the lake, remained to give the town a substantial look, but the O'Connor cottage was the simplest sort of place.

It stood at 101 Lake Shore Drive, behind the town picnic grove and recreation area, and lacked a view of the water. It had but three rooms and only one was heated, by an oil stove, but it was not far from the Stiles's compound, where Larry and Anne made them warmly welcome.

Ross was exalted to be joining the Wylies. Shortly after his arrival he was challenging the prevailing tranquility, telling stories and acting out their climaxes. He had paid nine hundred dollars for the Hudson, he announced, and it was proving an all-around disappointment. On the way up from Bloomington its brakes had been losing heart at Michigan's hills and in coaxing its gears into second for an exceptionally steep descent the lever had come off in his hand. Ross's miming of trying to screw the gearshift lever back into the floor while the car careened downward left Larry and Anne gasping with laughter.

But even as he entertained the Wylies he had them marveling

again over his naïveté. How could anyone with such a variety of cultural and academic experience be so unsophisticated in behavior? One evening at the Stiles's he drank some of the contents of a whiskey bottle which was actually water, colored and flavored with Kitchen Bouquet to thwart a tippling cook, but Ross pronounced it fine bourbon and claimed to be "high" on it.

But the balance of the summer of 1946 was a good time for all of Ross's family. They were used to confined quarters and Ross had no difficulty in getting down to work in the little cottage. He had placed his typewriter on the table in the front room, or Grand Central Station as he called it, and immediately after breakfast he would sit down there and work through the day, ignoring the children as they tramped by on their way to the beach at the far side of the sandy park.

In the late afternoon, Ross would rise from the table and with Vernice and the children stroll toward the lake, inspecting the discoveries Ernie and Larry had made earlier in the day, pausing to watch a tennis game before their stroll on the beach. Occasionally there was the treat of an ice cream cone bought at a stand.

Ross might then try to coerce the Hudson into a shopping trip. Although Vernice had not yet learned to drive, he thought it unwise for her to learn on an old car and the Hudson was all of that, more moody than ever, and he decided that "an automobile is really an ingenious hopper; you pour greenbacks into the bin-end and get grief out of the grind end."

He did enjoy the sense of reunion with Larry Wylie, particularly the long beach walks they took together in the late summer afternoons. Invariably Ross would overrule Larry's suggestion that they bring the children along. Larry, who was rarely out of the company of his own children during vacations, felt a bit guilty about abandoning them, while Ross was clearly indifferent.

The two young men would seek one of the dunes far up the shore for their conversations and Larry soon recognized that their roles had reversed—that his former protégé was becoming a successful author, while he remained a plodding teacher.

Here, looking out across the surface of the lake, Ross told

Larry that it was hard to describe *Raintree County*, for it couldn't be likened to any other book. There had been nothing like it, really. Plato's *Republic* was the nearest thing—but it was beyond that. Larry was astonished to realize he wasn't joking.

After the excitement of June and July, these days of late August and early September were discomfortingly anticlimactic for Ross. He felt isolated and could not rid himself of the notion that his accomplices in *Raintree County's* publication tended to apathy and inattention when left to themselves. There was a business-as-usual tone to the occasional letters from Boston.

In mid-August he learned from Paul Brooks that there had been some slip-up in a meeting between him and Jeff Wylie and that he was sending along a copy of Tom Heggen's *Mister Roberts*, describing it as "a great first novel in which we have a lot of faith."

Toward the end of September, Ross was discouraged by a bulletin from Jeff Wylie. *Time*, having found *Raintree County* to be somewhere short of the all-time champ in girth, had killed the news item.

Jeff confessed he had been busy with other projects, but when he had tried to stir up something at Houghton Mifflin he had met indifference. Paul Brooks had broken a lunch date with him and Lovell Thompson had "turned him over to Venn."

While Ross was sulking over the apathy in Boston, he learned through Mary Jane Ward that Bennett Cerf might mention *Raintree County* in his *Saturday Review* column. During a visit to her publisher, Mary Jane had been chided by Cerf for not seeing her cousin's book onto the Random House list. He had heard from Dorothy Hillyer that Ross was another Thomas Wolfe.

This galvanized Ross into writing Cerf and correcting the impression that *Raintree County* was in debt to Wolfe. Mann and Joyce were far more of an influence, he said. Indeed, he did not exist in the shadow of any writer and had written an unclassifiable book. Many literary tributaries had been drowned in the Mississippi of his long novel—Dos Passos and Hemingway, as well as Wolfe.

Simultaneously he wrote Dorothy Hillyer that while he didn't

fear comparison, "the label 'another Tom Wolfe' is pure poison
. . . Every year for ten years, 'another Tom Wolfe' has been
unveiled and promptly flopped. Such a comparison would be very
bad publicity in my opinion as Wolfe was never a best-seller and
the critics must be very skeptical by this time. Besides, nobody
wants another Tom Wolfe. One was quite enough.

"In publicity from the very start, I think it both true and
politic to play the book as unique, and not like any other book. Play
it strictly and fully on its own merits. No one really buys a book
because it is like Mann, like Tolstoi, like Wolfe, or anyone else.
But critics are much influenced by labels like that, and often these
labels get put on early and stick. For the reasons given, I would
prefer that the name Tom Wolfe never be mentioned in connection with mine by my publisher . . ."

It was this kind of wisdom that made Ross listened to at
Houghton Mifflin. For a first novelist with no publishing experience he was shrewd.

Late in October a note about Ross and his forthcoming novel,
the first public announcement of it, did appear in Bennett Cerf's
column. Direct comparison with Wolfe was skirted and Ross was
pleased, but he was dismayed by one line which he presumed an
error, that Raintree County would not be published until 1948.

Alarmed, he wrote Dorothy Hillyer to say that he had half-
killed himself to meet the agreed-upon schedule, which would
bring about publication in the spring of 1947, and he would be
displeased by any thoughts of postponement.

That he had "half-killed himself" with work was not entirely
figurative. He was tired and he had been ill for several weeks. With
the onset of cold weather the little cottage had yielded up some
arctic areas which the oil heater could not thaw, and a family cold
moved in with the Lockridges, presumably for the winter. Ernest,
who had been going to the local school, developed a tenacious
earache, for which the prescription was a return to Bloomington,
where he stayed with his grandparents for the balance of the school
year.

Ross himself was exhausted in a way which he knew was not

entirely physical. For the first time he felt he had overdrawn his energy account and, describing this to Dorothy, he vacillated between facetiousness and seriousness:

> I am really down and out right now and have been for a couple of weeks. Though I haven't yet babbled of green fields and pronounced last words, my fingers have been twitching at the sheets and my throat makes funny noises. I'm trying to find a medical doctor with a degree in Manistee who will hazard a guess as to how long I have to live. I don't think it will be 1948, judging by the way I feel right now, and I want to be alive when this book comes out.
>
> No kidding, I feel terrible and I keep thinking dismally of Keats' lines: "When I have fears that I shall cease to be Before my pen has gleaned my teeming brain," etc!
>
> Just now I don't mind resembling Wolfe in any way, except one. He's so terribly posthumous.

Presently he heard from Paul Brooks, commiserating about his health and assuring him that the schedule for summer publication would be kept to if Ross could supply the revised manuscript by early December. The manufacturing department had just told him they would need seven months between delivery of final copy and publication.

Ross responded with news of a complete recovery. The trouble, it seemed, had been with his eyes.

> I have the misfortune that one of them is perfect and one is better than perfect—or something improbable like that. As a result there is an imbalance and my brain was being pulled in two. On the basis of some such phenomenon, an oculist had given me a pair of glasses after I got back to Bloomington this summer, but I have been refusing to wear them. This, plus the untidy unmade bed of manuscript I've been wallowing in for months and, yes, years, had got me into a tizzy.
>
> Now I sometimes wear my glasses and feel fine.

Ross was so confident now that he spurned the *Ladies' Home Journal*'s interest in first serial rights, telling Paul Brooks that "the book would suffer so much from piecemeal treatment (a flashback here and there) that we would be wise to hold back . . . I need the money painfully, but I think the best strategy in the long run would be to evade, tantalizingly all pre-publication bids, whether from magazine or movies, keep *Raintree County* virginal, and let the overwhelming tide loose at once."

He was certain too about his progress with revisions, and as he posted more than half the book to Boston he let his editors know that he had improved work that was already near perfect and he was proud of himself. Incidentally, he had changed Shawnessy's middle name from Wesley to Wickliff, borrowing that of the English reformer who had made a translation of the Bible—appropriate he thought.

Also, he had some ideas on typography. "I *hate* quotation marks," he said. "They are cumbersome and ugly. This whole book was written with the long dash method in mind, and the conversations have all been arranged and proofed so that the method can be applied with equal clarity. The technique is intrinsically a part of *Raintree County*, and I would hate to see it changed simply because the other system has been conventionally used in America. *Raintree County* is not a conventional book, and it oughtn't to be thought about conventionally."

He summed up his state of mind for Dorothy Hillyer. "This last effort on the book has bled me white creatively, as far as *Raintree County* goes," he told her, clearly in want of motherly reassurance, but the mood of self-pity was linked to another of expectation—his great hopes for "the *annus mirabilis*, 1947."

On December 12, he heard from Paul Brooks, whose reaction to setting the dialogue without quotation marks was whimsical. But Ross was not amused, for the rest of the letter was a gloomy forecast about the schedule. Houghton could not possibly get the book out by July. Although Paul was sympathetic to Ross's urgency in seeing his book out, the only thing that really worried him about delay was the possible *Life* story on the Fourth of July. However, from what he knew of *Life*, the chances of that going through were small.

Although he was falling behind his own schedule, Ross was not about to capitulate and replied he was "violently opposed to seeing the early summer publication abandoned without at least a gallant effort. I can't agree that the *Life* possibility is small. Such chances are small or great depending on the materials promoted and the way it's promoted. I have a way of promoting things I believe in so that they come true, and I have no doubt Houghton Mifflin works the same way."

He urged a priority for *Raintree County* and went on to tell Paul that the *Life* story was no longer as important in his mind as promoting it hard for a Book-of-the-Month Club selection, from which everything else might follow. It was a natural for that, he said, since it had "sex, American vistas, volume, readability, novelty, depth, artistic stature, and an indefinable something called glamor."

He felt the Book-of-the-Month Club "ought to be darned happy to get a book like it to offer the *millions* of people—among them myself—who are fed up on the pitiful halfgotup offerings with which we have had to content ourselves."

Ross found an additional argument in his own well-being. While he had recovered from his illness of the fall, he knew it had resulted from strain and worry over the book and he told Paul that "the sooner R.C. appears in 1947, the better it will be for me personally, and I submit that this factor is—or should be—of some interest to H.M. as well. Like you, I'm not the least bit worried about the success of the book when it comes out. But unless it comes out well before Fall of '47, I shall be in woeful financial straits—a rather strange position for anyone sitting on a potential jackpot like *Raintree County*. People ought not to think of me as the typical irresponsible young author who can suspend time and twist himself into pliant knots while waiting for his first novel to come out. I find that my wife and four small children all have to go on eating and living through all my artistic vicissitudes. I don't want to have to grab some mediocre teaching position just before R.C. is published—and I ought not to have to. As a matter of fact,

I'm at least as valuable a literary property as the book itself, and I'm right now all ready to begin laying the ground for a book that will knock R.C. into a cocked hat."

On January 11, Ross telegraphed his editors the single word FINIS and amplified it with a letter announcing that the last of *Raintree County* was in the mail and "the battle's done." In suggesting to Dorothy Hillyer that she put this last part of the revised manuscript in the Houghton Mifflin safe, where he presumed the rest of it was being held, he said, "As for me, I'll stay out of the safe. I want to live dangerously for a change." He would be on his way to Boston as soon as he could. He was planning to stop in New York for a few days but he would turn up around January 15.

Ross arrived in Boston on January 16, a Thursday, and moved back into 46 Mountfort Street. In subletting the apartment he had been able to retain one room for his return, but he discovered the entire apartment had been recently vacated.

On Monday morning Ross was welcomed back to 2 Park Street, where he told Paul Brooks, Dorothy Hillyer and Craig Wylie, who was to work with him on final copy, what he had accomplished. There had been three major problems. First, there was Elsie's intrusiveness into her father's story. He was aware of their feeling that the section told from her point of view slowed the narrative. Second, the Reverend Jarvey and Mrs. Brown episode was a detour from the main road of interest—John Shawnessy's marriage to Esther. And finally, what was he to do about the dream materials which concluded the book?

He had made some modifications in the Elsie passages but retained them, arguing they were essential in showing John Shawnessy not as a questing hero but as "father-preserver, the progenitor of Raintree County as a way of life." Also, he thought the separate point of view an asset, preventing artistic monotony; he did not mention that Elsie was his mother in childhood portrait, and for that reason he wanted her to stand.

He had solved the Reverend Jarvey–Mrs. Brown problem by reorganizing these sections, assembling them at the midpoint in a new Day passage called "The White Bull," which brought bull, Reverend, Mrs. Brown and chorus together in a "noontime pageant of Eros."

As for the dream section, he had cut the three hundred fifty-six pages of old Volume V to a thirty-five-page coda. He had done so, he said, not as a concession to their views but in recognition of their wisdom. Although he was willing to subject it to criticism of detail, he wanted it to stand substantially as it was.

Also, he announced a new Susanna Drake, a richer and more significant character who greatly bolstered her story, which, he thought, had been the weakest part of the book. He had added a new sequence around her, "the story of Johnny's sojourn in the South and his honeymoon in New Orleans." It made a prelude to the Civil War and showed the Southern side of it.

Finally he explained that while his cuts and changes were so numerous it was useless to cite them, the book's size, even with lopping off the last volume, had shrunk very little. It would still be "The biggest book ever published in one piece by an American novelist of serious stature."

New readings left his editors feeling that Ross had done less cutting than he had led them to hope for and in fact had expanded some sections, but Craig Wylie gave him a generally favorable report. He did bring along a sheaf of proposals for further improvements. These had to do largely with stylistic and technical details but they included three fundamental structural objections.

The first urged more de-emphasis of Elsie's role as storyteller. Also, Ross's wanton woman was a disappointment. This was the actress who shows Johnny Shawnessy around town. "Edith Vaughn puzzled me," Craig Wylie told Ross. "As you present her, she seems a typical little cheap burlesque whore. But Johnny seems to see a lot more in her—she appeals to something more than his physical side. I think she is your weakest character and others who have read Raintree agree."

Despite Ross's warnings he was also unhappy with the "coda." "I know you have worked over the dream and reduced it drastically. I still don't think it adds anything and I think it is a bad note to end on." He proposed Ross finish the book "with the Perfesser tracing JWS in the air with his stick."

Craig Wylie had been a schoolmaster, a legislator and, most recently, a naval officer, and his good-natured authority was an agreeable complement to Ross's intensity. Despite an Eastern manner, Craig had Indiana ties. He spelled his name identically yet he was not related to Larry and Jeff Wylie's family. He was related to Louise Wylie (Ross's friend in Houghton Mifflin's college department), and his great-grandfather had been Indiana University's first president; the brick house he had built there was the current home of the Indiana University Press.

Most important, Craig was impressed with the book. He had never read a contemporary novel that had given him so romantic and enthusiastic a vision of the American scene. They got along so well that Ross took Craig's rather blunt criticism with good grace. While he did not agree on all points he would consider each in the final rewriting, which he now undertook.

Ross labored at the revisions. "I work every minute of the eighteen out of twenty-four hours that I'm awake," he wrote Vernice, "doing as much at home as I can and then rushing down to H.M."

Even his dreams were of book making and he awoke from one "in a feverish fury at 4:00 A.M. and sketched the most beautiful book jacket . . . simple, but terrific." He had drawn some rolling Raintree County hills which, on second glance, became a female figure, reclining, nude, her head thrown back in slumber or rapture.

Lovell Thompson was delighted with Ross's jacket sketch, as he was with his maps and decorative drawings for the text, and passed them on for professional rendering, while the editorial department made its proper genuflections when Ross appeared with an armload of corrections. "Wonderful, just wonderful" was Dorothy Hillyer's verdict of his new pages.

So he wrote Vernice, "Everybody around here treats me like the prince of the earth—and the general impression is that *Raintree County* is an all-time phenomenon."

Ross did find time for some social life, for a dinner with Steve

Tryon and a weekend visit to Jeff and Betty Wylie's house in Hingham. Over this February weekend at Crow Point he enjoyed some walks on the beach with Betty Wylie, was taken with her hearty humor and took part in the family Ping-Pong tournament, trouncing host, hostess and their expert sons to emerge, as usual, the champ.

But he did not use his liberty or the promise of his fame to make new acquaintances or, in spite of his threat to Dorothy Hillyer, for any romantic adventures. He was far too excited about *Raintree County* to want diversions.

When Craig and Angie Wylie asked him to dinner in Weston they made a party of it by inviting Dorothy Hillyer and some neighbors who, having been told not to dress, turned up in silk and pinstripes and set a formal edge to the evening. But Ross was undaunted and took charge at once.

He talked about his book without a pause. He explained that he and William Shakespeare had solved a particular dramatic problem in the same fashion and guessed that in two hundred years' time readers would still be discussing the symbolism of *Raintree County*. His amazed audience looked for some sign of jest, or the chance to join the conversation, in vain.

In mid-February Ross made it plain to his editors that he had gone about as far as he would go on revisions, that they could now begin uninterrupted typesetting. Throughout the rest of February and early March Ross kept just ahead of proofreaders at the Riverside Press and then, on March 14, he wrote Vernice, "I'm leaving today, Friday, at 5:00 P.M. for home, thank God, will arrive in Indianapolis Saturday at 12:00, and will get home from there to Manistee as fast as I can . . . Everything in connection with the book that I can do here is done."

When he said good-by to Dorothy Hillyer, she mentioned a much-publicized prize being offered by M.G.M. for new novels. Carl Brandt, the New York literary agent, had proposed the idea to Louis B. Mayer as a way of attracting the best books to his studio. Brandt had arranged that his dynamic wife, Carol, be put in charge of the operation. The huge sum of money involved, and the hoop-la, was sure to launch a book successfully, and Ross, who liked contests, thought it a fine idea to enter *Raintree County.*

Ross took several days returning to Lake Michigan and when he explained to the puzzled Wylies that he had come unquestioningly by way of Indianapolis, he was surprised to learn the Eastern service was excellent from Grand Rapids and he could have saved a day by that route, bypassing Indiana altogether.

He was no sooner home on Lake Shore Drive when the sample pages arrived, and he was delighted with them. Vernice shared in admiring the thick, creamy stock, the bold, antique typeface and the pleasure of seeing the first, tantalizing words of text in print. But then, as he awaited the first galley proofs, he found having nothing to do a strange experience. He had been in toil for a decade.

"I'm back in Manistee," he wrote Jeff Wylie, "and so bored with myself that I'm afraid I'm going to start writing another book. Everyone here is well and the family reunited. I plan to stay right here through the summer until Fortune, that fickle slut, starts giving me the eye . . ."

He had his jacket photograph taken by a local photographer and, in sending the proofs to Boston, marked his favorite. "Vernice says it's my 'Johnny Shawnessy' expression and that it has a Mona Lisa quality, now smiling, now not." If it was used he asked if it was "possible to touch out the shaving wound on the chin?" He ended with a gloomy "Just now I'm not doing anything newsworthy and am a bit bored with myself. It's taking a while to disengage myself from *Raintree.*"

In mid-April his sense of aimlessness was broken by the arrival of the first batch of galleys, one hundred forty-three of them, and he hurled himself into their correction. These went off to Lovell Thompson on April 22 with the warning he had had his "last crack at the text of *Raintree County*" and he trusted there would be no further change without consulting him.

He continued to dwell on the idea of the M.G.M. contest and reminded Lovell Thompson of the extra set of galleys which would be needed for submission before its May 12 deadline. Then he heard, in a telegram from Dorothy Hillyer, that typesetting was complete and a set of galleys was now ready for submission to the M.G.M. contest. Ross replied:

> I have your wire. It's thrilling. Wire me often. I'm sending herewith an application for the contest filled in as far as I can fill it. I have put pencil x's at the places where you folks can supply the additional information not accessible to me. However, as you see, I wish the application to be made over my signature.
>
> Since I have decided to enter the MGM contest, I'm for doing anything and everything we judiciously can to win it. *Raintree County's* disadvantage in a contest of this kind—where motion picture people are involved—is its technical novelty and its philosophical depth. If there is any way to commend the book to them for its Americana, its story possibilities, its "sensational" uniqueness without abandonment of readability, it ought to be done.
>
> In particular, I think it might be very wise to suggest that its picture possibilities are already being explored by *Life* magazine and have been under consideration there for over a year.
>
> Diggory, I recall, spoke of the inadvisability of trying to high-pressure them. True—but the principle mustn't be carried too far. It would be naïve not to present your book tactfully in a favorable light. If anything, motion picture people are more inhumanly human than the rest of us, and a little "education" with respect to the book will pay dividends.

He sent a more detailed manifesto on dealing with the M.G.M. people to Diggory Venn noting, "There are certain ideas in connection with the book that might be tactfully planted in the collective mentality of the contest sponsors and which would vastly enhance *Raintree County's* chances . . ." He explained its use of cinematic techniques and urged him "to present the book tactfully in a favorable light . . . probably word-of-mouth would be best, as and when opportunity presents. I believe too, in the efficacy of gracefully-expressed, unofficial letters, perhaps asking for further clarification of some point in connection with the Contest and offering some facts about author and book gratuitously."

Although Diggory Venn had already had some correspondence

with M.G.M. he felt it would be awkward for him to attempt any of these elaborate subterfuges and said so to Dorothy Hillyer. She agreed emphatically.

But Ross was giving Diggory Venn no rest and the next day his letter about the contest was followed by one reminding him of the possibility of *Life*'s Fourth of July story, noting that Jeff Wylie should have a set of galleys.

Then, on May 12, he received his own complete set of galleys, plus the title page and some paragraphs of copy describing the book. For Ross it was a Christmas stocking. The title was set in a massive, archaic, hand-cut typeface that delighted him. Under it ran the long, italicized subtitle, "which had no boundaries in time and space, where lurked musical and strange names and mythical and lost peoples, and which was itself only a name, musical and strange." Beneath that stood "Ross Lockridge, Jr.," in clean, eighteen-point Garamond type. He was enchanted with this and wrote Dorothy Hillyer that "it acknowledged in print for the first time that I am the author of a book. This left me gasping."

He went on to say that he was "frightfully excited about everything (you have to take your fun where you can get it during this production period)." He commended the anonymous author of the book's description, recognizing some of his own phrases but noting some new ones. However, in the last sentence there was an echo of one of the early readers' appraisal, that here was the novel Walt Whitman might have written. He did not want that last sentence used. He was aware that the statement was effective and that it was intuitive as well. Having chosen Whitman as subject for his unfinished Ph.D. project, he had read everything by, and about, Whitman and thus knew that some of the "Wolfean" influences noted in his work were more accurately Whitmanesque.

Nevertheless he objected to equations with any other writers as a matter of principle. "It's partly stinking personal vanity," he explained, "but there are other reasons. Whitman couldn't have written *Raintree County* and probably couldn't have written a good novel at all. This sounds like a scholar's quibble to what was meant metaphorically, but the objection goes much deeper. Old

Walt, America's greatest poet, was, as every student of his life and works knows, a not particularly virile person, despite his pretense of being so . . . There are well-known 'tendencies' in Whitman's poetry and life, inseparable from his genius, which have no counterpart in *Raintree County* . . . He was extremely protean in sexual matters . . . It's one thing to be called Whitmanesque, and another to have it said that Whitman 'might have written your novel.' "

Now Ross had news from Jeff Wylie which was difficult to see as favorable. Possibly as a result of Ross's original suggestion, Henry Luce was eager for a Fourth of July story on "pleasant America." There were to be twelve pages of color and a cover showing a girl on a merry-go-round. At present it seemed quite independent of, and might well kill, *Raintree County's* chances, but if the book could be made to fit—and this would depend on the editors' enthusiasm for it—they might yet ride in on the July 4 issue. He had not yet sent any of the excerpts Ross had loaned him to New York, but he had talked to Diggory Venn, who was sending him a set of galleys, and these would go off to Rockefeller Plaza on arrival.

On May 20, Ross returned the rest of his corrected proof and found himself restive and irksome over the intractableness of the great *Life* beast and the diffidence of those who were meant to be prodding it into his corral.

While he was casting about for a project to occupy him, the far-ranging Houghton Mifflin sales force was assembling at the summit of Beacon Hill to hear about the fall list. The salesmen learned that it contained not only *Raintree County*, but another massive, panoramic novel about the Civil War, *House Divided*, by the well-known author Ben Ames Williams. When they grasped the editorial enthusiasm for the Lockridge book, they immediately proposed it be put off until January so as to avoid an intramural competition as well as to give them time to read it and generate some enthusiasm in the trade.

Thus, on May 23, Paul Brooks approached Ross gingerly with this proposal, first mollifying him with an account of the enthusiasm for *Raintree County*. It would be exceptional commotion around any book, yet this was a first novel. He had not seen the like of it during his fifteen years in publishing.

Then he went to the unpleasantness. He knew it would be a blow but the reasons were so compelling and Ross's own interest so much at stake, he felt equally sure Ross would agree. He explained the desirability of having the salesmen read the book before selling it, but more importantly the certainty that *House Divided*, with its enormous advance sale, would get in the way of any major novel on the list. The bookstores were waiting for it. Ben's name was known, and they couldn't stop his book if they wanted to.

Thus, Brooks continued, the decision had been reached to publish *Raintree County* in January 1948, when it would get more review space and they could give it the promotional treatment that they had recently accorded Anya Seton's *Turquoise* and that Doubleday had given the previous year to Kenneth Roberts' *Lydia Bailey*.

He was aware, he said, that this delay meant Ross would receive no royalties until the following year and now offered him an additional advance of a thousand dollars to tide him over.

Ross bristled at Houghton's unruffled way of manipulating *Raintree County* as though it were so much merchandise—or worse, simply another book on the list. He saw Brooks's argument as a subterfuge for advancing another novel at the expense of his own and replied tartly that *Raintree County* stood above the merchandising tumults of this, or any, year.

On the other hand, Ross said, *Raintree County* and *House Divided* were competitors for Book-of-the-Month Club selection. Choice of one would preclude the choice of the other for some time to come, and he demanded a "fighting chance" for *Raintree County*. *House Divided* would have a huge popular sale in any case. That was not so of his book, and he reasoned it was in the interest of the publisher to see *Raintree County* be given every opportunity for a fair trial by the book club judges. The two books should be submitted at the same time.

Ross also wrote Lovell Thompson, disarming him somewhat

by saying, "I know that everyone must be goddam tired of hearing me sound off about my book, and I am getting goddam tired of sounding off about it—and even thinking about it, as I am deep in plans for another book," but then warned him against taking his present one casually.

"There is no doubt a tendency," he told Thompson, ". . . to look upon *Raintree County* as a very unusual 'first novel,' embodying in that phrase its unmistakable connotation of a work of promise (we look forward with eagerness to the more mature work of this author, etc.). Now, it is both inaccurate and commercially unsound to think about *Raintree County* in this way. It should never be referred to by H.M. in phrases such as 'A very unusual first novel,' etc. The fact of its being an author's first novel cannot of course be avoided, but 'first novel' has a penumbral meaning throughout the whole world of books that is inaccurate as applied to *Raintree County*. It should be thought of and sold as a book without precedent, a *monumental achievement.*"

Since it had "its own rightful destiny to perform," *Raintree County*'s publisher ought to be "a wise and willing midwife" to it. It was "going to cause an explosion *in the realm of ideas*—to which modern books seldom penetrate," Ross told Thompson, and his "salesmen will be selling that unique commodity—literature. This hasn't happened in America very often in the last ten years—I say it in all seriousness. *Raintree County*, whenever it is sold, will be without a real competitor . . . Reviewers in one way or another are going to say, 'My God, look what has been attempted here' and perhaps even, 'My God, look what has been accomplished here. Ladies and gentlemen, this is a book apart.' "

If another house were publishing *Raintree County* it would not be withheld because of *House Divided*. So, Ross reasoned, it would be both foolish and irresponsible of Houghton Mifflin to postpone his book until next year.

Ross's zealous interest in the publishing process, which had been seen as helpful, was becoming intrusive enough to nettle the most temperate Boston dispositions, so that Paul Brooks's reply had an edge of irony. He wrote Ross that they seemed to have achieved a remarkable meeting of the minds. Even as Ross was proposing his dual submission, it was done. Bound proofs of *Raintree County* and of *House Divided* had gone off to the Book-of-the-Month Club the previous Monday.

There would be no slackening of effort, Paul assured him. Houghton had a big investment in *Raintree County*, and he did not speak of money alone. They would do everything in their power to get a big sale for it. They had to.

Appeased, Ross replied in a sunny humor, implying that his demands had not been in earnest and hoping "you have relished the style and perfection of rhetoric in my two recent letters, since they had no relation to reality. Just warming up for my next novel."

"I promise," he ended contritely, "that the disgusting spectacle of the author's love-affair-with-his-own-book is about to end. I only hope that as my passion subsides, it will be communicated to you folks, who are going to have to carry the traffic from now on in."

Nevertheless, knowing that *Raintree County* had gone off to the Book-of-the-Month Club, Ross could not resist some instructions to Dorothy Hillyer on

creating the proper atmosphere for its reception. If it can be tactfully done, I think it might be wise to follow the line that they have a *responsibility* as well as a position of power when they are presented with a book like R.C. They have on their hands a literary phenomenon, which, whatever may ultimately be said of the book, surely will not come their way again in a lifetime or a lifetime of lifetimes.

I am a firm believer in the advisability of bombarding people with reminders of the article under consideration. What people like is additional *information*—RC is a book that excites speculation and curiosity as to how such a thing ever came into being in such a benighted age.

This is my perfessorial side, of course, expressing itself. But the nobler part, you will be happy to know, is up to his ears in neglected reading and absolutely drunk with vast projects, now that the massive labor of RC is behind. Honestly it is so far behind that I can hardly endure to read a page of it now.

And then to Lovell Thompson, Ross wrote:

I want to know whether to be nervous or not. Seriously . . . I think it very important to do some crusading for it. One reason why the book club membership is falling off is that they have ceased to give their readers quality books.

Some tactful appeal must be made to the latent sense of responsibility which must be lurking in the mentalities of people like Fadiman, H. S. Canby, etc. The BOMC, which missed taking Grapes of Wrath, cannot in the long view afford to miss taking books like Raintree County. Not for one moment—until you are forced to—would I yield to the thesis that Raintree County is too big for the book clubs to handle.

On June 4, Ross wrote to Diggory Venn:

I think it awfully important to crusade a little for the book. Has Dorothy said anything to you about Bernardine Kielty and other means of creating a little top-level atmosphere for a serious consideration of the book? The Book-of-the-Month Club needs Raintree County. I don't think they can afford to turn it down. Be sure, Diggory, that they have every reason to reproach themselves for it if they do.

Meanwhile, at the M.G.M. offices, John McCaffery was reading the galleys of Raintree County. McCaffery had been born in Montreal, Idaho, and had grown up in Madison, Wisconsin. He was thirty-three, Ross's age, and also had considerable ambition along literary lines, though less as writer than as editor and critic.

As he read, John McCaffery recognized the terrain and point of view as very much his own and acquired a strong empathy with Raintree County and the man who had written it. When he had finished, he carried the impressive bundle of galleys into Carol Brandt's office and announced, "This is the book. It's a work of genius—and if we are going to give a prize, this is the book to get it."

Thus, the first of Ross Lockridge's determined wishes for *Raintree County* began to come true.

Carol Brandt was not so overwhelmed by the novel as Mc-Caffery. She had reservations about its prolixity, its success as a salable book and its possibilities as a motion picture, but there was no doubt that it was an exceptionally vital and original piece of work and it was the likeliest candidate they had.

She conferred with Waldemar Vetluguin of the M.G.M. story department in California and with Louis B. Mayer himself, and it was thereupon decided to offer *Raintree County* the prize if it could be pruned of some of its excessiveness.

With this news she called Dorothy Hillyer in Boston and was surprised by her reaction to it. Although there was no doubt in Dorothy's own mind that the prize would have a salutary effect on *Raintree County*'s publication, if its award were dependent on further cuts or revisions, she doubted the author would agree.

Dorothy described Ross as a teacher accustomed to getting along with very little money who now lived with his wife and four children in a cottage on Lake Michigan. Hearing this, Carol Brandt felt sure she could persuade the young man that what she had in mind would benefit his book and she suggested that Dorothy bring him to New York for a conference.

Ross received word of the new excitement on June 27. A telegram from Paul Brooks asked him to "Please telephone me collect immediately." As Dorothy had predicted Paul found Ross chilly about further revisions but he was perfectly willing to come to New York and talk with the M.G.M. people. There was nothing to keep him in Manistee and he set off at once.

The Brandts kept an apartment at the St. Regis and with Ross on his way from Michigan, Carol Brandt reserved rooms in the hotel for both him and Dorothy Hillyer, who was coming over from Boston. Ross arrived at Pennsylvania Station in the late afternoon and took a taxi to the St. Regis, where Dorothy Hillyer was awaiting him. She explained that Carol Brandt was expecting them for dinner here in the hotel and in the course of the evening would propose some alterations to *Raintree County* that would make it acceptable for the M.G.M. prize.

There was no question but that the prize would benefit the book's publication and his launching as a novelist. Also, the money, somewhere between a hundred and fifty thousand and a quarter of a million dollars, depending on other achievements of the book, would give him the financial security for years of future work—but of course he must make the decision.

That evening Carol Brandt, a woman with the brisk air of a ruling queen, welcomed them to her suite, telling Ross how fine a book he had written. John McCaffery was also there and Ross knew his name as a magazine editor and master of ceremonies of the radio program *The Author Meets the Critic.*

While drinks were offered, Ross sensed that Mrs. Brandt was formidable but he felt his sponsor, Dorothy Hillyer, was her equal, and he turned to McCaffery. McCaffery claimed to have discovered *Raintree County* in a heap of submissions and seen it at once as a work of genius. He had already threatened to quit if Metro failed to give it the prize.

From his first whiff of the M.G.M. interest Ross had been confident about it and now this praise, which seemed to assure the outcome, had the heady effect of alcohol. He was high on it. With these influential people gathered here to celebrate his accomplishment he felt marvelously exhilarated and capable. The prize was all but his and he need only stick to his guns. Glowing, animated, bobbing this way and that as he talked, he assured his new friends that what they suspected was true—*Raintree County* was the great novel America had been awaiting.

Carol Brandt ordered dinner to be sent up from the hotel restaurant and over it she made her case for substantial cuts. She wanted some fifty thousand words of what she thought superfluous material removed. Over Ross's objections she explained her plan and assured him it would not be painful. She and McCaffery knew just what sections to omit and he could leave it up to them.

As she spoke, Ross's elation ebbed and when he turned to

McCaffery for support she clarified the situation saying, "Mr. Lockridge, I alone will decide whether your book gets the prize."

Ross protested that one simply did not cut a work of art, while Carol Brandt insisted that the cuts she had in mind would result in a better, to say nothing of a more salable, book. Ross held that gouging fifty thousand words out of *Raintree County* could only mutilate it. There was no point in discussing it.

But they did discuss it until past midnight. Obviously used to having her way and convinced this would prove no exception, Carol Brandt showed no sign of weakening. Nor did Ross. When he asked if she thought cutting would improve *War and Peace* she astonished him by replying, "I most certainly do," and arguing it forcefully.

But at two in the morning Ross was still maintaining that if *Raintree County* had to be altered to receive the prize he would refuse it, and at last Carol Brandt put an end to the haggling. "We aren't getting anywhere," she announced. "We're just repeating ourselves."

She was not going to change her mind, she said. The prize was contingent on the cuts. But she suggested Ross sleep on it and give some heed, if not to her own, to his editor's counsel.

Although Ross slept little he followed the rest of her advice. He accepted that Carol Brandt was not going to yield and he considered Dorothy's words that to refuse the prize would be to deny *Raintree County* the assurance of a big popular success and himself the time and peace of mind for several more novels.

If passing up the prize proved a lost chance, a deflation all around, he would be kicking himself for years to come. Besides, he trusted McCaffery. His suggestions were sound and had even opened fresh insights into the book. Of course there was no question of agreeing to Carol Brandt's "leaving it to them," but so long as he retained control he felt certain cuts could be made that would satisfy M.G.M. and yet do no real damage to his book.

In the morning, Ross put in a call to Vernice at the Stiles's number in Manistee, and when she came to the phone he explained that in spite of its being a pile of money, the prize was conditional on more revisions. Vernice sympathized. She dreaded his having to go back to work on the manuscript and was wholly behind him if he decided to refuse it.

O.K., he said. He would give it one last think as he walked across town and then, in about three-quarters of an hour, he would call her at the public phone across from the cottage.

Carol Brandt's office, in the Loew Building at Broadway and 46th Street, was a huge one, furnished with a Steinway grand piano and the paneling and eighteenth-century furniture from the London production of *Berkeley Square*. Dorothy Hillyer had been waiting there with Carol Brandt and John McCaffery since the appointed hour of nine-thirty and they were increasingly concerned as Ross failed to turn up.

He arrived at ten-fifteen, fresh and looking rested and in his exuberant mood. He apologized for being late, explaining that he had wanted to consult his wife and there had been some delay in reaching her. But yes, he told them, he *had* decided. He would accept the prize, and the cuts.

There was a burst of joyful congratulations and then Ross asked Carol Brandt if he could call his wife with the news. She offered her private phone on the piano. While awaiting his connection Ross explained that he was calling the booth in the park facing his house. When it was suggested that now he had acquired a quarter of a million dollars he might want to install a telephone of his own, Ross laughed. Yes, he thought he would. With all that money he might even buy his wife a washing machine.

Later, waiting with Dorothy Hillyer at the curb outside the Loew Building, searching the rush of traffic for an empty taxi, Ross turned abruptly melancholy—much as he had the previous evening when the cutting was first mentioned. It was so evident that Dorothy asked if anything was the matter.

Ross shrugged and said, "It's as if I've just sold my soul to the Devil."

VI

The celebration luncheon took place at Voisin, and arriving for it, Ross had lost his misgivings. To the festive table Dorothy Hillyer brought word that although the Book-of-the-Month Club judges would not consider *Raintree County* until a subsequent meeting, they were already interested and Amy Loveman, with whom Dorothy had just spoken, felt the new pruning would make the novel even more appealing to them.

John McCaffery spoke of the influences of Joyce and Wolfe on *Raintree County*, showing a preference for it over the work of those authors and a remarkable familiarity with its detail. Delighted, Ross turned to the others saying, "John knows more about my book than I do. I'll let him make the cuts."

Back at McCaffery's office it was clear that Ross had given no such license, but they did get off to a good start. He agreed in principle with what was wanted, promised to return to Manistee, reflect on it and do it all himself.

In parting, McCaffery asked if he was equipped to deal with his new wealth and Ross said he had done nothing about it as yet. McCaffery recommended an attorney named Martin Stone, who owned the radio program *The Author Meets the Critic*.

Ross went directly to the offices of Cohen, Bingham and Stone at 10 Rockefeller Plaza to meet Martin Stone, a big, genial man of thirty-two, well acquainted with authors and their problems. Ross told him how, while earning two thousand dollars a year as a teacher he had written this huge book, which was about to be recognized as a major literary achievement. He produced the proofs, indicated the cuts he had been discussing with McCaffery and urged Stone to read *Raintree County* at once.

Ross assured him that the book would be made into the biggest motion picture M.G.M. had ever produced, would be a selection of the Book-of-the-Month Club and would win the Pulitzer Prize, thereby riding the M.G.M. escalator clauses up to the full purse of the contest—over a quarter of a million dollars.

When Stone asked for details Ross explained he had no agent and thus anticipated receiving the whole $150,000 base payment. He expected Houghton Mifflin to regard a $25,000 publisher's bonus from M.G.M. as its commission on the motion picture rights. When the contest was first suggested he had mentioned this to Paul Brooks, who had told him that if so huge a sum were actually won there would be no difficulty in dividing it.

Ross told Martin Stone that the M.G.M. money was only the beginning of the financial harvest to be expected from *Raintree County*, there would be additional income and more books in the future, and thus he should lay plans for tax consequences on a grand scale.

Stone, marveling at the assurance of his new client, agreed to consider his problem and to come up with a proposal which might turn to advantage Ross's past lean years at Simmons.

When Ross called Jeff Wylie in Boston to report his own news and to inquire about any developments at *Life*, he was invited to spend the forthcoming holiday weekend at Hingham. Since he was already planning a visit to Boston, he accepted.

Next day at 2 Park Street Ross made the rounds of the editorial and promotion offices accepting fresh congratulations from old friends. When he pointed out to Paul Brooks that while his six years at hard labor were about to produce a bonanza for Houghton Mifflin Company and people talked to him as though he were a rich man, his actual assets were what you might expect of a fellow who had been supporting a wife and four children for a year on a thirty-five-hundred-dollar advance—somewhere around a hundred dollars.

Moreover, his publishers had so rigged his economy that he had no prospect of further income until after publication day, an event ever receding into the future. Paul Brooks, who had previously offered to increase his advance, admitted the justice in Ross's argument and agreed to an additional fifteen hundred dollars at once, thus bringing the total to five thousand dollars.

Ross's tenth wedding anniversary was a week off and he wanted to take an appropriate gift home to Vernice. When he told Diggory Venn that he was considering a good pen-and-pencil set, something she had always wanted, Diggory protested. Practical though a pen-and-pencil set would be, a piece of jewelry might be more fitting to a man who had struck so golden a literary vein, and he recommended Trefry and Partridge at the summit of Beacon Hill.

Later in the day Ross did call at the shop, bringing along counsel as he had to the Galeries Lafayette thirteen years earlier. It consisted of Diggory Venn, Dorothy Hillyer and Martha Stiles, all of whom watched while the clerk produced tray after tray of bracelets and necklaces.

The selection was bewildering and Ross was hesitant until his attention was called to a jade necklace. It was an old piece which Martha Stiles thought lovely and which, the clerk pointed out, was a particularly good value.

Ross decided on it instantly, causing Diggory Venn to suspect the necklace's sudden appeal to Ross was that of a bargain, while to Dorothy Hillyer it was instinctive knowledge of what his wife would like. The necklace "was" Vernice and Ross's act revealed how his wife, whom she had never met, was ever with him.

At Hingham Ross was his sanguine self, joining the boys again in Ping-Pong, sailing with Jeff Wylie and taking long walks. While striding along the beach with Betty Wylie, he spoke of his future. He wanted to go to California, possibly Pasadena, so as to be near the Huntington Library. He planned to resume work on his epic poem as soon as he had these last revisions out of the way. He still had faith in *The Dream of the Flesh of Iron* and he had only been diverted from it because of the need to make money from his writing.

In the evening, while they watched the town fireworks, Jeff and Ross agreed that the Fourth had a special significance for them both tonight and Jeff said he was newly optimistic about *Life's* using *Raintree County*.

On the long train ride home to Manistee Ross imagined what the effect of the M.G.M. prize was likely to be on his life and that of his family.

Carol Brandt and John McCaffery had told him that M.G.M.'s first trumpeting of the award would occur on July 14 and explicitly warned him against speaking to reporters prior to that date. From what Ross suspected of Hollywood's publicity apparatus, he and those close to him were about to be plunged into a bath of limelight. He had no objection for himself or Vernice, but what until now had been at the core of his anticipation—that the principals of his book were, in a mixture of fact and fantasy, his mother and her forebears—could become, not the gift-within-a-gift he had intended for her, but a source of embarrassment and ridicule.

He was so stricken with this thought that on arrival in Manistee he phoned John McCaffery to head off any possible mention of the sources of his book in M.G.M. publicity and then composed a letter to Diggory Venn warning him:

> For the time being, and until my family have read *Raintree County* (which will not be until advanced copies exist and shortly before publication) there can be *no references at all* to the existence of family materials in the book . . . no statement *of any kind* must appear that my grandfather influenced the character of Mr. John Wickliff Shawnessy.
>
> Please note that although Henry County is described as influencing the book, no specific statement is made to the effect that my mother's family influenced the book. In fact I regretted a little

last summer that this particular sentence was torn from a letter of mine to use with the early promotional material.

Therefore, at the risk of belaboring the point *ad nauseum* let me repeat that *absolutely* no official statement from any source can be released for the present in any way involving my family with the characters in *Raintree County* . . .

I assure you that an unwise early use of this stuff could conceivably cause untold anguish for me and trouble for us all. I know what I am talking about.

Early in the second week of July Ross got down to work. But he had scarcely begun when new irritation arrived in some suggestions for revision which Amy Loveman at the Book-of-the-Month Club had supplied to John McCaffery. He was particularly incensed by her remark that *Raintree County* "cries for cutting" and regarded her suggestions (among them a proposal he cut the entire Fourth of July footrace between Johnny Shawnessy and Flash Perkins) as "a series of blind grabs with no leading principle or motivation except to get something out of the book at any cost."

Suspense and anticipation were bringing Ross a new sensitivity to outside opinion. He did feel vulnerable and it was an uneasy, unpleasant sensation. Nevertheless, his and Vernice's wedding anniversary, which fell on Friday of that week, was joyous. The jade necklace was a huge success and, as he wrote Dorothy Hillyer, "It is a time of great expectations."

On that same Friday night, Paul Brooks was working after office hours at 2 Park Street when he received a call from an official at M.G.M. reporting that the contest judges had decided upon a co-winner for the prize. It was Maritta Wolff's novel *About Lyddy Thomas*. This was notification that the announcement, scheduled for the following Monday, would be so worded.

Paul Brooks's immediate reaction was that he could agree to no such thing. He made a note of where the man could be reached over the weekend and then notified Ross. Ross was dismayed at M.G.M.'s behavior. He agreed it was contrary to their contest rules, which declared the award would go to but one book, and that they must be held to their word. He would share neither the money nor the publicity. It must be all, or nothing.

Brooks delivered this ultimatum and the M.G.M. representative promptly capitulated. *Raintree County* would be the sole winner and Maritta Wolff's book would receive some auxiliary kudos. The matter was closed by John McCaffery's apologizing to Ross.

McCaffery did go on to ask if Ross would object to their saying in publicity that his funds had been low, down to a hundred dollars, say, in order to dramatize his achievement and lend the award story a bit of color. Ross had no objection.

Monday, July 14, the day of the promised announcement, began uneventfully. Despite the sense of expectation, nothing unusual occurred and Ross worked on the cuts without interruption. In the evening, when the children had been put to bed and the woods outside the cottage sounded with the customary shrilling of crickets, inside there was a feeling of anticlimax.

But Ross and Vernice waited up for the ten o'clock news broadcast and heard the familiar announcer's voice tell of the Marshall Plan meeting in Paris, a Truman veto of the Republican tax bill, the rescue of a mountain climber in Yosemite National Park and then—of Ross Lockridge, Jr., a thirty-three-year-old novelist living at Manistee, whose book had just won the one-hundred-fifty-thousand-dollar M.G.M. award.

So the news was out. They sat for a while guessing which of their family and friends had heard it, imagining their reactions, but in the enveloping lakeside quiet it was hard to believe anyone besides themselves had been listening.

But they had. In Hingham, Massachusetts, for example, Betty Wylie heard the announcement while ironing some underwear Ross had left behind. Putting down her iron, she told her husband, "I'm not going to send these shorts on to Ross. He can buy himself a new pair."

During his recent visit to Hingham, Ross had found a wallet containing a few dollars and turned it in to the police; now a few blocks away, at the Hingham newspaper, a reporter hearing the same broadcast recalled that the recipient of this golden shower was the fellow who had brought the lost wallet in a week ago, and realized that for the next edition he had a lead with both a local angle and a shining moral.

But at the cottage in Manistee, Ross and Vernice had decided it was unlikely there would be further excitement tonight and were about to go to bed when, shortly after eleven, they watched the lights of a car probe along Lake Shore Drive and stop just outside. Two men, one bearing a camera, appeared at the door and announced they were from the Manistee *News-Advocate* and had come for photographs and an interview. Vernice, who had on a house dress, excused herself, to reappear a few moments later in her "finery" and be photographed at the typewriter with Ross leaning over her shoulder.

Ross described this first encounter with the press facetiously to John McCaffery. "The editor of the local sheet staggered into our cottage at 11:30, his jaw ajar, his voice hoarse with disbelief. He shook hands, fumbled with a flashbulb, and in his confusion took pictures of himself, his assistant, and accidentally a couple of my wife and me."

But actually, Ross liked the picture and story the *News-Advocate* ran next day. Its inaccuracies (that his father was a professor, that he had received an initial advance of five thousand dollars) were slight, and his own.

He also approved of the stories which appeared in the Bloomington and Indianapolis papers for, like the *News-Advocate's*, they were based on interviews with him. But he was irritated by the wire-service stories about the manuscript which were appearing across the country.

On July 16 he fired off a barrage of nearly identical letters to Paul Brooks, to Diggory Venn (trusting no such story went out from H.M.) and to John McCaffery.

These atrociously misleading stories of huge cuts are the worst possible from the standpoint of the book's critical reception. The idea to keep first and foremost as *Raintree County* approaches the critics is that it is a work of art from first to last and that not one vulgar, ignoble, or commercial motive has ever prevailed in the writing or the cutting of a single word.

I confess myself a little worried [he told Paul Brooks] by the acquiescent attitude taken by my editors in this matter of cutting the book . . . there is no reason to give the least encouragement to the idea that *Raintree County* is an unpruned jungle from which thousands of words can be hacked at will and at the caprice of everyone who wants to reduce costs or attract a few thousand more moron readers.

Next day he wrote Diggory Venn of his suspicion that "the incredibly inaccurate story about 'cutting' *Raintree County* was in some measure officially inspired":

Look again at the publicity materials I submitted. There isn't a single word of confirmation for this distressingly erroneous story of a huge MS. cut in half at the suggestion of a couple of ladies at Houghton Mifflin. What kind of a book is it that an author sits down and cuts 300,000 words out of! If I were a reviewer and acquired such advance impression of a book by a lanky, pipe-smoking (I do not smoke), tweedy, slightly moronic (reckon I kin git muh wife that there washin' machine now) ex-college hack down on his luck, I would expect some kind of sloppily-written, sloppily edited, over-sized, half-baked horror—or at best a rather glamorous book with a possible movie future and no more. . . .

No permanent damage has been done, I trust. But let there not be another word of that "cutting" twaddle. This book must hence-forth be handled for what it is—a work of art, in which the highest and most rigorous artistic standards were observed in the writing from first to last.

But despite a testiness over the errant course of his public relations, Ross was enjoying their first fruit. Each day brought congratulations from old friends and acquaintances, from total strangers, from people who seemed to be deranged and from people who hoped to profit by his fortune, all drawn to the light of his new notoriety. He was particularly pleased by a telegram from

Mary Jane Ward, now in Hollywood as technical adviser to the motion picture adaptation of *The Snake Pit*. It read: *Gregory Peck says it must run in the family.* He told McCaffery:

> The Manistee Post Office and yours truly have been buried in an avalanche of fan mail. Some letters and telegrams I can understand, but there must have been something in that magnificently corny news story that touched the heart of the nation. Among the epistolary oddities is a letter inviting me to invest in an oil well (no kidding), and five (count 'em) letters from literary agents suggesting that I cut them in on a share of the proceeds. All this to a guy who has done fairly well representing himself.
>
> There's simply no getting out from under this mountain of mail. I would be a month answering it. I understand it is rule number one not to disappoint your fan mail, especially the first you ever get, and I have perforce answered a few of the more important ones—putting the others away to ripen, not that they weren't pretty ripe already.

Ross did enter this apprenticeship to fame with assurance and the promotional program he had promised Dick Scowcroft well in mind. His schooling in ballyhoo was his father's, its elementary lesson the cynical one that artlessness plays to an empty house while flattery brings in the customers. As he sat down to his fan mail, this was his guide.

He answered a note from his former professor, the distinguished Hyder Rollins, by recalling

> with pleasure and gratitude your kindness to me during my year at Harvard. Your faith in my future as a scholar meant a great deal to me, and although even then in '40 and '41 scholarship proper was second in my mind to my creative aspirations (at the time I was working on a huge epic poem!), your own superb example and the habits of careful scholarship that you—more than anyone else— helped to instill in me have certainly contributed much to the stature of *Raintree County*. It is, I hope, a genuinely creative work from cover to cover with the multitudinous detail of research carefully assimilated, but the research is there—years and years of it—

and it has given *Raintree County*, I believe, an impressive solidarity lacking to most of our contemporary novels.

This was Ross at his public relations, wholly absorbed with book and self in the anxious pre-publication months, and a little tipsy.

His risibilities were overcoming his pique about the "cutting" stories, so that he could now report to McCaffery:

By the time the rags-to-riches angle reached the Boston *Post* and banner headlines on the front page, I was reported to have landed in New York without carfare. That moron remark about the washing machine, which I really cannot remember uttering and was not my first historic reaction to the award—as you yourself testified over the phone—has brought on a shower of very smart telegrams and letters and will no doubt bring the washing-machine companies in no time at all with free machines and testimonial blanks in their hands.

He wrote Jeff and Betty Wylie:

Every time I open the door, I knock down two Western Union boys with handfuls of telegrams. We are using that yellow paper now to start the fire in the morning. People calling themselves my friends and whom I've never heard of in my life are wiring me congratulations. I have already had two requests from undoubtedly pretty girls to help them get the main role in the film version. A literary agent in New York who represents Somerset Maugham has suddenly taken a great interest in my future, wants to handle any old high school stories I may have lying around.

Thus *Raintree County* finds its way at last into the consciousness of the American people, along with Roosters, Seals and the Hippo at the Hub Zoo. Such is the reward for the long, conscientious labor spurred by a desire for fame. You can have this kind of fame.

Vernice too had reservations about notoriety. They had lived such private lives and she found the new curiosity about them unpleasant. People had taken to driving by the cottage, slowing down to stare at them, and neither she nor Ross liked that. Less specific, yet more important, it seemed that since the award announcement Ross's eagerness for publication had been dulled. The book had ceased to be a source of happiness for him.

Ross's fusillade about the cuts had a numbing effect on correspondence from Houghton Mifflin, adding to his sense of letdown. Since leaving 2 Park Street, he felt he had lost his publisher's full attention, that they were turning to other books and forgetting him. On July 23 he inquired of John McCaffery, "Are my publishers still in business? I don't hear from anyone these days. Tell 'em I'm selling the old City Section to Random House."

Yet he saw no further evidence of publicity blunders and his irritation was finally soothed by a letter Paul Brooks wrote him on the 24th. He fully understood Ross's attitude toward the "cutting" stories but dismissed his worries about "acquiescence" on the part of his editors. In any case, he told him, Raintree County would soon be speaking for itself and dispelling any false impressions of looseness or sprawl.

But no sooner was this concern put to rest than he found another. In Sheilah Graham's syndicated column, he was astonished to read that Raintree County had already been cast. Miss Graham reported that Gene Kelly was not playing the lead. It had been won by Robert Walker. Lana Turner, Ava Gardner and Keenan Wynn were to have supporting roles and the studio would spend five million dollars on the production, the largest investment since Gone with the Wind.

Ross was dismayed that M.G.M. might have cast and budgeted Raintree County without even consulting him and he decided that for reasons he could not fathom, Carol Brandt and John McCaffery were isolating him from the company itself and developments there.

Ross's itch for Hollywood was an old and not uncommon one. It was one indisputable ingredient of the tradition of fame and he wanted to see it and be a part of it. Lately this rather generalized yearning had been exacerbated by competitive feelings toward

Mary Jane Ward. Besides, like any devoted mother unwilling to abandon her child to strangers, Ross wanted to go west with *Raintree County*.

Consequently, Ross sat down at his typewriter and fired off a letter to the awesome head of M.G.M., Louis B. Mayer. He began by congratulating Mayer on the studio's grasp of his immense, revolutionary and complex book. He had not written it with a movie in mind, he said. Indeed, no commercial motive had prompted a single word of it. Nevertheless, *Raintree County* had "magnificent human content." It was the richest an American author had ever handled and it could be made into "the most magical and splendid medium that the world of man has ever devised."

As though Mayer had just emerged from the egg, Ross now told him that the so-called superiority of British films really depended on content, and the time had come for America to combine its commercial skills with some substance. *Raintree County* was its opportunity.

What worried him, he said, was the possibility of M.G.M.'s turning out a shoddy scenario and making a box-office success bare of art and originality. He had not been reassured by Sheilah Graham's announcement of a cast. Surely it would be to everyone's advantage to consult the author before taking so important a plunge.

But he was sure that Mayer, powerful representative of a great empire of art and money that he was, would not permit a botching of the job. In fact, his own decision to let M.G.M. have the book was in part his esteem for Mayer's perceptiveness and inspired delegation of authority.

This letter was a personal appeal to him to give the author of *Raintree County* his rightful share in making the picture. He had been told that in devoting himself to the novel he had robbed the screen of a first-rate scenarist. Whatever the truth of that, he did know his book as he knew the fingers of his hand and *no* one was better able to bring its spirit and content to the screen intact.

What he had in mind was a picture as glamorous as *Gone with the Wind*—but a greater work of art.

The reaction to Ross's letter was explosive enough, though not at all what Ross had anticipated. First word of it came in a phone call from Paul Brooks. Ross learned that a cross Mayer had bucked his letter back to Carol Brandt and John McCaffery, who, as it happened, were in California. They thought the letter naïve and tactless and they were furious with him for going over their heads.

The scolding Ross received over the Mayer letter did persuade him that he had made a fool of himself. He could even begin to admit it, but in the end, being wrong was simply intolerable. On July 28 he wrote:

> Dear John and Carol. It has come to me in a roundabout way that my "official" letter to MGM, addressed to Mr. Mayer, may not have been received in the spirit in which it was written. It must be my fault—the fault of my phraseology and of an honest but—shall we say—awkward sincerity . . . A careful rereading of my communication will show that I appealed for no more (and perhaps it was too much) than some as yet necessarily undefined share in preparing the scenario.
>
> Now in extenuation let me say that . . . I have received *absolutely no kind of official confirmation or notification of the Award or reference to the book from the people who I was told were official contest judges.* They are to me certain as yet unknown and therefore (I regret to say) unthanked people in Hollywood. Not one word has come to me from the people said to be producing the picture that they have in fact read the book and are eager to try its picture possibilities. I haven't had a chance to sign a contract on the book or discuss it in any way with anyone but you and John.
>
> It would be my natural expectation—and, I believe, you will agree, the natural expectation of any young author who had won that glamorous prize the MGM award—that the people who had given it to him and were preparing to budget perhaps millions on a picture etc., etc., would say, "Hello, we liked your book." On the contrary . . . there has been this rather long period of complete silence and darkness . . .

However, I wish to emphasize that the letter I wrote to Mr. Mayer was *not* written in personal pique. Far from it. I am a friendly person and I wanted to thank someone . . . Now, if I have hurt someone, I apologize—not for my intention (which was, I believe, good)—but for my expression of it which must have been very bad indeed.

As for my innocent offer to help in the picture, forget it. I withdraw the suggestion entirely, with the same noble and categorical finality with which John informed me that the Award was to be given me on the expressed terms of the contest . . .

Sending a copy of this to Paul Brooks, he confided, "I am as a matter of fact glad that I wrote that letter, as it confirms for me early and with finality, an impression I was reluctant to accept—that the best thing any writer of real stature can do is stay away from Hollywood . . ."

McCaffery was slow to forgiveness, and acerbity was unmistakable in his assurance that Ross was in able, understanding hands at M.G.M. and he should leave well enough alone. Carey Wilson was now going to direct the picture and the biggest publicity plans that any book had ever received from a movie company were in preparation. For instance, at Mayer's direction, a newsreel would be made of the formal award ceremony and distributed to theaters throughout the country. A jubilant Ross wrote Paul Brooks:

My now famous letter to Mr. Mayer has probably turned out to everyone's advantage. It blew Mr. Mayer's hat right off—that seems to be clear—but it seems that twenty or thirty people rushed into the breach and convinced Mr. Mayer that Lockridge, who is a very bad writer, had said the diametrical opposite of what his letter seemed to say. This was done, of course, not out of charity for Lockridge, but so that Mr. Mayer would not have the shock of discovering that people like Lockridge really exist and that there is such a thing in the world as candid and fearless sentiments fearlessly and candidly delivered.

The letter had excellent results. Lockridge no longer wants to have anything to do with making a motion picture called *Raintree*

County . . . and was subtle enough to withdraw the suggestion before he was turned down.

The Mayer letter added to Ross's reputation as *enfant terrible.* Now, as his multipage exhortations were passed from desk to desk at 2 Park Street, they collected such ironies as "Isn't it lovely to have someone so full of instruction!!" or "Authors are such *interesting* people—Why we love our work!" and there was growing feeling he ought to be told that an author does not question his publisher's competence at every turn without risking his displeasure.

Lovell Thompson tried an avuncular approach, but it scarcely distracted Ross. One of his editors noted that Ross seemed "unaware of the barbs in McCaffery's letter. I guess he is impervious to anything but a harpoon," he concluded, signing himself "Queequeg."

But Ross's fulminations were often rooted in some reasonable complaint and contained sound suggestions for launching his book. Moreover, as all parties knew, he rode the tradition of "the difficult author," the belief that eccentricity and genius are inseparable and make up a rewarding editorial burden. Thus no one, at this point in the delicate relationship, wished to be the disciplinarian.

Paul Brooks's cool, authoritative manner seemed the most effective. When, after talking with McCaffery, he wondered if Ross might take a hand with the Book-of-the-Month Club judges and jeopardize his chances there, he specifically warned him against it. To which Ross replied with a "Paul, I'm ashamed of you for thinking I might write a letter to the BOMC. Though my stratagems are sometimes pretty audacious, damn it, they aren't that dumb!"

But Paul Brooks was again uneasy when Ross told him that his cuts for M.G.M. might amount to only thirty-five thousand words. Dorothy Hillyer agreed that Ross had "an amazing forgettery." She had heard him meet the conditions, formally and verbally. The cut was to be fifty thousand words or *more.* Fifty was the minimum.

Ross verified his intention to fall short of his promise. He would keep to it if he must, but pleaded, "I'm a tired boy . . . six and a half years of effort have played me out and I'm not quite up to it physically."

Paul telegraphed Ross the next day, holding him to his agreement. "Believe we must stick to our promise of 50,000 words," he said and then, tersely, passed on news of *Raintree County*'s fresh triumph. "August 18 issue of *Life* will print story of The Race. Approximately 8000 words. Payment 2500 dollars. Am sending proof to you."

Ross wired back his jubilation that *Life* was using it, assuring Paul Brooks it would help *Raintree County* at the Book-of-the-Month Club deliberations, and he wrote his thanks to Jeff Wylie. There is "no way in which I can adequately express my personal gratitude for your share in the pre-publication excitement," he told him. "The *Life* interest in the book may have had no small share in the MGM decision, and of course you know that this was all your doing. The payment—which seems incredible—is $2500, exactly what I received for my last year of teaching at Simmons . . ."

With this news that he was to be introduced to American readers in the pages of *Life*, all in a matter of weeks, Ross could hardly contain his excitement or his anxiousness about how this foretaste of the book would be received.

He was sleeping poorly. Even when he was in bed with the house dark and still, his thoughts raced on, climbing and coasting over the hills of his accomplishment. He was intoxicated with the coming-true of dreams. His imagination was busy with more and more elaborate expectations, but at the same time it was harassed by actual events—by the upsetting results of the award announcement, by worries about financial and tax problems that Martin Stone's letters raised and by occasional, irrepressible doubts about the book and himself.

Nor were these the only distractions at 101 Lake Shore Drive. One of the children had been ill for several weeks and been quarantined throughout in "Grand Central Station" with his father. Terry, the baby, was suspected of having swallowed an open safety pin and Ross had had to rush him to the hospital for the reassurance of an x-ray. In the midst of another workday the table at which he had been typing collapsed, spilling notes, manuscript and typewriter on the floor. In the wreckage only the typewriter suffered serious injury, but this was enough, for it required scouring Manistee for a replacement, a machine with too many eccentricities for Ross's galloping pace.

As if there was not enough to occupy them, they had guests in early August. Ross's parents and Edward and Mary Jane Ward Quayle arrived, ready with care and advice.

Mary Jane maintained that the M.G.M. award was a contradiction for a novel with literary aspirations, a thought that had once bothered Ross, but now he argued that *Raintree County* was all-embracing, and then listened, fascinated, to his cousin's recent experiences in Hollywood. They stirred his just-thwarted intentions of following his own book to California.

But throughout this anxious, emotion-filled summer, Ross kept steadily at his work, all day and into the night. His industry, as he completed the promised cuts for M.G.M., had never been more grinding and indeed there was something self-punishing about it now. He complained that his heart was not in it, that he was making these changes only to please the Philistines. But it was gratifying all the same. It was his habit, this swinging along the corridors of his huge structure, toolbox in hand, pausing to refinish a piece here or there, and he could not conceive of doing anything else.

He was much like a builder, his house complete, yet reluctant to leave it as soon he must. The house he had made of *Raintree County* was more real, to say nothing of more appealing, than the world outside and he would far rather putter around in it, even to please the fussy new tenants, than to move on.

Moving on, the transition from a completed structure to the uninviting ground of a fresh excavation is hard for all writers but Ross had added difficulty in that work itself had become a refuge.

A day or even a few hours of idleness were insufferable.

Working on *Raintree County* had become compulsive. He was happy while doing it and miserable while not. It was the custom of six years, and moreover the discipline was lifelong. He had been trained to work at capacity since childhood. His mother's formula, directed toward scholarship, was laced with positivism. Winning out was assumed. He had the equipment, the fine mind and sound body; all he need do was energize them. The striving, of course, was up to him.

Ross took the formula a step further. Success was the only acceptable outcome and failure was simply not admissible. Effort was rewarded by accomplishment, which in turn was rewarded by approval, and over the years the formula continued to function for him, shortened like a telegram to read, "Effort equals approval." So, working—having all memory, perception, skill harnessed to his energy and applied to a single task—had become Ross's sanctuary. While he was at work there was no room for doubt about its goal.

On August 20 Ross finished his revision for M.G.M. and triumphantly mailed it off to Boston. An altered City section, renamed "Sphinx Recumbent," and the introduction of a new, urban temptress called Laura Golden, had eliminated twenty thousand words. Thirty thousand more had been pruned from other parts of the book so that his promise was kept, and he was happy with what he had done.

Once again Ross had gone reluctantly to a revision of his book and then, on completing it, admitted the new passages were vastly better than the old ones.

But he was exhausted. He could not seem to catch up on sleep. He had lost his appetite. He had to force himself to eat and he was troubled with constipation as well. He looked unwell and had lost a great deal of weight in recent months. His eyes continued to trouble him and even with the corrective glasses his vision blurred over clear, large type. He felt he had reached the bottom of a reservoir of energy he had always assumed was infinite.

During Mary Jane Ward's visit she had joined Vernice in

worry over Ross's appearance and she warned him he was pushing himself too hard. But he did not need to be told that he was spent, and he promised that with this final revision out of the way he would give the rest of the summer to restoring himself.

All along he had held the belief that a week away from the book, with some exercise and a couple of good nights' rest, would fix him up. Now, in late August, with the lakeshore inviting recreation, he set about it.

Across from the cottage on the park courts, he found the community tennis tournament in progress and after watching some matches he bought a racket and looked for an opponent. The man he chose turned out an excellent player and Ross was more out of shape than he had realized. He came home from the court defeated, purple-faced, having insisted on a return match. Terrified, Vernice persuaded him this was foolishness.

Ross conceded and settled for some pat ball with Vernice, a swim at the beach and some basking in the hot, late-summer sun. But he was listless. When their landlord noticed Ross's haggard looks and proposed the Lockridges join the O'Connors—for a trip up the lake to see the Great Bear Dune, Ross went along, but moodily, and his reaction to the spectacular cliffs was barely courteous.

During the World Series broadcasts he sat all afternoon by the radio, half-listening to the game. For Ross, it was curiously passive behavior. Only some event related to *Raintree County* could enliven his interest. When Martha Stiles arrived from Boston for her vacation, she brought over her cousin, Jack Stiles, a beginning writer anxious to meet his fortunate neighbor, and Ross enjoyed sharing some professional problems with him and agreed to read some of Stiles's work.

Then Carey Wilson, the producer assigned to *Raintree County*, at last made himself known to Ross, briefly but enthusiastically. As a result, Ross unearthed the idea of going to Hollywood and confessed to Carol Brandt that the place held a magic for both him and his wife. He wrote McCaffery to ask "About the newsreel of the official awarding of the Award; When and what is it? And who does what to whom? A recent letter of yours uses the phrase 'on the spot' filming. On what spot?"

To this McCaffery replied on August 26, "The time of the newsreel is still not definite but we expect to have the details worked out this week. Principally it will be woven around Mr. Mayer presenting you with the Award for the Novel Contest. (Maritta Wolff won't even be lurking in the background.) The actual filming will take place in Hollywood and we will whisk you out there and whisk you back again—and if you know Hollywood like I know Hollywood, that will be enough."

Delighted, Ross wrote Jeff Wylie: "MGM is planning to make a newsreel of the MGM Award winner accepting the award from Mr. L. B. Mayer. I am to be whisked to Hollywood for this charade and whisked back again—something like the magic carpet of the Arabian Nights."

In a valiant effort to provide the Book-of-the-Month Club judges revised proof by September 10, Houghton Mifflin was hurrying into final manufacturing and there was little more Ross could do to *Raintree County*, but on August 26 he did make one further, significant change. He composed and sent off to Boston the statement "I wish to acknowledge the assistance of my wife, VERNICE BAKER LOCKRIDGE, whose devotion to this book over our joint seven-year period of unintermitted labor upon it was equal to my own. Without her, *Raintree County* would never have come into being." Beneath it he set his name and explained to Dorothy Hillyer that he wished it to appear in the front matter. "It is intended to establish the fact of my wife's physical and—in a sense—spiritual co-authorship of *Raintree County*. It is not only her due but it will be of some help income-tax-wise."

He went on to say that in view of Vernice's special relationship to the book and this new acknowledgment, he was changing the dedication, formerly to her, to one which read: "For My Mother ELSIE SHOCKLEY LOCKRIDGE, This book of lives, loves and antiquities."

"That leaves my mother, to whom I originally intended to dedicate the book, in sole possession of that honored spot, which I think just as well. Each gets an equal but high distinction this way, but the honors are not shared . . . Besides, it is increasingly clear that I'm going to have another book to dedicate to my wife before very long."

Ross had indeed been making plans for his next project, progressing from that of a return to *The Dream of the Flesh of Iron*, through one which would make use of the bizarre effects of the award, to one which would draw on recollections of his childhood in Fort Wayne.

"My new book," he confidently told Dorothy Hillyer toward the end of August, "(which will have to be a *Sphinx Recumbent* to everyone but me for a long time) has already gone through thirty single-space pages of planning. It won't be anything like *Raintree County* and yet it will exist in an organic relationship to it—something like New Testament to Old Testament. If luck and health hold, I shall have it done before the bloom is off (and the hay is made) in *Raintree County*."

Ross's belief in his burgeoning income prospects had persuaded Martin Stone that the conventional backward spread of it might be less advantageous than some agreement which would distribute his income over future years, and the questions he, in turn, asked Ross about anticipated needs over the next few years had set Ross off on some financial extrapolations.

In New York, Stone had been led, in his first encounter with an M.G.M. lawyer, to believe that the hundred and fifty thousand dollars due Ross could be paid to him in regular installments over future years. But subsequently the M.G.M. lawyers corrected themselves, telling Stone that the money was an award and as such must be paid as a unit and could not be distributed in any way.

When Stone reported this and its serious tax consequences to Ross, he was once again dismayed by M.G.M.'s behavior. He recalled that in New York, prior to their agreement, McCaffery had assured him the money could be paid in any way that Ross wanted it—fifteen thousand dollars a year over a ten-year period, for example.

However, Ross agreed to forgo direct accusation and let Stone try to win some concession from M.G.M. He had just had an encouraging talk with Paul Brooks, who had indicated a willingness on Houghton Mifflin's part to consider making Ross a new contract with a larger advance payable in 1947. Paul Brooks had mentioned that Houghton was inserting a new feature into future contracts, an annual limitation of payments, the effect of which was to spread large incomes into the future.

It was agreed that Stone would now indicate to Houghton Mifflin that since M.G.M. was "letting him down" on his tax problems, Ross might turn to them for some pattern of income distribution. He would also remind them of Ross's contention that Houghton was not entitled to both the twenty-five-thousand-dollar publisher's bonus from M.G.M. and its 15 percent commission on motion picture revenue.

To Diggory Venn, who was about to leave for a long vacation abroad, he wrote: "I would be willing to lay a bet with someone that we get another spread from *Life* before the year 1948 is out, using some of the pictorial and background materials on *Raintree County*. These constituted the original idea for a *Life* article as conceived by Jeff Wylie and me, and are untouched as you see. *Life* now has a paternal interest in the book. They have deliberately scooped it as literary news and if it becomes a big hit book in prestige and sales they are likely to take it up again."

Yet despite his automatic pressing of the advantage, Ross's feeling about this first major exposure of himself in print was anxious. This fruit of the fourteen-month effort at *Life* was bringing him unexpected concern.

The Great Footrace excerpt appeared in *Life*'s issue of September 8, and with it before him Ross imagined its appearance at millions of doorsteps and newsstands across the country—the multitude of Americans who were picking it up, thumbing it and beginning to read the words he had written. He wondered about reaction to this section out of context. It laid such emphasis on the bawdy roughhouse in the Freehaven saloon, Flash and Johnny's bragging of sexual conquests and Cash Carney's blasphemies. In particular, he wondered what they would be thinking in Bloomington.

He returned from a trip to the village deep in reflection and broke a long silence to say to Vernice, "I walk past people and I wonder what they think." She took it as a revelation of what she had always known about him. Although he denied it he cared terribly about what people thought of him. He needed to be liked and he suffered under disapproval.

Confirming Ross's worst suspicions there was no response at all from Bloomington and each day the silence grew more howling. He guessed the piece had made a scandal, that family friends were passing it from backdoor to backdoor, whispering, no one daring to speak of it in front of his parents, thus realizing the nightmare of embarrassing his mother and the Shockley family.

Even while his mind rejected these Bloomington values it was Ross's nature to accept them in his heart as absolutes and to blame himself now for flaunting them. Shaking his head over these excommunicating thoughts of home, he asked Vernice, "Whatever made me think I could get away with it?"

Yet this was only the skin of a many-layered anxiety. When he reckoned that not all of Bloomington was bigoted, surely not his mother, he crept toward an even more agonizing conclusion. He guessed that his father had read the excerpt and reacted with a glacial silence that had enveloped the household, that while the offense he had taken was outwardly a moral one—How could the boy have breached these well-established fences of decorum?—he had been hurt in a far deeper way. First, five years of mutiny and then he had been licked grandly in the pages of *Life* magazine. There was no way to be patronizing about that, no way to pass that off. It was a stab at his father's vitals. While Ross had not intended this kind of overkill, and agonized over it, he could neither revoke it, nor ask forgiveness, nor change in the least his militancy about *Raintree County*.

And yet his anxiety about it grew, adding to his vulnerableness and uncertainty about the book and, remarkably, his avarice.

Money was becoming both a tangible assurance that the work itself was good and a solid retort to his father, whose own writing on Indiana history had never quelled worries about the rent.

Ross complained to Paul Brooks about the "neatly truncated check" of his *Life* payment, one from which Houghton had deducted its contractual fee of two hundred fifty dollars, proposing that Paul engineer further use of the book in the magazine "—and really earn that commission!"

His querulous tone reflected the conflict playing itself out in his consciousness, that of the idealism which Elsie had taught him to value as the only true gold and the materialism, by which even she had to admit, the real world kept score.

In a sense he had been answering both parents' voices in this year of seeing his book published—first his father's urging him to promote it, then, at the St. Regis, his mother's telling him to stick to his principles, then his father's suggesting he *could* juggle the compromise, and finally his mother's, telling him he had sold his soul.

So now, reflecting on what he had done, he seemed to be on a seesaw, tipping at one moment to feelings of being used, being someone's patsy about money, and in the next to a self-loathing for his greed. Even as he recognized this as the perennial conflict between art and commerce, and the threat of the bitch-goddess, he could not stop.

In excess, money was no longer carfare and groceries but chips of success and symbols of the world's love and thus it was becoming an end in itself. Pique about money, fuming about it with Houghton, was beginning to attract him for it offered an escape from other anxiousness and a substitute, like a lover's quarrel, for love itself.

The first stirrings of this new wind from Manistee eddied into the offices at 2 Park Street in a letter from Martin Stone raising the question of dividing the M.G.M. proceeds.

Paul Brooks replied by saying there was no question about the division. By contract Houghton Mifflin owned motion picture rights and could sell them, on approval of the author, paying him

85 percent of the proceeds. This had no connection with the twenty-five thousand dollars M.G.M. had awarded specifically to the publisher. He pointed out M.G.M.'s phrase "No stipulation is made as to its use, but it is expected that it will aid in furthering the sale of the novel," and said that was how he expected Houghton Mifflin to use it.

While Ross was keeping an eye on Stone's overtures to Paul Brooks, his worry about his father's behavior was resolved. What Ross had guessed was close to the truth. His father had been offended by the *Life* piece—saw no need for its profanity—and his silence about it was intentional but having made his point, Frank Lockridge was ready for a reconciliation.

In announcing his plans for a family reunion, he quickly accepted Ross's assurance that the excerpt *Life* had chosen did not reflect the whole *Raintree County* and he agreed to stay judgment until he had read the book.

On Sunday evening, September 21, Ross, Vernice and the children joined his aunts, uncles, cousins, nieces and nephews to descend on the little Methodist Church on Paw Paw Creek, some ten bumpy miles from Peru, Indiana. Here they all gathered around long tables in the church basement to feast on fried chicken and home-baked cakes and pies.

Frank Lockridge had seen to it that a reporter and photographer from the Indianapolis *Star* were on hand to record the occasion. As family patriarch and director of the Hoosier Historical Institute, he was photographed awarding the evening's literary prizes, generous slices of the mince pie, to Ross and to Mary Jane Ward.

He stood nodding with fatherly pride while Ross confirmed to the *Star*'s reporter Sheilah Graham's cast for *Raintree County* and said that for the present at least he would not be returning to teaching but might be moving to California and added that although he was not ready to discuss it, he was already at work on a second novel.

Ross returned to Manistee in good spirits, only to learn from Martin Stone about Houghton Mifflin's steadfast position on dividing the M.G.M. money. He wrote Paul Brooks immediately, pointing out that entering the contest had been their idea. Although he had not been particularly impressed by the two hundred fifty thousand (Lion Feuchtwanger had recently received three hundred fifty thousand for a novel set in eighteenth-century France), he had been persuaded by its promotional advantages.

At the time he had noted the twenty-five thousand dollars which M.G.M. would bestow on the publisher as well as the two hundred fifty thousand which went to the author and, with the contest rules and his contract in hand, he had come to Paul for a clarification of his motion picture clause, indicating that he considered these two sums made up the 15/85 percent division of the total and asked his agreement to it.

He reminded Paul that his answer had been "Look, Ross, if we win all that money, we can easily make a *division satisfactory to everyone*," whereupon Paul had "smiled paternally, I smiled, and that was that."

Now, with the money won, he was told it would be divided in a way which "*represents the maximum favorable interpretation for HM and the minimum for me*—i.e. all of H.M.'s $25,000 immune from me, none of my $150,000 immune from them—"

Ross argued that the publisher's award of twenty-five thousand dollars had been generated by him, that if it were used as Paul said, to promote *Raintree County*, it would displace some other twenty-five thousand dollars Houghton would have put to this purpose. So, in effect, he would be paying for his own advertising.

For this reason he insisted that the total proceeds, his award and theirs, be lumped, and then divided according to contract.

Finally, it was he, Ross, who had brought about the bonanza and he warned his publishers against putting too small a value on the talent and devotion that had made it possible.

"The future is no longer a vague promise," he said, "it is taking on an interesting specific character. My own belief is that the most valuable property in this whole transaction is not *Raintree County*, valuable as that is. It is the human property attached to it—namely myself, not simply because after all an author is his book, but because of the creative potential rolled up in me."

Paul Brooks wrote Ross the same day, reminding him of his publisher's contribution to launching *Raintree County*, and pointing out that it was the sort of effort Houghton Mifflin made not only for a single book but an author's career. In the light of this he was hoping to hear more about the book Ross had mentioned to Dorothy Hillyer and was willing, whenever he was ready, to discuss the long-term program.

Aware that Brooks's letter had crossed his own, Ross replied at once, describing

> . . . the project I mentioned to Dorothy. It's of course a novel, and I'm throwing myself into it with the same ardor that characterized my work on *Raintree County*. I made it a practise never to discuss with anyone the creative content of *Raintree County* while I was working on it, and shall observe the same general rule with the new novel. However I can tell you that it will be simply nothing like *Raintree County*, except that it will have an equal grandeur of design, though it may not be quite so long. I shan't spend any five years on it, barring mishaps. As I have pointed out before, *Raintree County* proper was written in its entirety in two years and a half after I ground up three years of false starts and experimentation that led up to it. The new novel will be advantaged by the maturity as a writer gained with *Raintree County*, less distracting working conditions, and the fact that this time I am treading on much more familiar ground.

Lovell Thompson was aware of the discontent rumbling in Ross's heart and he also recognized the part of Ross's nature, a delight in theory and reason, which was akin to his own. When he found the opportunity to involve him in a problem of the book's design, he did so. Defending his choice of red cloth for *Raintree County*'s binding, he wrote Ross on September 24:

> Martha tells me you are anxious to have a dark green cloth stamped in gold . . . I think there is no handsomer combination

than scarlet and gold. On my bookshelf it is the red and gold shelf-backs that really decorate a room. (Thoreau is one, Dos Passos another). The duller colored volumes merely serve to set them off. Moreover the reds are more apt to be enriched by dirt and dust, where many other colors merely lose their charm along with their freshness. I know that green is in a sense more appropriate, but I hate to let appropriateness interfere with our making the best-looking book we can contrive at the moment. There is also—to descend to a more sordid plane—the attraction value of scarlet. When the youths of the next generation begin to cut their teeth on the literature of this, they are almost sure to read the titles with the red backs first. Let me know what you think.

To this Ross replied:

Like you, I like a good shade of red (Tolstoi's *War and Peace* with the gold title stamped on a black panel on the back is one of my favorite jobs of bookmaking), but surely as between a good red and a good green, the preference is pretty much one of taste, as green is a beautiful primary color with plenty of eye-catching value. Now the question of aesthetic harmony and appropriateness is really a very important one here—much more so perhaps than you realize. Anyone who has read *Raintree County* can vouch for the immense aesthetic importance assumed by the colors green and gold almost from the first page forward—and one can literally say, *the title* forwards. One reader of my book, a woman, said that after reading a few hundred pages, she had the feeling of just having walked through a big green meadow with the sun shining. It is a unanimous reaction. The heroines are predominantly dressed in green, it is Johnny Shawnessy's favorite color, it is the color of summer in Indiana, and *Raintree County* is a very summery book.

Having prevailed, Ross promptly confessed to Martha Stiles that Lovell's "ideas about the red cloth were, as usual, so damnably eloquent and convincing that I hated to maintain my point in the face of them."

VII

At their meeting on September 25, the Book-of-the-Month Club judges did not reach a decision on *Raintree County* as had been expected but put it off until the next meeting in October, holding their Damoclean sword over the book for another month. However, what bothered Ross now was not the B.O.M.C. decision but how Paul Brooks would react to his strongly worded appeal to leave his prize intact.

He could not get it out of his mind that his publisher had at first doubted him (when he had asked to discuss the splitting of the award, Paul Brooks had been hard to reach, then depreciative of the possibility of winning) and then, when his own faith in his book had been vindicated and there was prize money to be had, made an unlovely grasp for it. If they were really inclined to take advantage of him, Ross felt he must make a firm stand against it. Paul's response, however casual and patronizing, was his word and he must be held to it.

He had the academic's suspicion of the business world and its motives. Although the people at Houghton Mifflin originally had disarmed him with their intelligence and by their response to him and his work, the M.G.M. episode was showing them up as wholly indifferent to him, hypocrites after all.

He was convinced, and felt it must be just as plain to others, that he had not the least selfish motive. It was simply a matter of principle.

Weeks went by with no response from Boston, and his feeling of being ignored increased. When at last a letter arrived from Houghton it was a request from Hardwick Moseley, the sales manager, to appear at an Indiana Library affair. Ross turned him down abruptly, saying he had received close to fifty such invitations and was refusing them all until the book had appeared, when he would "accept a very few special speaking engagements at a damn good fee. I intend to let the book sell me instead of vice versa . . ."

The stillness of Houghton Mifflin's editorial rooms was not the indifference which Ross imagined. Paul Brooks had found Ross's recent letter, with its ethical and emotional presumptions, a difficult one to answer and instead had decided to deal with the legal questions it had raised through a conversation with Martin Stone. He did so just before departure on October 3 for a week's vacation, leaving it to Stone to give Ross a summary of their talk.

Martin Stone's account of this conversation did not reach Manistee until October 9, and to Ross, Paul's long-awaited response was both dilatory and cruelly insensitive. He took it as a refusal to surrender any of the M.G.M. income.

That night, Ross sat down to talk it over with Vernice. In his view, Houghton had forced him into an ugly and impossible situation. In failing to recall his promise, Paul Brooks had repudiated it, leaving Ross to proceed only on his own recollection of it.

But even if there had been no such promise made, or even discussed, still an 85/15 percent split of the total award was surely a fair and reasonable way to go about it. Not only did Vernice agree with him but so had Martin Stone. Houghton's blunt rejection of the idea was a rejection of *him*—and the more he thought about that, the more bitter he became.

This was the most painful lump for Ross to swallow, that his publisher was so ready to alienate him, even when he had told it of "the big, new book in the making." This was what made its attitude unbearable.

Ross had gathered from Stone that it would take a breaking off of relations and a lawsuit to prevail over Houghton Mifflin and now Ross and Vernice seriously considered this. But in the end they saw the impracticality of withdrawing *Raintree County* at this late stage of publication. They talked on into the night and reached a feeling of exhaustion and submission which, they now agreed, was "throwing in the towel."

Ross felt they had been "beaten into submission," only because he lacked the money for a legal battle, and thus they simply could not "buck the wealth, power and ability to temporize, of Houghton Mifflin."

So, he now proposed to surrender his claim to both the publisher's bonus and the 15 percent commission of his prize money to which Houghton was entitled by contract—but to retain all three of the bonuses possible under the M.G.M. conditions, those which depended on selection by the Book-of-the-Month Club, the Pulitzer Prize, and exceptional bookstore sales.

When they reached this decision and at last went to bed, Ross found he could not sleep. Throughout the night he reviewed each incident that had led to this brink of desperateness. In the morning, that of October 10, he sat down to the typewriter and poured forth his indignation in a letter to Paul Brooks:

> The sum of money at issue is of course substantial, but it is not the amount of money involved which has caused my profound displeasure in this matter. It is something potentially much more dangerous from Houghton Mifflin's point of view. I cannot get it out of my mind that either I am being dishonest about this—and I am in a position to know that I am not—or else Houghton Mifflin is . . .

To this accusation of dishonesty, he added one of stupidity, for courting his own resentment. Even so, he offered the concession which he had discussed with Vernice and which Martin Stone had approved. Houghton could keep its twenty-five-thousand-dollar bird in hand if he could have the three—the bonuses for Book-of-the-Month selection, the Pulitzer Prize, and exceptional bookstore sales—in the bush.

Turning to the renegotiation of his contract, he warned:

> It will be all to Houghton Mifflin's advantage to play fair and straight with me. By way of comparison, I have carefully gone into this question of contract and author-publisher relations with my cousin Mary Jane Ward. She found herself in a very similar situation with Random House after an entirely unexpected pre-publication success of Snake Pit. Her contract, as originally drawn, was extremely unfavorable to her in many ways. Cerf authorized a complete renegotiation of her contract—and in such a way that the author is assured a lifetime income from her book. The handling of Mary Jane's whole set-up was, it seems to me, a model of its kind in generous and far-sighted management of an author—and in this case, by the way, an author who is, for reasons inherent in her art, not likely to repeat the immense "trend-novel" success of Snake Pit.

Ross ended by emphasizing "how seriously I regard the question of ethical treatment of a young author just at the time when, because he is neither wealthy nor established, it seems easy to put the knife into him without danger. It is just at this time that a fair and far-seeing decision on the part of the publisher is necessary to the publisher's own best interest."

Simultaneously he wrote Dorothy Hillyer, saying, "I am making a last offer based upon my faith in the book. The offer means in effect that I am assuming the whole risk with respect to these moneys at issue, while HM assumes none . . . This is a hell of a concession—from a man who will do a lot (short of calling himself a liar when he isn't) to keep other folks from being skunks. Honestly—what's the matter with you folks—don't you want my next commercially important book?"

He was, he told her, "already sitting on a new pile of swiftly growing MS. that any publisher in America would give $25,000 for—just as a bonus for the privilege of signing a contract on it. For God's sake, Dorothy, consider this whole question carefully, and do not encourage an unethical decision toward the one author in a thousand where it would be sheer stubborn business blindness—on top of dishonesty—to do so."

These truculent letters to Paul Brooks and Dorothy Hillyer consumed him. He detested unpleasantness and habitually shied from it, just as he had contempt for people who squabbled over money and was quick to ridicule them, but he was victim of a runaway emotion, the compelling need for his publisher's affectionate assurance. If his posture was undignified, possibly ridiculous, it only added to his impetus. Like a child making his scene in the lobby, the spectacle he was creating only fed his fury. That it was tolerated was assurance in itself and, of course, it added to his consequent remorse.

When Tuesday morning, October 14, arrived in Manistee without any response from Houghton Mifflin, Ross could bear the humiliating silence no longer and called Paul Brooks, just returned from his vacation. To Ross's restated demand, Paul replied that although he could not recall their discussion about the entry blank he would stand by whatever he had said in the way of a reasonable accommodation.

Nonetheless, the twenty-five thousand dollars was Houghton Mifflin's, no question about it or that as his agent, they were entitled to 15 percent of the proceeds of his motion picture sale. However, he thought that some of the bonuses, the B.O.M.C. and Pulitzer ones, for example, were negotiable as Ross had suggested in his letter. He would have to consult the M.G.M. rules again but supposed that if this were the only difficulty he might persuade his associates to concede them.

Ross was delighted. Of course there were no further difficulties. That he be left the escalator possibilities was all he asked. It was that simple. He ended with new expressions of fealty and immediately called Martin Stone in New York to tell him that the problem had been resolved. He then sat down to write Paul Brooks:

I can only express inadequately how pleased I am—how heart-warming it is—in these degenerate days to find a guy who is willing to stand by his word.

I am aware that my second letter began to acquire a tone which, strong as it was, did not fully express my heartbroken and indignant feeling at what I took for a breach of faith . . . I know now that this feeling of mine was founded in part on a misconception—not my fault, nor so far as I can tell my lawyers.

. . . I trust that the real subject of all this confusion—the book to which I have given so much of my youth and strength—will go serenely on to whatever destiny is appointed for it, superior as a work of art to the squabbling and confusion to which the author has himself so generously contributed.

Then he explained to Dorothy Hillyer:

My interest in the division of the MGM proceeds had long ago dwindled from any serious interest in the money involved to a terrific desire on my part to see my publisher keep the faith with me in a reasonable form—a faith which Paul has so magnificently vindicated.

I am going to try like the dickens to avoid ever getting into an unclear contract situation with Houghton Mifflin, as misunderstandings of that kind seem almost as hard on me as questions of artistic difference. I am no business man, as I trust I have now proved to everybody's satisfaction and dissatisfaction, and it is therefore all-important to me as a more or less dedicated artist to work with people who can be trusted to keep their word with a proper evaluation of all the human, literary, and legal realities at stake.

The truth is that I couldn't work during the last two weeks, so preoccupied and shocked was I by this situation. When I cannot write, something is really wrong, and normally I can write with perfect concentration while riding in a merry-go-round. Part of the trouble was that I had a terrible feeling that the big work that I am engaged in now was something I did not want to bring in with the childish glee and dump on the desks of Houghton Mifflin in due time, just as I did *Raintree County*.

I long to see you all again—especially for the time when I can bring Vernice in and say, "Vernice, this is Dorothy, this is Paul, this is Lovell, this is Connie, this is Diggory, this is Craig, etc., etc." You are all just characters in a very exciting storybook to her.

Ross's responsiveness in their telephone conversation had been such that Paul Brooks felt he might have given him an overoptimistic impression of the acceptability of his proposal. Thus he went directly to consult his associates.

There was substantial agreement that Ross's proposal they relinquish any part of the twenty-five-thousand-dollar publisher's bonus was unreasonable, and that the presence, in Ross's lawyer, of a middleman only complicated their problem. They had no inclination whatever to permit Ross, who had supervised every other phase of *Raintree County*'s publication, to usurp the ultimate function of management. Still, some kind of compromise was vastly preferred to a brawl.

The decision soon arrived at by Brooks, Hardwick Moseley and Lovell Thompson (the trade department's triumvirate), plus the firm's president, Henry Laughlin, was this: provided there were no legal objections, they would consent to a revision of Ross's contract that would ease his tax burden, and they would relinquish rights to his book club and Pulitzer Prize bonuses, but not to that contingent on sales.

As he was preparing to write this decision to Ross, Paul Brooks received a call from Martin Stone, to whom he gave a terse report of developments to that moment.

Paul Brooks's letter to Ross got off the following day, October 15, and it began by indicating certain grievances on his side of the argument. First, the tone of Ross's recent letters made reply difficult. Nor was it clear whether Ross expected to be dealt with directly or through his lawyer, who only lately had entered the picture.

In any case he felt they might dismiss the possibility of intentional deception on anyone's part. Undoubtedly there were misunderstandings and he was quite ready to accept blame for his part in them. They seemed to grow out of a conversation he, regrettably, could not recall.

As to revising the contract, there was no question but what Houghton was entitled to a 15 percent share in all payments to the author under the M.G.M. award. However, they were willing to waive their rights in the Book-of-the-Month and Pulitzer possibilities. They could not do so to further payments depending on sales. He was unable to defend any other point of view, either to himself or to his associates.

He explained that the M.G.M. payment began after twenty-five thousand copies had been sold, and Houghton's first printing of *Raintree County* was to be fifty thousand copies. Ross did not seem to realize how much faith his publishers had in his book.

Paul offered further assurances that they were in no way taking advantage of him, that the original contract was a fair one and that the revision of it, to conform to Ross's wishes, a very special concession.

But unfortunately, before this letter of Paul Brooks reached Ross, he had news of it in a telegram from Martin Stone. It reported that Houghton was agreeable to Ross's receiving 100 percent of possible book club and Pulitzer Prize income, but that they were "quote adamant unquote" in refusing to surrender 15 percent of the M.G.M. monies based on sales. He suggested Ross call him on receipt of the letter from Brooks, which was on its way.

The effect of Stone's telegram on Ross was immediate and explosive. In a rage, he sat down to his typewriter and wrote Paul Brooks:

> So far as I am concerned, if this decision is adhered to, we are right back where we were—that is to say—I shall be right back where I was on the whole matter—absolutely and unalterably convinced that you and your associates at Houghton Mifflin have completely failed in your reasonable and fair responsibility to the author of *Raintree County*.
> . . . Your decision to seize upon this last-ditch concession of mine and extort a further concession from it . . . is, believe me,

not consonant with the faith, pride, and trust that I have sincerely had in my publishers and which has so far been mutually profitable to us both.

He reviewed the history of his grievances, summing up:

> . . . in a fine and cordial effort to keep all the human and legal responsibilities represented by this problem, Houghton Mifflin now "adamantly" proposes to give up *exactly nothing*.
>
> I am tired of this issue. If somebody phones me up and tries to wheedle me into seeing how beautiful and reasonable this position of Houghton Mifflin's really is, they will find it very easy. I am writing a letter with this letter authorizing my lawyer to make the terms that you dictate on this point.
>
> This document if and when drawn up should have a border of black ink around it, as in it will repose, cold and recumbent, my faith in my publisher.
>
> It is only fair to add, however, that on this point Vernice and I have given each other a solemn promise, which we shall carry out immediately in such a tentative but palpable form that we couldn't go back on it if we wanted to. This promise—coming from a man who is not aware that he has ever broken a promise so solemnly given to himself or another—is that Houghton Mifflin Company shall never have another big book by the author of *Raintree County*.

"Do not misread your man—do not misread your man," he warned Paul Brooks above his formal signature. Then, before sealing the letter, he headed the first of its six pages with the longhand inscription "This letter must be read by all the editors at Houghton Mifflin—aloud preferably—and a joint decision reached. Ross Lockridge Jr."

Paul Brooks received this letter on Friday, October 17, and was dismayed. He shared it with his partners, among whom there was now agreement they had lost Ross as an author. Indeed, Hardwick Moseley felt Ross might make good his threat of trying to enjoin *Raintree County*'s publication. While it was unlikely he could actually do so, their announcement campaign was well advanced and Moseley could foresee a very public embarrassment.

From the tone of Ross's letter, Houghton Mifflin's management doubted that any appeasement of his appetite for M.G.M. income was possible and in any case felt it could not, in good conscience, indulge him further there. The feeling was general that they had reached an impasse, but Paul Brooks, noting the instructions to Stone and the sullen invitation to a phone call and remembering how responsive Ross had been in their last conversation, was more sanguine.

Brooks's instinct was sound. His letter of October 15 had by now reached Manistee and it was having a mollifying effect on Ross. This was enough so that on Sunday Ross put in a collect call to Paul, at home in Lincoln, to tell him that he now saw a certain reasonableness in his views and was willing to be persuaded toward them. He had had some poor advice he admitted. When Brooks spoke of the advantages of a renegotiated contract under which Houghton would take the whole responsibility for spread income, Ross accepted it eagerly, as though this were precisely the kind of compromise he had sought.

In a second phone call at breakfast time on Monday, Ross told Paul that Martin Stone had endorsed the plan for Houghton's releasing all future income to him under annual ceilings and had been working along these lines himself. Then Ross confessed that a letter he had written to Paul on Friday night was in the mail to him and he asked that he destroy it without reading it. Paul agreed and their conversation ended in warm reconciliation.

Ross followed up with a telegram to Paul saying, "Heartfelt thanks for your kindness to me in recent conversations. Thanks too for agreeing not to read my last . . . Here's to Raintree County and here's to a great editor and a great house. Ross."

His relief at the settlement of their feud again poured forth in a letter of thanks to Paul Brooks for his "forgiving attitude," for "helping a young guy out of a hole he dug for himself," and he promised repayment "with another book sooner, I think, than you would guess."

Yet alongside these hopes for an immediate reengagement in

work lay the sense of emptiness which led him to confess to Brooks in a P.S., "I feel as if I'd had it. You know men and books—is there such a thing as a writer being 'shell-shocked' from the battle of creating his own book?"

On Monday, October 20, he wrote to Dorothy Hillyer in a similar mood of contrition and self-concern:

> Never, never again. Honey, you have no idea how I bled on this thing. No doubt I caused some distress and consternation, but if it's any consolation at the other end, I have never had such a terrifying mental—not to say physical—experience.
>
> Just a case of sheer literary shell-shock, strangely abetted by confusing circumstances and some bad advice . . . Paul was simply magnificent . . . and as I have slowly perceived in anguish and despair did the wise thing in every crucial instance. I confided my case to Mary Jane Ward, had to, they thought I was taking a drubbing—but I know now that I was just drubbing myself. I was at one point all ready to discuss in a tentative way my future with some other house. Damn all other houses. Paul saved us all from catastrophe.

But from the sweet, fleeting joy of the reconciliation, Ross was drawn closer to the real crisis of the spirit which underlay his quarrel and to face some doubts about himself as a writer.

He was clinging to *Raintree County* in the way of a mother who has been living for the child within her and now, with its agonizing birth over, knows that even as it has exhausted her it has been the source of her strength. *Raintree County* had guided Ross for so long, giving purpose to each minute of his day, that he now felt a husk. It was as if he had yielded up his core.

He knew well enough that his salvation lay in getting started on a new book, but despite his assurances to Houghton Mifflin he was having trouble. There were moments of self-confidence when he recalled that the beginnings of *Raintree County* had been erring and uncertain but he seemed to forget that the grand designs of *The Dream of the Flesh of Iron* had led him into swampy, discouraging territory and that it was a very tangible grandfather who had led him to firm ground.

He was so determined to surpass himself with an authentic masterwork that he was losing his way again among ambitious abstractions. Beneath the heading "New plans for writing beyond *Raintree County*," he noted:

> The new novel to be worked out first on a religious and philosophical basis.
>
> The problem of life is, of course, its relation to Creation. What creates a human life? Has it purpose? What is the source of the good and evil in its private and yet shared universe . . . Old Socrates was right—Virtue is wisdom. Evil is error that mortal mind makes.
>
> The great unresolved problem—the problem of Time and the temporal world. Does it—did it—exist? . . . Is there a time that includes all things? No. Time is a mode of perception—human, erring, inexplicable. It is nothing outside the humanly perceived world. Kant resolved the dilemma of Time by merely admitting its inexplicability and by making of it an inescapable mode of human perception.
>
> How true and objective is the past recorded in literature and history? The records that we have are the subtle transformation of lost realities. One must never forget that there is only one eternal reality. Life and its Creator—or better still, a Life and its Creator.
>
> One does not simply disguise but transcends the merely personal. All great literature is of the nature of myth—legend, and when legend reaches its fullest character of wisdom, it becomes religious legend.
>
> The one indestructible substance is being. Thus in writing one should seek to divorce himself from the personal association . . .
>
> We look back over our life and see the highly personal and diversified character of it. There is a temptation to see too much pattern in it . . .
>
> It is possible to regain one's excitement about Life. One is not the creature of blind impulses, a random shoot from the great swamp, sustained briefly in a mesmeric dream of love and suffering and death.

Although he filled pages with such notes they grew more diffuse and led him further from the finite scene or situation or character on which to build. Ross had to face the actuality—that he had no start on a new book.

Moreover, this elusiveness of material made him question his powers—not his technical ability, which he knew was constant, but his motivation. He was now bewildered about the very purpose of a novelist, even of putting words onto paper. He had begun to doubt the act of writing itself. In putting himself these questions he felt the terrifying suspicion he would never write again.

Throughout the preceding week Ross had had more difficulty sleeping than usual. He would wake from only an hour or so of restless, nightmare-ridden slumber and be moody and depressed throughout the day.

With the peace-making on October 20 and the release of tensions which it brought, Ross hoped to make his way back to some shore of serenity, a restoring of his appetite for food and sexual pleasure and the healing of a few hours' deep sleep. But he lay awake the whole of that Monday night, reliving the episodes of his quarrel with Houghton Mifflin and blaming himself for them, worrying over the hazards of publication which lay ahead, and suffering the terrible sense of emptiness and falsity which came with not being able to work.

On the following day, Tuesday, October 21, he could eat no breakfast. He complained of a dryness of mouth that prevented swallowing and he avoided his worktable. He could no longer release his pressures with an angry letter to Boston—and there was no question of thinking about the new book. He had lost all interest in it.

As the morning wore away, his depression grew deeper. He spoke of his worries about *Raintree County's* appearance. To Vernice he seemed to be suffering a kind of acute stage fright about his publication. He was suspicious that various people were already at work to harm him and his book and he assured her that people were watching him. He had seen them.

He refused to go outside the cottage and he sat without

moving for several hours. He had a feeling of wanting to cry. The tears were there but he lacked even the strength to raise them. His expression was grief-stricken and when Vernice asked what was troubling him and what she could do to help him, Ross replied in monosyllables, softly, almost inaudibly, that he did not know and there was nothing she could do.

From his withdrawn, trancelike state it was as though he could barely hear her patiently repeated questions. "I feel nothing," he murmured. "I'm without any emotion. I know only that I love you and the children." A terrified Vernice recognized that the flame of her husband's spirit had just guttered out.

Vernice had had some experience with emotional disorder. When Imogen, her next older sister, was ten she came down with encephalitis and it left her subject to violent temper tantrums. One stemmed from a Parcheesi game and an accusation of cheating so fierce that Vernice was nearly persuaded of her own guilt. When the other Baker children turned on the raging Imogen, their mother would warn them she was sick and lie down on the bed beside the screaming child, embracing her until she subsided.

But Imogen did not get better. The Bakers had to commit her to the state asylum at Madison and when she returned to them she was a stunned, dull girl. A brain operation was recommended and although this raised hopes, it resulted in an infection and Imogen's death.

The Imogen experience had led Vernice to abhor emotional outburst and had helped to build her own unusual placidness and reserve. It had also made her wary of medical advice for nonspecific illness.

And yet in three months she had seen the vital, buoyant man she had loved from her girlhood turn into a man without spirit. The essence of Ross Lockridge had drained out of him as though from some hideous crack in his soul. She recognized it as the sort of collapse then euphemistically known as a nervous breakdown, but she knew that it was serious and that it was a mental as well as a physical illness.

Still she was convinced that its cause was exhaustion from the task of revisions and from the agonizing dispute with Houghton Mifflin. Now that both were finished she hoped that rest, her own loving care and the passing of time would restore his peace of mind.

Ross's depression and inability to write continued into these last days of October and yet he did respond to Vernice's treatment. He seemed better, particularly in the afternoons, and she took courage from that. Also, when friends called or there was some new demand in connection with *Raintree County*, he would rouse and become his old, exuberant self. However, the moment he was alone with Vernice, he would retreat into melancholia and she came to recognize those displays of cheer as protective and to describe them as "putting on the act."

There was soon another demonstration of Ross's chameleon spirits and a suggestion that beneath his apathy lay reserves of vitality.

Earlier in the month, John P. Marquand, a Book-of-the-Month Club judge, had been in Boston for the day and was shown a proof of the *Raintree County* dust jacket. It was John Morris's rendering of Ross's concept—rolling Indiana countryside which, on closer examination, becomes a supine female figure.

It amused Marquand and on returning to his home at Kent's Island in Newburyport, he described it in a note to Harry Scherman, head of B.O.M.C. in New York.

"You intrigue me greatly," Scherman replied on October 15. "I'll see if I can get one right away. Usually these birds use our jackets and I imagine they will, if you decide to use the book. It strikes me the pickings are awfully slim this month."

When, on October 23, the judges did convene at the B.O.M.C. offices, only four—Marquand, Henry Seidel Canby, Dorothy Canfield Fisher and Clifton Fadiman—were present. Christopher Morley, the fifth member of the panel, was in Europe, but he had left them a letter about *Raintree County*, which went:

> In spite of my prejudice against it for its enormous length—and I still think it doesn't need to be so long—I find it a remarkable

book. I think it better under control than Tom Wolfe, for instance. I hesitate to encourage the present passion for writing fiction of such gigantic longitude; I cast my mind back to Wilder's *Our Town* and see in how few words he conveyed the same fundamental ideas. Nevertheless there is something finely impressive about the book; the Day itself and the flashbacks dissolve into each other without difficulty. What makes the book very real to me is that I knew a Middle Western boy whose mind and dreams and family background and experience were very like J. W. Shawnessy's. (His name was Don Marquis.)

I am frankly doubtful of it as a choice. The mass-reading public is likely to be either bewildered or pained by it. If there is strong enthusiasm for it among my colleagues, I am quite willing to go along, but I want to inject a serious note of caution.

Christopher Morley's letter reflected the other judges' feelings, that *Raintree County* was unnecessarily long and undisciplined, but had rare qualities. Marquand liked its vigor and Dorothy Canfield its "deep-hearted love for our country." Clifton Fadiman thought it no more than "a try at that great gleaming illusion, the Great American Novel," but he liked its vitality and humor. Henry Canby was troubled by the time scheme but thought it a rich, vital novel. So, the decision was to take it as their January selection, provided the author would agree to further editing.

On Friday, October 24, Ross received the news of *Raintree County*'s latest victory as though he had expected it. But it promptly restored his spirits and on hearing there was the usual string attached, that they were asking for some new cuts, he responded like a veteran commander, leaping once again to defend his beleaguered bastion.

So, when Henry Canby telephoned him to explain what they required, he found Ross stubbornly resistant and the ordinarily mild-mannered Canby finally lost his temper, crying out, "My God, Boy—you've got an eleven-hundred-page book!"

Whereupon Ross listened to Canby and presently was persuaded that what they had in mind was artistically sound and not difficult to accomplish. They had found the scene which took place between John Shawnessy and Laura Golden in an upstairs room of her New York house unsuccessful. Ross's intent, to show "frustration and rejection," had gone wrong and the result was inappropriately "sour."

Agreeing, Ross confessed to Canby that he had been uneasy about it, that he had inserted it "under pressure and in haste" as part of the M.G.M. alterations but that "the best literary jury in America unerringly put the finger on the weak place."

Once again Ross returned to perform surgery on *Raintree County* and without difficulty eliminated several thousand additional words from its text. On October 28, he sent off these final revisions to Paul Brooks in Boston, telling him he had found Canby a "humane and wonderful gentleman" and that "it was as simple as this: the five eminent people who compose the jury of the Book-of-the-Month Club unanimously agreed that the book was fine but one scene ought to come out. The author unanimously agreed to take it out."

Ross's elation over the B.O.M.C. decision bubbled forth in a letter he wrote Dorothy Hillyer on October 29, saying:

> My God, Dorothy, is all this really happening? Of course I predicted it all myself and always believed it would happen this way, but now that it is happening it's as if a man had the personal power to shape his own universe, rub the magic lamp, etc., and project dreams—and that really oughtn't to be possible in the light of the Twentieth Century.
>
> I've been thinking it over to see if anything else can possibly come now to give *Raintree County* a pre-publication boost . . . and I've decided that there's just one thing left. I'll get one hell of a loud telephone ring and find myself holding an unexpected telephone, and a voice like John McCaffery's but two octaves lower and even more rich and mellifluous will say,
>
> —Hello Ross, this is God speaking.
> —Hello, God. What's up?

—Why, Ross my child, I think you'll be pleased to hear that I've just had a little Meeting with Myself and have decided to select your book for Our Book-of-the-Cosmos Club.

—Gosh! That's wonderful. What century?

—Why, the Twentieth Century Choice, son. I'm going to do the review myself.

—Swell. There's no one I'd rather have do it. I'm acquainted with some of Your own works, of course, the Bible, and all . . .

—Don't mention it, son. It's a pleasure. Of course, there are a few little deletions that I would like to see made—not to shorten the book, you understand, though my God, boy, why do you write such long books!—no, not to shorten it, but just to improve its artistic character. Now I've had some experience in these matters, been around a little, think my judgment is worth considering, and of course if you don't do it, we can always take Hemingway's forthcoming opus in place of yours.

—Well, just what did you have in mind?

—It won't be hard—I'm merely suggesting that you pull out the character named Professor Jerusalem Webster Stiles and patch up the book a little. Course there's an element of time. You only have to 1960 to do it.

—I've always sort of liked that character, fairly important to the book, sort of involved with the book's basic meanings, and——

—Remember, boy, all I have to do is issue a fiat. I just plain don't like that character. He's a discredit to your book, and I may say—though of course personal considerations are not involved— that the character of his comments upon Myself is not, shall we say, the sort of thing consonant with the high moral character of the literature we are accustomed to disseminating to the Book-of-the-Cosmos readers.

—Yes, sir, I'll take it under advisement, sir, and see what I can do. Naturally I want my book to succeed and——

—I know you do, boy, I know you do. It's grand of you, boy, to agree to do this thing. Get that stuff in right away, and don't let me catch hair nor hide of that infernal rascal in your copy. You understand, of course that when and as and if a satisfactory revision is made along these lines, you get one billion two hundred thousand dollars, all the gold from the Cosmic Reserve in Fort Knox, and a huge, big-as-life picture of Me as soon as the book tops the two billion mark.

—Thanks a lot, sir. I don't know how to thank you enough.

—Don't mention it, son. I'm sending the contract around to-morrow, and we'll expect an option on your next book. You're bought, boy, bought. Good-by, son, and keep your nose wiped. I think you have real promise.

Ross closed his exuberant letter with the observation "that I have really gotten over and recovered from *Raintree County* at last . . ."

But the elation over the B.O.M.C. selection and the satisfaction in further perfecting *Raintree County* was short-lived. Night thoughts still terrified him and his days were gray with depression. As he and Vernice talked of what could be done, Ross admitted his anxiety revolved around his family's opinion of the book.

He could not get it out of his head that his father was hostile to *Raintree County*. His censure of the *Life* excerpt was proof of it. Ross could feel the instinctive competitiveness between them and felt it was going to color his father's judgment of the book, and that he would try to influence his mother about it. He wanted his mother to make up her mind first.

Previously, Ross had wired his family news of "a very great lunar honor paid to a certain famous but fictitious piece of Hoosier real estate," but in calling them he found they had already known about the B.O.M.C. selection. They had learned about it first in a telephone call from L. S. Ayres, the Indianapolis department store.

Ross told his mother that the acclaim for *Raintree County* seemed to be adding to his plaguing anxieties about the book. He spoke of how his health had been affected and of his belief that her opinion of the book was involved. He asked her if she would come to Manistee at once in order to read *Raintree County*. Of course, Elsie agreed.

She drove up from Bloomington, arriving in Manistee during the first week in November. So that the children would not disturb her and she could give full attention to the book, Ross had taken a room for her at a nearby inn, and he provided her with a set of page proofs to which he had added the final B.O.M.C. corrections.

"It's your book, Mother," he told her as he left her alone with it. "You'll notice I haven't dedicated it to you—it's written for you and I want to have your approval before it's published."

Typically, Ross had burst from his melancholia at his mother's appearance, so that she was not as alarmed as she might have been, but she did recognize his failing health and realized he was passing through a major crisis.

While Elsie read her way through *Raintree County*, emerging from her hotel room at mealtimes with an enthusiastic report on each episode completed, Ross wrote Dorothy Hillyer on November 5, saying, "In some ways Publication Day is passing for the author right now, as my mother is reading the book with vast admiration and understanding. That has been all along with me the most delicate point of all."

Even so, he confessed, "I'm still far from myself, have been quite sick and the stresses and strains of contracts and successes aggravated the trouble. It's all part, too, of the big picture of readjustment that I have to make as my book approaches the world."

Next day he wrote to Paul Brooks, "I've had a severe bout with the flu and may be some time convalescing. Don't count on me for any very forceful cooperation before Publication Day." And in acknowledging a kindly letter from a friend, he told him, "I've been sick and am recuperating slowly. Along with it I realize that I am in the vast period of readjustment as I lay down the burden of *Raintree County* and let the world take it up."

Elsie's final verdict on *Raintree County* was a fervent approval. For Ross it was an enormous relief—and yet it was still not enough. With his mother's sanction won he was anxious about what his father, and indeed the rest of the world, was going to think of *Raintree County*. He felt acutely sensitive to hostile reaction from any direction and wished he did not have to endure publication at all. Desperately he said to Elsie, "Mother, sometimes it seems to me as if I wrote my book in a vacuum—that nobody else would ever read it but us."

Recognizing that he was indeed ill and the illness psychological, Elsie sat down with Ross and Vernice and discussed, with a characteristic force and practicality, the best way of dealing with it. As always, her belief lay in the power of the human spirit to overcome the most formidable difficulties.

Ross was not surprised when his mother offered her own medicine. She had confidence in his ability to help himself, and in the healing power of faith and prayer, and so proposed he undertake the Christian Science treatment. He agreed to read *Science and Health with Key to the Scriptures* and other books she would provide, and he would visit a Christian Science practitioner in Indianapolis whom she recommended.

As they talked, Ross took an objective view of himself and his problem. He suggested that although the cottage here had served them well, its associations were no longer good ones. With his frail health and the onset of fall there was no need to put up with its chills.

When Elsie suggested they come home, Ross said no. For the present, at least until *Raintree County* was published, the idea of settling down for an indefinite period in Bloomington was not appealing. What did beckon, he said, was California. Ever since Steve Tryon had come back with tales of its benign climate and sybaritic ways it had been in his mind. Besides, he would be following *Raintree County* there, assuring himself a cordial welcome in Hollywood. Regardless of whether he actually worked on the picture he would be keeping an eye on it and finding ways in which to influence its final outcome.

Perhaps they could go alone and make a second honeymoon of it. If they found some agreeable community and an attractive house they could come back for the children and settle there. He would soon have the money to do that comfortably. California might be just the place to live and work.

Elsie and Vernice agreed that a trip west, one that combined holiday and purposeful exploration, was precisely what Ross needed and they made arrangements for the children. Ernest, having spent most of the previous year with his grandparents, would have no problem readjusting to them and to Bloomington school. Elsie volunteered to take Ernest and Jeanne as well. Vernice felt she could leave little Ross with her brother's family in Martinsville, and Larry with her mother and father.

The decision made, it was carried out swiftly. While the children were being prepared for the new pattern of their lives, and the packing begun, Ross wrote Diggory Venn on November 8, ". . . we are planning an immediate change of residence from Manistee, probably to California . . . We need a warm climate— myself in particular, as I've had a bout with the flu and am not up to a Manistee autumn, let alone winter." Beneath a shaky signature, he added a P.S., "The one unbreakable rule as yet is—no direct reference to family materials until after publication day. My mother has read the book and loves it, but other members of the family would have to be sort of included on a release of those materials . . ."

"Other members of the family" were, of course, his father.

Finally, Ross composed a list of disciplines and prospects for his own use. Of *Raintree County* he told himself:

> I should exclude it from my thoughts or, if I think of it at all, simply pick it up and read one of the optimistic "sweet" parts of it. . . .
>
> Meanwhile continue searching thoughts into the nature of self and God, and the nature of Divine Love and Power, à la Christian Science, along with readings in the Bible.
>
> Confidently and fearlessly face every contingency of life, strengthened by a reliance on God, knowing the essential error of every dream of anxiety, fear, etc., and your ability to meet and master every problem in a material world, where strength of Spirit is always adequate. "Divine Love always has met and always will meet every human need."
>
> Look at some residences in California, but consider also the possibility of returning to Bloomington around Xmas . . .
>
> Begin extensive planning on a new book—planning of charac-

ters, situation, etc., whenever you feel at all like touching the necessary materials.

Although it was Ross's practice to begin important undertakings with such jottings, these seem to lack conviction. Even as a boy in the midst of the Epworth League's plentiful prayers he was not on negotiable terms with God. His mouthpiece, John Shawnessy, concedes only that *each self participates in God* and is about all we are likely to know of the mystery. Only a week earlier he had playfully cast himself and God in a skit. So this formal appeal to Him was a measure of Ross's wish to follow his mother's prescription.

But his anguish was real and deep. He saw it as a continuum of bad dreams from which he could not awaken. There was the bad dream of his guilt. He kept coming back to the idea that all his troubles were of his making, that if he had refused to change a word of *Raintree County* he and his book would still be whole. His insecurities centered on the money that had bought his compromise. He could see the reflection of a two-headed fool, the avaricious and the gullible one, and he loathed himself for both.

He also knew the bad dreams of lost love, of lost gift, of impotence and, finally, most terrifyingly, he knew the bad dream of patricide.

On Tuesday, November 11, Ross and Vernice left Manistee for Indianapolis, where Elsie had made the necessary arrangements with the practitioner. On their way south Ross found himself sharing his mother's faith in the efficacy of Christian Science treatment and looking forward to more of it. He spoke of the future with some confidence, agreeing, "There's no pill like the Gospel, Mother."

On November 12, while Elsie and Vernice settled his children at their temporary homes around Bloomington, Ross kept his appointment with the practitioner and, from an Indianapolis hotel, wrote Craig Wylie:

> I've been through a period of sickness—nearly beat me down, spirits low and everything, but I seem now to have the Perfesser

firmly by the throat and am dragging the scamp willy-nilly out of the Great Dismal Swamp, into which you will recall JWS refused to let him descend. We are all children when we are sick, and like children our discernments are simpler and clearer.

Just now I sit in a hotel room looking out upon the Circle in Indianapolis in the middle of which rises the famous monument discussed in the opening pages of "Fighting For Freedom," the Civil War battle section of Raintree County. The stone men are there, the bronze guns, the monoliths and symbolic shards of that legendary era that I attempted to recreate in Raintree County. So the past lives and moral convictions survive even in pieces of humanly altered matter—like the Gettysburg bullet you gave me on that memorable evening spent at your home with your lovely, lovely wife.

We are planning to travel slowly, Vernice and I, across the Republic. It will be a good day when you and I meet again and I have an opportunity to inscribe my thanks to a fine gentleman and humane scholar in the book he helped me to make better.

Next day, Ross and Vernice set out for California. It had been arranged that they leave the old Hudson at the Quayles' farm in Elgin, Illinois, and they paused there long enough for Ross to get a barbiturate prescription from an Elgin doctor and for them to make their farewells to an apprehensive Mary Jane and Edward Quayle.

For Vernice, who had not been free of the cares and hard work of her household in a decade, their journey promised some freedom and a holiday. Ross was hopeful too. As they boarded The Chief in Chicago's Dearborn Station, they were feeling adventurous and sure that awaiting them in the West was the tonic Ross needed, and a new life with some comfort and challenge for them both.

VIII

Arriving in Los Angeles, Ross and Vernice rented a Ford car, searched for a suitable place to stay and settled on the Peppertree Lodge, a motel in North Hollywood. There, on November 19, Ross wrote Paul Brooks that they would "stay awhile for a sort of rest cure. Our plans are pretty indefinite, but we should be here long enough to receive the author's 12 copies of the book."

Vernice had bought some new clothes and as she strolled the meticulously landscaped districts of Hollywood and Beverly Hills, marveling at the Elysian weather, she felt an agreeable sense of weightlessness. She was particularly intrigued by the Spanish-style houses festooned with bougainvillea and set against scythes of palm and tall fingers of cypress. The impression was of a community recently erected by a stage crew, one that would be taken down and packed off to the warehouse before she strolled this way again.

Her pleasure in these first few days in California grew from the belief that Ross too was enjoying, and already benefiting from, the change of scene. He seemed to be—and he spoke eagerly of what lay ahead for him at M.G.M.

However, when he reached Carey Wilson, Ross found him busy with other projects and he soon grasped that the studio's plans for *Raintree County* were, at best, prospective ones. Not only were the preliminaries of scenario preparation and casting in abeyance, it was no longer certain that Wilson would be its director. This time there was no mistaking the lack of concentration with which the studio headquarters greeted him, nor was there much he could do about it. Inquiring for his friend McCaffery, Ross learned he was leaving the firm.

Although he had no real knowledge of M.G.M. dynamics, his intuition was accurate. All was not well. Within the management there had been a conflict of theory on how good screen stories are discovered. Louis B. Mayer had been persuaded that a principal source was the New York literary scene, an area in which Carol Brandt was particularly adroit. Mrs. Brandt had convinced him of the efficacy of an elaborate New York operation for acquiring literary properties and of the consequent publicity scoring over his chief competitor, Twentieth-Century Fox.

She had then conceived the idea of the huge prize, one which would bring M.G.M. first choice of every available manuscript, thus allowing them to buy, at their own price, properties other than prize winners. Topping off her victory, Carol Brandt had made the terms of her own contract. They were such that she had been known to laugh over their dazzling generosity.

Kenneth Mackenna, head of M.G.M.'s story department, had an altogether different notion of how to acquire stories. He felt that no first-class author would submit his work to the uncertainties and possible humiliations of a contest, and that regardless of the purse, it would attract only second-rate material. But worse, in trumpeting the hundred-and-fifty-thousand-dollar prize, they had invited *all* writers to demand that sum on a noncompetitive basis. As a result, they had raised the floor of their own literary negotiations, without tangible benefit to Metro.

By November 1947, ominous portents and thoughts of retrenchment were in the industry winds; Mackenna's view was appearing the more reasonable one and the extensive New York acquisition program was being dismantled. The reaction to several years of promoting the prize had set in and within spheres of studio influence, the award winners—Elizabeth Goudge's *Green Dolphin Street*, Elizabeth Metzger Howard's *Before the Sun Goes Down*,

Mary Renault's *Return to Night*, Maritta Wolff's *About Lyddy Thomas* and *Raintree County*—now wore the leprousness of a serious miscalculation. This judgment was being confirmed by the release of Carey Wilson's production of *Green Dolphin Street*, first of the prize winners, to a dismal reception.

Not only were studio politics running against Ross but so was his reputation. It had been decided already that his zealous admiration for his own book and his lack of technical experience made him the worst possible medicine for the prolix *Raintree County*. Nonetheless, Ross was welcomed by Carey Wilson and arrangements were made for him to meet Mackenna and Milton Beecher, the man in charge of contract writers and their assignment to production.

When Ross spoke of his and Vernice's curiosity about the studio itself, a date was set for a visit and presently the Metro publicity department called to inquire how long the Lockridges would be in town and if Ross would be available for promotion. Ross agreed, for the first time since the family reunion, to be interviewed.

But the novelty of Wilshire Boulevard and its unusual people was no distraction for Ross's worries about publication day. These still centered on his father's possible disapproval of the book and lately his assignments in Christian Science reading had increased his dread of moral censure of his book. So he drew up a manifesto pointing out that *Raintree County* was essentially a moral novel, rooted in Christian principle, and that everyone who thought otherwise simply had not read it intelligently. On November 23, he mailed copies to Paul Brooks and Dorothy Hillyer.

"As *Raintree County* approaches the vast American reading public, and especially certain local scenes," he explained, "I have hoped that the sex, irreverence and profanity of some of the scenes and characters of this book will not get it blacklisted anywhere, including Boston, and will not obscure its nobler and deeper meanings too much. As you know I made a careful last refinement of the book with these matters in mind, toning it down and improving it considerably without loss of vitality or sacrifice of artistic principle.

However, in the event that church groups etc. should take a jaundiced view of the book I have prepared a special and pious little paper, enclosed, covering these questions and pointing-out the basic Christian and ideal symbolism and meaning of the book. You might keep it on tap as a rejoinder to any criticism of that kind."

On November 26, when Ross called at the General Delivery window of the North Hollywood Post Office for his mail, he was given a package containing the first bound copy of *Raintree County*. Ross bore it proudly back to the Peppertree Lodge. He admired the binding and its jacket, read snatches of it with fresh pleasure and then sat down to write Paul Brooks, "We have it! All the years of dreams, hopes, and hard work held at last between two covers in the right hand! After millions of words, you will be happy to hear that the author of *Raintree County* was simply speechless. Vernice goes around sort of cradling the book from time to time. Our fifth baby! The cover designs, end-papers, etc., are just bewilderingly, wordlessly beautiful. We can never thank you all enough for the faith, effort, tact and guidance that brought my seven years' dream to such a beautiful consummation."

Vernice, as Ross had indicated, was as pleased with the bound book as he, and she began to read it from the beginning. Curiously, Ross's pleasure was short-lived. He was finding something finite and irrevocable now in the very sight of the book and soon asked her to put it away.

Continuing sunny days tempted Ross and Vernice to daily drives and they prospected the neighboring suburbs trying to imagine themselves installed in one of these trim stucco houses and the children at play on the emerald, handkerchief-size lawns.

However, a trip to the beach introduced them to the California traffic jam and they found it appalling. Also a study of the *Los Angeles Times*'s classified advertising revealed that the modest houses they had been admiring were priced at about fifty thousand dollars. A "ranch" they noted might encompass only a pair of fifty-foot lots. To a couple with Indiana values it was preposterous.

Moreover, they felt alone here. It was not only the children they missed but friends and family.

It was in part loneliness that led Ross to a nearby Christian Science Reading Room, but beneath that lay a more significant urgency. He was not improving. Appetite and a night's sound sleep eluded him. He had not replenished confidence in his writing; he was so creatively empty that thoughts of a new book only depressed him.

Furthermore his sense of pride in *Raintree County* was shaken. Looking back over the parade of its revisions he saw both the compromising of his own integrity and a sure sign of the book's imperfection. He began to doubt it was as good a book as he had believed.

Together, Ross and Vernice went to a Wednesday "Testimonial Meeting," one of the regular functions of the Christian Science community in which members rose to describe their problems and how their faith had saved them.

Vernice was very doubtful that Christian Science theory and practice, particularly this kind, was any staff for Ross. With the dimming of her own California hopes, she began to share his fear that he was drifting toward another collapse here, far from the understanding help they could summon at home. As her thoughts turned there, Vernice wrote her sister Clona Nicholson, whose job at the Citizen's Loan and Trust Company required a knowledge of such things, to inquire about available houses in Bloomington.

Meanwhile Ross had arranged that an advance copy of *Raintree County* be sent to South High Street and on November 28 a letter from his father brought the news he was so anxiously awaiting. If anything, he was more understanding and wholehearted in his praise of *Raintree County* than Elsie had been, and Ross rejoiced. He wrote his father:

> Dear Dad. I have your wonderful letter and can only say that somehow you have captured and expressed—in a way I couldn't have done myself—what I tried to do in creating *Raintree County.*

I am really not at all worried about the public reception of the book. Every indication is that the book will be a winner in every way, with or without controversy. Indeed, I never thought of mere commercial or contemporary success in writing *Raintree County* but tried to create a book for Humanity. Strangely enough, at the very pinnacle of RC's remarkable prepublication success, the strength that enabled me to write it seemed to desert me, and I have been at odds and ends with myself. During this time, however, I have reminded myself of the grand old truth, "Whom the Lord Loveth, he chasteneth." And I have had vast comfort and strength from a direct reliance on the Scriptures and the great symbolic truths everywhere expressed in the Old and New Testaments. When our strength deserts us, there is a greater Strength.

We are just going to take it easy for a while, keep our business appointments with MGM, of course, and in due time make the necessary decisions about residence, etc. . . . . I don't feel like public appearances as yet . . .

He explained that he would soon have his first royalty payment and from this he would be sending along an endowment gift for his father's Indiana historical foundation—"a very small and humble return to you and Mother for years of splendid example and guidance and also for the deep understanding which you have shown for *Raintree County*."

They were cordially received at M.G.M. While Ross got down to business, Vernice was entertained with a commissary lunch and a glimpse of the fifteen-year-old actress Elizabeth Taylor, already a veteran of several "Lassie" pictures and *National Velvet*.

Ross's conference with the big shots, which he had been anticipating for so many months, was a surprise. Where he had expected a council of Caesars, these were affable, businesslike fellows and they were plagued by all sorts of financial and scheduling difficulties. His worry, that they were going about *Raintree County* in slapdash fashion, was soon put to rest.

He liked both Carey Wilson and Milton Beecher, the man who could hire him for work on the screenplay, and Beecher did say that when the time came they would welcome Ross's advice and help, and they would pay him for it of course. But there was nothing immediate to be done. They would let him know when there was.

Although they parted with handshakes and promises, by the time Ross joined Vernice for a visit to the set where *The Big City* was in production, he had the numbing feeling that he had just been through a brush-off.

It was now plain that there was nothing whatever for Ross to do in California and next day he wrote Martha Stiles of a change in the weather which was as much spiritual as climatic. "We're enjoying one of the heaviest rains I've seen in a long time," he told her. "I'm all for heading back to Manistee." He asked her to ship the original *Raintree County* manuscript to him there, along with thirty-five copies of the book, which he wanted to inscribe for friends and helpful acquaintances.

But then Clona Nicholson's reply to Vernice brought an interesting alternative. She had found a house for sale in Bloomington. It was in a newly developed neighborhood, South Stull Avenue. The house itself—a trim, gray-shingled colonial with a garage and pleasant yard—was just completed. Its price, twenty-five thousand dollars, was as inviting as the thought of leaving Hollywood to its own and of returning to friends and family. Ross wired her to buy the house for him.

The means were now at hand. He heard from Paul Brooks that a check for $122,500 (M.G.M.'s $150,000 prize, less Houghton's commission and Ross's $5000 advance) was off to his Bloomington bank account. Paul added that he had wrist fatigue from writing greetings to be enclosed with the *Raintree Countys* now going off as Christmas cheer to Houghton authors everywhere.

After three weeks in California, Ross was as eager to leave as he had been to arrive and on December 11, as they were ready to quit the Peppertree Lodge, Ross wrote Paul Brooks that henceforth "all mail to me should be sent to my name RR. 3, Bloomington, Indiana. We plan to be back there soon."

But the return journey was an anguished one. As Ross and

Vernice traveled eastward toward home, his depression deepened, and he confessed to Vernice that he did not think he was going to get well. By the time they reached the Quayles' farm at Elgin to reclaim their car, he was desperate, and they turned to Mary Jane for advice.

Mary Jane Quayle, who had been concerned for Ross since her visit to Manistee in August, was dismayed by the change in him. During the three weeks he had been in the West, he had lost even more weight and his thinness was alarming. An even more dramatic symptom of his illness was his quiet. She knew that the normal Ross would have returned from California bursting with observations about the fantastic place—but he was mute. All the reactions of this man, who had so consistently vibrated with energy, had slowed. She recognized an invalid's inability to react to outside stimuli and now saw the trip to California as an attempted flight from the closing net of his illness which had proved, quite naturally, inescapable.

What gave her hope for Ross was his ability to speak rationally of his own plight. He considered himself mentally ill, he told her, and yet felt he should be able to lick the problem by himself. When Mary Jane Quayle proposed that he could not, that what he needed was professional psychiatric help, Ross agreed. Still, all three of them knew this would be opposed by Ross's parents. Elsie, with her increasing dependence on Christian Science, had rejected medical advice. Ross's father, though for different reasons, would be as stoutly opposed. He knew Ross's mind from having trained it, knew it to be a superb and healthy one, capable through discipline and exercise of any necessary adjustment. The suggestion of unsoundness was shameful. His reason for opposing psychiatric care for Ross was simply that none was needed.

However, both Frank Lockridge and Elsie, her Christian Science notwithstanding, had faith in the wisdom of Ross's uncle, Dr. Robert Peters, and now at the Quayles' farm it was decided that all three—Ross, Vernice and Mary Jane—would go at once to his Indianapolis office and insist that Ross needed psychiatric care.

At this meeting with his uncle, Ross was explicit, telling him he believed he should go to a sanatorium. Dr. Peters, who shared many of Ross's father's views about mental illness, was reluctant, but, facing the unified opinion at his desk, agreed and made arrangements that Ross, under an assumed name, be admitted to Methodist Hospital in Indianapolis for treatment.

The psychiatrist who took charge of Ross's case at the hospital made his examination and prescribed a program of electric convulsive therapy. This raised immediate anxieties in Ross because of a childhood experience. Some twenty-odd years earlier, he had climbed onto a dressing table in the bathroom at South High Street and reached for the light which hung above it. His outstretched fingers touched the cord, which was faulty, and he took such a strong jolt of current from it that he was knocked to the floor and left with a lifetime fear of electricity.

Although he was assured the treatments would not be painful he dreaded the preparations, whose unpleasantness was only exceeded by the aftermath. Because of the possibility of voiding during the convulsion he was offered little to eat beforehand. Then, in the treatment room he was directed to a table on roller casters and told to lie down there and make himself comfortable. Stout straps for restraining him hung from it but these were not fastened, for the danger of breaking bones was less with arms and legs unconfined.

A nurse swabbed his temples with alcohol and coated them with jelly and the therapist clamped on the headgear, a large forceps with the electrodes attached to its blades. These were pressed firmly against his skull while a gag, rubber tubing wrapped in gauze, was placed in his mouth to prevent his biting his tongue or damaging his teeth.

With the electrical equipment ready an attendant took a position at the table's head, his hands resting on Ross's shoulders, prepared to pin him down, and then the first stimulus, some seventy volts of current, flowed, for about two-tenths of a second, through the electrodes into Ross's brain. As he lost consciousness his legs flew up like a jumping jack's, then straightened again, beginning the tonic phase of the convulsion.

Seconds later, under a stronger electrical impulse, he went gradually into the clonic phase, his body shaking with small, jerky spasms which became slower and more pronounced until they faded out, leaving him still as a corpse, not even breathing. When he began to breathe regularly again he was wheeled into another room and there, after a quarter of an hour, Ross emerged from his coma into twilight consciousness.

His brain cleared slowly. Voices drifted to him and he responded drowsily with no notion of where he was. As he was wheeled back to his own room his head swirled and ached, his stomach was queasy and his recollection was a drifting fog.

The treatments were given several times a week and although Ross assured his psychiatrist that he already felt improved, the reverse was true. They were gruesome ordeals. He told Vernice that he dreaded them beforehand, never lost consciousness during them and, far from helping him, they were destroying his mind. "The Middle Ages had their snake pits," he told her, "and we have our shock treatments."

He wanted to get out of the place as soon as it could be arranged—by Christmas if possible and in any case in time for the autographing party L. S. Ayres department store was planning for his publication day, January 5.

Dr. Peters, sensitive to the distaste and embarrassment Ross's hospitalization was causing in Bloomington, was quick to arrange for his release. The consulting psychiatrist objected that the complete course of electric convulsive therapy offered Ross a good chance of recovery, but he was still ill, surely no reliable judge of his own progress. It was unwise to interrupt it now.

Over these objections Ross left Methodist Hospital just prior to Christmas and set out with Vernice for Bloomington.

Home again, driving a brand-new Kaiser, about to move into a brand-new house, and with all the unrealized hopes of publication coming in the new year, it seemed life's promise might yet be fulfilled. As though to confirm it, New Year's Eve brought Ross a telegram from Paul Brooks with advance news of his critical reception. "New York Times, Tribune, and Saturday Review notices wonderful. Happy New Year. It should be."

The first, and most influential, reviews were indeed all Houghton Mifflin had hoped for. In comparing it to *Main Street* and proclaiming its "mountainous integrity," James Hilton's *Tribune* review was the first of a battery of salutes to *Raintree County*.

In the *Saturday Review of Literature* Howard Mumford Jones suggested that with its vision, gusto and skill, Lockridge's novel could mark the end of a long slump in American fiction. Although balanced by reservations about murkiness and excessiveness, equally radiant tributes came from Orville Prescott in *The New York Times's* daily book review and from Kelsey Guilfoil in the *Chicago Tribune*.

The one which pleased the author most was Charles Lee's for *The New York Times's* Sunday *Book Review*. In noting and approving the scholarship, particularly the interlocking, symbolic structure, Lee won Ross's approval as the most careful reader of his book.

On publication day, the Monday of January 5, Ross kept his promise and appeared at L. S. Ayres in Indianapolis. At the height of the party, he was photographed behind a barricade of *Raintree Countys* and surrounded by a Norman Rockwell composition of American faces, down to the little girl peeping over the guest of honor's shoulder, mischievously delighted to be sharing the viewfinder with him.

Ross, freshly barbered, sporting a flamboyantly scenic necktie, was obligingly ready with pen and smile. But his eyes were heavy-lidded and Vernice saw them and knew how weary he was, what an effort he was making, and knew that he would not be repeating it soon.

Good news continued to arrive from Boston. The first edition of fifty thousand copies had been sold prior to publication and Houghton was back to press for a second. In the three days following publication they had reorders for three thousand copies.

Reuters, the European news agency, had acquired rights for international serialization, and *Omnibook* for condensation, while Spanish and South American book rights had gone to Louis de Caralt. In passing on these bulletins, Paul Brooks asked about his plans and urged him to come east in the spring since they had many things to talk about, notably Ross's next book.

With the anxiousness of publication day itself now in the past, Ross could turn to some necessary business matters. The final purchase and furnishing of the house at 817 South Stull Avenue was now completed and they were able to move in during mid-January. Next Ross settled his account with Martin Stone and set aside his considerable payment to the Department of Internal Revenue. He was also able to buy some government bonds and to take out insurance policies on both his own life and Vernice's. When he had done all this, only a small fraction remained of the $122,500 which had been his bumper 1947 income.

But of course the graver, and still clandestine, problem to be met was that of his health. While his mother and father recognized this and were kept alert to it through Vernice's continuous concern, it was often difficult for them to credit, for Ross had become adept as a professional actor at the alternating of his roles, and their presence invariably brought forth his rational, optimistic one.

But if Ross's parents underestimated the gravity of his illness, they did know that he was in delicate health and that he was suffering an undefined emotional conflict, and they soon proposed separate, though nonexclusive therapies.

Elsie urged Ross to continue his Christian Science treatments in Indianapolis. Ross consented and the practitioner agreed to set aside a part of each Tuesday afternoon in which to meet him, until satisfactory progress had been made. Vernice, who was learning to drive the new Kaiser, would arrange her life and that of the children so as to make the trips with him.

Frank Lockridge's plan drew on a steadfast belief in his son's essential soundness and in the efficacy of exercise for the mind. He planned that they meet in regular sessions now, as they had when

Ross was a boy. Together they would read and commit to memory the best of mankind's inspirational thought.

While *Raintree County's* press continued to be a largely favorable one, the second wave of reviews, which Ross saw toward mid-January, were more severe with him.

The *Christian Science Monitor* found the minor characters, the women in particular, disappointing and sounded a faint but unmistakable note of moral censure. Then *Time* magazine, which Ross had been counting an ally, praised it, but with the damning faintness of "an assignment brilliantly completed" and a work "of the second order."

Newsweek's critic was devastating. "It spreads everywhere, like beer slopped on a table," he said of *Raintree County* and ripped on to fulfill Ross's own premonition with "If Lockridge had found an editor as capable as Wolfe had found in Maxwell Perkins this might have been a really magnificent work. Obviously there was no such word craftsman about. The result is one grand gush of words that makes the reader wonder what kind of English it can have been that Lockridge taught for five years in Simmons College, Boston."

But unkindest of all was Hamilton Basso's lead review for *The New Yorker.* "American fiction writing has for a long time been building up to *Raintree County* by Ross Lockwood Jr.," Mr. Basso began. "It is, it seems to me, the climax of all the swollen, pretentious human chronicles that also include a panorama of the Civil War, life in the corn-and-wheat belt, or whatnot . . . For here, in a thousand and sixty-six pages of a novel, equipped with such guides as maps, chronologies, and illustrated endpapers, is *everything* that happened in this country between 1844 and 1892—"

Persisting in that ultimate humiliation of getting Ross's name wrong, Basso had further sport with *Raintree County's* technical devices and wondered why the publishers "didn't go the limit and provide a compass. I could have used one just to find my way from the end of one chapter to the next."

He summed up the novel as "just the sort of plump turkey

they bake to a turn in Hollywood." But then, in an unexpected act of clemency, he decided that "unlikely as it may seem, Mr. Lockwood does have talent. When he stops trying to write like the author of a pageant of America and just goes ahead and writes he can be read with interest and enjoyment. Nearly all his major figures are failures, but he succeeds splendidly with a few minor characters. One of them, a Professor Jerusalem Webster Stiles, is in the native comic tradition of Mark Twain. This is Mr. Lockwood's first novel, so there is still time for him to learn that bulk is not accomplishment, that fanciness is not literature and that Thomas Wolfe, while an excellent man in his way, had defects that look absolutely terrible second-hand."

Ross was gravely wounded by these reviews and claimed that neither the *Newsweek* nor *The New Yorker* man could have more than skimmed the book, but this was thin consolation for he had often admired the judgments of both magazines and knew they commanded an audience of discriminating readers. He could no longer shake off these scoffing appraisals of *Raintree County*, nor a deepening sense of artistic failure.

However, there was cheer from the mails. Letters from friends, acquaintances and total strangers brought daily praise and admiration, and he found time to answer almost all of them. To friends and strangers alike, he confessed that he didn't feel successful at all, that on the contrary publication had brought him only stress, and its aftereffect was illness, confusion, fatigue and a feeling of being crushed by it all.

To his oldest friend, Malcolm Correll, then completing his doctorate at the University of Chicago, he wrote, "I am so 'sat on' by old Father Fate these days that I haven't anything good to say for myself. What with family trouble (new house, sickness— mainly me, children everywhere as usual, etc.), celebrity trouble and general exhaustion from too many years too hard at the same thing, I am far from the old Lockridge just now and am trying hard to get out of the woods. Believe me, Fame—if you can call it that—ain't what it's cracked-up to be."

But his misery could not suppress a patronizing wave for a stay-at-home from a battle-weary conqueror. "Go on, my friend in the paths of service and scholarship to which you are devoted," he told Correll. "Honest, I was happier when we were exchanging ties back in the old high-school days and courting our now respective wives."

When a free-lance writer, Nanette Kutner, wrote from New York for an interview, he begged off, but when she called he relented and in mid-February she appeared at the house. He admitted to her that the Newsweek and New Yorker reviews had angered him and then, when Miss Kutner asked how he was getting on with his new book, he pointed to the scattering of papers on the desk of his little study and said it was "terrible going."

Taking her back to her hotel, Ross drove badly, with sudden starts and stops, and when she told him he seemed awfully nervous and unsure at the wheel, he admitted that he hadn't been sleeping and that even pills were no help.

"Maybe you ought to get drunk," she suggested.

"Maybe you've got something there," Ross replied. But he declined to come in with her for a drink.

Although he still could not write, Ross was discovering some bright moments in the short, gray days of mid-February. He anticipated the mail each morning and from one letter learned his biography would appear in the new edition of Who's Who in America. Also, he had selected members of the Indiana University faculty whom he admired and he presented them with autographed copies of Raintree County and he renewed old acquaintances around town.

Ross often dropped in on the nearby Dowlings for a chat with his old schoolmate Leo, who once delighted him by reporting that a Lockridge boy had found him washing diapers and assured him his father would not do "that kind of work."

For the first time Ross had the leisure to enjoy his children, and he did. One afternoon shrieks brought Ross to his basement, where he discovered five-year-old Larry entertaining two contemporaries, the daughters of neighbors. Larry had persuaded them to take off their clothes and was now pursuing them around the furnace. When Ross had seen the girls dressed and sent home, he lectured Larry on the proprieties, but could not help laughing over his son's precocity.

At his father's urging, Ross agreed to a couple of speaking engagements at the university. For both, he planned to talk about writing his book, a subject that usually ran away with him, but he took the precaution of some rehearsals and when he appeared before the Men's Faculty Club, the citing of his literary influences came forth by rote and the disappointment of his audience was plain to him. One of his former professors noted that the only spontaneous moment was when Ross was asked what he was going to do next and he had replied, with a startling candor, "I wish I knew."

A week or so later, at the Rotary meeting in Alumni Hall, Ross acknowledged his debt to his father's love of history and paid sure-to-please tribute to Bloomington, saying that after all his travels he'd found no place like home, but again the response was little more than polite. Although he had tried, he had not been able to produce the vitality, the histrionics and imaginativeness which his friends in Bloomington had come to expect of the *wunderkind.*

The worst part of it was that his father saw the talks as encouraging steps to recovery, and Ross felt the reverse was true. They were not only agonizing for him, but displayed his terrible emptiness. While he could pull himself together and don the cheerful, self-deprecating mask, his performance was so far from the truth of what he was feeling—or failing to feel—that the result was a further depression.

So he was firm in declining urgent appeals from Boston to make an appearance in the East. Diggory Venn had some tempting invitations for him, one from the New England Press Women, another from the *Herald Tribune*'s annual book-and-author luncheon; when Paul Brooks suggested *Raintree*'s sales would benefit, Ross promptly replied, "For an indefinite period, the book will have to hobble along on its own merits as I am under doctor's orders to take it easy—that is, as easy as I can with the hullabaloo that's going on around here. We have a good deal of sickness in the family with me as leading contender. So we shall simply have to temporize in the matter of personal appearances until further word from me. I will definitely not be available this month."

On February 16, Ross told Paul Brooks that "After a careful check-up over the week-end with my physician, I regret the necessity of curtailed activity for some time to come. Naturally I want to help out with my book in any way possible that doesn't jeopardize too much my health as father of four. Even a couple of local appearances I have made have been pretty strenuous."

The *Christian Science Monitor's* temperate moral warning about *Raintree County* had been followed by a handful of letters from Indiana readers protesting the book's licentiousness, and one of Ross's children reported a disquieting incident on the playground. A schoolmate had pointed him out, saying, "Oh, it's his dad that wrote the dirty book." Also, when some of Elsie's friends learned that *Raintree County* dealt with sex they made it known they would not read it. While this did not imply any shunning of Ross himself, it was distasteful to him. Still, all this had been local and private, and in his frequent rationalizings, Ross had been able to dismiss it as gossip.

By mid-February, however, *Raintree County* was climbing the best-seller lists and Houghton's advertising campaign was touting its popularity and future on film. It made a fat, tempting target and Ross was not to be spared the sanctimonious broadside he had dreaded.

On the evening of February 18, Father A. J. Barrett, a Jesuit priest from Fordham University, rose to tell an audience of three hundred gathered to hear a discussion of "Catholic Thought on the Best Sellers" that *Raintree County* was "one thousand sixty-six pages of bombast, rank obscenity, materialist philosophy and blasphemous impudicity." He declared the book "patently falls within the general prohibition of the Index. It is a book inimical to faith and morals," and "For most readers it may be a proximate occasion of sin."

Father Barrett pointed out "The Birth, the Resurrection, the virginity of Mary, the divinity of Jesus Christ Himself are derided in terms of lascivious and unquotable blasphemy."

The story of this denunciation appeared prominently in *The New York Times* and the wire services carried it westward, so that it came promptly to Ross's attention—adding more weight to his burden, more envelopment to his sense of failure and more mindless speed to the runaway his book had become.

He heard from Diggory Venn that the "pious little paper" he had sent from Hollywood had served his publisher well, for he had based his successful rebuttal to Father Barrett on it. The priest had not been heard from since. But Ross found neither humor nor pleasure in this heartening dispatch from the battlefield. He had lost all such resilience.

When his old English instructor and chess coach, John Robert Moore, found Ross pushing a cart along the aisle at the A.&P., he could scarcely believe this was the man who, summer before last, had been so jubilant over his publishing prospects. The shoulders drooped; the face was gray and haggard and the eyes were dull. Ross told him that he was drained by his seven years of work on the book and that he was depressed over the adverse reviews and the attack of the Fordham priest.

When Ross called at the Dowlings in search of one of the children, he paced the living room several times, preoccupied, oblivious to questions, and then left with scarcely a word.

Don Smalley, with whom Ross had exchanged houses in 1941, saw him coming down Maxwell Lane one morning and though he scarcely recognized him with his stoop, his gaunt face and exhausted eyes, hailed him and asked him in for a cup of coffee. Assuming his friend's mood was temporary he tried to cheer him by praising *Raintree County*, but he couldn't break through to him. He was cloaked in apathy and hadn't the least interest in what Smalley was saying about his book, listening only out of politeness.

At home, Ross spent much of his time in the downstairs study he had pointed out to Nanette Kutner. It was a bare place, but he kept to it, night and day—most often stretched out on the narrow bed, staring at the ceiling. He scarcely slept. The strong barbiturates which had once been effective now anesthetized him for only a couple of hours and left him wearier than before. Remarkably, at the sound of the doorbell, he could still leap up and if the caller was one of his own parents or Vernice's, he would drop his apathy as though it were a garment and behave normally, speaking of plans and of family affairs in a way that consistently reassured them.

A doctor in Marion, Indiana, to whom Frank Lockridge had described his son's attacks of despondency, suggested they might be suicidal ones. But the elder Lockridge dismissed his friend's warning, for he was convinced that Ross was making progress in the program he had laid out. Since Ross was having trouble starting his new book, his father had suggested he try his hand at something unrelated, poetry perhaps, from which he used to take such pleasure. While Ross had not yet been able to write any poems he did strive to please his father in exercising and strengthening his weakened memory. There was disappointment for them both in these early sessions. When Ross tried to memorize the Patrick Henry speech he had known so well as a boy, he failed.

Ross was just as dutiful toward his mother's prescription. He kept his scheduled appointments with the practitioner, assuring her of his renewing strength through the healing of Divine Principle. He did enjoy the Tuesday trips to Indianapolis, though less for the benefits of Christian Science than for the drive through wintry countryside and the opportunity to be alone with Vernice, suspended for a few hours from the cycle of his purposeless day with its regular evoking of his anxieties.

At other times he was less rational. He spoke of fears, of plots against him, and he was occasionally incoherent. When Vernice found him making a round of their kitchen, opening the cupboard doors, peering in, closing them, she asked what he was doing and Ross replied gravely, "I'm looking for a way out."

She had been awaiting the chance to consult her own family doctor about Ross and suggested that Elsie substitute for her on one of the Tuesday trips to Indianapolis, but Ross wouldn't hear of it. He liked the arrangement as it was. He argued that she needed the practice in driving.

Then, on February 27, Ross received a jubilant telegram from Houghton Mifflin, telling him that *Raintree County* had just attained the number one position on the *Herald Tribune*'s national best-seller list, that which would appear in the Sunday edition of March 7, eight days hence. "Good Going" were Paul Brooks's final words to him.

During the following week Ross seemed to find new heart. His depressions were less frequent and he spoke with fresh hope of taking Vernice and the children to France while he wrote his next novel.

The whole family rejoiced at the change. Elsie in particular thought him "more like himself." Together they looked into his tiny upstairs room and Ross, stretching out on the narrow child's bed, recalled how his father used to sit on the end of it and tell him stories. He said he wished he were a boy again.

Noting that his hearty laugh was coming back and that he had begun joking with his family in a way he hadn't since his return, Elsie felt sure he was "beginning to come out of it."

On Saturday, March 6, shortly before noon, Frank Lockridge left his office in the university library and as he passed through its main doors he glanced overhead at the inscription, John Milton's "A good book is the precious life-blood of a master-spirit." He was struck by its aptness to his son's state of mind.

He was still thinking of this when he reached home, where he was surprised and delighted to find Ross awaiting him. Father and son spent the afternoon together. They spoke of the offer Ross had received from a lecture bureau and the possibility he would be able to accept it before long. Ross brought a special enthusiasm to his declamation practice that afternoon and afterward sat by the radio enjoying the broadcast of the regional high school basketball tournament.

Later in the afternoon, when Ross returned home, he put in some further work on his tax return before Vernice called him to the supper table. They dined together, finishing about five-thirty.

While Vernice went off to do the dishes and put the children to bed, Ross finished his work on the tax return. He also wrote a letter to Martin Stone, describing the deductions he was taking and asking for advice about what would be allowable for Vernice's typing services. Finally, he warned Stone that his tax problems would grow with future books.

At about eight o'clock, still in the excellent, even gay, spirits he had enjoyed throughout the day, Ross told Vernice that he was going to the post office to mail the letters in his hand and that on the way back he might stop off at his father's to listen to the Martinsville-Solsberry game, the finals of the basketball tournament.

Several hours passed and then, at ten forty-five, with Ross not returned, Vernice telephoned Frank Lockridge to ask if Ross had started home. He had never arrived, her father-in-law told her. This was bewildering to them both and he said he would come right over.

With mounting alarm, Vernice looked out toward the front of the house where the car had stood. There was no sign of its return. But when she stepped out of the back door and looked toward the garage, she saw a light burning through its windows.

Walking toward it she saw that both the large, overhead door and the side entrance door were closed and then, as she drew closer, she heard the sound of the car's running engine. She tried both doors and, finding them locked, turned back toward the house.

When Ross's father arrived they both hurried to the garage and managed to open the doors. Inside, the air was stifling and foul. They found Ross seated behind the Kaiser's steering wheel, his left foot dangling from the open car door, hands to his sides, his head resting on the back of the seat.

Vernice turned off the ignition switch and pulled Ross from the car into the cold, clear air of the driveway, pleading with him to respond to her. But Ross showed no sign of life.

Her call for help reached the Bloomington fire department at eleven thirteen. Her frantic question to the man who had answered was "Can you do anything for carbon-monoxide poisoning?" Within moments an emergency truck was on its way to 817 South Stull Avenue and, arriving, the two firemen found Ross's father, mother, sister and wife trying to carry him into the house. The firemen helped and when they had stretched Ross out on the kitchen floor began the resuscitation procedure.

The firemen were relieved by teams of police officers and although the attempt to revive Ross was continued for over an hour, it was futile. Dr. Robert Lyons, Monroe County coroner, who appeared shortly after the firemen and police, pronounced Ross dead and subsequently fixed the occurrence of his death at about nine-thirty.

Despite family hopes that the inquest might rule Ross's death an accident, the coroner reasoned that although Ross had left no written evidence of suicidal intent, the overhead garage door could not have been closed without his knowledge, nor was there a radio in the car to explain his lingering with the motor running. Thus, on Monday, March 8, he released his verdict, that Ross had taken his own life.

All across the nation, the radio and newspapers added the baffling final chapter to what had been the season's favorite success story. On the hall table at 817 South Stull Avenue, telegrams of dismayed condolence were accumulating from those who, only a few months ago, had been sending their envious congratulations.

On Tuesday, the day of Ross's funeral, Lockridge friends and relatives assembled in Bloomington from all over Indiana, and while no one came from Boston, two of Houghton Mifflin's Midwest representatives arrived from Chicago. By two-thirty in the afternoon, several hundred people had filled the pews of the First Methodist Church.

The service was begun with prayer led by a dear family friend, Reverend Will Wylie. In his sermon the pastor, Dr. Merrill Mc-Fall, drew a parallel between Ross's life and John Wickliff Shawnessy's, pointing out that at heart, Ross was an idealist and he had written that into his book. Those things which had been criticized, he assured the moral watchdogs, had been necessary to bring forth the true ideals and faith which were not only Johnny Shawnessy's but Ross's own.

Then Dr. William Lowe Bryan, president emeritus of the university and most esteemed of Lockridge family friends, rose to give the eulogy. "Ross was always first and best," he told the silent congregation, "and his book was an expression of genius." He viewed the day's sad task as a logical consequence of Ross's extraordinary dedication to his work. "Ross Lockridge, Jr., wrote with a passion," he said, "never once wanting to turn back, and believing throughout seven years of trial that his faith would create the greatest achievement."

"Nothing burns a man up like writing with an impassioned mind hour after hour," Dr. Bryan later explained. "It resulted in a deadening of emotions—I wish I could say that better. There's an exhaustion of whatever it is that is the mother of emotion, so that the ordinary impulses of youth, of joy and satisfaction are dead for a time."

After the funeral, Mary Jane Quayle stood for a moment with Dr. Peters, waiting while Ross's coffin was loaded into the hearse for its journey to Rose Hill Cemetery. The inquest had been a farce, Dr. Peters told her emphatically. Ross's death had been an accident. He had never been suicidal. Mrs. Quayle agreed, recalling Ross's habitual carelessness with automobiles. She had seen him finish using his car and walk away, leaving its motor running. Moreover, knowing Ross's thoroughness, she was certain he would not have intentionally ended his life without some word, some instructions for Vernice.

"Ross seemed to feel that his work was done," his father said. "I think too his work was done. His reward came quickly. His wife and children will be well provided for. I think his work will endure."

"He lived seven years with that story. It sapped his very heart's blood," Elsie Lockridge said. "Ross was a deeply spiritual boy, always. He believed in God."

"It may be a long time before there is another man with Ross's spirit and ability," Vernice wrote Paul Brooks, "but if such another one should appear, everything should be done to preserve him. I feel no bitterness in my heart, nor any regret, because as Ross kept saying, everyone did what he considered right and what he felt had to be done. No one could anticipate—least of all Ross—what would happen. Ross died as a result of overwork, but he suffered much from what he called the Sickness of this Age—materialism—which he had so hoped to counteract in some small measure by giving *Raintree County* to the world."

Thus, Ross's mourners explained his death—feeling they must in order to reconcile their own consciences to it, or before he could lie at peace in the earth.

There is no longer need to bury Ross properly, only to clear away the mystery he left us—that astonishing, still tantalizing gesture of rejecting what he had sought so single-mindedly.

It is hard to dismiss the notion of the bitch-goddess, success shaped like a Circe, who with her potions of money, flattery and celebrity transforms the private poet into a pig for the public roast.

But success was not thrust upon Ross. He sought it. It was young Lockridge, dreaming of *Life's* pages, Book-of-the-Month Club announcements and Hollywood, who rounded up Houghton's startled flock and sent it flying along the promotion trail. And in any case, I am convinced that success was not in itself a spoiling force for him, but rather the warm, propagating culture for a vulnerableness he might otherwise have carried safely.

There were so many optional situations in Ross's life that there is an illusion of accidental pattern to it. *If only* he had left the promotion of *Raintree County* to his publisher and gone on to another book. *If only* he had not been offered that monstrous prize, or had refused it. *If only* Elsie had been less sure of the human spirit's capacity for miracles. *If only* Frank Lockridge had heeded his doctor friend's warning, placed less stock in the soundness of Ross's mind and exercise as its restorative. *If only* Vernice had been spared that searing experience with her sister Imogen. *If only* all the family had been less alive to appearances and faced up to his real illness. *If only* Ross had finished his course in electroshock therapy.

And underlying all this seeming bad luck, *if only* the rise of *Raintree County* had been less spectacular. *If only* his progress as a writer had been more gradual. There is a temptation to put it, *if only* it hadn't been America where overnight success is both a legend and a major industry. One of the arresting features of Ross's story is its Americanness—the native dream of conquest and triumphant homecoming, turned nightmare.

Of course there was nothing accidental about Ross's life. It is true tragedy, the end inevitable, carefully prepared in the beginnings—in Elsie's will to fulfill her father's dream of literary accomplishment, then in the promise and death of her first son, then in vague disappointments by her husband, a second son and daughter and, finally, in Ross's acceptance of her challenge.

As a child, Ross's acceptance was mere wish, a stage for his fantasies, but as he matured and saw the shape his energies might take, the will to write a book for his mother became more elaborate and more focused. The force grew. He had no doubt about what force it was. He even wrote about it in his first bid for publication. Without any attempt at disguise, he built *The Dream of the Flesh of Iron* around the protean family triangle and the energy generated by its perpetual conflict—the fair, love-bestowing woman being tyrannized by the old, powerful man while she is adored by the young narrator.

Ross made his purpose as explicit in *Raintree County*. He put himself into the composite character of his mother's true love, her own father. "It's your book, Mother," he told her when she came up to Manistee to read it. "You'll notice I haven't dedicated it *to* you—it's written *for* you." Elsie Lockridge's challenge to Ross had become the necessary will, with all the emotion and energy he would need to fire it.

A book is often revealing of the caves of its author's soul. It blows up out of primary tensions, out of anxiousness rooted in childhood, out of his original need for love.

Nearly always, good writing is an act of love—a plea, an offer, a demand for love, but somewhere along the line the author must acknowledge that he is in fact making art, not love. This is a disengaging, a maturing, a tempering act and in essence it is the discovery that he must write only to please himself, that a *genuine* egoism is a writer's only defense against the enemies of indifference, disparagement, flattery, that are surely awaiting him. This was a discovery Ross had yet to make.

When he said, "Mother, sometimes it seems to me as if I wrote my book in a vacuum—that nobody would ever read it but us," he had been seized by a foreboding that his innocent wish for attention had released a torrent of it. He could hear it, tumbling their way, and was frightened. But he certainly had not intended *Raintree County* as a private affair between them. The good opinion of others, *fame*, was the essence of *The Great Stone Face* and, at least in Ross's mind, of the American dream itself.

Success was an essential part of the gift he had intended but he had not anticipated this would attract moral and literary criticism and show up such flaws in his gift for his mother.

But *Raintree County*'s success plunged on. It was even accelerated by the controversies. It fulfilled to the letter Ross's reveries. He had rebelled, left his father's workshop to set up one of his own, and there he had fashioned a gift so wealth-and-fame-producing, so much more glorious than anything his father had ever done, and all of it such a public spectacle that there was no denying it. To his own astonished eyes, Ross had demolished his father.

Nor was that all. In toppling him he had broken the relationship, snapped the circuit of love and jealousy which joined his mother, his father and himself. Finally, it was his own disaster, for that triangle was the source of his creative stream.

While Ross's patricidal act was a symbolic one and all three could, in their affection for each other, cover it over with gestures of congratulation and assurance, the damage was real. For Ross the result was guilt—lonely, paralyzing and, in the end, unendurable.

TOM

IX

My ship was a destroyer escort, U.S.S. *Elden*, and I spent much of World War II in her narrow, steamy hull cutting a perpetually dissolving pattern into the surface of the Pacific and swearing that if ever there was an end to this stupid performance, I would spend the rest of my life doing something I wanted to do.

What I wanted, of course, was to write a novel about my wartime experience and I was still tinkering hopefully with this idea one night in the spring of 1948, when I entered the Alvin Theater. There, in two hours of delighted and dismayed recognition, I found that another ex-sailor named Thomas Heggen had scooped me. On the stage, my semimutinous ship had come to anchor. It was complete with my maniac of a captain, my blundering fellow officers and my heartbreaking crew. Even *I* was there. I was Doug Roberts.

So, a year and a half later, when Paul Brooks interviewed me for a job at Houghton Mifflin and asked me what kind of contemporary fiction I liked, I told him that what came first to mind was not a novel but a play called *Mister Roberts*. In setting me right, that it was both a novel and a Houghton Mifflin book, he lamented there would be no sequels. Heggen was dead. His lack of explanation is the earliest point to which I can trace my curiosity about Thomas Heggen.

My active inquiry began five years ago when I arranged a lunch with Tom Heggen's sister Carmen and then missed it. From the midst of a traffic jam on the San Diego freeway, I watched the airplane which was to carry me to that lunch rise from the Los Angeles airport and disappear toward Minneapolis.

It was the first of a series of frustrations, but I did meet Carmen and, in the course of the next several years, I talked with others who had been close to Tom—his older sister, Ruth, his wife, Carol Lynn, and his father, T. O. Heggen.

I knew his collaborator on the play, Joshua Logan, through a couple of books I had edited at Harper's Publishers—Sumner Locke Elliott's *Careful He Might Hear You* and Gay Talese's *The Overreachers*—and I knew Tom's influential cousin, Wallace Stegner, from having publicized his *The Preacher and the Slave* at Houghton Mifflin and from having visited his writing seminar at Stanford. Both Joshua Logan and Wallace Stegner had had a great deal to do with Tom's life and had much to tell me.

Also, when you become obsessed with a search, as I have with that for Tom Heggen, you have your lucky strikes. Most of mine have occurred since coming to the Writer's Workshop in Iowa City. I'm thinking particularly of Seymour Krim's leading me to Tom's girl, Helen Parker, and of Ellie Simmons's leading me to Tom's shipboard roommate, Alfred Jones in Osceola.

But the Iowa strikes were not all due to luck. Tom was born in the state.

In Iowa, where they are likely to call any cluster of houses a city, Fort Dodge is a real one. In the twenties, when Tom Heggen was a child there, it was a rail center for hog and cattle shipping and, thanks to beds of pure gypsum thereabouts, the home of half a dozen gypsum plants.

The Des Moines River cuts deep into the land, dividing Fort Dodge, and "The Flats" along its banks were slums. But there were also an active business district and pleasant, residential neighborhoods.

The Heggen family lived in the north, the good, end of town

and the white stucco house at 629 Forest Avenue was a source of pride to all five of them. It was not a farm but a city house and it was theirs, a hopeful, upward-bound kind of house.

Tom's mother, Mina, was a slender, angular-featured woman and she kept a careful eye on the mirror, not out of vanity but a belief in appearances. She was proud and anxious that her family look well in the neighbors' eyes. However pinched her budget, the children went off to school immaculately dressed. Only with herself, her children and her house trim and shining did she feel free of reproach.

Mina Heggen turned her vigor to the scouring and primping of that house and when Tom was six he would take mop and pail from the kitchen closet and swab down the linoleum to earn her approving smile.

Tom was frail and she was careful of him. On raw, wintry days when the neighborhood kids came by dragging their sleds and shouting, "Orlo! Hey Orlo!," for that was his name, Mina would go to the door to say, No, Orlo wouldn't be coming to the hill today. Then, his nose to the window glass, he would watch the boys go off, calling out and sailing snowballs to burst on woolly hats.

Throughout his boyhood Tom fell shy of five feet and weighed less than ninety pounds, but in class he was clever and competitive. His teachers favored him, visited him when he was ill, gave him As and Bs and let him skip two grades of elementary school so that, alongside his classmates, he was smaller than ever. He was always the little guy, a head shorter than his friends, yet always trying to match them.

By Fort Dodge standards Duncombe School was not a rowdy place but the fourth grade was the dominion of Paul Somerville, a red-headed Hercules to whom Tom and his friend Herbert Lefler paid grudging tribute. Walking home one day they were deploring Somerville's rule-by-fist when Tom noticed they were being trailed by a classmate even smaller than himself. With a backward nod he said there was at least one fellow *he* could beat up.

Next day Lefler, walking alone, found two boys punching each other on the pavement ahead and catching up he was in time to see the smaller boy triumph. Lefler helped Tom off the ground and they went along silently until Tom announced through his blood-dappled handkerchief, "I should have known better."

Tom's two sisters were attractive, able girls. Ruth, two years older, was a tall beauty with black, curly hair that came to her shoulders. Everyone fell in love with Ruth, not just her school-mates but her men teachers. Carmen, though younger than Tom, was a pretty, vivacious child with her own enthusiastic following. Between them, Ruth and Carmen set Tom an exacting standard of popularity and achievement. They also doted on him. He was their irrepressibly spunky darling and their joy.

The prevalence of dynamic women in his household contrib-uted to Tom's crush-proof adolescence. One exception was Ruth's closest friend, Isabelle Hurst. When Isabelle came to the house Tom would challenge her to a furious game of Ping-Pong. He always won and then dragged her off for private talks in which he would confess his secrets: of his most recent mischief and how, with poker-faced cunning, he had talked his way out of the conse-quences. She won his highest compliment. "Isabelle," Tom said, "has more innate poise than any woman I've ever known."

Fort Dodge High School was bursting with fourteen hundred students. It was a brawling place where the tidal rush between classes might eddy around a teacher just losing a half-nelson on a student neck. Ruth, the first Heggen to try these swirling waters, sailed them serenely. She became a star of the debating team and a favorite of its coach, Ralph Nichols.

The debaters were state champions. They traveled as widely as the football team and enjoyed, in some quarters, comparable pres-tige, so that when Tom followed Ruth into high school he hoped to qualify. Recognizing some of his sister's articulateness in Tom, Nichols encouraged him to try out. But Tom foundered. In the pinch, words failed him and realizing Tom had the will but lacked the discipline for debate, Nick cut him.

Nick was also the tennis coach and Tom tried that too, dili-gently turning up for practice only to reveal his poor coordination.

In telling Tom he would never make a varsity tennis player, Nick offered an alternative in his chess club. But when Tom competed in a field of thirty chess hopefuls he failed to climb above tenth place and quit, allowing Nick to write him off as a second-rate kid, unfortunate in having a pair of first-rate sisters.

Tom was still an able student but at Constantine's Olympia, the high school's favorite soda-parlor, scholarship was not a recognized asset. As he strove to make his reputation in some, in any kind of extracurricular activity, Tom was gaining one as a cutup. Whatever he said brought laughter.

David among the Goliaths, Tom was developing an elephant boy's knack for manipulating the lumbering beasts toward his own mischievous purposes. In the school library Tom sat with a husky fellow named Bob Whalen and goaded him to disruptions which would bring old "Biddy" Cruikshank down for a scolding. In the midst of one, Tom piped up, "That's it, Biddy, give him hell!" and she fled before the thunderstorm of laughter.

At home Tom was the same. His behavior with his sisters, his parents and his multitude of sober, industrious aunts and uncles was equally impish. He was always up to something immoderate, outrageous and defiant that ended in laughter and forgiveness.

All four of Tom's grandparents were of Norwegian stock. They had come to farm the rolling, fertile land of northern Iowa in the 1880s. Thirty-five miles to the north of Fort Dodge lay "Grandma's Farm" and when, on a summer Sunday, the Heggens drove out for a visit, it was like drifting backward in time.

Mina, smart and citified in a new dress and felt toque, T.O. proudly steering the latest model Buick north along the gravel road to Renwick, did not hide from Tom their ambivalence about the journey. Their recollections of farm life were nostalgic and yet they could remember the loneliness. They knew it as wholesome but also boring and brutal. It broke youth in half. Death was commonplace on the farm. It came early to the farmer and his wife as it did to their animals. T.O. and Mina felt a condescension toward the farm, and relief at having fled it.

Tom's father, born in 1885, had been raised on that Renwick

farm and even as a boy he had been knocking the soil from his shoes and thinking of town. At Waldorf, the Lutheran school in Forest City, he had seen an escape through teaching and he had taught a couple of years in a country school, but one day the proprietor of the little Renwick bank offered him a job and introduced him to the business of land assessment and the mortgaging practices that balance the farmer's seasonal income.

At the same Waldorf School T.O. had met Mina Amelia Paulson, a slim, dark-haired girl with deep-set eyes. She was from Lake Mills, a rural town near the Minnesota border and both her background and her reaction to it were like his. Mina's father had been a vital man with the immigrant's faith in the equality and opportunity of his new country and he recognized optimism and competitiveness as the twin virtues which would carry a man to achievement here. Mina shared his belief in what life held for a twentieth-century American.

A love of fine things had drawn Mina to city shops and city convenience and when T.O. caught up with her she was working at Holtzermann's, an importer of fabric and china in Minneapolis, and he courted her there and asked her to marry him.

Tom's grandmother still presided over the Renwick homestead and as they approached it along the tree-shaded lane, Tom's aunts and uncles would be lining the porch as though at the rail of a steamer. While most spoke as flawlessly American English as his mother and father, here with the matriarch they were apt to lapse into the tongue of their ancestors.

Tom was first to tumble from the car, not to embrace his relatives but to organize the day's athletics. He would start with field events between himself and his sisters. When he had exhausted them with running and jumping he would lay out a croquet set or a miniature golf course on the lawn and turn the rest of his kin out of the house, pairing them off and making prizes for the winners. In the lulls between contests he could be seen belting a tennis ball against the side of the barn.

By evening, when he climbed back in the car and T.O. headed it toward Fort Dodge, Tom shared in the sense of relief that they were bound not only for home but out of the past and into the future.

Tom was always ready to dismiss the past. The day he was born, December 23, 1919, was also the birthday of Ole Heggen, his grandfather, and T.O. and Mina agreed their son should have his name. Yet it was such an ancient Norwegian one, so hoary for a brand-new American, they altered it to Orlo and at Saint Olaf's Lutheran church he was christened Orlo Thomas Heggen.

Tom did not like to be called Orlo. It was diminutive and sissy and its Norwegian root meant nothing to him. He was embarked on an American journey in which old values were an encumbrance and old badges an embarrassment. Early in high school he cast off that slender link with his past.

One day Ruth, hearing a classmate shout, "So long, Tom," to him, asked about it at the dinner table and he explained that although he would remain Orlo within the family, henceforth he would be Tom to the world.

The family accepted this latest insurgency with good humor. At home his plans were seldom thwarted. Ruth and Carmen paid homage to his princely rulings and his father had long ago surrendered to them. Only his mother might have challenged his decision, and she did not.

Tom's father was short and foursquare, a mild, pragmatic man given to waving at the children when he came home from work and disappearing behind his newspaper. He left whatever discipline was required to his wife. T. O. Heggen had found a pattern of existence that suited him here in Fort Dodge. He had come here from the little bank in Renwick to set up a business of his own. In 1919 he had rented an upstairs office in the Carver Building on Central Street, opened a mortgage-loan company and been here ever since.

T.O.'s chunky figure had become familiar in town, as had his reputation as an earnest, ambitious, if occasionally unlucky, businessman. He found pleasure in his tidy home and his three fine children, and indulging them became his habit.

Mina Heggen, while not greatly dependent on friends and acquaintances, left everyone with an impression of refinement and unusual serenity. This was no dissembling. Her tidiness included emotions. She could be firm with Tom, even sharp with a reprimand, but there was never any careless spilling of emotion. For her to have lost her temper at him would have been as odd as an outburst of affection.

Mina's self-possession, that quality of poise which so appealed to young Tom, encased a dynamic nervous energy which ran the Heggen household and, with never a hint of self-pity, set an example of spirit and courage.

In the summer of 1928 the Heggens took a long summer vacation at Lake Le Homme Dieu in Minnesota, where they were joined by Mina's sister, Hilda Stegner and her son Wallace. Like Tom, Wallace Stegner had been a scrawny kid but he had grown into a strapping, good-looking fellow of eighteen and Tom admired him no less than his mother and sisters did.

Although Tom's Aunt Hilda was just recuperating from an operation she would lead the children far out into the lake, catching minnows with a net and singing "I'm Forever Blowing Bubbles." She seemed so young and merry he could scarcely believe the news which came soon after their holiday, that she had died.

There was one happy outcome. Wallace, who had never been very close to his father, now became wholly absorbed by the Heggen family. Mina could see in him a splendid, manly projection of her own father, and in turn Wallace thought of his "Aunt Min" and "Uncle Tom" as foster parents. To his cousins he was a dazzling older brother.

Later, while Wallace was earning his master's degree and doctorate at the University of Iowa, he would hitchhike the several hundred miles from Iowa City to Fort Dodge, often bringing along a friend for the weekend. He was already interested in writing and his enthusiasm for ideas was contagious. When he picked up a question book to entertain Tom and his sisters all three were eager to give him the best answers and from that time there was no warmer sun for Tom than Wallace's approval.

During the thirties Wallace was off teaching in different parts of the country—Wisconsin, Illinois, Utah and California—settling, in 1939, at Harvard. Although Tom did not see him during this period, they wrote to each other. Wallace would urge Tom to read a new novel that was being talked about and make him think of writing a story of his own to send off to him. He was often in Tom's mind. It was this enduring admiration for Wallace that helped pull Tom through the powerful, curiously sublimated crisis that ended his childhood.

In 1934, when Tom was fifteen, his mother told him they were leaving the house on Forest Avenue for a rented one on Second Avenue South, across from the Congregational Church. Her persistent optimism and his father's oaken quality, the unvaryingness with which he went off to work and returned, had led Tom to think they were immune to the effects of the Depression.

They were not. The slump in agricultural prices had started a cycle of mortgage foreclosures, undermining the rural credit structure and toppling just such businesses as the one T.O. had spent sixteen years in building. The New Deal's rescue operation through the F.H.A. was too late to save it and, in 1935, when he was fifty years old, he closed the door of his office for the last time and went looking for a job.

The one he found was as an evaluator for the F.H.A. and it was six hundred miles to the south, in Oklahoma City. The uprooting and transplanting of the family to the Southwest was especially hard on Mina. For twenty years she had been striving to make actuality conform to her dream of what life held for her and her family. She was so determined on a favorable course that she often saw their situation as rosier than it was. She was always assuring the children of their present good fortune and the future's promise. There had been lean times in Fort Dodge and it was characteristic of her that friends, neighbors and the children themselves were unaware of them.

But this failure during the Depression was too catastrophic to be denied. The aspiring design by which Mina Heggen lived had cracked and all her pride and discipline could not conceal her disappointment.

Oklahoma City was a big, wicked and relatively sophisticated town but its worldliness was wasted on her. While the bungalow they rented at 1014 N.W. 22nd Street suited their needs, she was openly unhappy. She complained of the muggy climate and the persistent gray film the dust storms left on her furniture and windowsills. She missed the clear chastity of her northern climate and said so.

Ruth, who was eighteen that year, entered Oklahoma City University while Carmen, who was thirteen, entered junior high school. Both accepted their mother's assurance that nothing important had changed and they adapted easily to their new environment. But Tom was not deceived. He went into an emotional nosedive that reflected his mother's despair.

Two separate but related demolitions had taken place and Tom felt subconsciously the effects of both. The family's evolution, begun with a journey from Norway to Iowa and now concerned with getting off the farm and in on the big American promise, presumably a steady, upward climb with growing assurances along the way, had collapsed. Incredibly, twenty years, a lifetime, of hope and effort added up to nothing more than a humiliatingly red-inked ledger.

But T.O.'s business collapse was not the only casualty. It carried along T.O.'s image as proud, self-sure father-husband. That image, and Mina's counterpart of devoted mother-wife, had enabled Tom to find his own role of lovable imp, with its rewards of laughter and forgiveness; but it took no more than a suspicion of pity toward a blundering father and a resentful mother to expose the reality that was always there.

In contrast to the strength of his mother and sisters, Tom's image of himself was at best a shaky one; and now, with the appearances of success—so important to his mother—spoiled, and his father revealed as an uncertain provider, Tom lost his tenuous hold on a gratifying self-image and a sense of confidence in the world around him.

With a senior year left to finish, he entered Classen High School. It was a huge, bustling place offering far more than Fort

Dodge had in sports and fraternity life, but he was too miserable to take any part in it. He had lost all desire to excel. He kept to himself, sleeping, reading away a whole Saturday. He made no effort toward new friends and did so poorly in his studies that he came within a hair of not graduating.

The crisis in his family's fortunes had set off an equally dramatic one in Tom's spirit. From an exuberant boy, brimming with devilishness, he had turned into a moody, diffident one. He had lost all interest in the world outside himself.

X

___

In the long, humid evenings of the summer of 1936, Ruth's beaus came to perch on the front steps of the house in Oklahoma City like birds on a wire and they noticed the change in Tom. Looking up from the endless Monopoly game they asked, "Hey, why not have a party and invite your pants down to meet your shoes?"

Tom's first dismal year in Oklahoma City ended in the discovery he had sprouted a couple of inches, had turned from a runt of a boy into a gaunt, lanky one. It was as though his body was taking on a shape more fitting to his changed nature. From this new altitude he allowed himself to hope that, like his cousin Wallace, he was a late-flourisher and that college would provide the environment.

Oklahoma City's well-to-do families sent their sons and daughters away to complete their education, to the university at Norman usually, but for stricter budgets there was Oklahoma City University, the "streetcar college." Ruth, who had discovered herself an actress at O.C.U., liked it and in September Tom entered its freshman class.

His hopes were pinned to new friends and new interests and although he would be living at home, he wanted to become as independent of his family as he could. As soon as possible he wanted to be rid of obligations to his father and to pay his own way.

Fraternities gave campus life its shape and he entered Rush Week anxiously, to emerge a pledge of Phi Chi Phi. While it was a local, neither the least nor the most illustrious of the five clubs, he was glad enough of the caste mark and its certification of being somebody. However, within a few weeks he was discontented with fraternity life. At its core he found little more than clannishness and besides, the boys he liked best had been chosen by the more prestigious Delta Psi Omega.

Classroom instruction was also disappointing and as he grew bored with his studies Tom began to take a pride in the microscopic effort he put into them. A string of Cs suited him and he was not much disturbed to find he had miscalculated and was flunking French.

He had known the university was run along austere lines by the Methodist Church but now he began to see the administration as self-righteous and wrong-headed and he resented every evidence of its authority.

Reaching for something to believe in, some style and attitude, some notion of self to sustain him, Tom kept returning to thoughts of Wallace Stegner. Wallace, recently married, was teaching at the University of Utah, writing stories and trying to publish them. A long one called *Remembering Laughter*, reminiscent of Edith Wharton's *Ethan Frome*, concerned an Iowa farmer's infidelity with his wife's younger sister.

When Wallace wrote that this story had won a Little, Brown novelette contest, had been chosen from a field of thirteen hundred competitors and would be published as a book in the fall, Tom tried his own hand at serious writing. He worked the same ground, describing a stoical Oklahoma cropper with powerful hands "endlessly whittling," who discovers his young, "coarsely pretty" wife in the arms of his "nervous, greasy" hired man. Tom finished by having the powerful hands break the villainous neck, and called his story "Like a Dry Twig."

It was rudimentary and revealed little of himself beyond a wariness toward pretty girls but each of its seven hundred words was useful and it had force. When Wallace wrote him encouragement about it, Tom offered it apologetically to Stan Pate, editor and publisher of the unofficial *Gold Brick*. Taking it, Pate made "Like a Dry Twig" Tom Heggen's first published fiction.

Wallace's belief that good writing was important, that it sought in the most direct way the truth and essence of life, was becoming Tom's. Early in that year it had led him into the office of the college weekly, *The Campus*, and the discovery that this was his true fraternity. Its staff—especially Paul Bennett, the knowledgeable editor, and a quirky, twenty-nine-year-old fellow freshman named Larry Myers—became the admired and admiring friends he had been seeking.

Tom showed himself an able reporter and an even better contributor to the midnight bull sessions. Over bottles of contraband beer he revealed the two keen edges of his mind—a savage wit, ever ready to snipe at O.C.U. stewardship, and an impressive acquaintance with contemporary writing. He seemed to have read everything from Mark Twain to the latest fad.

And in fact Tom's education was proceeding independently. He was prospecting American fiction and feeling like a man who has stumbled on the mother lode. Each trip to the library brought discovery, now Marquand's *The Late George Apley*, now Steinbeck's *Of Mice and Men*, and he took to strolling into English class with his own text, the latest *Esquire*, under an arm.

In his sophomore year Tom was licensed to write a column for *The Campus*. He called it Pi-Lines, the printer's term for a stick of scrambled type, and clearly delighted with his new social leverage, tried his voice as social commentator. At first certainly, there was nothing original about it. He borrowed the coy style of his neighbors and dealt in personalities, singling out the attractive coeds and firing off spitballs of interfraternity persiflage.

A suspicion that he lacked authority, was not half so sure of himself as Hi Doty in the adjoining space, was confirmed when he had to deal with tragedy. Red Griffin, *The Campus's* business manager, was returning hobo style from a weekend at home when he fell from a moving freight car, rolled under its wheels and was killed.

Tom had never been close to death. There had been no recent ones in his family and it was so rarely spoken of that he had come to believe it happened only to the old and sick. Heggen custom was to suppress powerful emotion. The heritage of all those stoical, callus-handed forebears was the discipline to smother heart and mind in platitudes, and he was beginning to sense the hypocrisy of it—that this was lying about the nature of life.

Red Griffin's death was a sudden, knelling *memento mori* that hypnotized Tom. But even among his friends there was a hasty burial of its implication under euphemism and sentimentality, and his rebelliousness stirred.

For Tom, the allure of writing was that on the page you could tell the truth in a way you could not, face-to-face, with others. Now he wanted to write an honest epitaph for Red Griffin. Although he tried in Pi-Lines, the result was unfelt and lame, not as good as Hi Doty's. Tom decided he had failed not only poor Red but himself.

But gravity was not called for again and the experience had sharpened his pen. He brought a fresh, caustic honesty to the ever-bearing preoccupation with dating. He drew an accurate self-portrait as an uncertain lover and blamed his shyness on the perversity of the girls.

It was his own innocence that contributed to his shyness. For an eighteen-year-old boy, Tom was remarkably innocent. Although Ruth and Carmen were habitually involved with one beau or another, he had still not had anything resembling an infatuation of his own. Nor was he well informed about sex.

With the Heggen family, sex had been far too personal, too painfully embarrassing, to be discussed—ever. Both parents had shied from any instruction and presumed the children would find out whatever was necessary, all in good time, and from some source outside their home. That was the way it was done. Among themselves, Tom, Ruth and Carmen were similarly inhibited. The family reserve was reinforced by a reluctance to reveal their own ignorance.

In his Pi-Lines confession, Tom did admit to an abstract but carnal attraction to girls, dropping a gratuitous "We still don't know the name of the blonde in our lap" into his stream of comment. It was a common undergraduate wish for love without obligation, but for Tom it was to lose only its facetiousness with the years.

Tom led a conventional social life. His father was permissive about the car and Saturday night would find him behind its wheel drawing up to some girl's house. The double-date, more likely to be conversational than romantic, was the custom and Tom usually teamed with Paul Bennett to make a foursome.

There would be a movie and sitting around afterward, and here he would strive to make a new girl laugh at his cleverness. He was not drawn to any one but he was polite and considerate with all, so much so that he built a reputation for quaintly chivalric behavior—the result, it was decided among the girls, of a strict upbringing.

But Tom's notoriety was growing and it was due neither to his popularity with the coeds nor to his readers, but to his capers. From the start of freshman year he had seen the O.C.U. landscape as dominated by infantilism among the students and hypocrisy in the administration and he harassed both wherever he found them. In his first month he presented a fraternity skit so offensive to the dean that the outraged man had climbed the stage to order the curtain down and to announce it would never rise on another Stunt Night.

Later Tom led a consumer's revolt against the Gold Bug, a campus restaurant operated under university franchise. When his crusading journalism failed to improve its sanitation and service he brought to bear his bullfrog talent for fly catching. From his habitual slouch position, Tom's hand could spring forth to snare the wariest of Gold Bug flies. A score of angry customers, waving glasses with Tom's quarries afloat in their dregs, demanded refunds and brought a stubborn management to terms.

These were self-conscious college antics cut for the general amusement and yet they bore the Tom Heggen stamp. They were statements about the O.C.U. community and they were related to his struggle for an authentic attitude and voice for his Pi-Lines column. The pranks bridged the gulf between his sanctuary of conventional collegiate frivolousness and the powerful rebelliousness he was not quite ready to display.

But the rebelliousness grew and took shape in two incidents, separate but related, that were far more significant than the others. At the start of his freshman year Tom told Paul Bennett that he wanted to be financially independent of his father and was determined to pay some part of his way through college. Although jobs were scarce, Bennett knew of one and he walked Tom around to the University Press to meet its superintendent, Reverend H. E. Brill.

Brill was a retired Methodist preacher and a seventy-eight-year-old bantam of a man. He had founded the press a dozen years earlier and he ran it zealously with regular reminders to the composing room that alcohol and tobacco were the world's greatest evils and that he required abstinence as well as precision in press work.

His interest in his boys was genuine and he was known as "Daddy" Brill but there was some irony in the nickname. He was not just a cantankerous boss, he was rarely mistaken. He offered Tom his first job, setting type at forty cents an hour. Each week thereafter, Tom set the body type of The Campus and he was soon a swift, accurate compositor. He got a kick out of his new expertise equal to the feeling of independence he collected every Friday with his twelve dollars.

But to know Daddy Brill was to discover he was the self-appointed watchdog of student morals. As copy arrived from The Campus's editors Brill would scan it for unsanitary thought and when he found something that displeased him he would simply change it. Tom fumed over this and the rebel within him stirred.

In October, while setting the guest list for the Delta Psi pledge dance, Tom substituted the name of Oklahoma City's most celebrated whore for that of Stan Pate's girl. It was the perfect three-way joke, taking a swipe at a big-man-on-campus, the Delta Psis and, sweetest of all, slipping right by Brill's censorious eye. But Tom's job was too dear for further jeopardy.

In the summer of 1937, Ruth decided to transfer to the University of Iowa for its program in dramatic arts and Tom, who had spent a score of evenings at College Players' rehearsals watching her, was not surprised. Sitting alone in back-row shadows, admiring her crisp performance in a Barry comedy and her moving portrayal of the mother superior in *Cradle Song*, he could dream her onto a New York stage and even imagine writing a play for her. Tom could not fault Ruth's plans but he was going to miss her, and during the summer he felt stirrings of last year's blues.

Hoping to keep busy and to bank some money, Tom offered to stay on at the press during the summer, but there was little printing to be done and Reverend Brill gave him the chore of sprucing up the building and grounds. One scorching day he put Tom to work demolishing a shack in the rear yard and when he came to help out, Tom was sure the old man's heart would stop.

Instead it was Tom who wilted under the stevedoring. Panting, he watched Brill lug off heavy chests and planks and cheerfully load them into the truck, with accompanying comment on the frailness of youth.

This besting made Tom decide he had had enough of Brill disciplines, of Brill notions of what was fit to print and of his own compromise. So, in the fall, he quit the University Press and distilled his indignation toward its superintendent into a piece he called "Censorship" and persuaded the *Gold Brick* to print it.

In this article Tom drew a vicious portrait of Brill as "a little man with a stunted, handle-bar moustache, and spry as the devil . . . To his major evil of suppression, the Reverend has added a little sheer cussedness for good measure . . ." He described Brill's censorship as unauthorized and arrogant, listed its recent, innocent victims and concluded, somewhat disarmingly, with an illustrative farce. In this, Reverend Brill, glowing with fanatic zeal, sharpens a huge pair of copy shears on a grindstone and shreds the day's copy while a horrified *Campus* editor is strait-jacketed and carried off screaming.

Brill, lacking a trace of humor, was furious over the article and Tom, just as predictably, suffered remorse about it. While he hoped for reconciliation he made no effort toward it for he had won a public victory and some self-respect. But the Brill episode ended all Tom's prudence over money. Henceforth he thought of it not as freedom, but bondage.

Later in the year Tom's insurgent spirits broke forth in another episode, dramatic enough to end his career at O.C.U. On a fine spring evening he was sitting with Larry Myers in Beverly's restaurant, enjoying his favorite dish of shoestring potatoes and discussing the annual rising of the sap. They agreed it took its silliest form in the ritual of queen-making. The recent coronation of a freshman queen had required two flower girls, seven coed attendants, each with an escort, and a three-year-old boy as crown bearer.

It was especially galling to Tom and Myers that their friend Bennett, as editor of *The Scarab*, the yearbook, was presiding over another of these follies. Tom noted that *The Scarab*'s promotion called for sending the photographs of the six candidates (one each from the five sororities and one from the non-sorority group) to Paramount Studios in California for "judging by company directors and screening experts." They shuddered at this hogwash.

Should they kidnap the queen? How about stuffing the ballot box—electing a particularly hairy member of the football team? Then Tom proposed it would be more imaginative to steal the ballot box itself. Imagine the excitement in the sororities. What howls of rage from the girls who believed themselves front runners. What a dilemma for Bennett. What a storehouse of Pi-Lines material. What an altogether lovely idea it was!

It remained to decide how the ballot box was to be hidden so as to baffle search parties and, in turning up, cast no suspicion on the conspirators. Myers knew a laundryman who, he felt, could be persuaded to keep it for three days and then, under cover of early-morning darkness, return it to the campus.

They carried out the plan expertly, with Tom snatching the box from the Great Hall and delivering it unobserved to the waiting laundryman. But they had failed to take into account Tom's reputation. When the ballot box was missed Bennett, in his role as student council president, sought him out and, under questioning, Tom confessed.

The student body thought it the funniest Heggen caper yet but the college president, Dr. Williamson, was not so easily amused. Meeting with members of his staff he reviewed Tom's record of unruliness and suspended him for the balance of the spring semester. In a private talk with Tom, Dr. Williamson told him he was really more than a suffering administration could bear and he thought it would be an excellent idea if Tom went elsewhere in the fall.

T.O. and Mina Heggen were stoic about this development and Tom finished up the things that were important to him—helping Paul Bennett edit *The Scarab*, adding a section of student writing and seeing that Larry Myers's fine, melancholy story, "Suicide Note," was included.

He was content to be leaving and to have the future uncertain, even though his optimism was due to his success here—the success with which he had moved his boyhood role of mischief maker out of the family and onto the campus. His pranks had matured. They were still capers, calling attention to himself, provoking outrage, laughter and eventual forgiveness but they were also compulsive expressions of his feelings. They were protests against the adolescent student behavior so blandly approved by convention, and they were insurrections against an administration he thought incompetent and arbitrary.

In Daddy Brill he had found a special adversary. Brill, with all his strong self-righteousness, had become the substance out of the abstract idea of authority. He was administrative authority and parental authority in one. Brill played the role of stern father so realistically that Tom was attracted and repelled by him. There was an inevitableness to their confrontation, as though Tom instinctively stalked such men and fought them, but whether he won or lost the conflict, the relationship was unendurable.

XI

In the fall of 1938, when he was eighteen, Tom enrolled as a sophomore in the Arts and Sciences School of Oklahoma Agricultural and Mechanical College at Stillwater. A. & M.'s orientation was intrinsically barnyard and oil rig and he was braced for that but not for a life so ritually social.

The half-hour "dance-date" was celebrated with the constancy of a sundown ritual. Weekday evenings at seven a loudspeaker system broadcast popular tunes throughout the women's dormitories and sorority houses. The male caller was expected to choose a partner and foxtrot to "The Dipsey Doodle" and "Moonglow." Seven-thirty marked the beginning of the "Coke-date," a pairing-off for soft drinks and conversation.

On weekends the fraternities had closed dances, some of them elaborate affairs requiring the girls to wear their "formals." The boys supplied corsages, and those fortunate enough to have them turned out in tuxedos. With odds of two and a half to one in her favor it was an unlucky A. & M. coed who had not won a fellow student's heart and fraternity pin by her junior year, and was not married within a few months of her graduation.

Tom made one concession to this tower of conformity by joining a fraternity, but this time it was convenience, not social aspiration, that made him a probationary Greek. The need for a job had taken him first to the *Daily O'Collegian*. He found its office and press in a building that had until recently housed the Dairy Department and his first look at the cratered newsroom walls pinned with urgent personal notices, a Western Newspaper Union calendar and a huge publicity photograph of Myrna Loy was reassuring.

Producing a handful of Pi-Lines columns from O.C.U., he talked Joe Synar, the laconic editor, into continuing them in the *O'Coly* and taking him on as a reporter. And it was Joe Synar, a prominent Sig Ep, who introduced Tom to his fraternity and fixed it so he could pay part of his room and board there by waiting on table.

The *O'Coly* attracted the only group on the campus which held unorthodoxy to be a virtue and Tom was soon manipulating these irregulars and, when work was done, gathering them around the copy desk. George Sherrick, a pressroom apprentice, particularly appealed to him. Although he was the son of a Ramona, Oklahoma, barber, Sherrick neither shaved, cut his hair nor, for that matter, brushed his teeth. He wore the blouse of an R.O.T.C. uniform, jeans and cowboy boots and he took pride in never changing them, even to sleep. Tom dubbed him "Two-gun" and made him the hero of one of the episodic tales he improvised to keep the newsroom from bed.

When the office session did break up, Tom could find some *O'Coly* staff members still up at The Roofs, an apartment over a Stillwater grocery occupied by Richard Venator, Truman Mikles and Scoop Farris. There was an ancient Underwood typewriter there on which he would tap out parody soap operas for the general amusement and, one way or another, keep the talk going until two or three, when he would bed down reluctantly for what remained of the night.

During the fall semester Tom proved an inventive reporter. He brought a colloquial immediacy to routine interviews, hurried off to Stringtown to do a piece on the model prison and to Oklahoma City to cover a sensational murder.

When an anonymous note threatened the dynamiting of the chemistry building he spent the night in a bush just outside awaiting developments. There were none beyond those induced by "purple passion," grape juice mixed with alcohol he obtained from a friend in the biology department, but these were enough for a wry, musing piece on a favorite subject, the nonevent.

Then, in midyear, Tom picked up a lead on a story about a Communist Party cell on campus. He authenticated it, plugged it deftly into the national anxiety, wrote it with care and then stood back to enjoy the fireworks. But they never came. Joe Synar was wary of the Communist Party headquarters in Oklahoma City. After a recent unfriendly editorial it had threatened the *O'Coly* and him personally with a forty-thousand-dollar lawsuit. He killed the story and Tom was stunned. He saw it as witless censorship, another demonstration of narrow-mindedness and conformity. He said nothing, just thrust his hands deep in his pockets and walked out of the office into the night.

He wanted no more of Synar's help and he defected completely from Sigma Phi Epsilon, moving out of the house. While it was not the end of his *O'Collegian* career, for he continued to supply Pi-Lines and an occasional feature, with the death of his Communist Party story, Tom's attitude changed. He showed scorn not only for his editors but for his readers too. When the film of Shaw's *Pygmalion* came to town and proved a hit with Aggie audiences, Tom told them they were too dumb to appreciate it.

"Neither the picture nor the play were meant for mass consumption," he explained. "What I suspect is that people are swallowing the picture whole . . . without once sinking their teeth in and tasting the flavor of Bernard Shaw. The audience comes away bragging on *Pygmalion*. Probably most of them are dull-witted sluggards, even as you and I and Richard Venator, yet they say they liked the picture, they rave about it. I say they lie. Most of them were probably bored or at least bewildered. If you pin most of the audience down they would confess the show wasn't as funny as they thought it would be. The Ritz Brothers are a hell of a lot funnier, they'll tell you. They, like their fathers before them, missed the fine points Shaw has hidden through the play."

But it was in his Pi-Lines column that Tom's point of view

changed the most. He had begun the year in a familiar mood, challenging the University of Oklahoma for parity, spoiling for a joust with some columnar counterpart at Norman. But in midyear he lost interest in entertaining, or even communicating with, the O'Collegian's readers and instead reflected the introverted zaniness of a midnight session at The Roofs.

Reverting to minimal study and ravenous reading, he displayed his fictional enthusiasms by imitation, and the result was like a child's dressing up in adult clothes. In the guise of a Zane Gray, an E. Phillips Oppenheim or an Erskine Caldwell, Tom would pose for an instant's glimpse of himself in his Pi-Lines mirror. He also tried experiments in poetry and run-on stream-of-consciousness prose that seemed at least one part "purple-passion."

He was bent on patronizing his readers, provoking them with purposeful obscurity and daring them to complain of his flouting reason and logic. Unable to forgive or forget that his spirited story on Communism had been shot out from under him his resentment spread throughout the college community. He lost some affinity with his fellow rebels and felt himself outbound again, toward someplace where the standards were worth admiring. But along with the rise and fall of his newspaper career, Tom was enduring a new and, as it turned out, even more significant experience. For the first time in his life he was falling in love.

A small, high-spirited classmate named Carol Lynn Gilmer had seen Tom in the O'Collegian office, noted the out-at-elbows sweater and the brooding shyness in his eyes. When he was pointed out as the Tom Heggen who wrote those odd columns she was intrigued. An aspiring reporter herself, she had read them with curiosity and then, getting the hang of them, decided they were hilarious.

When she came upon one about the campus night watchman she thought it the best yet and, passing Tom, introduced herself and told him so. He was pleased and thereafter stopped to talk whenever they met. Her figure was compact and with her dark, almond-shaped eyes, turned-up nose, cloud of curly brown hair and above all her sparkling enthusiasm, Carol Lynn was the essence of dynamic, wholesome American girl. Although aware that some of his *O'Coly* associates found her frosty, humorless and an altogether unpromising novice, Tom was not afraid of an opposing view.

The Chi Omega house, where Carol Lynn lived, adjoined that of Sigma Phi Epsilon so that they met often and when she was not dashing off to class they would drift off to the Coke shop for a few minutes' talk. Here he learned that she was serious about a news-paperwoman's career, so much so that she was planning to flout family tradition and quit A. & M. for Northwestern's Medill School of Journalism. Her older sister, her mother and her father, a utilities executive in Okmulgee, had all gone to Stillwater and her maternal grandfather had claimed a part of what was now college grounds in the homestead run of 1889.

Carol Lynn was wary of Tom's raffish friends, "Two-gun" Sherrick in particular, but she understood his attraction to mav-erick spirits and knew that it tied in some important way to his writing. He was casual about his newspaperman's world and his effortless accomplishments, but Carol Lynn recognized that even though the *O'Collegian* was permissive, it took nerve to write as he did. She was in particular awe of the Steffens-like attack he had made on the Stillwater Public Library for withholding John Stein-beck's newly published *Grapes of Wrath* because it put Okla-homans in an unfavorable light.

"Steinbeck ought to occupy every library in the country," Tom had written. "His characters live and breathe, also they cuss and drink and carry-on, but only because their real-life prototypes cussed and drank and carried on."

For Carol Lynn, Tom himself was as remarkable as his writ-ing. He was so strikingly intense, seeming to *feel*, whether happi-ness or sorrow, far more keenly than others. It was this sensitivity to emotion, his joy in discovery, alternating with black moods, she found so fascinating.

Tom told her about his cousin Wallace, already successfully published, and he talked about other books and writers he ad-mired. When he pointed out the gaps in her own acquaintance with modern fiction she vowed to close them at once. When he ticked off his favorite authors, Wolfe, Hemingway and Steinbeck, she inquired which he most wanted to resemble and Tom replied instantly, "None. I'd like to write like myself."

From this earnestness he could turn playful and delight her with fantasies in which she figured. A favorite was that of the city room, derived from the Hecht and MacArthur *Front Page*, and Tom's version had them playing the dual role of "Scooper," rival reporters whose sharp-toothed competitiveness hints at an embrace in the final episode.

Carol Lynn's first indication that beneath Tom's enthusiasm for making a literary convert lay an interest that was, after all, the conventional one came when he turned up to watch her tennis class. She was too poor a player for him to be taken with her court performance and yet he would sit alone, watching, absorbed in her play.

When he told her that the last page of Hemingway's *A Farewell to Arms* was the best writing he had ever read she looked it up and in reading Frederic Henry's farewell to Catherine Barkley felt certain it was a declaring of Tom's own love.

But unlike most A. & M. coeds, Carol Lynn was not ready for romantic commitment. As a child she had had a cast in one eye, the more humiliating since her older sister, Nina Emily, was a flawless beauty. When she was twelve an operation had corrected the eye but Carol Lynn still felt she was in her sister's shadow and she was determined to succeed by her wits. She kept her marks uniformly high and had barely begun on what she expected to be a long climb.

Arriving at Stillwater the previous year she was surprised to find herself popular, but curiously, the recognizing of her attractiveness made her uneasy. She liked having beaus but she liked her independence more. While Tom Heggen was different from the others and his style of courtship far more beguiling, Carol Lynn was still not ready for a love affair.

However, Tom had fallen with the delirious impetus of a first time. Beneath his world-weary manner lay the knowledge of his own vulnerability, the dread of rejection and the fear of moving into a new relationship where an open exchange of affection would be required. The effect was paralyzing, and when they were together, even for a moment over Cokes, the tension was so oppressive that he took to bringing along an acquaintance, a tennis player named George Counts.

Tom's infatuation was apparent to everyone now and the advice of friends was to seize the day. In spending so much time with him, they counseled, she obviously liked him. Time was ripe for aggressiveness. At first the suggestion only added to Tom's constraint but he did decide to follow it. He asked Carol Lynn for a real date and made plans to declare his heart.

The evening began awkwardly with Tom ill at ease among the members of the Sigma Phi Epsilon house. Although it was prior to his break with them he seemed neither to know nor to have the least use for them. As hours passed, the pressure of what he had to tell Carol Lynn built in his chest so that when he did contrive to be alone with her he blurted out his desire with a terrible intensity. She was fascinated, repelled and thoroughly frightened by his emotion and she fled, leaving him on the steps of the Chi Omega house, as frustrated and bewildered as ever.

Safe behind Chi Omega's doors, Carol Lynn ran up to the room she shared with Nina Emily and there, to the astonishment of her sister and friends, wept.

But for all its inconclusiveness the date did clear the air. Carol Lynn soon indicated that she liked him and she was moved by his yearning for her, but she was not about to capitulate. As a mere sophomore with all kinds of promises to herself she was committed to playing the field.

Carol Lynn's indefinite postponing of the passionate developments he had in mind was withering to Tom but it was not a rejection. It was a relief. He found it acceptable, and Carol Lynn more alluring than ever.

On Valentine's Day Carol Lynn received a dozen fine red roses, with a card enclosed which simply read "George." This confused her for she had two beaus by that name, a George Kohler and a George Storms. Weighing the probabilities, she decided on the former but when she thanked him Kohler replied that although he wished he had sent them he had not.

She was about to thank Storms when she ran into Tom's friend George Counts. Smiling, he asked if she had received the roses, and then explained he had not sent them but Tom had, enclosing a card with *his* name. It was a characteristically oblique Tom Heggen act and it was equally typical that he was delighted with the result, Carol Lynn's confusion over the Georges in her life.

But it was hardly a courtship to cheer the gray days of late February. While stretched full-length on a desk in the *O'Collegian* office, Tom proposed to his friend Truman Mikles that since it was dull as hell where they were, they go someplace else. Mikles agreed. They settled on the Mardi Gras in New Orleans and put a notice in the *O'Collegian* of their urgent need for travel expenses. It brought no response of course and although Tom hocked his golf clubs they were well shy of the price of bus tickets.

So they hooked their thumbs southward and embarked on a larky, collegiate victimizing of the wayside, each hitch, each hood-winked railroad conductor, each setback more hilarious than the last. In Dallas they flagged down an amiable woman, a recent widow with time on her hands and pleasure on her mind, and gleefully persuaded her to drive them all the way to New Orleans.

Arriving, they abandoned her for their own revels in the French Quarter but two days later with their money gone, Tom's conscience awoke to an upcoming examination back at school. Searching, they found her, jollied her out of resentfulness and convinced her to drive them back to Dallas. However, as they paused for the night in Alexandria, Louisiana, she asked for the fare—inviting one or both boys to bed down with her.

In the next room Tom and Mikles's laughter was edged with anxiety. Their bluff—were they the men of their boasts, or callow, mischievous kids—was called. They flipped a coin to see who was to join their chauffeur, and although Mikles lost, at the last minute he balked and it was no longer a merry widow who drove them into Texas and dropped them on the outskirts of Dallas. They walked, carrying Tom's heavy suitcase, into the center of the city, where he called home, asking his father to telegraph bus fare.

Tom arrived back on campus too late by several hours for his examination and confined again in a chilly lock-up of editorial and sexual frustration. Lingering shamefully in his mind was the recollection of that lusty, laughing Texas woman and the initiation she had offered him. He blamed himself for his fastidiousness and cowardice, because for all her coarseness she *had* appealed to him, at least she did now, and in failing her he had failed himself. It was a lesson in lost experience he had learned for good.

But he took up his pursuit of Carol Lynn where he had left it and saw her often. When she went to Oklahoma City for a weekend visit with relatives, they met there. Tom called for her in the family car and met her parents, and they spent an evening together free of the tensions which plagued them at college.

However, Tom could see no progress and he wore his pierced heart publicly. A March Pi-Lines column written in verse and apparently out of alcoholic despair, noted that while two could live as sweetly and cheaply as one, Carol Lynn had rejected all such romantic arguments:

> What's the diff if there's a moon?
> A moon and you, hounds a-baying,
> Owls hooting and you saying—never.

When the term closed in May Tom was feeling especially thwarted and it was not only the stalemate with Carol Lynn that caused it. What small enthusiasm he had shown for formal education in the fall had collapsed and the year-end evaluations of the *O'Collegian* staff were predictably disappointing. His skit for the gridiron show earned only "several laughs," and while he was certified a "brilliant writer," his increasingly subjective work had landed him as an also ran in the list of the promising.

But new plans were developing at home. Mina Heggen often spoke of the years before her marriage, recalling how she had enjoyed her job at Holtzermann's and Minneapolis itself with its many pretty lakes and parks. Her yearning for the northland persisted.

T.O. shared the optimism which, with the rumblings of the war in Europe, was creeping back into the national consciousness. Although fifty-four, he was sure he could rebuild a business life for himself and he was perfectly willing to do so in Minneapolis. He would quit his job and they would move north during the summer.

Tom was delighted. "Minneapolis is Mother's utopia," he told Carmen when he came home and immediately he made plans to transfer to the University of Minnesota, which was a utopia of his own.

But during the summer of 1939, while he was helping with the packing and moving, Tom's thoughts returned to Stillwater and Carol Lynn. Thinking of his unfulfilled love affair he began to see it as narrative and as a comment of his own on collegiate love.

Manipulating his two characters' motives in ways that suited him relieved some of the frustration and melancholy which lingered over the actual experience.

He called the story "Comedienne" and opened with a portrait of a sorority girl, Lou Myers, who "has everything"—looks, figure, brains and wit. Since she is "all-around," she permits the boys who date her a little necking but the consensus is that Lou is steadfastly virginal.

However, she has let it be known to the narrator, Jim Dougherty, that she is in love with him. A sorority sister has found her customary gaiety shattered by tears and Lou has confessed it. Jim cannot believe this, for when he and Lou are together they play a sharp-edged, flippant game of wits in which there is no hint of affection. The story describes the evening in which Jim hopes to discover the truth.

Calling for her at a sorority house Jim finds Lou her crisp, independent self. When he admires her dress she has a hard-shelled reply and when he proposes they drive to a popular road-house, she says, "Why not? I'm democratic."

On arriving they meet friends, and Lou, unaccustomedly, has a drink. They dance very close so that he is bold enough to suggest they go to a well-known lovers lane and she agrees. There she welcomes his kiss and turns helplessly ardent. When he puts a hand on her bare breast she urges him to "go on."

But perversely, Lou's encouragement curbs his aggressiveness. He pulls away, fiddles with the radio and starts the car. Driving back to the sorority house Lou huddles miserably against her door. Arriving, she bursts from the car and runs up the steps, where Jim catches her, embraces her and, realizing she is crying, comforts her.

When Lou asks if he has found her disgusting Jim denies it. When she asks if he will call her again he assures her he will. But as he drives away from the curb he laughs in victory.

"Comedienne," Tom Heggen's second serious story, is expert in several respects. The dialogue and descriptive detail are accurately observed and he has made an effective, dramatic situation out of his own experience. It is a far more convincing demonstration of ability than "Like a Dry Twig."

"Comedienne" is a fantasying of his first infatuation in which he attributes his own runaway passion to a fictive Carol Lynn. He made it an emotion strong enough to shatter the girl's light-hearted façade and betray her into an offer the boy spurns. Tom caused her tears to flow from desire rather than dismay and then allowed the boy, in a self-preserving withdrawal similar to Carol Lynn's, to triumph.

The boy has shamed the girl. Although, in a moment of compassion, he comforts her, she is his conquest. If it is a love story it is surely an unromantic one. Tom, in the person of Jim, rejects the offer of Lou's virginity and scores just as surely as if he had made off with it. Moreover he has kept his freedom.

Whether from uncertainty over this reasoning or an awareness that the story revealed a bleak side to his own nature, Tom did not offer "Comedienne" for publication but he kept it, thinking he might revise it some day.

He also kept his instinctive wariness, which the Carol Lynn experience had reinforced, of wholesome, marriageable girls. It was a competitiveness that reached toward misogyny; it was an inclination of his heart that would require a generous and devoted girl to change.

XII

Tom was right about the University of Minnesota. Its broad, bustling campus lay along the Mississippi's west bank, facing the provocative white towers of Minneapolis, and its newspaper, the *Daily*, swarmed with bright, journeyman journalists. It was just the ground for his flowering.

The *Daily* office was in the basement of a red stone, Romanesque building called Pillsbury Hall and Tom, a new member of the junior class, installed himself here at once. From the opening of that fall semester in 1939 he was a fixture, his scrawny figure hunched over a typewriter or indolently splayed across several pieces of furniture, gassing away in his mock-serious fashion.

Whatever the season he wore neither hat nor tie. His uniform, a fraying, green corduroy jacket and baggy pants, completed the scarecrow effect. Yet he was clean and fresh-looking and now at nineteen, although he still did not believe it, he was attractive to girls. His chin was strong. From plentiful brown curls his large ears pricked up alertly, like the god Pan. His eyes, set wide apart, were narrowly watchful. The impression he gave was one of faunlike shyness.

Tom lived at home, commuted, as did half the students at the university in these Depression times. While tuition was low, only thirty-five dollars a term, pocket money—money for drinks, books, movies and gas—was scarce.

So the pay was a fundamental part of the *Daily*'s allure. During his first year as reporter and desk man Tom earned thirty dollars a month. It made all the difference between anxiousness and an easy hand with a buck. But the *Daily* was far more than a means. As at O.C.U. and Stillwater, the paper was his classroom, laboratory and fraternity.

Beneath the logotype, the *Daily* proclaimed itself "The World's Largest College Newspaper," and whatever the truth of that, it was distributed free to all the university's sixteen hundred students and its faculty of five hundred. Its eight pages provided university and local news as well as two columns of world and national news culled from the wire services. For most it was the only newspaper they read. The *Daily* had a decisive leverage on the community and the idea of moving such a body of people with words fascinated Tom.

But the *Daily*'s greatest appeal by far was its staff. His fellow journalists were kin. Most shared his contempt for conformity and the fatuousness which abounded whenever faculty or fraternity brothers got together. Most were after some aspect of the bare-assed truth and that was all he asked of a man. Among them Tom found men to admire, men who challenged the best he had.

The editor that first year was Chuck Roberts, a big, long-faced, unflappable fellow from Evanston with some city newspaper experience, a talent for having things his own way and a generous hand with the bottle he kept in his desk drawer.

Tom liked his bravura. When Chuck followed the illustrious newspaper *PM*'s bold example and changed the *Daily* to a tabloid format, Chuck laughed off the protests (To hell with the doily, Give us back our *Daily!*), tinkered the polls and published self-congratulations until the readership believed that, journalistically, it had emerged from the Dark Ages.

Once a week, when Tom was night copy editor, he joined Roberts at the second-floor office of the Commercial Press in downtown Minneapolis to put the paper to bed. He wrote up late news which came in by A.P. ticker and by phone from the locker rooms and lecture halls, then laid out and pruned the stories that had been prepared during the day.

As each page was fitted around the islands of advertising and borne off to be set, there was time for a refresher at the corner bar. It was here, in the sharing of political views, that Tom found he thought much as Chuck did on the national controversies. They both liked New Deal medicine for the still-faltering economy, but they were unshakably pacifist toward the war. While they thought of themselves as politically daring, as Midwesterners they were stoutly anticommunist. They snickered at the possessed youths forever hawking Trotskyism or Coughlinism from the Union steps and suspected that all herding ended in a shearing. Individualism was their heritage and only religion. They scorned group action as strictly for the looneys and they believed in laughter as the only effective weapon against a complacent establishment. Jesting was not just fun. It was indignation. It was serious business.

Most importantly, they agreed about writing. In Wolfe, Steinbeck and, above all, Hemingway, they had found things to marvel over. They compared their discoveries, the words that had made them grasp, in one insightful flash, what life was all about.

Vic Cohn, the meticulous, scholarly copy editor, was very different from Roberts but Tom liked him too. He was drawn to Cohn's unassuming intelligence, found his eye as quick to spot pretention as his own.

The *Daily's* art critic was an unapologetic bluestocking and when she turned in an enthusiastic review of the abstract show at Northrop Auditorium, Tom and Vic were skeptical. She argued that their views of contemporary art were "know-nothing" and thus meaningless, while Tom insisted that in half an hour they could splash up something as good as the stuff she had praised, she challenged him to prove it.

At the art studio the two editors daubed exuberantly at a canvas, titled it "Abstraction," signed it Heggen-Cohn and carried it into the gallery under Cohn's overcoat. Unobserved, they took down a painting, slipped it into a closet and hung their own entry in its place.

"Abstraction" did not go unnoticed. Tom and Vic were summoned to the office of the university vice-president, but instead of a reprimand they were congratulated and presented to a reporter from the *Star* for an interview.

Trudging back to Pillsbury Hall, Vic contended that if they had not prevailed over a girl with superior airs, nor over hypocrisy in general, they had at least made everyone laugh. Although Tom was just as pleased with the outcome he did not show it. A hoax, he fumed, was an art form in its own right and should be protected from poachers. It was one more sleazy victory for public relations.

In their senior year, 1940, Cohn replaced Roberts as the *Daily's* editor and he gave Tom not only his own former job as copy chief but a choicer plum, a once-a-week column. A *Daily* column was the most prestigious space in the most prestigious of campus publications, and it was the goal of every literary wit.

The single shadow across this prospect was that Tom's column was to appear only once a week, and on Saturday at that. In handing out the assignments, Cohn had given two columns a week to Max Shulman, establishing his supremacy.

Max Shulman was as urban as Tom was small-town. He was from the Jewish section of St. Paul and he was poor even by its standards, poor enough to make Tom feel rich. Because he had had to drop out of college to work for a year he was a class behind Tom, and yet he was Tom's goad. Max was a driver: a small, oval fellow with sharp, handsome features, blue-black hair and the stance of a bantamweight. He was always smiling, but ready with a thrust that might catch you—not hard, but unawares.

As a writer Shulman was exuberant. He gushed words. He drowned *Ski-U-Mah*, the university's humor magazine, with traditional, antic pieces. Some were inept while some were made extremely funny by his gift for wild exaggeration. Equally hilarious in conversation, he was the champion of campus jesters.

Tom was not happy with Max's advantage—being bested so certainly was enough to turn a clown from clowning. Indeed Tom chose the title Saturday's Child for his column and under this waiflike legend surprised his readers with a wistful irony and such earnest themes as dangers to academic freedom and the threat of the war in Europe. But Tom could not keep a straight face for long nor could he stop competing with Shulman for the title. He was always spoiling for a match, in print or out, just so long as there was an audience.

At noon it was customary for *Daily* staff members to carry their lunch bags into the adjoining *Ski-U-Mah* office, where the "exchanges"—*The Lampoon, Purple Cow, Octopus, Tiger*—could be thumbed and, over the sandwiches and milk, local wit could be matched.

From his editor's desk, Max Shulman presided over a loyally risible audience but when Tom appeared he would leave off the preliminaries and get ready for the main bout. As competitive comedians what they said was less important than how they said it. It was important to keep their nonchalance (very big, nonchalance), to top their opponent or at least pretend to. Sometimes they refined their drollery in ever-subtler circles of incongruousness and absurdity. At others it was very broad.

While passing a wintry noon hour in the *Ski-U-Mah* office, Tom proposed the place needed an office whore, an able, willing girl who could be chained to the editor's desk. This brought noisy argument over which of the coeds was most fitted. Tom interrupted to say they were being very unscientific. Offering to show them how to select the right girl he made a tour of the classrooms and the reserve reading room at the library announcing that all female journalism majors were wanted in the *Ski-U-Mah* office. Tom reappeared before the eager jury herding about thirty girls, galoshes aflap, laden with coats and books.

Over their protests of "Hey, what's this all about?" Tom called out, "Is the applause meter ready, Dr. Shulman?"

Shulman pulled out the lower drawer of his desk and peered in. "Yes. All ready."

Dividing the girls into groups of five, Tom passed behind them, holding a hand over each in turn for a response. At the height of the clapping Shulman would glance into his drawer and make a note on paper. One from each group was chosen for the final heat and when this was run off he congratulated the winner and dismissed all the contestants with his thanks.

"But what *is* it," the victor insisted, "some kind of beauty contest?"

"You'll be notified," Tom said showing her out the door. He turned, poker-faced, to accept the jury's gleeful approval.

Tom's humor was not just clowning. His wit was mordant. Behind the poker face and diffidence you could catch a glimpse of horns and switching tail, the hint of a wild, angry nature and a disposition to beware. He made contemptuous fun of fools and his jokes were particularly cruel to girls—girls of all kinds.

When he was with Shulman, girls were only game. The contest itself was what mattered and Tom sensed Max's weak point was a certain squeamishness where he had none. Walking along a corridor with him, Tom sighted Marjorie Searing, a coed so immaculate and virginal-looking she seemed to have stepped from the pages of a Louisa May Alcott novel. As she turned toward the ladies' room, Tom barred the door saying, "No, Marge, there's no need to keep up the pretense. We all know you're too pure to have natural functions." And some things were sacred to Shulman, for he was as tongue-tied as she, and Tom chalked up a score.

At parties Tom and Max would argue some nonsensical fine point and then clown out their competitiveness with boxing gloves. They agreed to no hitting in the head but they slugged away at each other's trunks for hours, pausing for more drink and then resuming. They were drawn to each other as rivals but they were not, as most thought, friends.

Tom found nothing at the Minnesota School of Journalism to change his belief that there was little truth to be found in classrooms. Aside from the novels that interested him he rarely cracked a book.

Although he was tireless in helping a friend prepare for a test Tom would wait until the last moment before a deadline of his own, then wander around the *Daily* office asking what others recalled that might be useful to him. So armed he would go off to the examination room.

During the 1939 Christmas vacation Tom had a warning from the director. His work was hasty and careless, far below the level of his ability, Dr. Casey told him, "and it is of utmost importance to you to adopt a different attitude." Tom stirred himself only slightly and skimmed by, occasionally dazzling his instructors with a perceptive paper on contemporary fiction, but more often infuriating them with his indifference. When he was called upon for comment about a piece of writing by a girl classmate, he did not straighten the impudent curve of his spine or withdraw his gaze from the window: he only replied, "I wasn't listening."

Tom was agreeably surprised by a lecture on Vachel Lindsay, the vagabond poet who had walked the countryside exchanging his poems for food and lodging. Telling Shulman about it he talked him into visiting a Washington Street bakery for an experiment in literary barter.

Their duet of Shulman's "The Black Hole of Calcutta Was She" scandalized the good women behind the counter into filling their arms with day-old bread and urging them toward the door. Overcome with bountiful feelings they hurried back to journalism's new home, Murphy Hall, where they passed along the corridors tearing off chunks of the loaves, pelting clusters of startled classmates, crying "Food! Food for the starving peasants!"

Tom's most famous jape was that of the Copyreader's Ball. It stemmed, at least in its dramatic finale, from his ambivalent relationship with Bob Wadsworth, head of the *Daily*'s radio station. At one time they were close enough to co-publish a literary magazine, *Drafts*, which survived for a single issue. Their bond was Wadsworth's reckless willingness to be Tom's pigeon. He quickened Tom's sadistic impulses. When there was nothing better to do he would think up new ways to taunt him. One February night when he and Shulman were in a room at the Leamington Hotel, Tom called Wadsworth at home to report they had some wild broads with them and he had better hurry down.

Minneapolis was in the grip of such a freeze that Wadsworth had to pour boiling water over the radiator of his car to get it started but he did arrive, to be doused with the pail of water Tom had rigged over the door. Wadsworth suffered this kind of torment resiliently, as he might the bullying of an older brother, but not without resentment. He was always talking about getting even.

The idea for the Copyreader's Ball came to Tom late in the winter of his senior year, high season for all the big campus social events which brought to page 6 of the *Daily* a glut of announcements, guest lists and photographs of partygoers smiling stiffly out of their boiled shirts and long dresses. It seemed to Tom that the whole world was bent on dancing, except for the slaves of journalism. So, in his March 1 Saturday's Child column he announced the First Annual Copyreader's Ball.

He called on the proprietor of the Trail 'Em Inn, a roadhouse on Medicine Lake—a summertime place, boarded up this time of year—and urged him to open up for the party and get in with the free-spending college crowd. The man went to work prying the boards off the windows and decorating the dancehall with paper streamers and brewery posters, while Tom and Wadsworth got out the ballyhoo.

The ball was to be held the following Friday night. Admission was by invitation only and the price was one dollar. Dress would be semiformal which, Tom explained, meant tailcoat and tweed trousers. At this, Wadsworth swore that if Tom came in tails he would cut them off.

On the night of the ball the crowd descended on the Trail 'Em Inn, bringing its own bottles and promptly tore down the streamers and poked fists through the cardboard cutouts. The only lonely part of the hall was the bar where, at the party's height, the proprietor was seen to be weeping. Tom had brought a girl but he did not dance with her. He did not dance well and it was accepted that he never danced with anyone but Max Shulman. This was a customary part of the revelry and the crowd was not to be denied. While Tom and Max circled the floor getting a hand for their whirls and dips, Wadsworth appeared behind Tom brandishing a pair of long copy shears, trying to make good on his promise.

Tom felt a tugging, heard a cheer from the crowd and saw Wadsworth wave one tail in the air. A moment later when Tom noticed him lunge again, shears flashing, Tom put a protective hand to his seat just as the jaws closed. He felt a stab of pain.

The crowd was still laughing as Tom dragged Max to a halt and looked at his left hand. The tip, the whole first joint, of the fourth finger was gone and the raw flesh bubbled with blood. As Shulman and Wadsworth realized what had happened they opened a circle to search the dance floor. It was Tom who spotted the missing part of his finger. He picked it up, studied it and said, evenly, "This is the most significant moment of my life."

In spite of pain-killing drugs, Tom suffered. He was at home in agony for several days, but he was stoical. On the Monday following the Copyreader's Ball Tom posted his chart for nine-fingered typists on the wall of the *Ski-U-Mah* office and noted that a columnist didn't need ten fingers. In fact with nine he aimed to write a better column than Shulman did with ten.

Just behind the curtain of Tom's clowning and his service to journalism lay his commitment to "real" writing. In these Minnesota years, as he was turning into his twenties, his skill was growing. Even better, so was his perceptiveness about subject. He was drawing, as he had in "Comedienne," from his own background, always closer to the bone.

In the autumn of 1939 he wrote "Albert" and submitted it to *The Literary Review*, a quarterly of serious writing published under the *Daily*'s auspices. They immediately accepted it.

"Albert" is a story about boys, their cruelty and occasional compassion for one another. The hero, Carly Holmes, is a small boy but a selfless one, capable of pity for an outcast, a retarded child named Albert. When Carly's gang bullies Albert, Carly risks the scorn of his friends to defend him with his fists, walks off as his protector.

"So Albert had a friend," Tom wrote. "That is not quite true; Carly was not his friend in the sense that he was Jim's friend or my friend. It was more of Carly's great sympathy for suffering. It was the same thing that made him cry at the movies; his heart was simply too big for his small body."

Albert becomes Carly's shadow, wordlessly bringing him simple presents. When Carly's cold turns to pneumonia and he dies, Albert cannot accept it. In the final scene, with the fourth grade assembled at the cemetery in a snowstorm, Albert emerges alone from the woods. He is the last to leave his friend's graveside.

The virtue of the story is its restraint. Tom did not overdo poor Albert's bereavement or Carly's heroism. Carly's straightforward behavior, as though it were the natural thing to do, saves the story from bathos. Carly Holmes, incidentally, was the first of Tom's heroes to die—and, in death, to be exalted.

In the spring of 1940, as Tom was completing his first year at Minnesota, he finished another story, "First Anniversary," and submitted it to Ski-U-Mah. Conventional college humor was on the way out and Ski-U-Mah was striving to change its nature into a magazine on the order of The New Yorker, combining cartoons with serious fiction.

" First Anniversary" was serious and, like "Albert," an exploration of Tom's childhood. It describes a middle-aged couple at their evening meal. They speak rarely and then it is of the food on their plates, the possibility of rain. At the start they are privately recalling what day this is but only when the dishes are washed and put away does the reader learn this is the anniversary of an automobile accident which has taken the life of their son and only child.

They are a gentle, homely couple. The husband is a stooped, discouraged man with thinning hair who speaks in a soft, folksy voice, calling his wife "Mother" and telling her the ham "looks pretty doggone good." He is resigned to their son's death while she is still angry and resentful about it. She wishes that instead of her son, one of the other boys in the car had been killed. She weeps over it and is consoled by her husband, and yet she is the one with guts. An irrepressible will to keep up appearances has her propose in the midst of her sorrow a row of petunias for the backyard and a scattering of grass seed for the bare spots.

Their son is also mourned by a girl. Although she does not appear, they note that in the accident's aftermath she could neither eat nor sleep. She "about had a nervous breakdown." From the scraps of writing the boy has left they suspect he would have become a writer, perhaps a journalist or, as his mother puts it, "something better." She is sure it would have been "something better," while the father is content to imagine his son a reporter. "That's real good work," he tells her. "You don't make a lot of money in newspaper work, but if it's work a fellow likes, that makes up for it."

Tom gave the couple his mother's maiden name, Paulson. It was as precise a portrait of his parents as he could draw. In "First Anniversary" he had postulated his own death and the fantasy that his mother and father were not just bereaved by it, but permanently stunned and sapped of purpose. The story was a fulfillment of the death wish—*they're going to miss me when I'm gone*—of the self-centered, lovelorn child.

Above all, "First Anniversary" reveals Tom's ambivalence toward his parents—a sympathetic and yet unmistakable patronizing of their rustic simplicity, along with a terrible hunger for their admiration and affection.

XIII

The war was drawing closer but it was still unreal. The concern Tom felt about it only intensified the pleasures at hand, which, for him, were plentiful. He had built an extraordinary reputation and now in his senior year he had only to maintain it. It was of three parts, nested one within the other like a Russian doll. The howling buffoon enclosed the witty, perceptive columnist who, in turn, cloaked the inmost Tom—the somber, easy-bleeding writer.

Publication of several stories in *The Literary Review* brought praise from gray eminences in the English department as well as from friends. Then he capped his success in fiction with half a dozen pieces of able criticism. He revealed his disappointment in Thomas Wolfe's posthumous *You Can't Go Home Again*. He was impressed but disturbed by Carson McCullers's *Reflections in a Golden Eye*. His admiration of Hemingway's *For Whom the Bell Tolls* was nearly cloudless.

Then, as if there were not fruit enough, these bright Minnesota years brought Tom Frances Solem. She was a classmate, a journalism major, one of the scores of girls who milled about the *Daily* offices hugging their books, hoping, asking to be noticed. Her forebears, like Tom's, were pure Norwegian, and she had grown up in Fergus Falls, Minnesota, her family only lately having come to the twin cities.

She was short, Tom's size, and she had the fair Nordic looks that even on gray February days give the Minnesota campus the appearance of a daisy field. But she was not a beauty; her eyes were too small and deep-set, her mouth too wide and prone to grin, her figure too sturdy. Perhaps it was her own forthright nature, but there was no guile, and very little pride, in Frances Solem.

But she was easy as an old slipper, warm and responsive, with a sunny enterprise that made her attractive, the delight of her sisters in Gamma Phi Beta. Even Tom Heggen tolerated her. He liked her intelligent, often comic, curiosity and he recognized a vulnerableness, a tendency to ache, not for herself but for the pain of others.

Frenchy, as friends had called her since childhood, was quick to sense her own affinity to Tom, to the outrageous jokes and the painfully thin skin that went with them. Everything she learned about him seemed to be further knowledge of herself. She began to feel as though she really were a part of Tom Heggen, that she was whole only when she was at the *Daily*, somewhere in the room with him, or trailing him on some errand across the campus. She could not help herself. Throughout their junior year, when his indifference was enough to break her heart, she suffered and hoped.

Tom's apathy was in part a longing for Carol Lynn. Just as planned, she was at Northwestern and he kept up an occasional correspondence with her there. In April, apologizing for a long silence, he noted that letters were a poor substitute for seeing her:

> People, myself included, lie so damn much in letters. Not intentionally perhaps, perhaps none of the information is in itself a lie. But often the whole tone is. It may be just a theory of mine, but it seems to me that when you are removed from someone, the temptation is great to write yourself out the way you'd like to be, not the way you actually are.

To her question about his writing he replied:

> I do not have any delusions about being a great writer. Or even of making a living from writing, although that is easy enough to do in its lowest forms. What I want to do is write, not be a writer. I

hope that doesn't sound too theatric. Anyone can write but mighty few can be writers. So I take the humbler ambition. Whether or not I can write well remains to be seen. Right now I am doing a minimum of fiction writing because I have got some good things to write, but I am afraid now that I would only spoil them.

About my equipment as a writer: I don't know much. I have a certain amount of intelligence, I suppose, a greater amount of sensitivity, and I think I have been hurt more than most kids my age. Those three things, I think, are what makes writers. Particularly the last. I don't know. It may be that I haven't been hurt enough.

He closed with plans for a summer journey in which he hoped to see her. It was to be a bumming trip with the admittedly fanciful goal of reaching a Gulf port and then working his way by boat to South or at least Central America, but in any case he would pause in Oklahoma City for a week during which he hoped she might arrange a visit to her aunt there.

In June, Tom set off to the south, but he got no farther than Oklahoma City. There his luck at cards emptied his pockets and he fared no better in love. Carol Lynn was in the Ozarks.

Returning to the tedium of summer school and the family routine at home he was stifled with disappointment and yet his trip, particularly the visit with old friends in Oklahoma City, had stirred memories of other travels, of his trip to New Orleans with Mikles and of the tragic end to Red Griffin's weekend at home.

Tom closed himself into the small back bedroom and wrote a story that wove past experience and present longing into a bold pattern. He called it "Passing Through Kansas."

It was a first-person account of riding a freight, the final leg of a bumming trip. It began with homeward-bound anticipations of "our house on the wide street beneath the canopy of cool trees," of "driving my father's car on summer nights," and of Carol.

So there could be no doubt Tom did not alter her name, nor was there a suggestion that the narrator differed in any way from himself. "Mostly I thought of Carol . . . in the dark on the cool screened porch of her home, the radio turned low, kissing and touching each other, listening to the murmur of people strolling by and all the other sounds of a summer night. I thought a long time about Carol, so long that I could not see her face clearly in my mind."

Clinging to the catwalk of a tanker as it thunders across the plains he is frightened by an approaching figure, but it is only a young Negro also heading north. Shouting over the roar they share thoughts, a pack of cigarettes, a handhold on the catwalk. When the train slows for a town, Tom jumps off to avoid the brakeman. Following, the Negro stumbles, falls beneath the wheels and is decapitated.

". . . I remember most of all the Godlike precision of it. It was so simple, so impersonal, and so final that it could not possibly be tragic. It was clean as a knife flashing through the air . . . One moment he was alive, and the next moment he was dead; there was no in-between."

Hidden in a boxcar, Tom watches the brakeman's discovery of the body, the arrival of a stretcher. "The reason I know the human head is so heavy is because I saw one of those brakemen, a large man, pick it up and carry it to the stretcher. It made him stagger all the way."

If it was reminiscent of Hemingway it was also controlled, scrubbed clean of the mawkishness which had sapped the childhood stories of the previous year. It gleamed with a manly coming of age, a tough-minded tolerance and a dawning acceptance of impersonal violence and death. "Passing Through Kansas," which was soon taken by *The Literary Review*, was easily his best story to date.

He also wrote to Carol Lynn, saying:

> Scooper, I called you . . . and your mother allowed you were at some damn girl scout camp in Rush Springs, Arkansas. I will give you an opportunity to deny the charge before I believe it. I had greater hopes for you than that: attending a girl scout camp!

Then he took a bold new offensive, proposing, whimsically yet earnestly, that she transfer to Minnesota:

You could live at the Chi Omeger house and work at the *Daily*. What greater joy hath any man? The Chi Omegers, so far as I know, are good girls here. The *Daily* is a veritable hotbed of them— I think there are four working on it.

Not only that, Scoop, but I will get you a job paying $8 a month as queen of the copydesk. All you have to do is sit on a desk in the corner and look pretty, which would certainly be no task for you . . . I swear you would really like it here.

But Carol Lynn had no intention of leaving Northwestern and as autumn came to the Minnesota campus, bringing its bustle of new enterprise, Tom realized that he and Carol Lynn had gone separate ways and at last put her from his mind.

Tom was among the last and most conspicuous of the loners. All his friends had paired off and went about their daily chores and pleasures as inseparably as married couples. While he had no objection to uniqueness he did to consistency and now, in the fall of senior year, he turned to Frenchy Solem and to her enormous relief suggested a date.

Frenchy was remarkably, happily effortless and the habit of being with her was easy to acquire. Gently, as though from a lifetime's experience with wariness, Frenchy coaxed him close enough to feel her warmth and sureness. The effect on Tom was magical. She emerged from the blind of familiar, genderless palship as that willing, adoring girl he had been seeking through thickets of self-doubt since adolescence. In the winter of 1941, just as he reached majority, Frenchy taught him all the truth she knew about love.

By early spring he had become an accepted member of the Solem family circle, so much so that when Helen Solem found her sister at home alone one evening she asked for an explanation and learned from a disconsolate Frenchy that Tom had gone fishing.

Continued exposure to Tom's humor made her an addict. Strolling homeward together singing the season's craze, "Beat Me Daddy Eight to the Bar," Tom paused to pick up a twig and then, chasing her, flogged out the rhythm on her back, and she was still laughing about it when she got home.

They appeared together on a radio quiz show and when asked the meaning of the word "calèche" Frenchy answered that it was a sort of carriage and bore off the prize. Tom was impressed and his uncharacteristic response touched her. He bought her a gift, a silk scarf imprinted with the drawing of a calèche.

In their serious talks about the future Tom confided that even though it might disappoint his family, he hoped to find some kind of writing career, one that would bring in enough to live on. When Frenchy suggested they could hardly be displeased if he did what he wanted to, Tom shrugged and described a summer afternoon in which he had stretched out on the lawn and spent a while gazing up through the tree branches. His mother had thrown open a window and called to him, "Are you going to spend all day on your backside? How do you expect to make anything of yourself?"

Lately, anxiety about Tom *had* fractured the parental permissiveness. It had been one grand hell raiser of a spring and he had brought his hangover to the breakfast table regularly. To his father Tom seemed to be completing his education without a livelihood.

Frenchy assured him his instincts were sound and he oughtn't to worry about this—why should he try to fulfill other peoples' ambitions when he had a perfectly good set of his own? To hell with them. But that voice from the upstairs window was troublesome to Tom for it spoke his own conscience.

Ironically the war, which would surely be reaching out for a fellow just graduating and turned twenty-one, seemed to intensify the queasy awareness that the college holiday was over and it was time to go to work. By graduation day Tom had to make two adult decisions, one about a job, the other about Frenchy.

Early in May he had unexpected help toward a job through the appearance in Murphy Hall of a man named Pendleton Dudley. Dudley was a friend and representative of DeWitt and Lila Wallace, proprietors of the *Reader's Digest*. Because they feared the magazine's becoming too Eastern in its viewpoint they had sent him to search for talent in the Midwest journalism schools.

Ralph Casey was hesitant about recommending Tom. He was

shy, he told Dudley, not much of a scholar and not always dependable but his talent was unquestionable. In his interview with
Dudley Tom made a favorable impression and listened attentively
to a description of the editorial life in Pleasantville, New York. To
a man without prospects it didn't sound half-bad.

Dudley left for other hunting grounds but Tom learned he
was being seriously considered for the job. In the first week of June
it was offered to him and he accepted at once, agreeing to come
east and start work on the first of July. His family was overjoyed.

Then as graduation approached he and Frenchy became closer
than ever. He had no claim to a fraternity pin and could not give
her that customary symbol of a tentative betrothal, but he wore a
team jacket with "Frenchy" written in felt script across its back
and thus proudly displayed his own commitment. He was deeply,
gratefully, wholeheartedly bound to Frenchy now. She had become
a second skin. But whether it was the time to make formal marriage plans was puzzling and Frenchy left it, as she left all decisions, to him.

At the end of June they parted with an understanding that
they were in fact engaged but before they told anyone he would go
and see what life was like at the Reader's Digest. If it looked okay,
they would make their plans public. He would send her the ring
from Pleasantville.

XIV

DeWitt Wallace had conceived the idea of a monthly, pocket-size digest of magazine articles while in France recuperating from a World War I chest wound. In 1922 he had raised sixty-three hundred dollars, made an office under a Greenwich Village speakeasy and published his first issue—an edition of five thousand copies.

The *Reader's Digest* to which Tom came in midsummer of 1941 was enjoying the greenest of its many eras of growth. Circulation had spurted to two million and the staff, having overflowed the Westchester village of Pleasantville, had just moved into palatial new quarters crowning the hills outside neighboring Chappaqua.

The white-towered, red-brick Georgian building housed all *Digest* operations but printing, and as Tom was shown around he knew he had arrived in somebody's idea of paradise. Beyond the walls lay a maze of manicured hedges and flowerbeds, while within, American antiques and French paintings shimmered with authenticity. Wonders everywhere, it seemed less a place of business than a museum.

By the time he reached DeWitt Wallace's office Tom was awed and anxious and he expressed a shy skepticism about his future here. This did not go down well with the big boss, whose doubts were obvious as he passed Tom on to Peter Cary for apprenticeship. But Cary, a man of twenty-nine with a husky voice and an easy smile, liked him and put him to work selecting and cutting articles.

Tom was a quick, self-confident student of the *Digest* process. Articles were to be labeled "U" for usable, "P" for possible and "N.U." for nonusable, and in his second week he gleefully confounded the senior editors with his recommendation "Damned fine article—N.U."

Tom's humor tickled Peter Cary and they took to bearing their lunch trays to a table by the cafeteria window where they ignored the view of the valley to share their enthusiasm for "Scotty Fitz" and "Ernie Hem" and to have sudden hysterics over jokes their associates failed to understand.

As Tom grew to know the *Digest* he was of two minds about it. He admired the shrewdness and professionalism of its staff, which accounted for the technical excellence and readability of the magazine, but he reckoned that the editorial attitude, uplift and self-help, was fatuous. Moreover he suspected the cloistered, essentially euphemistic dominion the Wallaces had built here was false as a wax apple.

The parallel between this and the campuses of his past put mischievous thoughts in Tom's mind. But while the masthead offered a tempting gallery of targets he found few accomplices. Among *Digest* employees there was a feeling of hardly credible good fortune at being here.

The other newcomer was a 1941 Columbia graduate named Jack Beaudouin, obviously an able and energetic fellow anxious to do well at his job. Tom would appear at his desk in the midst of a busy afternoon, prop his feet on Beaudouin's assignments and while away a half-hour in deliberately casual conversation. With Beaudouin, as with all his new acquaintances here, there was nothing casual in Tom's intention. He was challenging, testing each one to discover which were the company men and which the possible recruits, those hearts where he might find some independent and combustible spark.

In a group he was poker-faced, listening to the run of the

others' conversation for a while before speaking out to contradict something that had been said—not because he disagreed but because unison and congeniality bored him. Difference and perversity were his joys.

He was as abrasive as ever toward the girls, trying them constantly for their tolerance. If one showed a trace of prissiness he reacted with a profane barrage. His "shittys" and "fuckings" would ring down the corridors to brazen the slightly open door of Lila Acheson Wallace herself. Within a few weeks of his arrival Tom had divided his fellow workers into the half that he liked and was devoted to him, and the other which he openly scorned and which, in turn, despised him.

The girls among the editorial assistants had a professional contempt for flirtatiousness which suited Tom perfectly. He treated them as sisters, teasing them, borrowing from them and, on a warm afternoon, spiking their Cokes with contraband rum so as to study their reactions.

One charming redhead did attract him. She was Helen Firstbrook and, as he put it, "Helen happens in the library." He often came to sit by her desk and steal some company time for gossip and making fun of the bowling leagues and singing groups the Wallaces urged on their "family."

Most afternoons he would visit Helen at three to announce, "It's about time to begin to start quitting," but on one of these he shuffled around her corner making uneasy noises. "Why don't we . . . Wouldn't it be . . . ," he stammered before managing to get out, "What about this summer theater? Should we go to that?"

Helen accepted enthusiastically and evening found them enjoying an intermission cigarette outside the playhouse. They withdrew from the crowded entrance to lean against a fence and in the moment's darkness and quiet Helen felt a soft nuzzling against her cheek. Tom's shyness and their comradely relation had not prepared her for this and her recoil was instinctive. But not wanting to offend him she turned to Tom apologetically and faced a horse, poking over the fence for her attention.

The ludicrousness of the horse's anticipating him made Tom

roar but it did not ease his inhibition. Much as he was attracted to Helen and longed for one of these bright, ambitious *Digest* girls to love him, when he was alone with one he felt the implausibility of it. Sex was as formalized as the tulip beds and the girls too brittle, too able and independent to be interested in him.

So, most evenings he went off with an amiable, epicene bachelor named Eddie Schmidt, whose apartment door was always open and hand ready to pour the drinks; or else he kept to the room he rented from Dr. Shaw in the village, and went to sleep with his fantasies.

Throughout late summer and early fall he thought a great deal about Frenchy and his promise to her. In contrast to these nimble fillies there was something ruminant about her and he wondered if she might be *too* content for this fast track, but still her easy embrace seemed a rare, good thing.

Tom had been keeping careful watch over Jack Beaudouin as he went through the ordeal of Jack's engagement, envying him the pleasures of his fiancée's weekend visits from New York. One late September afternoon Tom turned up at the Beaudouin desk to stare out the window for a while and after some grunts and half-sentences, to confess he had to go buy "a goddam engagement ring." Would Jack come along? It was a first public admission of his own plan to marry.

Together, Tom and Beaudouin motored into White Plains and spent a half-hour at a Main Street jeweler's. There Tom made his painful choice, and mailed it off to a joyous Frenchy in Minneapolis.

As the year progressed the draft was an increasing threat for Tom but he was no longer thinking of resisting it. Along with many of his countrymen he had traded in his belief in neutrality for sympathy with Britain's courage and anger toward "that son-of-a-bitch Hitler."

Some of Tom's classmates were already in service and of these Tom was especially fond of Doug Whipple. In June when Doug had joined the Marines, Tom had thrown him a splendidly de-

praved party at a South Minneapolis motel. Unlike Tom's introverted writing friends, Doug was an able athlete, not only good-
looking but charismatic. He moved with effortless grace and spoke
with a quiet confidence that attracted men as it did girls.

Doug's style was easily convertible to war and when Tom read
accounts of military bravery he often thought of him. Then,
learning that Doug was in training at Quantico, Virginia, Tom
wrote to suggest they meet in New York. Soon, on a Saturday
night, they met in the city and began planning a debauch. In uniform, Doug Whipple was more dashing than ever and Tom imagined that just being with him would bring a girl to his own bed.

Doug's unerring nose for pleasure led them to Greenwich
Village and into a party with a tempting display of women. But
before they could single out the likeliest, Tom lost interest. The
prospect of a double seduction, so alluring in the abstract, now
daunted him and the party seemed repellent. When he found a
child coughing pathetically behind a screen his last predatory
thoughts dissolved in indignation.

On a second evening they went off to prospect Harlem,
promising to find and bed a whore. They prowled Lexington
Avenue and 125th Street, having a drink in every bar they passed,
but no girl approached. At three they returned downtown scoreless,
with Tom more relieved than disappointed.

But these abortive evenings with Doug Whipple nourished
Tom's sprouting patriotism. As they talked about the German
advance into Russia and the sinking of the Bismarck, Doug seemed
a part of these stirring events while Tom felt left out. He could
even exhume a boyhood vision of himself in khaki, pistol slung
from web-belt, loyal troopers following, as well as more recent ones
which had him off in Spain with the Lincoln brigade or flying with
the Canadian Air Force. It was juvenile romanticism and he could
ridicule it as quickly as he could dream it, and yet it played through
his thoughts like a fresh wind.

As though in response to the wish, Tom's draft board drew his
number and in mid-November notified him he would soon be
wanted in Minneapolis for physical examination. He presented this

news to the *Digest* and at the end of the month packed his bag and quit Pleasantville with little regret.

Home again, Tom behaved modestly, spoke pleasantly and politely to all. His friends, marveling at this unaccustomed civility, this sheathing of the famous Heggen needle, decided his Eastern experience had been chastening. Only once did Max Shulman and Bud Nye notice the old malevolence. Tom had been awaiting Wadsworth at a party, preparing a torment for him, and when, wisely, Bob failed to show up Tom angrily threatened to find him and cut off *all* his fingers.

But Tom's detachment was due less to his recent than to his present circumstances. He had returned to aimless days of waiting for something to happen. All other purpose was dwarfed by the giant purpose of war. And yet there was nothing but time. He seemed to be drowning in it.

As for Frenchy, he had imagined that seeing her again would clear away his indecisions, but New York had done something to his eye. She looked careless of herself, a bit dowdy, and his ring on her finger had a perverse effect. He suddenly wanted to hold onto his freedom and was more confused than ever. The war with all its uncertainties argued against commitment of any kind. If there was adventure to be had he wanted to be free for it.

One night he emptied his pockets before her, counted out two dollars and change and confessed it was all he had left from his *Digest* earnings. They would have to wait, he told her, at least until mid-December, when he would learn whether he was to be inducted.

Frenchy, who had imagined they would marry immediately, could not hide her disappointment and they quarreled, Tom saying he doubted that she would like the *Digest* and that she would ever be much help to him in such a place.

When she grasped he meant inspiring him to accomplishment, Frenchy guessed she was in some kind of contest with his mother. She had already decided that Mina, with her ideas of life as striving, always urged Tom to conventional achievement and that her own role was to defend him against such destructiveness.

In the past he had been drawn to her for just that acceptance of life-as-it-came, and now she asked *why* he must accomplish something. What was the struggle *about*? Life was not for winning but for living. Why not be content with what he had? But he would not explain. If she didn't know that instinctively there was no way to tell her.

Frenchy sensed it was Mina Heggen speaking, in Tom's voice, telling her she had lost.

The Japanese attack on Pearl Harbor was inconceivable, surely some master fantasy of Orson Welles, but when the smoke of disbelief cleared from the wreckage of the Pacific fleet, the nation beheld the real myth, that of its impregnability.

Tom Heggen's reflex was to enlist. Recalling that Chuck Roberts had joined the Navy as a yeoman, Tom hurried downtown and lined up at the recruiting office. He was given a typing test and then directed to a desk where a sailor, preparing the forms for his enlistment, asked, "What is your reason for volunteering?"

Tom fingered the draft notice in his pocket but, knowing the Navy could not accept draftees, said, "I don't know."

"I'll give you a hint," the recruiting yeoman said. "It begins with a P and ends with C."

"Panic?" Tom asked. The yeoman shook his head and wrote in "Patriotic."

On December 15 Tom raised his right hand to swear the oath of his country's service and he felt the war machine enclose him. Time itself changed. Hours that had been infinite and cheap he now counted out like a miser. He saw familiar, homely sights as though for the first time, knowing it might be the last.

When he turned up at the Solem house in St. Paul he was feeling remote, as though he had already gone to war. Walking with Frenchy Tom explained that although he felt about her as he always had, what lay ahead was too uncertain for marriage. He might be shore-based, of course, but it was more likely he would go to sea or somewhere halfway around the world.

Frenchy told him these were the very reasons she wanted to marry now, to give what stability they could to the present and hope to the future. Tom argued that it would be unfair to her, tying her down for the duration. He might not even survive and he saw no advantage to either of them in Frenchy's widowhood. They would have to await what the Navy did with him.

She made the best of it and looked on indulgently while Tom celebrated his last day and night in town. With Bob Litman, an ardent Heggen fan and comrade from the *Daily*, Tom joined in a drinking marathon. At its peak they called a Minneapolis radio station to fake a press bulletin on the invasion of a fictitious Philippine island.

When the midnight news brought their account in doomsday commentator baritone they had hysterics. The war itself seemed less awesome and tamper-proof. It was the last jest, one to put the mark of the era they were reluctantly quitting on the era they were, even more unwillingly, entering.

The next morning was gray and brought such agonies that as Tom posed with other recruits entraining for Great Lakes and waved good-by to Frenchy, he welcomed what he had dreaded most—the loss of identity and of all control over his destiny. There was relief in wiping his slate clean. Like a prisoner delivering up his possessions until some infinitely distant day of release, Tom relinquished his collection of ambitions and obligations and for the present he was glad to see them go.

The bulk of the new Navy was still on paper but its vanguard, skeletons on the ways of shipyards from Bremerton to Newport News, was fleshing out. When he finished boot training as yeoman 2/c, Tom was assigned to the battleship *South Dakota*, fitting out at the Navy yard in Philadelphia. He spent the early months of 1942 in the shadow of the great ship and of the spidery cranes, criss-crossing the sky to install her vitals.

Typing a nautical mile of BuShips requisitions in quadruplicate gave Tom a loathing for stenography. While he got along with his barracks companions, the Navy's class distinction, the four years of college that made a gentleman, was conspicuous and he felt he did not belong.

While scarcely wizards, the officers he encountered were from just his middle-class background and he spoke their language. He observed their relatively cushy life and noted the cheerful sounds emerging from the officer's club.

So he wrote Chuck Roberts, now in the Navy's public relations office at Chicago, asking if he could find a way around the math requirement that had kept them both from midshipman school. Chuck could, and did. In April he and Tom were admitted to the V-7 program and ordered to Notre Dame University for a month's preliminary training as apprentice seamen.

On the way to South Bend Tom had a few days at home, time enough to discover that a former classmate, Harry Reasoner, had sold a story to *Liberty* and that Max Shulman, now completing his senior year at the university, had made his first professional score. Ken McCormack, an editor from the New York firm of Doubleday, had come to town, sniffed out Max's "Sauce for the Gander" columns and was impressed enough to offer him a book contract. Along with a publisher Max had acquired a literary agent and, it was said, called him daily for the latest quotations from the marketplace.

Tom found Max's news hard to stomach. He was aware of Max's advantage in single-mindedness and yet he felt himself Max's equal as a journalist and far more able as a serious writer. Max with a *book* out?

Tom had no such prospect, not even an idea for one, and the Navy was taking him further from the possibility. It was more besting than Tom could hide behind a quip. He left town grimly for what he called his "goddam war," and neither Frenchy Solem nor his other friends in Minneapolis were to hear from him for a long time.

XV

Once more on a university campus Tom was at home. While his four months as a tar had been landlocked, alongside his classmates he felt salty. With Chuck Roberts he probed the order of the day for vulnerableness and at the end of their first week they hitchhiked to a nearby town, set their white hats at a jaunty angle and stepped up to the rail of a family tavern.

Sailors were still a rare sight in Indiana and Chuck's pre-Pearl Harbor ribbon, the mark of service prior to December 7, was taken to mean he had been under attack in Hawaii. The drinks flowed generously and it seemed an unkindness to correct their new companions. When a little girl came for his autograph, Tom signed her book with a hero's flourish, "Best wishes, Bela Kun."

Chuck alone knew the name as that of a Hungarian communist leader and it was the kind of old-style, private joke that kept them laughing through a week of calisthenics and seamanship.

When the possibility of a weekend pass was posted, Chuck proposed a visit to Chicago. His family and his fiancée lived in Evanston and he wondered if Tom wanted a date arranged. Tom thought no—for an enticing idea had occurred to him. He put in a call to Carol Lynn Gilmer, now in her final year at Northwestern.

Carol Lynn was surprised and a little bewildered to hear from Tom. He had to remind her that they called each other "Scooper," and she was hesitant about meeting him. She had only six weeks before she took her degree, she explained, and was busy with final papers and her part-time job at the dean's office. Reluctantly she agreed to meet him on the following Saturday.

Actually, Carol Lynn was engaged. She wore the fraternity pin of a Northwestern student from Kentucky named Doug Johnson. Over the Easter holiday earlier in the month she had taken him home to Oklahoma to meet her family. She was able to accept Tom's invitation only because Doug was in Louisville taking civilian flight training.

When Tom called for Carol Lynn his first glimpse told him he was still attracted to her. There was the faintest smarting of a three-year-old wound of disappointment but it was overwhelmed with present buoyancy, a self-confidence the Minnesota years and Frenchy Solem, as well as the Navy blues, provided.

Chuck and his fiancée made a model of romantic contentment and the perfect foil for Tom's courtship. With all four of them gathered at a café table he was ready to show off, to say something clever, to write something fine for Carol Lynn to admire.

Carol Lynn's defenses soon gave way before Tom's contagious high spirits. She was stimulated by seeing him again. Forgotten responsiveness to his intensity was awakening. Clearly, important changes had taken place in both of them. He had matured since Stillwater and so had she. She was no longer afraid and when they parted at midnight she admitted she was looking forward to seeing him again.

She spent Sunday morning studying in the house she shared with other students and when Tom called at noon to ask if he could see her next weekend she hesitated for an instant, thinking of Doug Johnson, and then agreed.

The following Saturday, after a week of drills and classes, Tom covered the hundred miles from South Bend to Evanston and found Carol Lynn waiting. She had spent the week on job interviews, she told him, talking to people at *Coronet*, *Home Life* and the *Chicago Times*. Now she was carefully weighing them for the experience and future they offered.

What a contrast she made with Frenchy, who, though a gifted

editor, had accepted a routine job with the Minneapolis Athletic Club magazine. It pointed up the essential difference between the two; what had seemed a matter of vividness and style was really purpose. Carol Lynn had an unswerving idea of her direction and went about the choosing of her first job with a thoroughness and intensity that put Tom in mind of the women of his own family.

He told her about his *Digest* experience and recommended Carol Lynn write Pen Dudley there. He guessed that he would be making his rounds of the journalism schools and that she ought to see him. He thought she would like it in Pleasantville and as for opportunity, it had her Chicago jobs beat by a mile.

The following Saturday, Tom's last in South Bend, he telegraphed Carol Lynn asking for a third date and that evening gathered her up for another meeting of their café seminar. As the glasses and cigarette butts multiplied Chuck, his fiancée and Carol Lynn became Tom's audience for an episodic fantasy which involved them, their waiter and the people at an adjoining table in a German intelligence plot to extract their new knowledge of flag-hoist signals. He kept them bewitched and laughing all evening.

Carol Lynn, to whom he played directly, was hypnotized. She had lost all wariness. Learning that Tom's class was coming to the Northwestern campus for its three months' midshipman training she rejoiced at the further possibilities for seeing him. During the week while she awaited Tom's arrival in Chicago, Carol Lynn wrote to Doug Johnson in Louisville, returning his fraternity pin.

To most officer candidates the shedding of jumper and bell-bottoms for brass-buttoned coat and visored cap was a leap in self-esteem and smartness but Tom's indifference to clothing triumphed over naval tailoring. His new uniform rumpled in such odd places it seemed intended for someone else and he bitched about it constantly.

But in all other respects he took cheerfully to the new life at Abbott Hall. The regimen was intense, a forced-feeding in ordnance, navigation, communication and gunnery that would simulate an officer's technical training in ninety days, but Tom was in a mood to thrive on it. In the midst of reading Scott Fitzgerald's recently published *The Last Tycoon* he gave enough time to his Bowditch and *H.O. 214* to pass his tests, even the math-ridden navigation, with high marks.

In the frantic schedule of classes, drills and inspections which took the midshipmen from reveille to taps there was one scant hour, that just prior to the evening meal, for repose. At the end of his last class at five, while others collapsed into their sacks or shined their shoes, Tom led Chuck Roberts and a classmate named Arnold Reed at a trot, two blocks up to Chicago Avenue, then three blocks over to Michigan, a nine-minute race to Madame Galli's bar.

Beaming, the lady herself would set a bowl of shrimp before them and the three midshipmen, beers in hand, relaxed and laughed over the day's events—for exactly forty minutes, whereupon they would jog back to Abbott Hall and, fresh from "Madame Galli's muster," step into the platoon formation for inspection and the march in to dinner.

Although the Navy provided him little time for it, Tom was equally pleased with his wooing of Carol Lynn. She lived and attended classes on the Evanston campus but her part-time job in the dean's office was a fifty-yard dash from Abbott Hall. He saw her not just on their weekend dates, but for a few minutes every day.

On a typical Saturday night Tom and Chuck Roberts debated whether Wolfe or Fitzgerald was the better writer, Tom claiming that Fitzgerald would be read and admired long after Wolfe was forgotten. He spoke of "this writer from St. Paul" as though they were related in some way.

He was fascinated with *The Last Tycoon*, the devastating account of the author's battle with drink and mental collapse. There was a terrifying caution in those night thoughts. Tom told them what he knew of Fitzgerald's life and how he had died only recently in obscurity. He could admire all the man's excesses because of his devotion to writing a good novel. *Gatsby*, with its understated clarity, was a masterpiece. No, Fitzgerald had no peer in Wolfe.

Tom loved this kind of talk. Humor and cleverness and shiny

phrases came dancing off his tongue. Beside him, Carol Lynn had the feeling that everything he said was newly minted, shaped with that special intuitiveness. She would try to gather and keep these conjurings of Tom's as he gamboled on, but they defied her. They dissolved like the smoke over the table and that, she felt, was a lamentable loss.

When he saw her alone—and they did find time for leisurely walks along the lakeshore—he did not speak in conventional affectionate patterns and yet they did talk earnestly about marriage and what it ought to be, particularly now, in relation to a great war. He used a complex, private language which held meanings within meanings. He was unequivocal about one thing. He wanted to be with her whenever the Navy made it possible. He was as powerfully in love with her as he had been at Stillwater.

Moreover, he had the joy of watching her fall in love with him. He stated nothing. Everything was oblique and yet an understanding beneath the surface of their words was growing strong.

On Memorial Day, May 30, they sat on the grass in front of the Deering Library talking about themselves and their luck at finding each other again. Who could say that a Navy which brought that about was all bad? Tom suggested they were serious enough about each other so that neither would want to go out with anyone else, and Carol Lynn agreed. This was as close as Tom, in his perverse way, could come to a proposal. Carol Lynn recognized, and accepted, it. From that moment it was understood between Tom and Carol Lynn that they had promised to marry.

It was typical that as they reflected on this decision, Carol Lynn swept out all her old uncertainties and set to plaiting her new emotions and old aspirations into a single braid of love for Tom while he, though no less enchanted, was pricked by misgivings.

First, he had no idea how to confess his heart's change to Frenchy Solem nor of how to face himself in the light of her affection and trust.

There was a second concern in the obscure suspicion he was not a domesticatable animal, but this was easier to dismiss. Just beyond the horizon lay the tumult and the dark seas. It was easy to imagine them lit with a burst and to have a moment's view of a ship upended. In the North Atlantic and the South Pacific men lived and a moment later they existed only in the memory of someone waiting. It was all in your luck.

Everyone shared in the urgency of present moments. It was a time for style and grand gestures. Only idiots thought of consequences. Besides, Tom felt quite certain that Carol Lynn's vision of marriage and of him as her husband was strong enough to carry him into the role. She would be a hard girl to fail.

As for Frenchy, he tried a dozen letters before he gave up and wondered if his sister would take his old heart's comfort off for a womanly talk—if she could explain what an incorrigible son-of-a-bitch he was and how she was well rid of him.

On the afternoon of June 2, Carol Lynn met Pendleton Dudley for an interview and in the evening Tom was able to get away from Abbott Hall and join them for dinner at the University Club. Tom did not hide his eagerness to sponsor Carol Lynn but Dudley made it clear he had several well-qualified candidates and that the decision was the Wallaces', not his. They parted without any idea of Carol Lynn's chances.

When days passed with no slight encouragement from the *Digest* Carol Lynn looked for a stopgap. Since it would allow her to stay on here through the summer and thus a few minutes of each day with Tom, she accepted a job with the *Chicago Economist*.

The awarding of Carol Lynn's M.A. in journalism took place on June 13, a Saturday. Tom sent her flowers, came to the ceremony and took her out for a celebration dinner. Over this they talked about when to marry. Until Tom had his commission in August the Navy would not permit it and afterward there was no assurance of time enough for a wedding in Oklahoma. Carol Lynn had no taste for one of the ten-minute, justice-of-the-peace ceremonies that Chuck Roberts was planning.

During her first week at the *Economist* Carol Lynn received a telegram from Pendleton Dudley asking her to call him but when she did he was as inconclusive as ever. The following Monday brought a second telegram from Dudley asking Carol Lynn to come to Chappaqua for further interviews.

Tom guessed this summons held a reasonable certainty of the job and she ought to go. Pleasantville, he said, was not a bad place for a wedding and, incidentally, as good as any for her to wait out his return.

Carol Lynn reshuffled her plans, found a friend to replace her on the *Economist*, called her family in Okmulgee and shopped for the clothes to take her into new territory. At noon on June 17 she met Tom on the steps of Wieboldt Hall to say good-by. Then, sure she was doing the courageous thing and determined to make Tom proud, Carol Lynn boarded the three-thirty train for New York.

Tom began to hear from her every day. She told about her interview with DeWitt Wallace. It was cordial but formal, without commitment. She had lunch in the cafeteria and met some of Tom's friends, then went off for a week's wait at the Commodore Hotel in New York. Her anxiousness ended in a return to Chappaqua for a meeting with Lila Wallace—who told her that the job was hers.

Then, toward the end of July Tom's orders arrived. He was assigned to a tanker, U.S.S. *Salinas* (AO 19), operating in the North Atlantic. It was a disappointment alongside Chuck's prize, a cruiser fitting out in the Puget Sound Navy yard. Still, he had a few days' leave before reporting in Boston, time enough to get married.

Carol Lynn received the news with joy and wrote that wartime or no they were going to have a *wedding*. She shared quarters in a Pleasantville boarding house with Vera Lawrence, another newcomer several years her senior. Carol Lynn explained that Vera had become a tremendously close friend and an absorbed listener to descriptions of her marvelously talented "Scooper" and the exciting plans in the making.

With Vera, she had decided on the Presbyterian Church. A friend from home, now in New Jersey, was coming up to be her one attendant. Peg Shay, head of the excerpts department, had offered her apartment for the reception and Barbara Preston was giving them her house in Connecticut for a foreshortened honeymoon.

To Tom the program did not sound at all his style. His preference lay with minimum fuss, but he could not bear to puncture Carol Lynn's ballooning enthusiasm.

Graduation Day at Abbott Hall was August 3 and Tom's first act as a fully sworn officer and gentleman was to look in on Chuck Roberts. He found him packing in furious and uncharacteristic haste. Chuck explained that he was leaving directly for the West Coast. The wedding, which was to have taken place that afternoon, was off. At the very last moment he had canceled everything and was hurrying on his way still a bachelor. No, he could not explain it, didn't understand it himself beyond its being buck fever.

It was a peculiar irony for in a way Tom's own engagement had sprung from an envy of the pleasure and composure Chuck drew from his. As Tom saw his friend off for Seattle, puzzling over the reversal that left him, not Chuck, on the altar steps about to face those responsibilities, he felt a twinge of buck fever all his own.

Before taking the train east Tom dawdled an extra day in Chicago trying to shake off his misgivings. With his wedding a couple of days off he could not imagine himself as a husband. For him, ardor was so much a matter of excess, a midnight emotion, and it occurred to him that in the complex patterns of courtship you played a game of want and frustration, one which screened the real issue of whether, once the barrier was removed, a man could sustain day-in, day-out, morning and afternoon, his desire for a woman.

Eddie Schmidt, who had agreed to be his best man, met Tom in Pleasantville and drove him around to Sunnyside Avenue, where Carol Lynn lived. It was the eve of the wedding and Tom, in uniform, waded through a roomful of girls busy with clothes and boxes.

Seeing Tom, Carol Lynn ran to greet him with a single cry of "Scooper!" When she turned to introduce him to this nucleus of the wedding party as "My Scooper!" he scowled at her and said

"For God's sake, don't call me that." The girls, as well as Carol Lynn, were stung.

The wedding next day, August 6, was to be at four and Tom spent a bad day at Eddie Schmidt's apartment on Manville Road. He was nervous and jumpy and to Eddie and Jack Beaudouin he looked unwell. He told them he didn't think he could go through with it.

While Schmidt and Beaudouin agreed between them that Tom was unusually apprehensive they assured him these were normal qualms, gave him more to drink and, as the hour approached, buttoned him into his high-collared white uniform. With one last drink for the road Eddie got Tom into his car and on the way.

The groom's appearance at the church door ended a few minutes of concern about him. Tom was flushed and unsteady enough to require Eddie's guiding hand on an elbow but he was here and the congregation bobbed like a flowerbed before a sudden breeze, smiling its relief.

The ceremony went without incident and at the reception afterward Tom floated agreeably among the guests enjoying himself until it was time to leave. On the station platform the New York-bound wedding guests tried to board a different car but Tom rounded them up and insisted on keeping the party going. As the train scurried through Westchester toward the city he left Carol Lynn to move among the others and they could not tell if he was serious when he put his arm around Eddie Schmidt, urging him to come along on the honeymoon in Connecticut.

But he was unmistakably in earnest when he sat by Barbara Preston to say, "I don't know what I got married for . . ." and beside Vera Lawrence to confide, "What a goddam stupid thing for me to do . . ."

Barbara Preston had gone to some pains over the honeymoon cottage, stocking its refrigerator with food and champagne and making up the bed with pink sheets. But Tom found the little house on Wire Hill Road equally well provided with anxieties.

There were those of the unknown future, the tensions of being brought together in this pressure cooker of intimacy only to be separated indefinitely, plus those he had acquired at the altar earlier in the day.

Being alone with Carol Lynn, knowing she was his for life and that his debt to her of satisfaction, love and assurance was outstanding, dismayed him. Tom suspected that their marriage, only a few hours old, was already a calamity.

XVI

The blue water Navy in which Tom embarked was an escape. From the moment he reported to the Navy yard in Boston he felt a sailor's freedom, and even though he entered communication school to await *Salinas's* readiness, he now felt itinerant enough to find fresh joy in his wife.

Carol Lynn was able to visit nearly every weekend and they had good times together. They stayed at the Statler, danced at the Ritz Roof and visited Carol Lynn's sister, Nina Emily, who, with Dwight Evans, her husband, had an apartment on Commonwealth Avenue. Boston had taken on a vivid wartime excitement. There were uniforms of different services and nationalities in the restaurants and curiosity put Tom up to his games of dramatic improvisation. Most happily—when he and Carol Lynn were alone their lovemaking was gratifying for them both.

But in November when Tom did ship out on the *Salinas*, he was again irked and rebellious at domestic obligations; the need to commit himself and the future to the pages of V-mail was distasteful and it made him question again if there was anything substantial in his marriage.

In port, whether Boston or New York, the call to Pleasantville became a burden, and when they sat together, it was often in silent agony. Carol Lynn would want to know about life at sea, whether he missed her as she did him, when he thought the ship might be in port again, and Tom became sullen and unwilling, finding perverse pleasure in withholding what she wanted of him. All that he could communicate to her was despair, the antithesis of the ebullience which had attracted her. Although Tom was physically beside her, it seemed to Carol Lynn that the real man was receding, drifting farther toward the horizon each time they met.

Once in New York when he excused himself early in the evening, saying he had to return to the ship to stand a watch, she found herself doubting it, wondering if he hadn't other plans, and her dreadful suspicions were confirmed when he let slip that he'd been in Boston without letting her know.

At sea, her bunkers brimming with diesel fuel and aviation gasoline, *Salinas* was a great, nearly submerged cow wallowing with a herd of the beasts to Africa and back. It was such endless, boring duty, month after month of it, unfolding like the constant expanse of sea ahead and the healing wake astern, that he found himself wishing for an enemy attack.

In the course of his watches he thought about Carol Lynn and his ambivalence toward her. In spite of his apparent indifference when they were apart, her effect on him was powerful and pervasive and the guilt over his own behavior constant, leading him on to feelings of his own worthlessness and a despair which, strangely, seeing her in port for a few days did nothing to set right.

His head seemed to be full of mush and although he had resolved to do some writing, in the six months at sea he failed to put a word on paper. He told Carol Lynn that he could see no end to the war and thought it would last forever. But his own was sharply interrupted in August. *Salinas*'s call in Bermuda permitted him a spectacular liberty. The benign climate, the pungent smell of lime and rum in the Front Street bars started him on a glorious drunk. At the peak of it he felt a recurrence of belief in his own magnificent destiny and a control over it.

But Tom's descent was disastrous. His teasing horseplay turned ugly and in returning to the ship by hansom cab he scuffled with another officer and put his hand through the cab window, raking his wrist so deeply on the jagged glass he nearly severed it.

This second damaging of his right hand was severe enough to require his detachment from *Salinas*, an operation, and a two-and-a half-month convalescence at the Chelsea Naval Hospital in Boston. During late summer and early fall of 1943, while he sat on the hospital veranda, fingers taped back to his wrist so the tendons would knit properly, he recognized that if the Navy had provided him an escape, it had surely not made him a haven. He was an unhappy and indifferent officer.

Everyone bitched about service force duty, envied the men of combat ships, but his wretchedness lay deeper, rooted in the premise of this infinite war. He believed so passionately in individual destiny, in the right of every man to pursue some unique, personal truth, that this dragooning of millions of youths into so elaborate, expensive, wasteful and in the end absolutely futile enterprise was the ultimate humiliation.

If his heart was not on *Salinas*, neither was it in Pleasantville. When Carol Lynn came to visit him now he gave off a tangible chill. He would stare down at his cast, much-autographed by the nurses, and give the impression of a man who wished she had not come. When he spoke hopefully of reassignment to the Pacific theater and his belief that if you had to be involved in a war it might as well be where the danger was, she took it as a further rejection of herself.

Walking back down the hill from the hospital, Carol Lynn could no longer doubt that her marriage was in peril but she believed the cause was some failure of her own.

It was Carol Lynn's nature to believe that all human problems would yield to earnest siege and she made plans. She realized she scarcely knew Tom. The more she was with him, the more mystery he became. She wondered if, unconsciously, he felt she had usurped his job, and while she loved the *Digest* and life around it, she considered quitting and making some sacrifice of her own toward the winning of the war. She also determined to seek Tom's family's help in her dilemma.

When Tom's sister Ruth turned up in Boston one day he took her into Schrafft's for lunch, enjoyed the speculation of ladies about his arm sling and told Ruth with a wink that he had never done so much for the war effort. Ruth said she had come from Pleasantville and a visit with Carol Lynn, making it plain she had liked her, that they had shared some confidences and would, if she could, find out what was troubling him, help in some way. But Tom was mum about his marriage.

The big reward of Tom's convalescence in Boston was renewing the powerful boyhood relationship with his cousin. Wallace Stegner was an instructor at Harvard and Tom went over to Cambridge to visit him and his wife, Mary.

Wallace took Tom to some of Bernard De Voto's Lowell lectures, to some nightclubs to hear jazz combos and to the Howard Mumford Joneses to listen to some literary conversation. Wallace also let Tom read the galleys of his forthcoming novel, *The Big Rock Candy Mountain*.

Tom thought the book was the best Wallace had done. He was overwhelmed by the vivid sense of the northern plains and the strong family situations Wallace had drawn from their common past. Grasping how rich this was in fictional possibilities, Tom recognized his own blindness to it. Nevertheless, being with Wallace, admiring his work, was stimulating. It restored his own confidence and he vowed to begin writing soon.

Just prior to his release from the hospital Tom was allowed some leave in Minneapolis and when he returned he wrote Carol Lynn a careful letter admitting the visit home had disappointed him.

> Of course I was glad to see my parents, and they were glad to see me, but the thing that I suppose I went home to find they couldn't give me. It is some measure of peace of mind. Since I went home it's become quite clear to me that no one can give it to me; that the only way to have it is to create it, and that's what I've got to do now.

You see, for a long time now I've led myself to believe that some day I would write some good prose. Some day, not now, but some day. I am a lazy bastard and I could always say "What the hell, there's plenty of time. Go have a beer." For a fellow who wants to write I must be the most unwritten fellow in the world. All of my stories are still in my head. And for a long time now I have been aware that perhaps I would never write them. The habit of wishing stories instead of writing them is a vicious one, and even now I don't know if I can break it but I'm going to try. That's what I got the typewriter for. I have written one story up here, and it was pretty bad, but perhaps not too bad after two years of purely mental writing.

It's not enough to say that I'm in the Navy now and that's a full time job. Nothing on earth is a full time job if you want to do something else. And what I want to do now is write a long story, maybe a short novel, maybe nothing at all that's recognizable, but anyhow words on paper. What's been festering for a long time is whether or not I have the talent and the guts and the vitality to write the things I want, and I figure now is as good a time as any to find out. If I could demonstrate conclusively that I don't have them, after a fair test, then I could probably drop the whole thing and not feel too badly. But to let it go by default, as I've been doing, was getting me down.

I don't much like myself, and I was no good to anybody. I believe this is the thing that you disapprove of. It will exist, I suppose, until I get some work behind me, and some sort of a decision. So wherever I am sent when I get out of here, I must spend every possible minute working on this thing. For I know that nothing will be settled until I get forty thousand words down on paper.

It was the kindest, and at the same time an honest, way to tell Carol Lynn to forget him.

Tom's orders were disappointing, sending him to New Orleans to await commissioning of U.S.S. *Agawam*, another tanker, and from December 1943 through the first six months of 1944 he was at donkey work, plying the glassy Caribbean to Aruba and back to

New Orleans with a cargo of aviation gasoline. He performed his communication duties listlessly and he was unable to write. He felt dull of mind and wasted in spirit. He was sick of himself and each day sank another fathom in despair.

Then, in June, his request for transfer was granted. He was ordered to U.S.S. *Virgo* (AKA 20), an attack cargo and troop ship of the Pacific fleet's amphibious force. He flew from the war's backwaters, via San Francisco and Hawaii, into the center of the combat zone on July 12, reporting aboard *Virgo* where she lay in Eniwetok atoll. *Virgo* was a veteran of the Tarawa and Kwajalein assaults and was presently readying for Guam. The 3rd Marine division was already aboard and she was embarking the Army's 77th infantry.

It was a big ship, a floating city with a cargo of anxious warriors about to make some history, and Tom was soon finding himself at home. As assistant communications officer he stood no deck watches and his duty was to keep up with the required changes in the secret and confidential documents. It cost him only an hour or so a day, leaving the rest of it free.

He shared a stateroom with Alfred Jones, a fellow officer from Osceola, Iowa, and Tom liked him at once for his honesty and spirited independence. Jones had some advanced political ideas, and a photograph of Norman Thomas shared a frame with that of his wife, Kay. He spoke of Kay often and wrote her at every opportunity, but never questioned Tom's silence about his own marriage.

He had a box of watercolors with which he daubed views of Iowa landscape, the Clark County courthouse and, with equal nostalgia, nudes. Tom kidded him about the last, pointing to the pubic hair and saying, "That's vulgar, Alfie. An *artist* doesn't paint hair down there." Jones defended himself not on artistic but on naturalistic grounds, insisting he wouldn't want a woman without it.

They were soon sharing a ritualistic humor, most of it centering on their acute loathing of the ship's captain, Lt. Commander Herbert Ezra Randall. Randall was a short, bull-headed, merchant mariner with sparse education and an undisguised dislike for his college-graduate staff. With the other ship's officers they called him "Old Stupid" behind his back and agreed he had qualified for command on only two counts, his ability to bring the ship alongside a dock and to anchor her on bearing.

Virgo stood off Guam during the last week of July, landing her troops and standing by during their victorious progress across Orote peninsula, then withdrew to rehearse for General MacArthur's promised return to the Philippines. In late September she took a Marine assault force into Peleliu and again waited out the bloody battle ashore. Although Virgo was part of the armada now thrust at the Philippines, she was suddenly withdrawn and ordered to Hawaii and on to San Francisco. With her homeward-bound pennant streaming aloft there was general rejoicing and an anticipatory celebration during the stopover in Pearl Harbor.

From his first day aboard Tom had been a newly happy man. He slept late, played acey-deucey with Al Jones in the wardroom, made friends with Lippincott, the ship's doctor, and with an agreeably indolent ensign from Pennsylvania named George Mascharka.

In his top bunk he arranged fan and light to his liking, his copies of Erskine Caldwell's *God's Little Acre* and of Steinbeck's *Cannery Row* within easy reach and presently felt that sense of fertility he had been awaiting for two years. The story idea that first took shape, like Jones's watercolors, drew on home thoughts, the Minnesota campus and college doings. When he typed it up he asked Al Jones to read it.

Jones returned it with kindly contempt, saying that in the light of the war they were temporarily quitting, the story was superficial and then suggested that the material for a fine story lay around them, in the officers and men of the AKA 20.

They talked about characters and a particular incident at Pearl Harbor in which a signalman found that his glass could be trained to advantage on the uncurtained windows of the nurses' quarters. Tom had done some peeping himself, using the telescope on the five-inch gun. What appealed to him about the situation was the irony of the ship's grimly cross-haired optical equipment being turned to carnal purpose, and he also liked the idea of the officer–enlisted man caste system bending to the common urgency. He decided it could be a romp.

As he lay in his bunk feeling the roll and thrust of Virgo's eastward progress, scenes took shape and characters fused and spoke with their own tongues. Then, toward the end of the voyage, he sat down at the desk and typed the story. He had no great opinion of it but when Jones came off watch Tom gave it to him and asked what he thought.

Reading it, Jones laughed several times and when he put it down said, "Yes. That's it. Now you're on course. Why don't you do some more?"

The morning of October 29, the ship's company had been up since dawn awaiting a first glimpse of San Francisco's hills and the tall white hotels which crown them, but the fog was dense and gliding through it, barely underway, they saw nothing until a seaman on the forecastle cried, "There—look up!" and they saw the fretwork of the Golden Gate Bridge passing slowly overhead. It was the first of the contrasts between how they had imagined homecoming and its actuality.

The second was far more thwarting. Captain Randall permitted no liberty during the first days in port and mutinous thought rose in every man on the ship. But working parties did get ashore and Tom came by enough whiskey for a monumental drunk in his stateroom. At its height he decided to burn some secret and confidential documents in his wastebasket and, later, to take a hot, freshwater shower. He fell in the stall under a jet of scalding water and could not rise but was dragged out by other officers who marveled he had survived without serious burns.

Tom was not certain what he would do with his week's leave. Going home had occurred to him and remarkably so had Carol Lynn.

With the "Nurse's Story" his two-year block had been broken and in a way that indicated more to come. The promise he had made, as much to her as himself, might be kept and that seemed to dislodge another old block. However, when he tried to reach her he found that Carol Lynn had just quit the *Digest* and was on her way home, preparing to enter the Red Cross for overseas service.

When Al Jones brought his wife, Kay, aboard for a glimpse of officer life they found Tom unshaven, suffering from the night's excesses and the stateroom which had been the scene of them, more than usually untidy. He had no idea of his effect on propriety until he saw the reflection in Kay Jones's eyes. He had collapsed her whole shining concept of the naval tradition.

This made him decide to spend every moment of liberty in lovely, pleasure-bent, easy-virtued San Francisco. It was a wartime heaven, teeming with pretty, willing girls. There was drink and music in abundance. Its lobbies and bars jostled with officers on their way to and from the war, and Tom plunged into its midst.

Ensign Mascharka shared Tom's ideas on recreation and they made their liberties together drinking their way up Nob Hill until Tom discovered that Bob Litman was in town. Litman, now a resident at the University of California Hospital in San Francisco, promised a week of glorious dissipation and set up dates with nurses and dieticians he guaranteed to be viable.

On the first of these they ran out of money and were stranded in Berkeley without the price of a taxi. Next time Tom decided Bob's girl was better than his and argued for a swap until both girls took offense and fled for home. On a third, Tom was put out of a nightclub for smuggling in his own bottle and the girls were mortified. Each of these evenings ended in sexual frustration, and yet Tom found them hilarious, gratifying in their very perversity.

The girls were not important but dissipation was and he went about it zealously. As in the past, dissipation was the defiant flag of confidence in his secret gift. Al Jones was right. He was on course. That elusive talent was safe on board.

On January 4, Tom was at sea again. *Virgo* was steaming toward the Philippines carrying reinforcements for the Sixth Army, then battling its way across Leyte. And he had indeed tapped a creative well. Throughout the early months of 1945 more stories took shape in his mind and the best was "Night Watch."

"Night Watch" was an account of a routine midwatch on the bridge of U.S.S. *Reluctant*, no more than a conversation between the officer of the deck and his quartermaster, Dolan, but it gave Tom an opportunity to describe the nature and the sound of such time- and pain-killing exchanges, a mixture of ship's gossip and the dreamlike yearnings of shipboard loneliness.

The O.D. appeared as Tom felt a good man should. He was an amalgam of his friends Doug Whipple and Chuck Roberts. He named him after both, Lt. Doug Roberts.

Tom suspected the story was boring to read because of course it was *about* boredom, specifically the wartime boredom which erodes youth's precious hours and kills individual hope and courage. However, Al Jones told him he need not worry. It was good.

In mid-April, while *Virgo* lay in Leyte Gulf, embarking Marines who had survived the bloody fighting in the Philippines for the invasion of Okinawa, Captain Randall sighted a sister-ship, *Bellatrix*, at a nearby anchorage. *Bellatrix* (AKA 19) was commanded by another ex-merchant mariner, thus Captain Randall ordered the gig alongside and went calling.

He returned from his visit to report that *Bellatrix*'s skipper had a coop of chickens on his signal bridge, and while he chuckled over this foolishness he was clearly nettled to find that in this vast expanse of military conformity his friend was expressing, in chickens, his right to individuality.

Next morning, Captain Randall called Wolff, the bos'n, to his cabin, pointed out the fringe of trees on the beach and sent him ashore with a working party. Wolff returned with a small palm tree transplanted into a five-gallon paint can.

That same night Tom went up to the flying bridge for a chat with Al Jones, who was standing the midwatch there. The ship was at anchor and as he took bearings on the shore, Jones pointed out the tree on the starboard side of the captain's bridge. Peering down at it, Tom found it a particularly objectionable symbol, a claim, like MacArthur's hat and Patton's pistols, to absolute authority. On his way below, Tom paused on the captain's bridge long enough to heave the palm tree overboard.

Next morning the captain began an inquiry into his missing property and at the same time sent Wolff and his working party ashore for a replacement. Wolff returned with two potted palms, installing them on the port and starboard wings of the bridge. It was the eve of Virgo's sailing for the Ryukyus and the captain posted two Marines, one for each tree, in a sunset-to-sunrise watch over his palm garden.

That night Al Jones had the evening, eight-to-twelve, watch and since Tom never went to the movies he paid him another visit on the flying bridge. From here Tom could see the screen on the fantail, and the horsemen galloping across it were assurance enough the captain was in the audience. Tom proposed that two bright and resentful Marines with knowledge of the captain's whereabouts might have abandoned their posts for the rail astern of the captain's cabin, the better to watch the film. He was right. Together, Tom and Al Jones crept down the ladder. Each seized an unguarded palm tree, heaved it over the side and withdrew undetected.

Steaming northward in the morning, they could hear the captain's fulminations and guessed his suspicions would soon get around to them. Hoping to confound him they had a machinist's mate strike a medal from a brass shell casing. It was inscribed: *The Order of the Palm, for service above and beyond the call of duty in the face of the enemy.* That evening, with the officers assembled for dinner in the wardroom, Tom arranged that Ensign Mascharka present the medal to Ed Fahl, a fellow officer who always joined in the protests against the captain but was in perceptible awe of him.

While the captain regularly ate his meals in his cabin and was not at the award ceremony, his executive officer, Mr. Lermond, was. Lermond was another merchant mariner with traditional loyalties to the captain, and Fahl was in acute discomfort. He first insisted he was the wrong man, then warily accepted, and there was a moment of suspense before the exec joined in the laughter.

The captain's determination to punish those responsible for the theft of his palm trees was diverted by the hazards of the Okinawa invasion. As *Virgo* approached the island on May 1 there were frequent *kamikaze* alerts, thirty-two during their stay in the area, and the ship's company was habitually rushing to battle stations. During these emergencies Randall showed a noticeable preference for his cabin, leaving the ship's maneuvering to Alfred Jones, whose general quarters station was officer of the deck.

After the assault, with troops and cargo successfully unloaded, *Virgo* was forming up to withdraw under the darkened-ship precautions which made collision at sea a constant peril. Jones had just complied with a convoy command and ordered half-speed when the captain appeared on the bridge. Ignoring Jones, he asked the engine room why it was at half-speed and on being told it was the O.D.'s order, called for full.

Seeing a ship loom directly ahead, Jones ordered full right rudder and rang up stop on the engine room telegraph. While collision was avoided, the captain spluttered that he would put Jones in hack for ten days. Jones not only rejoiced in being confined to quarters, but when Captain Randall tried to pardon him, insisted on his punishment. Tom thought it all wonderful.

It was during the Okinawa campaign, while *Virgo* lay offshore, that an explosion of rockets lit up the anchorage. Tom went into the radio shack and discovered the pyrotechnics were no last-ditch enemy attack, but a celebration. The Germans had surrendered. The war in Europe was won.

In this Pacific vastness where all but man had seemed eternal, Tom now saw the lightness at the horizon that was his own war's end. While he shared in the general jubilation and thoughts of release, he felt a new anxiousness about time; what had seemed infinite now might not be enough to do the work he had promised.

Thus he decided to expose two of the stories he had written to sympathetic assessment. He mailed a copy of "Night Watch" to Wallace Stegner in Cambridge, telling him that the war, being the big bore it was, had driven him to writing out his frustration. He had not done it for fun but to keep from losing his mind, he explained, and, in asking Wallace to look over this sample story, begged some honest advice. If he thought it worthwhile going ahead with more, he could say so in two words, "Go ahead." If he felt otherwise, he need only write three, "Knock it off."

Tom also sent the "Nurse's Story" off to Carol Lynn's fleet post office address telling her, not quite truthfully, there was no one on board who could give him any understanding, and asking her opinion of it.

Tom had no idea of Carol Lynn's whereabouts but knew she was on her way to the forward areas and any day could materialize out of a group of uniforms at Virgo's ports of call. Actually she had sailed from Puget Sound on April 12, the day President Roosevelt died, and she was in Hawaii sharing a house near Pearl Harbor with other Red Cross girls when she received the "Nurse's Story."

In an immediate reply she said that she was feeling very near him, having just talked with a man on a yard tug who recalled AKA 20 from a recent visit. Not only was she enchanted with the "Nurse's Story," but so were her housemates. She had read it aloud to six girls who had been experiencing the other end of the woman shortage, feeling ranks of hungry eyes feeding on them from ships just in from sea, and finding it more agonizing than pleasurable. They had recognized how the story contained the force of mass sexuality and released it in humor. Its accuracy had brought forth a burst of laughter as the girls found an emotional release of their own.

Wanting to share the story further, Carol Lynn sent it on to Vera Lawrence in Pleasantville, and Tom soon had a letter from her saying she had read the story aloud to friends there. They had settled in with mild anticipation, Vera wrote, but as she read they had become hypnotized and when she finished there was absolute silence for several seconds, and then they all howled. It was an acknowledgment, she told him, of what only she and Carol Lynn had known before, that Tom Heggen had a touch of genius.

More good news followed. A note from Wallace Stegner suggested that Tom's humility about "Night Watch," if not just pretense, was unnecessary. He saw things in it that Tom had no notion of putting there, the emphasis on passing time, for instance—the clock ticking away the seconds, Dolan talking away the minutes, the watch creeping through the hours to join an infinity of them.

He recognized the conflict in Roberts's suppression of real, remembered, intensely felt life, through the opiates at hand, and how he is never quite successful, how longing is always threatening to break through. He felt Tom had wrung from these elements a remarkable tension and suspense. It was a damned good story.

"Keep them coming," he wrote, adding a tantalizing, "and we'll see what we can do with them."

As Tom reread that instruction, he assumed Wallace meant magazine submission, but his approval added to Carol Lynn's and Vera's encouraged Tom to think he had written two exceptional stories and to wonder whether, if he could indeed "keep them coming," they might not be collected in a book. He thought the crew's term for the ship, "The Iron-Bound Bucket," might make a good title.

As *Virgo* steamed among the Ryukyus, swinging stores up from her hold and across twenty feet of streaming Pacific onto the decks of the cruisers and destroyers of Admiral Halsey's Third Fleet, Tom rarely left his stateroom. Ideas crowded his mind and he grew buoyant with confidence. He felt he could do anything, and could scarcely wait to prove it.

With Al Jones he would talk over a remembered incident and a character involved, trying ideas until one seemed right to them both, whereupon he would spend several hours flaked out in his bunk, staring at the overhead while the blower whispered in his ear and story pattern took shape. Characters came readily from the fo'c's'le, or the bridge, to tell what was on their minds. The stored observations of four years at sea, the men, the moods, the look and sound and smell of a ship, all stood within his reach.

At a particular moment he was ready and he would draw a chair to the desk leaf, roll a sheet of paper into the portable and write with a concentration that enveloped him. It would have taken a well-placed enemy shell to intrude on his steady pace.

Incidents, characters, conversations, crowded upon him, pushing and elbowing each other like refugees boarding a departing train.

Even when *Virgo* returned to San Francisco for fleet stores in late June the city scarcely distracted him. When he did go ashore it was to find a quiet hotel room in which to write. In July he sent off three more stories to Wallace, telling him he could barely keep from gagging as he wrote them, but since he was committed, he would finish. There would be more coming.

Wallace replied enthusiastically, this time with news that he was leaving Harvard and would resume teaching at Stanford in the fall. Before leaving Boston, however, he would show "Night Watch" to his friend Edward Weeks, editor of the *Atlantic* and at the same time propose to Dorothy Hillyer at Houghton Mifflin that she read the stories and consider publishing a small book of them.

In Tom's heart, where dark and stormy weather generally discouraged growth of any sort, there was an insemination. At first its effect was uncertain, scarcely discernible, and he was wary of acknowledging it. Yet when he permitted himself to dream the seed was unquestionably there, glowing, and shedding a remarkable comfort. He had never in all his life been happier.

Tom sent a duplicate set of the three stories she had not seen to Carol Lynn and while he was offhand about his long-awaited productivity, he did report that Wallace had been "shockingly enthusiastic" over what he had seen, and that it was great to be at work and know that *it* was working.

A radical change took place in his thoughts about Carol Lynn. This good, hopeful time was not only a fulfillment of his own desire but of hers for him, and he began to foresee a postwar life attached in some fortunate way to the stories, and bound by his and Carol Lynn's love. Pleasantville was halfway around the world and recollections of the summer of 1941 were blurred by four comatose war years. At this remove he could share her dream of domesticity—though not without some bohemian touches of his own.

They would be poor, he wrote her, as any self-respecting writer and his wife should be, but they would not mind the privation. When their garret grew too cold for comfort, they would burn their *New Republics* in its fireplace.

On August 6, an Army B-29 dropped its hideous load on Hiroshima and while the event was largely ignored on board *Virgo*, its effect was swiftly felt. On August 15, as the ship approached the fleet base at Ulithi, Japan surrendered. The huge United States armada now converged on the Japanese coast and by early September *Virgo* lay at anchor in Tokyo Bay.

Tom walked among the silent, bending crowds which made way for him in the streets of Yokosuka. A middle-aged Japanese approached to tell him he had opposed the war and that his countrymen had always had a great sympathy for the Americans. Tom could not tell if he spoke the truth or only courtesy, but either way it depressed him. He would have preferred some evidence of hatred.

Although scuttlebutt had it that the geisha houses, or more accurately, the brothels, of Tokyo were elegant and no disappointment at all, Tom was too preoccupied for diversion. He was working, completing more stories, against his crazily accelerating clock.

With the signing of the peace accord on September 2, he had accumulated enough service points for release. By that date he had completed a third batch of stories and these he sent off to Wallace and to Carol Lynn. Then, on September 18, he was detached and found a berth on a tanker leaving for Oakland.

Alfred Jones came to the gangway with him and, shaking hands, they agreed to get together at home. As Tom went over *Virgo*'s side for the last time, his friend wished him luck with *The Iron-Bound Bucket* and Tom thanked him for his help. Then, with the lighthearted wave of a man who is almost a civilian, he promised to share with him in whatever came of it.

XVII

Tom arrived in San Francisco on October 6 and immediately telephoned Wallace Stegner. Now a full professor, Wallace was beginning his first year at Stanford, and his resonant voice was all the welcome home Tom had hoped for. Wallace said that he and Mary were eager to see him. They had taken a house in Palo Alto and there was plenty of room. He must come right down. Yes, he had some news.

It was an enthusiastic reunion. Wallace had few regrets in abandoning the Harvard-Cambridge scene and he was happily confident over his prospects here in California. But the best of his news was this: in leaving Boston he had been commissioned Houghton Mifflin's West Coast editorial representative and it looked now as if Tom would be his first addition to the firm's distinguished list of authors. Dorothy Hillyer, a Houghton editor, wanted to take an option on the book.

Nor was that all. Wallace's friend Ted Weeks, editor of *Atlantic Monthly*, had read and liked "Night Watch." The chances were good he would publish it, but he wanted to see more of the stories and Dorothy Hillyer was making copies of the others to send across the Common to him.

Tom had brought with him three new stories and when Wallace had read these, they sat down to plan the book. First off, Wallace did not like the new one about Solomon, the steward's mate, and Tom instantly conceded that all three of his new stories were poor and should be junked.

Wallace disagreed, saying the story about the big liberty in Elysium would benefit from cutting but otherwise he thought it could stand as written. He did feel it would be a mistake to let the stories go simply as a collection when there was a chance of tying them together and giving them some aspect of a novel. He saw just such a possibility in the character of Lieutenant Roberts. He was Tom's own reflection and a superb figure, Wallace told him, and with very little rewriting he could be made to dominate the book, even the episodes, such as the nurse's story, in which he did not appear. Let the book begin and end with Roberts, he proposed.

Reassured, Tom not only agreed with this editorial wisdom but felt confident he could bring it off as easily as Wallace had suggested. In the morning he set out for home, promising a finished manuscript within a couple of weeks.

San Francisco was a brimming funnel of returning warriors and the ticket counters were six-deep with frustrated travelers, many of them bristling with priority. Settling in for a wait, Tom felt an expectancy about his writing, a sense of tunneling out at last. While he knew that disappointment was the natural order and always anticipated it, still he trusted Wallace's optimism more than his own pessimism and guessed that before long there would be tangible good news about the book.

If there was one person he wanted to have share in such pleasures, it was Carol Lynn. The promise had been to her. Still waiting, he wrote to her, commiserating over her island-boundness and reporting that homecoming was not a bit overrated.

Then, with a wink, a girl at the ticket counter sailed him by the queues onto the next flight for Minneapolis and as he flew eastward he could not get over the elating notion that a change had taken place in him, one that involved the war's end, the new, private life before him and the special gift becoming ripe within him. In any case it shone from him and the girl had recognized it and given him this prized, winged seat.

As he turned over Wallace's idea of making Roberts dominate the book from the start and tie it up some way at the end, it occurred to Tom that Roberts might leave the ship just as he had, with warm wishes of good luck. Then, instead of coming home, he would have his combat duty at last, and it followed that he would be killed by it—fulfillment and apotheosis in a stroke.

Never mind if a tragic end was at odds with the rest, it was appropriate. Since at least his twentieth year, when he wrote "First Anniversary," he had known with the sureness of a petulant child that death is the only road to full appreciation. In one final, tragic episode Roberts's hero death could give the book a wholeness and dimension he had never anticipated.

Some twenty thousand feet in the air, staring down at the snowy folds of the Continental Divide, he reckoned on the possibility for the book's success. The idea that he might have a taste of it in this, his twenty-sixth year, had a nice irony to it.

What if success did come to the Tom Heggen who had always scorned it, been drawn instead to the misfits and losers? He guessed there would be satisfactions. Who didn't dream of prevailing? He had. He could fix the times of its intensity—at Duncombe, the hopeless year at Classen, recently in his raw envy of Shulman's easy accomplishment and widening fame. Yes, if he were to have some flirtation with success, he imagined he would find her sweet. Meanwhile he was going to turn his back on her for he knew she was a capricious guest and rarely visited where the place was laid.

Home, 4621 Beard Avenue, was a joy, its illusion of changelessness complete. Installed in his second-floor back bedroom among familiar smells, pictures, the books of his teens, he could stretch out on his bed and believe himself a child again, with time infinite and nothing to do but dream.

Squatting on the front steps he looked around at nearby houses, noting that while some of the most magnificent cities in the world had been turned to rubble, not a shingle had fallen here. A neighbor was raking leaves in his driveway, just as Tom remembered him. Nipper, a springer spaniel from next door, clearly

embarrassed by a recent shearing, came over sidewise to say hello.
What a faraway innocence lay here at the foot of Beard Avenue.

His mother's sunny reflection on the war was that it had
multiplied her family and she was looking to the day when,
doubled, it would gather under her roof. Ruth was already home
from Red Cross service in England. While stationed in Worcester
she had met and become engaged to Duval O'Neal. Dee, as she
called him, was from St. Louis, a technical sergeant in the engi-
neers, and they planned to marry on his return.

Carmen's husband, Jim Billings, was still in China with the
Marines and Tom took to teasing her about him, conjuring scenes
of Jim sharing the warmth of a campfire with some fierce Communist Chinese.

To celebrate Tom's return Ruth made up a family theater
party. Ethel Barrymore was in town with *The Corn Is Green*,
Emlyn Williams's play about a Welsh schoolteacher and her
affection for a bright student, and all five Heggens trooped in to see
it. It was the first professional play Tom had attended and he was
impressed, not only with the Barrymore performance, but by the
play itself.

A letter from DeWitt Wallace had awaited Tom, congratulating him on his defense of the nation and suggesting he would be
welcome back in Pleasantville. Tom's objections to *Digest* disciplines lingered so that for a week the letter lay unanswered, but as
he reflected on it he realized that once the book was finished he
had no idea what to do with himself. He most certainly did not
want to stay here. In a month he would have a wife to support.
They must live somewhere, and he was sure Carol Lynn would
approve of Pleasantville. It was *their* place. On the whole it did not
seem too bad a prospect.

On October 15 he wrote Carol Lynn to say that yesterday he
had been "paroled" from the Navy and to urge she too get herself
sprung. If they were reluctant to let her go she might give that Red
Cross outfit "some treason to make the most of," and then hurry
on home. He was finishing up his foolish book, he reported, and
looking forward to doing nothing for a while. Nevertheless, he

supposed he would take up DeWitt Wallace's offer of a job as he lacked the energy and initiative to look for another.

Tom gave himself wholly to the book now. In his mind he had worked out most of what remained to be done. Lines were stretched and situations drawn so that as he bent over his old desk in the upstairs room, missing pieces unfolded swiftly and so easily that he was suspicious of them. Writing had never been so effortless.

Then, on the 19th, he had a letter from Dorothy Hillyer enclosing a two-hundred-dollar option payment and the promise to replace it with a contract as soon as he sent her more stories. She had other news. Ted Weeks was taking a part of what she had sent him for the *Atlantic*, and paying three hundred and fifty dollars for it. He wanted an option on further stories too, as they became available. "They couldn't be in a better place," she assured him, "and it will be good for the book."

He wrote Dorothy Hillyer at once to say he had finished four more pieces, leaving him two to write, and these would require another week. However, he thought he might wait until he had the whole thing finished when he would "send it all in prettily typed and maybe bound with a ribbon. My reason is simply that this book seems to me very bad indeed, and would I could present it in the most favorable light possible."

"I hope my pessimism doesn't annoy you," he told her. "This whole project went sour in my hands shortly after its conception, and I haven't been able to really believe in it since. It was conceived in a big hurry, and once started I of course had to stick with that scheme or have nothing at all. I would like someday to write you a good book, but I doubt that this is it. But anyhow I will write you a book now and hope it is just that my viewpoint is jaundiced from too long an immersion in the Pacific, a most unattractive ocean."

The last day of October, Carol Lynn telephoned. She was "stateside" at last, at a demobilization center near San Francisco, and her voice sang with prospects of release. She was still feeling "sandy," she said, from her months on Guam and Saipan, and furious with a luck that had kept her a jump behind him for a whole year, but she rejoiced in the hope that no more than a week now lay between them.

She whooped at his news about the two hundred dollars he had received for the book and was relieved to know he had gotten off the letter to DeWitt Wallace. As they talked about the future they found themselves in perfect time, a pair of good dancers reunited to familiar music, anticipating, supplementing each other. When Tom spoke of a job that would pay the rent while he found his way to a new book, Carol Lynn noted that the housing situation in Pleasantville would be even worse than before and she would be thinking how to deal with it.

At the end of the first week of November Tom went to the airport to meet Carol Lynn. Waiting at the gate he could not dismiss some apprehensiveness, for he had not seen his wife in over two years, not since the day he had told her he had this feat to perform before he could love her.

But now it was done. He had put his talent and guts on the line and won his forty thousand words, better than fifty thousand at last count. He was purged and proved, ready now to share his life with her. It would be a fresh start and he felt a rush of confidence about that.

His first glimpse of her was enough to wring his heart. She still wore her uniform and the deep glow of Pacific sun. She looked indomitable, evoking old Stillwater yearnings for her and of having to earn her because she was top. He felt a flush of pride as other heads turned to see who the pretty, purposeful, flashing-eyed girl was running to meet.

Tom wore civvies, the look of the future he felt, and they were the first thing Carol Lynn noticed. As they kissed, her fingers plucked at his sleeve. Walking through the terminal, waiting for her luggage, Carol Lynn was laughing at the unexpectedness of seeing him in mufti. She couldn't get it out of her mind. It wasn't important, she said, just strange. And yet Tom got the idea it was important to her, that she had been anticipating a reunion in uniform, a symbolic act that would justify some past sacrifices and bury some old humiliations—and he'd managed to gyp her out of it.

Mina Heggen performed her act of welcome by turning the downstairs sunroom into Tom and Carol Lynn's bedroom, while Ruth and Carmen arranged an evening's entertainment. In the first heavy snowfall of the year, Tom, his wife and sisters laughed and shouted to each other like children while they shoveled the car out of a drift and drove off to see Tallulah Bankhead, who had followed Miss Barrymore into town.

Physically, Tom and Carol Lynn's reunion was gratifying. Together on the sun porch, with the rest of the house hushed, their love-making was food for a long famine. By day it was easy enough to dismiss a certain awkwardness together as just another part of "the readjustment problem" everyone talked about. It was simply a matter of their getting used to each other again.

Mina and T.O. took Carol Lynn for granted as Tom's sensible choice for their daughter-in-law while Ruth and Carmen, now certain of her loyalty and belief in Tom, welcomed her to sisterhood. Nevertheless, Carol Lynn found the Heggen family less effusive than her own. The Heggens disciplined their feelings. They were considerate, and yet reserved, not only with her but with each other.

Carol Lynn did make them smile with tales of Tom's awkwardness as a householder, in particular his struggle with the hot water heater at Barbara Preston's. She felt sure he would learn though, and they shared her confidence that she could tame the beast, could lead his occasionally maverick spirit gently but firmly into the Pleasantville pasture for schooling in the useful gaits.

Tom knew that in Carol Lynn's vision of the future stood one of the lovely old houses that dot the upper Westchester countryside, complete with sloping lawn, sprinkler and the kids running through its pinwheel spray. He knew how strongly that vision motivated her, but he also knew that it was balanced by a good sense. It was that good sense she now transmitted in the note to Vera Lawrence asking her to find them a place to live. Their only two requirements for a first home, she wrote, were that it be inexpensive and within walking distance of the *Digest*.

In their first "serious" talk, Carol Lynn assured Tom he need not fear that his nighttime bedfellow turn into a daytime competitor. She had no use for that kind of relationship and was going to be a twenty-four-hour-a-day wife to him. She had decided against taking her old job or, for that matter, any job.

Recognizing this as self-sacrifice Tom suggested there was no need. While he had qualms about going back to the *Digest* they sprang from the humdrum nature of the job and not from anxiousness that she, or anyone, would threaten it. What was important to him about the *Digest*, he explained, was that it give him time for his next writing project—whatever *that* turned out to be.

Now, when they were alone, they could feel tension between them, some not yet satisfied expectations lingering from that first glimpse of each other at the airport. When Tom asked if anything was the matter, she said No, nothing she could put her finger on really, but she did feel shut out from parts of his life. There were walls. She supposed it was simply the readjustment, but she felt he wasn't integrating. He kept his life in parts. The Navy life, which he continued to reflect on, was one part. Being home with his parents and sisters was another. Then there were the friends who called but never appeared. Life at the *Digest* was a fourth part. Their marriage was a fifth, an altogether separate part. Finally there was the book, and it was separate too. Why was she not being any help to him with it? Had he stopped work on it?

He didn't need any help, he said. For better or worse the book was finished; only some tidying up to do and Carmen had agreed to type it. But even as he protested he recognized that he was provoking her. He sensed they were sliding into a familiar, involuntary conflict, one that was not really between him and Carol Lynn at all, but within his own heart. It was as though his nature was divided against itself, one half struggling to mature, the other reluctant to abandon childhood's pattern.

Still his anxiousness took shape in argument. He supposed there were compartments to his life, and why not? Not all the elements in one's life are compatible. When Carol Lynn contended that they should be, he proposed a trip downtown.

Tom's tour of *his* Minneapolis began with the orderly places, the Viking Room and Harry's, where he found some presentable ex-*Dailians*, fellows like Bud Nye and Harold Chucker, newly discharged from service, but then he led her on to meet his *gurus*, the reporter-reprobates who, he told her, were not only the funniest, but wisest men in town.

There was George Pritchard, a magnificently pungent man, given to regular alcoholic punishment of his failing heart and kidneys. During the war, lack of money had forced him to leave college and take a job on the *Trib*, where he turned out to be a brilliant journalist. Now he was back at the university, living with a derelict of a woman in a squalid on-campus apartment where the debris of nightly parties was never swept up but simply ground underfoot. It was Tom's idea of what home should be.

And there was John Cotton, a once-great basketball player now grotesquely, humiliatingly stooped by spondylitis and yet, Tom thought, even more splendid in his cynical professionalism as a newspaperman and the fierce, fluent pride he took in his talent as a procurer.

Tom glowed with admiration for these two. He explained that they lived with, had a downright affinity for, disaster. He loved them for that and for their clear, ninety-proof vision of life. They knew what it was all about and their laughter was the most admirable sound he had ever heard.

To culminate Carol Lynn's introduction to saloon society, Tom announced a party in her honor at the Club Bar, a Chinese place with booths, beaded curtains and a flock of canaries that was permitted to fly the premises. It was favored by Tom's friends in spite of the canaries and a misanthropic proprietor who clearly preferred his place empty.

Among the guests were Max and Carol Shulman. Max was just out of the Army and bristling with enterprise. His second book, *The Feather Merchants*, a satire about civilians in wartime, had not met the solid success of *Barefoot Boy* but it had increased his fame and he was now well along in a third novel.

As he left, Max extended his sympathies to Carol Lynn for

suffering Tom's idea of a party, and although she laughed at that she was by now conceding that Tom had made his point about the walls. At its worst the party had been an agony and she had not enjoyed his gamier friends.

As she had to the Shulmans, Carol Lynn warmed to Vic Cohn and his wife, and she happily went along to dinner at their house. In the sea of Tom's erratic acquaintance, the Cohns were an island of sanity and constructiveness, but even their quiet hospitality did not reconcile her to the twin cities' bohemian life. She felt on alien ground.

In spite of Tom's intention to share his book's adventures with her, he tended not to. Talking with Cohn about it, the book became a private matter between them. He had given Vic a copy of the manuscript, describing it as "this half-assed novel I've written," and in returning it Vic told him it was "damned good." He thought Tom had caught the war in such an original way that the book's success was assured.

Typically, and enthusiastically, Tom protested. He thought that no writer would be able to catch the World War II experience as Hemingway had in the first one. Our war was too big, Tom insisted. It involved too many people in too many experiences. Fear could not be the theme, for not everyone fought, nor anger, nor sorrow nor, it seemed, any other single emotion.

When Vic suggested that Tom had come close to doing just this, Tom scoffed. And yet the idea plainly intrigued him, kept him silent for a while, seemed to lead him further into the world of his book and, as Carol Lynn had noted, away from her.

Now, after several weeks in Minneapolis, Carol Lynn was anxious to get home. Her mother's birthday was approaching and she intended to be on hand for that and for Thanksgiving. She also felt that she and Tom would be easier with each other on her ground and under the more demonstrative influence of her family.

But when she urged him to come along, Tom spoke of having to tidy up his manuscript and get the verdict from Boston. She left for Okmulgee without him.

Earlier in November he had sent Dorothy Hillyer five more

stories saying "the way I see it, they pretty well finish the book," and while there was a "piece of a prefatory nature yet to come . . . the book lies pretty well exposed for what it is." Now he heard from her that she thought the new stories wonderful. Although she was confused about the order in which he intended they appear, she was certain "that the book must end with Lieutenant Roberts' death, which made me water my desk with tears. It is very rare for a series of stories to achieve an emotional climax like this and we don't want to lose such an opportunity."

Three days later he mailed off the fair copy, prepared by Carmen on her office typewriter, of *The Iron-Bound Bucket*. He wrote Dorothy Hillyer he was "so sick of the book that my primary purpose was just to get it off," that he had made a provisional arrangement of episodes and "like to kid myself that these stories reinforce themselves thematically."

With his book complete, Tom celebrated. But the party was incomplete. He found himself apologizing for Carol Lynn's truancy. That smarted and aggravated his sense of abandonment. Then, as they had in the past, Tom's revels aborted and the result was a crunching of the family car. No one was hurt, but there was a widespread creasing of fenders, a shattering of glass and, by dawn, waves of remorse.

He had brought inconvenience to his father and Ruth, who used the car to get to work, and Tom spent an agonizing day on the telephone. He had just learned from a body shop that the repairs would come to two hundred dollars, exactly what he had earned from three years of writing, when the phone rang and he picked up the receiver and heard a familiar voice.

"Tom, it's Al Jones. I'm in town. I'm down at the station." Jones was cheery with the thought of reunion and he was summoning Tom to keep his gangway promise.

Al Jones told of how he had arrived in Seattle aboard the destroyer *Halsey Powell* and was on his way to Great Lakes for discharge with plenty of time for a stopover. When and where could they meet?

Tom found this an irritating proposal and rationalized his

contrariness with the thought that these old wartime associations led you smack into Legion Hall but at the same time he knew it was more personal. He did not welcome Jones's partaking interest in the book. Whatever the joys and agonies his Navy stories were to bring, he could not share them.

When Tom admitted the book was all set for publication Al Jones crowed his delight. "My God, Tom," he cried from his steamy booth, "you're really going to do it aren't you? You're going to get rich out of this thing."

"No," Tom assured him, "not a chance of that. You have to have a movie sale to make money out of a book and the movies won't touch this one because of the tough language. And I'm not taking that out for anybody."

Then, blaming his accident, Tom begged off on a meeting. With reassurances they would get together soon he wished his old shipmate luck and said good-by. But afterward he was ashamed at having failed Al Jones and conceded that Carol Lynn had been right about his Navy. It was a separate sphere of his past, a place of memory and imagination where he liked to withdraw—but it must not intercept his present, surely not in such tangible shape as Alfred Jones.

Tom wrote to Carol Lynn in Oklahoma telling her he had wrecked the car, making a fine, thorough, two-hundred-dollar job of it, and then, at the end of the month, he set off for a visit to Okmulgee.

Since Stillwater days he had admired the Gilmers' easy ways with one another and his welcome to their big, comfortable house had some of the tranquilizing effects Carol Lynn had hoped for. Mr. Gilmer was a utilities man and there was evidence of a professional zeal even in the family album. He had photographed his giggling daughters against a background of hydroelectric works in every corner of the Southwest and Tom joined Carol Lynn and Nina Emily in good-natured ribbing of their father. As he fell into the role of being another of the children, the constraints of Minneapolis seemed to melt. He found a pleasure in being displayed—naval hero, magazine editor and promising author—to Carol Lynn's twenty-eight cousins. He was just the prize they had expected her to bring home.

When Tom and Carol Lynn returned to Minneapolis together in mid-December he wondered what to give her for Christmas. In the end he left the decision to Ruth, who chose a pair of pajamas and a matching robe and these, with their suggestion of long cozy nights and sunny breakfasts to come, were a great hit on Christmas morning.

Tom was to report for work at the *Digest* on January 2, and Max Shulman's New Year's party was a leave-taking for him. It was also the local literati's celebration of the new year and the new future opening before them all. Even Tom turned generous and mellow in this mood. Climbing the Shulman stairs, he accepted a compliment from Bud Nye, who had just gone to work for the Emporium's advertising department.

"You know I'm coming around to realize I'm not much of a humorist," Bud said. "My columns weren't really funny—certainly not in a class with yours and Max's."

Sharing the toilet bowl with Bud, Tom shook his head. "No, I wasn't funny either," he said. "Max was the only funny one."

Tom and Carol Lynn left for New York in bad weather, expecting to fly out of it but finding worse as they lurched across the country. Arriving over La Guardia in a dense sleet storm, the airplane circled for an hour before reaching down, like a swimmer with his toes, for the ground. While they landed safely, they learned that another plane had gone off the runway into the bay and they were left with a sense of peril and nearness to death they had thought behind them.

In Pleasantville, Vera Lawrence had found them a place on Mountain Road. It had evolved from a garage but a gallery with overhead skylight entitled tenants to call it a studio and made a good place for Tom to work. Carol Lynn rejoiced over its decorative possibilities and, until it was ready, they accepted Vera's invitation and moved in with her.

Passing through the Georgian entrance to the *Digest's* main building had the same constricting effect on Tom's innards as going back to school. He found a new face at the reception desk, fresh chintz here and there, but nothing essential had changed. The florist was standing back to admire his bowl of yellow chrysanthemums and an authentically reproduced Hepplewhite table was having its daily buffing from a real maid.

In the corridor friends offered what he decided was a cellmate's welcome, the fatalistic grip a prisoner extends to the returned fugitive. Across the desk from Ralph Henderson, his old boss, Tom learned that news of his book had preceded him and won him a new assignment. He would no longer be concerned with magazine articles but with the increasingly popular novel condensations.

Maurice Ragsdale headed the book department. "Rags," as he was known, had tousled, sandy-gray hair, a choirboy smile and a mild, nearly inaudible voice, but it was immediately clear these features camouflaged a will of flint. Alert to Tom's reputation, Ragsdale wanted it plain where he stood on mavericks. There was too much work for any horsing around. Tom enjoyed an instinctive bristling at the collar and a sharp recollection of "Daddy" Brill.

But Tom was grateful to Ragsdale for his first assignment, which was to cut Frederic Wakeman's *The Hucksters*. Tom had admired Wakeman's *Shore Leave*, a raw, funny novel about Navy revels in San Francisco. He thought it an honest account, superior, since it was a proper novel, to his own and wished it were the book he had written about the war.

Although *The Hucksters* pioneered a new school of satire directed at the advertising business and was to have a far greater success than *Shore Leave*, Tom was not nearly so reverent toward it and in making the condensation found himself touching up the exposition and occasionally writing new dialogue for Wakeman's characters.

When Ragsdale caught him at his charities he was quick with a reprimand and instructions to redo the cut, sticking to the author's own words. "Don't be so goddamn creative," he ordered and left Tom smoldering.

The massive *Digest* machinery and its demands for conformity evoked all Tom's mischievousness. With Peter Cary he would lark away a half-hour each afternoon, snickering at the latest organizational fatuousness and the enthusiasm with which their fellow workers complied. Merle Crowell, DeWitt Wallace's stoical assistant was known as "the wooden Indian," and when he delivered a batch of difficult letters from subscribers, Tom called after him.

"Just a minute, Merle." Glancing over the letters, Tom returned them. "Nope. I don't want to answer these."

As Crowell's eyes rounded Tom felt he had a good view of the Pleasantville state of mind—Depression memories; lines of watery-eyed men, their threadbare collars turned against those bitter winds, and in contrast the incredible good fortune of those who had found sanctuary here in this benign, prosperous utopia. Convinced of Tom's lunacy, Crowell backed off, never again to ask letter writing of him, but news of the encounter spread quickly, and in the cafeteria there were expressions of satisfaction that Tom was back, doing the unexpected.

Although they had not yet moved into the Mountain Road apartment, Carol Lynn was busy furnishing it. Each night she awaited Tom with an armful of cretonne, news of some bargain in housewares and the hope they could give the evening to decoration. As a rule he disappointed her. He complained that the endless fussing with samples and curtain rods was only to impress friends, and he revealed himself as even more helpless than she recalled.

To thwart all possibility of becoming a handyman he would announce as he left the office, "Vera's giving one of her parties tonight," and lead a file of expectant thirsts to Vera's. Although he pretended to be unaware of Carol Lynn's disappointment and Vera's dismay he felt it keenly. Their vexation with him was part of the pleasure.

Having assembled the party he took no responsibility for it, preferring to listen to, rather than lead, the conversation. His favorite blind was Vera's sofa. He would stretch out there, drink on his chest, to await targets of opportunity. The embarrassed silence was a tempting challenge and the *Digest's* table of contents rarely failed with game. When he offered "I wonder if they really will take the hush-hush out of hernia?" he was rewarded with an outcry of laughter and there was forgiveness even in Carol Lynn's eyes.

When the party was over, the guests sent on their way and the clean-up done, there were new strains for their three-way dependency. Vera was ten years Tom's senior and his feelings toward her were filial ones, just as hers to Tom were those of a kinswoman. But he was always testing her indulgence. He would borrow small sums, forget to pay them back, then react with surprise and hurt when she asked.

Vera's affection for Tom was becoming an alternate for Carol Lynn's, which, despite its patience and sympathy, was far more demanding. Tom's and Carol Lynn's arguments, which had turned on his multiple, exclusive worlds, now centered on his distaste for the *Digest* and the effect it might have on his writing. Carol Lynn not only liked the *Digest*, she saw it as their citadel and when Tom fumed about it, she humored him, explained away his rebelliousness as one more peculiarity of his talent or his readjustment problem—perfectly natural after his years of service.

To this Tom would reply, "Goddam, it *is* the service. Ten times over."

Some nights, as he sat on the edge of their bed, a feeling would steal over him that climbing into the opposite side was really his boss "Rags," or maybe the willful Lila Acheson Wallace, overseer of English antiques and French Impressionists, disguised in his girl's Christmas pajamas. And what a wilting of ardor *that* brought.

Watching Vera make up the studio couch for herself and Carol Lynn preparing to retire in the bedroom he would wander about, poking into Vera's books and pouring himself a nightcap. Then, at the last minute, he would say, "Look, Vera, I'm not sleepy. I'll probably toss half the night. Why don't you go sleep in the bedroom? No, really, I'd rather. I'll sleep on the studio couch."

And so, reluctantly, Vera would go off to share the bedroom with Carol Lynn.

Tom dreaded the breakup of his family of three and when, in mid-January, despite all his malingering, he and Carol Lynn moved into the Mountain Road studio, he clung to Vera. The three dined together several evenings a week and he kept a bottle of Scotch at Vera's so he could drop by for an hour on the way home.

In these twilight sessions he thrust the role of confessor on Vera. Her fondness and concern for both Carol Lynn and himself gave her the power of absolution and he had a swelling list of transgressions for it.

He had brought home a puppy and named him after Hemingway—Ernie. While Carol Lynn had also wanted a dog, Tom looked after it with such unusual and proprietary affection that Ernie became his alone. He had made the poor pup into another instrument of his attrition.

When Helen Firstbrook came for dinner she found Carol Lynn pretending cheer. She had obviously spent the day in preparation and now bustled in with elaborate dishes, while Tom sulked. He replied to Helen's coaxing with grunts and refused to speak to Carol Lynn at all. He was a stone straight through Helen's goodnight at the doorstep, making a ruin of his wife's eagerness to be a good hostess and humiliating her.

On another evening he suggested to Vera she stop off at the studio and on arriving announced that she had come to dinner. Delighted, Carol Lynn explained it was her birthday and, in celebration, she had made Tom's favorite dessert, lemon meringue pie. Then, as they sat down, he bristled at something she said and in no time was mute, refusing to answer her amiable questions. The more tolerant she was of his behavior, the more sullen he became and he ended her birthday party by refusing his portion of the pie.

He carried his contrition to Vera and explained that he

could not help inventing and administering to Carol Lynn a dozen little tortures every day. While Tom opened his heart to Vera Lawrence he could even make out the fuzzy outline of his motives —how his eagerness to display the bankruptcy of his marriage was both self-punishment and a cry for help.

At Vera's he could see, with the objectivity of a man writing about it, how his cruelty sprang from his own fright of failing her, physically and spiritually. Carol Lynn asked so much of life. She had such an elaborate idea of what marriage could, and thus should, be. She clung so firmly to that vision of a fine house with the coming and going of charming people, the children and, of course, endless, beautiful sex, at night and in the morning too.

But Vera felt that what he had begun in self-indulgence was becoming grave and runaway. Although she bled for them both, she could no more help him than he could help himself. Tom admitted it, along with the terrible irony that he did not want to hurt Carol Lynn. He loved her. He was always sure of that.

For all this self-knowledge he could not stop their quarreling and in the sulky intervening truces, while they dressed their wounds and buried their dead, he could read their hopeless future. Carol Lynn refused. Even when he told her bluntly that she no longer attracted him, that he could not even simulate desire for her, she insisted their trouble came less from physical polarity than some spiritual fault of her own, some failure to understand and to cope with his moods, which she continued to attribute to his genius. Confidence in her love for him, and in herself as a woman, may have been shaken but it was intact. To fail in marriage was unthinkable. She was determined to make a go of it.

It often seemed to Tom that Carol Lynn was viewing her marriage through a pair of *Reader's Digest* editorial glasses, rosy with the positivism, optimism and euphemism they must impose on a perverse, untidy world. But she was right in one respect, that under the surface of their quarreling lay the tidal pull of Tom's writing. He knew that he ought to be started on a new book and he was putting the blame for that failure on Pleasantville's antiseptic environment. "A writer," he told her fervently, "must keep going and going. He must have *all* the experiences, and they must be intense."

Bolstering this belief that he was wasting his time were the bulletins from Boston. Early in January, Houghton's editor-in-chief, Paul Brooks, wrote him, "Your manuscript seems to me the most exciting thing that has turned up at Park Street while I've been off in Europe vacationing with the Office of War Information. There have been plenty of attempts to do the sort of thing that you have done here, but this is the first one I've read that has really touched off the magazine. We shall try to see that the explosion is heard for some distance."

Brooks was "not too happy about the title. Do you think it would be possible to find something that would throw the spotlight more on Roberts? He is the one who holds the ship together. Anything we can do to emphasize the continuity of the story and play down the conventional 'war book' theme will be all to the good."

Then, on January 23, Brooks came up with his own answer, saying, "What would you think of calling it simply *Mister Roberts*? This has the virtue of simplicity and I think it is more arresting than a fancy phrase. Also it puts the emphasis where we want it. What do you say?"

Tom replied "By and large I think I concur on *Mister Roberts*. It seems to me very appropriate, and I raise only this question; does it sound too much like a biography title, as for instance of Chief Justice Roberts? Is it misleading in that respect? I'm for it though, and if you are too why don't we let it stick."

One propriety remained and he wrote Chuck Roberts to warn him "that the title of my book, out in July I guess, is *Mister Roberts* and the hero is a Navy lieutenant of that name. 'Roberts' has always seemed to me a nice name and so I appropriated it. The hero is quite a nice guy, I think, and not at all libelous to anyone named Roberts . . ."

The next week he learned the *Atlantic* was taking not one, but three sections. The first, which would run in the April issue, would be the "Night Watch" chapter preceded by the introduction. In

May they would use the episode about the captain and his palm trees, preceded by the news of V-E Day and Roberts's discussion about the war with the ship's doctor. In June they would conclude with "So Long, Mister Roberts," which would include Ensign Pulver's pranks on the captain, the farewell party with its firing of the five-inch gun, Roberts's departure for combat duty and the subsequent news of his death. As an "*Atlantic* First" he would receive their top story fees and be a candidate for a Metro Goldwyn Mayer award of fifteen hundred dollars.

At the same time, in early February, he received his publishing contract from Houghton, stipulating an advance of seven hundred dollars, of which he had already received two hundred as an option. Next he learned the *Digest* itself was taking a short excerpt from the "Nurse's Story" and for it they had agreed to pay the impressive sum of twenty-five hundred dollars.

On March 7 he wrote Paul Brooks that he had been reflecting on the book and if there were any themes to it, "then certainly the contemplation of women is a recurrent one." Two stories which drew on that, the "Nurse's Story" and "Flare-up on the Gun Watch" (the taunting of Red Stevens for trust in his wife), should be separated by a "sexless" story. He wanted the "Nurse's Story," now up front, made the seventh of the fourteen episodes. He wanted to put the Ensign Keith story up to the number two position because "it is in itself prefatory and because it introduces at some length a character, Dowdy, who becomes quite important to the book." Finally he proposed moving the episode about Roberts trying to get a change of duty to the eighth position. Paul Brooks liked Tom's reordering, and that is the way he sent the manuscript to press.

His publisher's burgeoning enthusiasm for *Mister Roberts* prompted Tom's first real threat to quit, whereupon Carol Lynn urged him to wait and see. She pointed out there were only a few months until publication, when they would be able to decide if the book was going to earn enough to support them for a while.

He took Carol Lynn's wary eye on their new bank account as doubt of his ability. She denied it. She believed in his talent as she believed in nothing else in the world and wanted only to protect it. That was why she felt they should stay on, so that he would have a place of his own to write in, so that they could build realistically for their future.

Now Tom told her that all she implied by "future" meant nothing to him. Writing was all that mattered. Without that the trappings she had in mind were meaningless. He could hardly hope for her to share that, and then, overruling her protest, he told her it was right she shouldn't.

It was the beginning of their climactic quarrel, one which ended in Carol Lynn's surrender. At last she was persuaded that their marriage was hopeless, that there was nothing more she could do. Carol Lynn's words etched themselves so deeply in his memory that later he set their essence down in the story "We Used to Own That Town":

> ". . . When you come home now and don't talk," the young wife says in a dead voice, "when you just sit and smoke and never say a word, or go off somewhere by yourself, Bill, I sometimes think I'm a little crazy when I remind myself that you were ever different. But you were. When I first knew you, I thought you were one of the most terribly alive persons I'd ever seen. You used to laugh so much, and you were interested in everything. You had so much, Bill. And then since we were married I've just had to sit helplessly by and watch all that go out of you . . . I used to wonder if it was my fault. If it was being married to me that was doing this. I've worried about this for a long time, Bill. But I don't think it's me. I love you, Bill; but I'm quite sure that you don't love me. I'm also quite sure that you're incapable of loving anyone, and so I don't blame myself for losing your love."

Tenderly and with all the candor he could command Tom told Carol Lynn that it was because he loved her and feared for her that he wanted her to leave him—before he hurt her more. Now he confessed to her his feeling, carried since his teens, of being doomed. The feeling centered on his recollection of a particular night when the Heggens lived in Oklahoma City. It was winter, freezing weather, and he had been drinking and having a wild time, when he blurred out. As his perception cleared he found himself at the end of a diving board preparing to jump, while friends cried a warning. The pool which lay below him was empty but that did not surprise him. Now fully conscious, teetering at the end of the board, he knew he had been aware of the danger as he made his way there.

Although he did inch his way backward to safety and, rejoining his friends, made a joke of it, he knew that for one instant the vast concrete floor of the pool had seemed soft and welcoming as a huge bed and it held a powerful allure.

Carol Lynn was bewildered and frightened by his confession but it helped her to accept the collapse of her marriage. In mid-March, their friends at the *Digest* learned what they had been dreading, that Tom and Carol Lynn were separating.

He wrote Chuck Roberts on March 26: "Carol Lynn and I have at last separated, and she will divorce me. This break was, I suppose, inevitable and for all considerations is probably for the best. Still, it's not pleasant."

Out of habit, Tom and Carol Lynn had one more rousing quarrel. It was over the division of their belongings and at its end he pawed over the carton in which he kept his writing. There were the yellowing columns of college days along with the scraps of typescript, the notes and false starts for a dozen stories. He found it all so trivial and amateurish that he carried it into the driveway and set a match to it.

Catching sight of his pyre from the door, a horrified Carol Lynn ran to snatch a couple of *Daily* columns the wind had freed. Bearing them off she slipped them into her packed suitcase. Then, numbed by all her disappointments of these last months, unable to conceive a new direction for her life, Carol Lynn left for home.

Ruth Moore, a *Digest* employee whose first novel, *Spoon-handle*, was having success, wanted to sublet her house in White Plains. Since it was removed from the *Digest* compound Tom took it. But neither the change of scene nor Carol Lynn's departure had the hoped-for effect. He could not write. He was moodier than ever and an increasing exasperation to his friends.

After a cocktail party Tom joined the merry crowd piling into a car and insisted to its owner, a girl named Marjorie Nicholson, that he would drive. Once out on the treacherous Bedford Road, his passengers' laughter turned to frightened silence. Pressing the accelerator to the floor he took the blind curves wide. Then as he watched the speedometer climb past sixty-five he announced that he had no driver's license. Minnesota had revoked it, he said, after he had killed a man.

With his hair streaming in the wind Tom cackled like a maniac and shouted, "I'll show you!"

When one of the girls in the back seat turned hysterical and begged to be let out, he did stop the car at the Valhalla railroad station. But he would not relinquish the wheel until Marjorie Nicholson wedged herself into his lap and refused to budge until he did.

Most often, Tom was pardoned his offenses. Among his friends at least, there was awareness he had thin, not thick skin, that he was in some kind of trouble and that perhaps it would be better once the book was out.

As he wrapped the corrected bundle of page proof for return to Houghton Mifflin he was satisfied it was as good a book as he could make of it but he felt it was limited in scope. Somewhere a larger theme, one that would do for a far more ambitious book, was awaiting him and meantime he was satisfied with what he had done.

Sending *Mister Roberts* off to Paul Brooks on April 16, Tom asked him to make one last addition to it, saying, "Would you have set up please this dedication: For Carol Lynn."

XVIII

When Vera Lawrence looked in on Tom she found him in hand-to-hand struggle with a hangover. He moved about gathering bottles and dirty glasses, hustling them off to the sink and mumbling about his thirst for ginger ale. Although he did not speak of Carol Lynn he admitted it was the first time he had lived alone and he found it unpleasant. He needed people around him to feel alive; they primed him creatively. The lack of stimulus was troubling him. He felt empty.

On the table was a letter from Paul Brooks. "Publishers are insatiable," it read, "and I am already beginning to think of the book that will follow *Mister Roberts* . . ." Tom was too and the evidence lay all about the room on scraps of paper, but he could not get started. "Honest to God, Vera," he said, "I don't know what to write."

While his search for a theme strong enough to sustain a novel continued, it bore some small fruit. In picking over the shambles of his marriage, hoping to draw a truth from it, Tom fastened on Carol Lynn's belief that he missed wartime excitement and that this nostalgia was at the core of their unhappiness. Using situations, blocks of dialogue still painfully fresh in his memory, he wrote a short story called "We Used to Own That Town."

It describes a precarious marriage between a sensible young wife and her veteran husband, who longs for wartime San Francisco. When he plans a return visit without her he puts their marriage in final jeopardy. "What I keep remembering about the town," he explains, is "the feeling—even when you couldn't see the Bay—that the war was there all the time, waiting outside the nets and just beyond the Fairlands . . . I guess that's what made the parties so wonderful—that end-of-the-world feeling. Because they were wonderful parties. Violent. Violent as hell. Whenever we got in, the room clerks always found us a suite. The Sir Francis Drake, The Palace, The Mark—they always got us the best.

And the girls would come in, all the fine, pretty, war-crazy girls, and the party would start and it never stopped until we left. We might be there a month and the party would go on all the time; it never stopped. The girls changed from time to time, that was all . . . They were violent parties . . . but somehow they were awfully fine. Once when we left The Mark we had to pay four hundred dollars for ruined furniture."

"It's *pathetic*," his wife replies, "to go on reliving a period of your life. That's what you're doing," and presently she asks the question that bothers her most. "You'll have a girl?"

"I suppose so," he says, "but it doesn't mean anything. All I want is a party . . . The girl doesn't matter. She's just necessary to the party."

When they have exhausted themselves in this dispute, he changes his mind, decides against the trip and goes for a walk along the familiar street "that led to the carline, the street that was grooved with the monotony of his daily footsteps. It was a soft night, and all down the street, windows were open in the lighted houses. Whalen walked along, listening to the sounds that came out into the still night. From one house he heard music and loud, excited voices and the sudden rich laughter of a girl. A party. An intensification of living. He listened, and with a dull terror, instantaneously aware of what it portended for him, he knew that the charge was right. He knew that he wished the war had gone on forever; that outside the nets and beyond the Fairlands the war forever waited."

It was a concession to Carol Lynn's belief that the foundering of their marriage was due to the war. While Tom did not wholly share that belief he saw some truth in it and wanted to see more.

One reason was that he felt the logical sequel to *Mister Roberts* would have a postbellum theme, that it would expose the aftereffects of war on a man. He often thought of Hemingway's *The Sun Also Rises* as the model of what he wanted to do.

Although *Collier's* bought "We Used to Own That Town," the story itself seemed to have exhausted the idea of a war-loving veteran. He found nothing more to say. So he turned to the converse, that of a veteran with a dread of war's death. He wrote a second story on that theme and called it "The Survivors."

A veteran and his wife, driving from New York to Minneapolis, are recalling a man, "a great hand with the ladies," who was killed in the war. Still under the shadow of his death they pause at a roadhouse, dance among the youngsters there and are exalted at being a part of this weekend rite. But the story ends with the veteran's terror, ". . . suddenly he was afraid of the outside edge of the floor and fiercely glad they were here in the middle, shoved and jostled and surrounded . . ."

In manner "The Survivors" is even more facile than "We Used to Own That Town" and the frivolousness of the dialogue disguises Tom's serious theme. It had little narrative and Tom suspected *Collier's* would find it "too slight." They did, returning it without the least enthusiasm.

Nor did he have more to say about the dread of war. The theme of a veteran in the postwar era had brought him to a dead end.

Nevertheless, the spring of 1946 came in on a rising tide of expectations. The *Atlantic's* serialization had begun and Ted Weeks reported that his readers' reaction was the most enthusiastic since he had introduced Betty MacDonald's *The Egg and I*. Tom found the fan mail less interesting than the hate mail. He was intrigued with one subscriber who thought "The Captain's Palms" was "a filthy story, its flagrant violation of the third commandment," and "its gutter profanity, unworthy of the *Atlantic*."

But the response which delighted him most was that of *Yacht-*

ing's columnist "Spun Yarn," whose appraisal for the sailing community was nicely technical. Taking the description of the heavens and the ship's course from "Night Watch," Spun Yarn demonstrated that Tom had put the U.S.S. *Reluctant* in the Antarctic.

Tom learned that "Night Watch" had been selected for the annual O. Henry Award collection and there was even a flurry of motion picture interest. Ted Weeks wrote, asking him to sign the M.G.M. option form but, encouraged by Paul Brooks, he declined it as unenticing. This brought Olin Clark up from the M.G.M. office in New York to call on Tom and to read the book. He saw nothing in it that he wanted—"which," Tom told Paul Brooks, with his usual modesty, "can hardly be considered surprising."

Henry Canby, one of the Book-of-the-Month Club judges, confided to Paul Brooks that their first readers had been put off by the profanity in *Mister Roberts* and thus did not make it an "A book." He felt that if it had been an "A book" it would have become a selection. Although the Literary Guild also failed to select it, advance reports from the trade were heartening. Virginia Kirkus's forecast admired *Mister Roberts's* "undercurrent of pathos," and Donald Gordon's *American News of Books* said it "sticks out like MacArthur's hat in a flophouse checkroom."

In early May, Paul Brooks wrote that Houghton was putting *Mister Roberts* at the top of its fall fiction list and it would be a principal subject of the sales conference in Boston on May 29.

It has been a custom to have luncheon guests at this free-for-all, beginning back in the days when Amy Lowell used to come and smoke her cigar and tell the boys what her stuff was all about. Will you add lustre to the present occasion by coming to Boston at our expense and lunching with us on May 29th? You will not be put on a platform or under a floodlight. But it will be a good chance to meet the people at 2 Park Street, a corporal's guard compared with your vast organization in Pleasantville, and at the same time, the men who will be running around the country selling your book. You will probably be the only guest. I hope very much that you can make it.

Tom accepted and on the morning of May 29 flew to Boston, arriving at 2 Park Street just before noon. On entering the oak-paneled editorial rooms he had the impression he was being admitted to some exclusive Boston club and felt very much the awkward Midwesterner. In this first confrontation with his editors he felt a resentment toward the high New England gloss which sales conference excitement made the more daunting. Although it was cordial, Dorothy Hillyer's grand-duchess manner raised his guard and Paul Brooks's top-loftiness did little to lower it.

Fortunately a small luncheon had been arranged in the grill of the Parker House and here, in the flow of drinks, his publisher's real enthusiasm for *Mister Roberts* as well as the genuineness as editors and individuals came through. Paul Brooks spoke lovingly of the out-of-doors and revealed his woodsman's knowledge of the upper Minnesota lake country, to which Tom confessed his own ignorance. He preferred interiors and no more vigorous exercise than the bending of his elbow. Nevertheless he liked Paul and they agreed to meet again in New York.

But as Tom was led into the sales conference itself, his discomfort returned. Some thirty-five strange faces wearing waxy smiles were gathered around a huge U-shaped table in the Bellevue Hotel's ballroom, and space was made for him at the table's head.

Beside him, and sharing the curious stares, was another guest and newcomer to the Houghton list, John Dos Passos. As Brooks explained his visitors, Tom learned that *Tour of Duty*, the celebrated novelist's account of wandering the war fronts, was also to be published this summer. While the buildup for *Mister Roberts* began, Tom examined the ladies around him, wondering what went on behind their eager countenances—and then he heard Paul Brooks introducing him.

Tom had not been given nearly enough to drink to make an impromptu speech appealing, nevertheless, at Brooks's bidding, he rose into a cathedral of hushed expectancy. While the red patches brightened in his cheeks, tongue and mind rebelled. He was speechless until a lady in a conspicuous hat came to his rescue.

"Mr. Heggen," she proposed, "perhaps you could tell us how you wrote your book."

Tom scowled, then burst forth, "Well, shit . . . It was just that I was on this boat . . ."

For a moment it was very still in the Bellevue ballroom and smiles faded all around. Tom reflected another moment but he could think of nothing to add and sat down to a spatter of applause. Dos Passos offered him a commiserating hand and wished him luck with the book.

Tom was not entirely displeased with his own performance, particularly since Dos Passos fared no better. When it came Dos's turn he was just as embarrassed and tongue-tied and seemed to outdo Tom in fumbling at his lapels and saying nothing.

Throughout the spring, Tom vacillated about quitting the *Digest*, but he clung on out of economic prudence until the end of May, when an interesting compromise appeared. Peter Cary, now married to Barbara Preston, was sent to New York to preside over the expanding book department, and with Peter's enthusiastic approval, Tom asked to be transferred to the New York office.

His two bosses, Ralph Henderson and DeWitt Wallace, were aware of Tom's emotional problems and forgave him much on their account. They were also proud of him, believed in his future as a writer and hoped to claim him as their own for as long as they could. They granted the request and in June he went to New York, found an apartment in a West Side brownstone and made his first appearance in the desirable role of an unattached and literary young man-about-town.

The *Digest* offices were high in the Grand Central Building, commanding a dramatic view up Park Avenue, and from here he was soon roaming publishers' row. He was meant to fraternize with editors and screen their lists for possibilities, and he did so, keeping an eye out for pretty girls and agreeable drinking companions. Evenings, he would turn up at the Carys' apartment on 75th Street to have a drink, to talk earnestly with Barbara's eight-year-old daughter, Sylvie, and, if he had no other plans, to stay on for dinner.

The freedom of the city was no help in writing, but the concept of a novel was beginning to emerge for him. Its theme was related to the one he had touched on in "We Used to Own That Town." He felt he could write something meaningful about his own generation of amateur warriors and its difficulty in finding a purpose in this new, civilian world.

Early in July Tom wrote Paul Brooks that he would devote his August vacation to "meditating on what can I say that might make a novel. Right now a book is very, very vague indeed in my head. About all I can think of is to do a rewrite job on *The Sun Also Rises* with slapstick touches."

He had planned his two-week vacation so as to be home in Minneapolis on August 20, publication day, but he also wanted to see Wallace Stegner. There were thanks for a decade of encouragement to deliver, and congratulations to collect. These last meant as much to him as any reward he expected from *Mister Roberts's* publication.

The first weekend in August he flew up to the Stegner summer house in Vermont, carrying a copy of his book for Wallace and Mary. It was glorious summer weather and together they loafed around the house in Greensboro doing fine, aimless things, playing tennis and shooting at targets. Best of all there was a long, sweet-smelling evening to drink with Wallace and to talk about writing.

Wallace held the slim book in his hands, examining the unprepossessing jacket with its drawing of a vast ship's side, and predicted a major success. Tom was pleased, but skeptical and moved on to tell about the kind of novel he wanted to write now, and his difficulty at getting into it. It was frustrating not to be able to write at will, but stuff came to him only in fragments, and in its own sweet time.

When he had heard Tom out, Wallace had some suggestions. There was always a fallow period after a book. You had to accept that. And by now he knew something of Tom's method, of how, instead of starting with an idea, a hypothesis with which to seek a fictional solution, he immersed himself in his own feelings, gradually giving them shape in people and story, and contriving a piece of autobiography in disguise. It was a fine method, proved by its working, but it was indirect, perhaps only semiconscious, so that he had the illusion he had found the story rather than made it.

Tom recognized just how well his cousin understood him. Even better, he was enjoying, fully as much as Tom, this reaffirming of the warmth between them. If Tom looked upon him as a sort of literary father, so Wallace returned the affection, feeling toward him exactly as if he were a richly talented son.

In mid-August, with twelve hundred and fifty dollars from the *Digest* selection and an additional thousand from an *Omnibook* abridgment just received, Tom left sweltering New York for home. Arriving at Beard Avenue, he produced a copy of *Mister Roberts* with appropriate diffidence and had his reward in family pride. Even his two brothers-in-law, customarily a bit stand-offish, approached with congratulations.

Publication day itself began with a telegram from Paul Brooks reporting: "Advance sale thirteen thousand two hundred. This is very good going for a first novel. Sending check for three thousand seven hundred eighty-two dollars."

Mina Heggen made the rounds of the Minneapolis bookstores to assure herself that copies of *Mister Roberts* were on hand. They were, although not always prominently displayed. When she told of making surreptitious rearrangements and leaving with *Mister Roberts* crowning several book stacks, Tom warned her, "They've got you spotted downtown, Mother."

Subsequently she even agreed to be interviewed on a local radio station. Even though public appearance was just as agonizing for her as for her son, she went through with it. Listening to the broadcast Tom heard her voice break with emotion when she spoke of him, and was moved too, but by dinnertime he was able to make light of it and tease her about her "big success on the radio."

Until this moment, T. O. Heggen had been indulgent about his son's writing, making no secret of a belief that it was unlikely to be of any practical value to a man's livelihood. But a glance at Paul Brooks's telegram and the knowledge Tom had already received about eight thousand dollars from his book impressed him. When he found the local reviews were enthusiastic, he read them aloud to people at his office and then went out to scour the stands for the magazines and out-of-town papers.

These made equally exhilarating reading. "All in all," said *The New York Times*, "Mr. Heggen has written a little classic. It invites reading aloud; it stirs vivid memories of other captains, other ensigns. By the chemistry of contrast, moreover, Mr. Heggen's book may remind some readers that in general, war writing has arrived at a debunking phase." The *Herald Tribune* called it "Some of the truest and funniest writing you are ever likely to see about the wartime Navy of the greatest sea power in history," while the New York *Post* man decided, "It comes very close to being perfect. I would be inclined to call *Mister Roberts* the best novel of the year."

In Chicago, the reviewing fell to two old friends. In the *Sun*, Chuck Roberts was faintly cool in his praise, calling the book for which he had loaned his name "an honest, behind-the-scenes portrayal of the Navy as it actually is—in dungarees rather than dress blues, written with a skill and assurance rarely found in first novels."

But in the Chicago *Tribune*, Tom's old scourge Max Shulman called it the best World War II novel so far—better than Hersey's *A Bell for Adano*, unpretentious, yet distinguished by compassion, humor and validity. "For his first novel," Shulman said, "Thomas Heggen has picked a small canvas and has turned out a small masterpiece."

Shulman's review was another kind of triumph, and a juicy one. In one jump he had overtaken his gut rival and been welcomed by him to his own plateau of accomplishment. It was an acknowledgment that Tom's rather more idealistic path led there too. And what a remarkable bond success was; he realized it made a man generous.

Shulman was in New York, aswim as usual in enviable activity. His third novel, *The Zebra Derby*, was a best seller, and even more to be desired, George Abbott was about to produce the musical comedy version of *Barefoot Boy With Cheek*. Max was busy on Broadway with final revisions and casting.

Tom's thoughts had also taken a theatrical turn. While he had seen few plays in his life, he had an itch to write one. Even with Broadway now in easy reach he seldom went there—twice so far, to see *A Bell for Adano* and *The Glass Menagerie*. The previous summer he had seen a stock production of *Arsenic and Old Lace*, and prior to that had to reach back to the two Emlyn Williams plays which had impressed him, *The Corn Is Green* and, in his freshman year at O.C.U., *Night Must Fall*. But in that same year, when he was seventeen, he had watched from the shadows while his sister Ruth rehearsed for College Players' productions. His stage yearnings had rooted then, in a fascination at how, with the playwright's help, she could grow into a girl that a whole audience could love.

When Tom returned to New York at the first of September, he called Max to thank him for the review, to bring him up to date on the latest hometown gossip and finally to let drop that there was some interest in making a play of *Mister Roberts*. "Of course it can't be done," Tom told him.

Shulman correctly interpreted Tom to mean, "Can you do it?" and he said that he thought he could.

Houghton Mifflin had indeed received some inquiries about dramatic rights to *Mister Roberts* but nothing had come of them and there was no difficulty in making arrangements. Max had his agent, Harold Matson, draw up a collaboration agreement under which Tom and Max would share equally in any proceeds. Then he made a hasty outline of the play, offered George Abbott the option and since he too planned to be home in Minneapolis over the holidays agreed with Tom to begin work there with the New Year.

Tom was impressed by Shulman's relationship with Matson and went shopping for an agent of his own. Diarmuid Russell was recommended and he called on him, bringing along a copy of his unsold story "The Survivors." Russell was an urbane, tart-tongued Irishman whom he liked at once and he not only agreed to represent Tom, but promptly sold "The Survivors" to Cosmopolitan for eight hundred and fifty dollars.

But a far more important outcome of his agreement with Shulman was certainty over what to do with himself. He was going to learn how to write a play and then make one out of Mister Roberts. When he spoke of quitting his job, Peter Cary suggested he take a leave of absence until he saw how the play took shape and if there were takers for it.

So he went on suffering ambivalence toward the Digest and his chronic irritation with it was inflamed by what they had done to the "Nurse's Story." Ragsdale had laundered it for the wholesome American family by replacing its climax, Sam Insigna's accurately rendered, "You stupid son of a bitch, that's the one with the birthmark on her ass," with "You stupid lunkhead . . . that's the one with the birthmark on her fanny."

When friends laughed at this encroachment and told him he should be happy with his twelve-fifty and the little disinfecting job the Digest had done on behalf of the wholesome American reader, Tom muttered, "Christ—what American reader is imbecile enough to believe a sailor would use the word fanny?"

In the midst of his fuming, an invitation arrived from the Ragsdales for their annual party. His first inclination, to stay away, was overwhelmed by wanting to let Rags know he had not been bought. Soon after deciding to go he noticed in a shop window a British trench coat. It bristled with flaps and grommets and summoned favorite boyhood images of a determined man in far places on dangerous business. While clothes rarely interested him this party called for a new jauntiness. He bought the coat and, before setting off with the Carys for Pleasantville, loaded its big pockets with a bottle of Scotch and another of cognac.

Showing Tom down to her guest cottage, where a bar was open for business, Betty Ragsdale was clearly put out that he had brought his own liquor. Nevertheless he showed no preference, helping himself and others from both his hosts' and his own supply.

When Maurice Ragsdale appeared to ask how the book was doing, Tom was pleased to tell him that *Life* was using the piece about Ensign Keith for an October issue, that *Liberty* had bought something too, and condensation rights had just been sold for the British Empire. Yes, it seemed O.K. so far.

Tom said he had nearly forgotten to speak of the *Digest's* condensation. To his old taskmaster's questioning look, Tom's sardonic reply was, "I thought you made a fine, creative cut."

Rags laughed and turned away, smiling his unflusterable smile.

Peter Cary knew the signs. He saw the flush deepen in Tom's cheeks and guessed accurately that he was primed for mischief. As they trudged up the path to the main house, where dinner was being served, he kept a worried eye on him. Tom paused in the living room to admire the picture window with its view of hillside dipping to the lakeshore in a blue dusk. Then, hefting his heavy-bottomed tumbler he speculated on what sort of hole it would drive in the great sheet of glass.

Pleading for caution, Peter Cary looked around for help and signaled to Vera Lawrence. She came hurrying over and, with Peter, soothed, distracted and finally delivered Tom from temptation.

While the picture window was spared, Tom did slip away to the guest cottage, where he scandalized an audience by pouring a bowl of salted peanuts into the keybank of Ragsdale's typewriter.

Next day, when Rags called to tell Tom he had left his trench coat behind, he did not mention the peanuts, although he had just spent some time explaining them to his wife. With hardly a trace of rancor, he admired Tom's new coat and told him he suspected that he could never, even after a lifetime of toil, afford such a garment.

Tom knew, as every male writer knows, that the spoils of literary victory are girls. Girls are the tribute, the proof and measure of his success. It was reputation itself, wanting to get in on it, he supposed, which made successful writers irresistible to some women, but it was also the writer's subtle power, his ability to manipulate people through words.

In any case, Tom was not disappointed. The successful publication of *Mister Roberts* did something fine for his sex appeal. Even girls who were not particularly interested in him could not bear that such a prize went unawarded and they bent to their matchmaking.

Helen Greenwood, a *Digest* alumna and friend of Carol Lynn's, asked Tom to a cocktail party at her apartment in the Village, saying she had an attractive girl for him to meet. She was a fellow editor at *Liberty* named Helen Parker.

At the party, Tom found no one to interest him until late, when a stunning, red-headed girl came in. Accompanied as she was by an attentive, darkly handsome fellow and two small children she hardly seemed the one intended for him but when he asked, Helen Greenwood said yes, this was Helen Parker. She explained the children as fruit of an unfortunate marriage and the young man as just a friend. He was a writer, late of *The New Yorker*, named William Gaddis, and if any romantic feelings had existed between him and Helen, they did no longer.

Helen Parker had greenish eyes, a husky, uninhibited laugh, a Scandinavian inheritance of fresh, fair skin and she radiated vitality. From the first moment, Tom was drawn to her. She had come from Chicago to New York, she told him, and for two years she had held a series of interesting jobs in the literary world. She knew *everybody*. Now she was on the point of quitting *Liberty* and striking out as a free-lance writer. The *Times* had already promised her book reviews and she hoped to do some articles.

Helen now told him she had read *Mister Roberts* with more pleasure than any book in recent years and she spoke perceptively of the episodes she most liked. Incidentally, she had noticed that the current *Digest* carried an excerpt.

Yes it did, he admitted, and what a massacre they had made of its editing. They had ruined it, and while it could be argued this was of slight importance to anyone but himself, this kind of hypocritical small-mindedness added up to a lie, and as these lies multi-plied the Digest made liars of its staff and fools of the ten million people who accepted the lies and, sooner or later, preferred to live by lies than by the truth. At the close of his censuring Helen praised his editorial integrity and added, "Gee—feeling that way it's a shame you have to go there and work."

The green eyes challenged him, questioned whether his bark wasn't that of a small dog on a leash, and sent him scrambling in reverse. He defended his employers, pointing out the breadth of the magazine's appeal and the combination of imaginativeness and professionalism with which it was edited.

But across Helen's pretty face spread clouds of dimming interest. She drifted away to talk with others, leaving Tom to realize he had just had a collision and been left with a serious crack in his pride. He watched her gather the two small boys and the dark, good-looking man and, with scarcely a glance in his direction, depart.

Thoughts of Helen Parker lingered and in the morning Tom was newly resolute. He told Peter Cary that when he left for Minneapolis in December he would quit. It had to be a clean break, with no promise of return. As of the first of the year he was going to be a full-time playwright. Then he called Max Shulman, told him about the beautiful redhead and asked him to come along and see for himself. When Max agreed, Tom called Helen Parker to say that he and a friend were on their way downtown to take her out for dinner. Helen had no objection.

They went to the Lafayette Hotel on University Place and as they were finishing the meal, Tom noticed a commotion at the entrance to the dining room. A familiar-looking man was arguing with the headwaiter and looking in their direction.

"It's Willie," Helen explained without the least surprise and presently Gaddis was making unsteady way toward the table. Without invitation he drew up a chair and glared at Tom. Al-though not in full control of his tongue he made it clear that he was unimpressed with Mister Roberts. He told Tom that it had been shamefully overpraised by the reviewers and now he wanted to know what he thought of himself as a writer. "I suppose you think you're pretty good," he charged.

Plainly, Gaddis did not share Helen Greenwood's opinion of his relation to Helen and since Tom felt this might taint an intelligent discussion of his book, he said nothing. In the silence, Gaddis's eye fell on Tom's jacket and, plucking it, he told Tom that it did not fit and if it actually belonged to him he did not like his clothing any better than his writing. "Where did you get a jacket like that?" he wanted to know.

Scenting a brawl, Shulman tried to divert Tom's rival with literary talk, and mistaking Shulman for Budd Schulberg, whose book he *had* liked, Gaddis listened respectfully. Indeed, as Max went on, Gaddis became so absorbed that he allowed himself to be led from the table and out into the lobby.

But moments later Gaddis was back, his fury centered on Helen this time. Seizing her water goblet he threw it at her but it fell short, shattering on a carafe, spilling on Helen's dress and piercing her serenity at last. While the waiters were sorry to see an end to the entertainment they now marched Gaddis out and asked Helen if she wanted a cop. She did not.

Coming out of the restaurant they stopped to buy a bottle of whiskey and headed for Helen's apartment at 30 East 13th Street. Predictably, Gaddis had preceded them and on the door he had hung a glowing red lantern. It was more appropriate here, he announced, than marking the hole in the street where he had found it.

While Gaddis raved about Helen's inconstancy, Tom quietly suggested to Max that they maneuver him to the head of the stairs, where, if he would but kneel behind him, he would do the rest. But Max preferred diplomacy and proposed to Gaddis that he join him at Schrafft's on Fifth Avenue for a cup of coffee. As they disappeared together Gaddis was still proclaiming his enthusiasm for *What Makes Sammy Run.*

Alone, Tom and Helen went over the fine, outrageous events of the evening, recalling every detail down to the expressions of the waiters, and as they laughed together they recognized that they were in perfect pitch. Helen's lustiness, her appetite for everything and the keen explicitness of her wit excited Tom. When they could laugh no longer, they felt immensely close. He had never known a girl so responsive, and making love was the natural consequence. It was a glorious discovery for them both.

Tom moved into Helen Parker's life. Within a few days he was monopolizing every moment of it, bringing her gifts, advising her on her literary odd jobs and career, and trying to ingratiate himself with her boys. In this last he was only half-successful. He fell naturally into collusion with them against their mother's authority and while Tom II, the older, found this interesting and took to him, Bruce, the younger, made his loyalty to the past and Willie Gaddis plain—with a kick to Tom's shins.

The essence of Helen's allure was candor. She was six months younger than he and had been born in Langford, South Dakota. Her childhood in Chicago had been bleak, dominated by a no-nonsense mother who, the moment Helen graduated from high school, saw her off to work with a mandate to bring home money for her board and room.

Deprived of college, she spurned dates to spend her evenings with a friend who had enrolled at Northwestern. Enviously she read her friend's assignments and lecture notes and developed a wistful taste for higher education.

At the same time she was holding down a job and earning extra money at fashion modeling. One day while posing she was asked to join the chorus of pretty girls at the Sherman Hotel's College Inn. Helen's mother was horrified but her father gave his permission, along with a warning against "getting mixed up with any of those musicians." Helen's compressed resentments led her to flout that advice. She was soon very much mixed up with Thomas Parker, a man with hair as red as her own, first alto saxophonist in "Happy" Felton's band.

Marriage to Parker gave Helen two children and a two-year opportunity to observe touring musicians. She was particularly pained by the subordinate relationship her husband—a small, frail man—tolerated with the huge, domineering Happy Felton. For

Helen, the music ended in a humiliating return to her own family, trailing her two children and her irresolute husband.

In the wartime winter of 1945 she came to New York alone, found the 13th Street apartment, took a job at the Office of War Information and entered her children in City and Country School. At the war's end she moved to publishing, made troops of new friends, fell in love with and planned to marry William Gaddis. He was a recent Harvard graduate with hopes for a novel and he had quit his job to write it. However, events of the summer had made Helen decide that marriage was no longer possible.

In December, as Tom was ready to leave for Minneapolis to work on the play, Helen had some blunt parting advice. She felt he deferred to Max when he might better trust in his own talent and judgment.

He read this as simple, womanly resentment over being left behind and assured her he would be back in a couple of weeks with the play finished. She laughed at the idea of such short-order dramatizing and predicted its doom.

But Tom was feeling too pleased with himself to pay heed. He had confidence in Shulman's know-how and his access to a first-class production. Meanwhile, the rest of his literary garden was coming along. The December 14 issue of *Collier's* carried "We Used to Own That Town," and "The Survivors" was due in *Cosmopolitan's* January issue.

Under the Christmas festoons in Scribner's and Brentano's he saw the piles of *Mister Roberts* diminishing, and a letter from Paul Brooks assured him the book had sold upward of forty thousand copies and was "still going strong." He enclosed a new royalty check for two thousand four hundred forty-five dollars.

The *Digest* management said farewell with customary indulgence, offering the possibility of one of its choice writing assignments usually reserved for the "roving editors." As he flew home to Minneapolis for the holidays his prospects were so plentiful it seemed his only want would be in hours of the day.

XIX

Tom's holiday week was interrupted by Helen's voice. She was calling from Barrington, Illinois to say that she and the boys were visiting Ernie Byfield, her former boss at the College Inn. She invited Tom down for a New Year's Eve party, and he accepted.

Byfield was proprietor of three Chicago hotels as well as the widely publicized Pump Room and Tom did not expect to like him. He was acutely aware of the man's fondness for Helen and he sensed that her turning up as his guest was intended to incite Heggen jealousy and punish him for leaving her.

However, the houseparty went well. Byfield was a genuinely good host. On Christmas morning he had delighted Helen's boys by donning a red beard and playing Santa Claus and with Tom's arrival he made much of *Mister Roberts*. He explained that he had put in some time as a war correspondent, and the two men were soon talking about writing and at the height of the party they welcomed 1947 in song.

Still, Tom nursed the thought that Helen's visit to the Byfield farm was at once a faithless and aggressive act, a test of his independence. Even when Helen explained that a snowfall had combined with his absence to make a New York Christmas unendurable and that it was a hope of seeing *him* that had brought her west, Tom withheld all promises. Writing came first, he insisted, and he did not linger in Barrington, for to the north, construction of the dramatic version of *Mister Roberts* was about to begin.

Max Shulman kept an office in the Pence Building, on Hennepin Avenue in downtown Minneapolis and he had hired a stenographer for the two weeks which, he assured Tom, was all they would require.

On the morning of January 2 Tom and Max rode up in the crowded elevator like a pair of actuaries. Hanging up his coat, Tom sat down in a corner of the office as far as he could get from the stenographer, whose pad was open and pencil at the ready. The bare room with its expectant audience drove all thoughts and the hope of them from Tom's head. But Max, the seasoned commander planning his campaign, got right to work.

The problem, he said, was to find a central dramatic situation to link the separate episodes and since there was nothing strong enough in the book they would have to invent it. He felt it might involve a threat to the captain's authority over the ship, that the crew might find the leverage to blackmail him. This would require an indiscretion of the captain so he proposed they introduce a native girl into his quarters. With this for a starter, he dictated some opening lines.

Max identified with Ensign Pulver and skimmed ahead when he could focus on him or the crew, but he could not get Roberts right. Roberts thwarted him and he finally admitted, "I can't write your hero. I can't write this guy who wants to *die*," and gave Tom his custody. Thus they found a working arrangement, one in which Max sketched in the narrative, whereupon they filled in the dialogue together, Tom speaking for Doug Roberts and Max for the others.

On January 17, after exactly fifteen days of work, and right on schedule, they finished a complete draft of a play. Although privately Tom was doubtful, Max bundled up the manuscript and hurried it off to New York for George Abbott's approval.

While Tom waited for news, he wrote Paul Brooks that he was "out here in the tundra again," and that he and Shulman had finished a draft. "The rewrites are yet to come and I dread them," he admitted. "I find it very painful, this exhuming of a book." Then he wrote Chuck Roberts in Chicago to say, "Shulman and I have been working here on a play which he has just taken off to New York. It is a very poor play as it now stands, and I am quite depressed about it. It's going to take a lot of sweat to get it into any sort of producible shape."

There was plenty of diversion in town. George Pritchard, Vic Cohn and Harold Chucker were there to talk and drink with—and then Tom met a girl. She was not an entirely new girl. He remembered her from university days. She had a fine-boned, pert-nosed, China-blue-eyed face, framed in ringlets of hair as red as Helen's. She had been Minnie Freudenfeld but, thanks to a fleeting marriage, she had become Minnie Brill and, more important, an actress.

Minnie, the bright star of the Minnesota Drama School productions, had made a hit with her Juliet and was now rehearsing a Chekhov play. She was hopelessly stage-bitten, determined to escape her family's stifling ambitions for her and the sparse opportunity Minneapolis offered. London, she told Tom, was the place for an actress to launch her career.

When Minnie Brill learned Tom was writing a play, she pried it out of him and hauled him off to Eric Bentley's playwriting seminar for some pointers. In her enthusiasm was assurance they were kin, similarly gifted and with equally dazzling futures.

Tom thought of Helen often and it was not just her absence that made this new romance possible, but also a certain spitefulness for her New Year's intrusion. Helen was strong and he had to defend himself. Thus, toward the end of January, Tom and Minnie became inseparable.

At the end of the month Shulman called with the news Tom had been expecting. George Abbott was unimpressed and had dropped his option. Shulman claimed not to be discouraged by this. He was busy though, with *Barefoot Boy* rehearsals and his fire of many irons. The moment he had some time they would get together for revisions. After all, there were plenty of other producers.

Tom read these assurances as the unctuous evasions of the

funeral director and realized that Helen's forecast had been accurate, that the collaboration was a mistake. Once he accepted this, the *Digest's* offer of a writing assignment looked attractive and he decided to go back to New York and take it.

As he was leaving Minneapolis an unexpected call restored some hope for the play. It was from Leland Hayward, the producer of *A Bell for Adano* and *State of the Union*. Hayward, in California, told Tom that he had enjoyed the excerpts from *Mister Roberts* in the *Atlantic* but he had neglected to buy a copy of the book when it came out in the summer. In the fall he had seen a copy in a bookshop, bought it and in rereading it thought for the first time that there was the germ of a play in *Mister Roberts*.

At that precise moment, he said, he fell critically ill and was taken to a hospital. As he battled for his life he would emerge from unconsciousness thinking about *Mister Roberts* and muttering, "Oh goddam, there's a *wonderful* play in it."

On his recovery he inquired about rights and learned the author was preparing a dramatization. Was it available? Tom hesitated for just an instant, long enough to weigh the possibility this was some kind of joke, and said that as a matter of fact Shulman and he had just completed a draft and it was available. "I'll buy it," Hayward said, "sight unseen."

Tom mailed it off, not permitting his hopes their full scope, but thinking that the book itself was sound as ever and in spite of his blundering might make its own way to the stage.

At the *Digest* office in New York, Tom learned the editors had nothing to offer him at present but they would have an eye out for an assignment and meantime Helen Parker welcomed him back to 13th Street. He spent nearly all his time there waiting for something to happen. He took her to meet Peter and Barbara Cary, but for the most part they saw her Village circle of dedicated writers, drinkers and nonconformists. Tom particularly liked the Carl Carmers, who lived across the street, and the young novelist Merle Miller, who admired both Tom and his book.

With Tom's return these friends of Helen's accepted them as a couple and assumed they would marry. Also, without conscious decision, Helen and Tom accepted that marriage lay somewhere ahead and spoke of it freely. It was as clearly understood between them that first he must settle the fate of his play. It was his entire preoccupation.

Paul Brooks warned him about it, saying, "I've never understood the metamorphosis of a book into a play, though I've heard the scream of the patient often enough. When the screams become loud enough, they always seem to call in a 'play doctor' who then carries off a considerable share of the dough. Perhaps you can explain it all to me."

Tom understood the wisdom beneath the whimsy of Paul's reminder that the theater had been quicksand for any number of fine novelists. It set him to puzzling over his obsession, wondering if it stemmed from old Shulman envy. If so, it had survived a most disenchanting collaboration intact.

During his fifteen-day struggle with the dramatization Tom recognized that he had written the original stories with a stage in mind. *Mister Roberts* was virtually without exposition. He had revealed his characters and told his story in action, as though seen through his own proscenium arch. It was an unconscious practice and he sensed it was rooted in his past. Since College Players' days he had marveled at how powerfully a writer's imagination is extended in the theater and at that divine leap from writer's mind to the tongue and body of a live actor.

Tom's second call from Leland Hayward came from Palm Springs, where he was still recuperating. He had read the dramatization and told Tom bluntly that it was hopeless, not just from a technical standpoint, which was not serious, but from their butchering of the original material. The heart of the book had been destroyed.

Tom said he knew that. He had had little part in the play's composition and felt an even greater loathing for it. As he apologized for wasting Hayward's time over an irreclaimable disaster, the producer told him to hold on, that it wasn't all *that* bad. He continued to believe there was a play in the book. He also felt that Tom had good dramatic instinct and thus had nothing to be afraid of. Why didn't he try a new version by himself? Any lapses in technique could be fixed later. While Tom was unconvinced that he was any kind of playwright, he took a deep breath and agreed.

Simultaneously the *Digest* called to propose a writing assignment, a profile of Louis B. Mayer, the head of M.G.M. It would require his going to Hollywood for the interview and Peter Cary suspected Tom would find a reason to turn it down. But Tom liked the prospects, in particular the chance of a side trip to Palm Springs and a talk with Leland Hayward, and he accepted.

He promised Helen to return shortly and in the first week of March, with a hint of better weather coming, flew off to Los Angeles. He was met at the airport by a brace of M.G.M. publicity men and whisked to impressive lodgings at the Ambassador Hotel in Santa Monica. Then, after two days' briefing, he was brought for an audience with Mayer himself.

Sitting across the commissary table from him, Tom found a bond in insomnia. Mayer had no use, he said, for sleeping pills. His antidote was the rumba. He had taken it up several years ago and assured him that a couple of hours of it before retiring guaranteed a sound night's sleep.

When Tom asked if he had any advice for a young man with ambitions in his business, Mayer corrected him. "You mean advice for you. All right, you want to know how to make a million dollars in the movies?" When Tom nodded he said, "I'll tell you. Figure out a way to put fucking on the screen."

While Tom could not see how he was going to work this sound advice into the profile he tucked it away as the perfect souvenir of California for Helen.

He wrote up the piece swiftly, relying on anecdotes about well-known stars and their relations with Mayer, painting him as a man with an acting skill of his own, one which gave him a decisive edge in casting and contractual disputes with his celebrated employees. Satisfied, he mailed it off to the *Digest* and went to call on Hayward in Palm Springs.

Tom knew that Hayward was tough, calloused by his apprenticeship as a Broadway and actors' agent, feared even by the formidable Mayer, but he was not prepared for the man's polish, a quality that intimidated Tom more than the marauder's reputation.

Hayward, who was surprised by Tom's wispiness and timidity, made an effort to put him at ease so that after an awkward start Tom lost self-consciousness. He saw in Hayward's rugged features, the laugh lines around his blue eyes, a man he could admire. Tom learned he was the friend and agent of Edna Ferber, Howard Lindsay and Ernest Hemingway. He was a literate man with enthusiasms similar to his own and before they parted Tom was trusting him and beginning to believe himself capable of writing his own play.

With a hard job to do he considered where to go. In New York, hearing strange voices through the walls, he had been paralyzed with loneliness. To write with concentration he had to be enclosed by people who were concerned for him and one place he could be sure of that was the house at the end of Beard Avenue. Here he would be encircled by the household's loving insulation.

In Minneapolis at mid-March, he started a new first act. In the beginning his characters kept dumb as stones but within a week he began to hear their voices. A scene took shape, and by the end of the month he felt a glimmer of self-confidence as a playwright.

Minnie Brill's departure (as promised she had gone off to be an actress) left a gap, but in April Helen wrote to say that she was missing him terribly and in fact had a case of "the empty bed blues." She threatened that since he would not come to her, she would to him. Coincidence, or fate, had brought her parents to Minneapolis and a house only a few blocks from Tom's. Unless he forbade it, the moment school was out, she was going to bring the boys west for a visit to grandma and grandpa. Tom thought it a fine idea.

While he was living by choice an orderly, immaculate family existence, a perverse part of him revolted against it. The need to jostle propriety was quickened by Helen's lurid declaration and it prompted him to leave her letter temptingly on his desk.

When Mina Heggen asked Tom about Helen he described her as a friend from New York who was coming to Minneapolis to visit her parents, that she had two children and was divorced. His mother, alarmed and disapproving, did not want to meet her. And that, he realized, was just what he was after—some assurance he could keep the parts of his life separate, and come and go to them as he pleased.

In late May, as fields and lawns turned green and afternoons warm enough for shirtsleeves, Helen came to Minneapolis and Tom began a new, though in some ways retrogressive, courtship. Each evening he would drive his father's car around to the Bells' house, where he was greeted warmly by Helen and with the flirtatiousness of a future mother-in-law by Mrs. Bell, who was busy with patterns and yard goods for Helen's trousseau.

Then he would drive Helen off to the Club Bar, where they were sure to find a table of his friends. They had never seen anything quite like Helen, a bona fide, incandescent, red-headed beauty, seemingly unconscious of her looks, but smart and funny, and they loved her. They huddled around Helen as though she were the only phone at City Hall, sometimes looking up at Tom in wonder to say, "No, Heggen, you can't have this girl. She's too pretty for you."

When he could pry her away he would drive her to one of the lover's lanes near the university and to the radio's dance music they would neck with the fervor of teen-agers, pausing to share their thoughts, Tom's of whether the play would get on and Helen's of the sort of place they would be able to afford in New York. Her heart was set on a house of their own in Greenwich Village. Ultimately, they would climb into the back seat of the car, where Tom would make love to her.

Once, on their way home, Helen looked out at the rows of darkened suburban houses and noted what adolescent behavior this was for a divorcee with two children. Tom began to laugh at the irony, and Helen joined in, helplessly, sharing a suspicion this was not the least of the indignities Tom's ambition would impose on her.

Helen thought it equally odd he did not take her to meet his parents and he had to explain his mistake with her letter. When she asked if there was no way to repair the damage he thought it best to leave that to time. His family lived in a sphere all its own, he explained. She would not enjoy it, and Helen shrugged her acceptance.

In June, Tom finished a first act and mailed it off to Leland Hayward, who, within a few days, called back with some guarded encouragement. It was good. There was some extraordinarily funny stuff in it now, but it didn't build. It was a string of fragments, not yet a play.

Yes, he did have a suggestion about what to do next. Did Tom know the gifted director Joshua Logan? Although only thirty-eight he had a string of hits to his credit. Two, *Annie Get Your Gun* and *Happy Birthday*, were current. He had a reputation as a theatrical wizard. Hayward had just heard from Logan, who was vacationing in Cuba, that he wanted to work on *Mister Roberts*. Did Tom have any objection to his seeing the first act? Tom, who had none, sat back to await the Logan reaction.

In mid-July, Bob Litman turned up, home from his two years' service in Korea and of all Tom's friends, Helen liked him best. He made her laugh over Tom's enthusiastic ineptitude at tennis, at how they had tried to set fire to the Excelsior amusement park, and the famous tale of the Copyreader's Ball where Tom had lost a finger to Bob Wadsworth's clippers.

Bob Litman was not a handsome man but he had a strong intelligent face, a warm voice and his prominent forehead tended to knit with a mixture of amusement and a concern for those around him. He and Helen were so drawn to each other they made Tom uncomfortable. Their heads were always together, whispering. When he found they had left the table and someone said they had gone off together in Bob's car, he had a tantrum of jealousy and when, half an hour later, they turned up, Tom astounded Bob by snatching Helen away to take her home.

"But he was only telling me how much he thinks of you," Helen tried to explain. "We talked about you the entire time." Bob admired and envied him, Helen said. He had spoken seriously about his destructiveness too, warning her it would be a real problem for anyone who cared greatly about him, but above all he thought Tom was God's favorite, the only truly talented man he had ever known. In the end, Tom was shamed by his jealousy and when he saw Bob, managed to turn it into a joke.

Tom also told Bob Litman that uncertainty about the play was making him tense and jumpy and he probably would not be himself until its outcome was settled. He was having trouble sleeping. What had begun as the consequence of fretting about the future was now a full-blown anxiety in itself. Sometimes he lay awake the whole night and could not write the next day.

When he asked about pills that might help, Bob Litman wrote him the first of many prescriptions for fast-acting barbiturates, and they brought Tom the composure he wanted.

Then he heard from Joshua Logan in New York. On the phone his voice was very different from Hayward's, its warmth and enthusiasm an immediate reassurance. He began by saying how much he liked the book and that he wanted to help in any way he could, to turn it into a play. He told Tom that while waiting for his script to arrive he had tried an approach using Doc as a narrator, but reading his, he had liked it far better. Tom's was faithful to the book, not just in incident but in theme.

The problem, of course, was to inject dramatic structure into what he had done, to provide some conflict to link the episodes, and one of Tom's scenes had given him a hunch about that. Now he wanted to explore that hunch with him. How would he like to come to Connecticut for the weekend and have a talk. Any companion he wanted to bring would be welcome.

The telegram Tom sent to Logan went: "Will arrive Friday afternoon with one redhead" and, on a warm, early August afternoon, he and Helen got off the train at the little station of Brookfield Center and looked to see if they were being met. He spotted Logan, a big, commanding fellow with a soft, rubbery look. His bland, oval face was etched with a thin moustache. Beside him was a stylish-looking man, handsome in the vain and spurious way of actors. The two were searching the few arrivals, but overlooking them.

Tom's usual discomfort about first acquaintance was multiplied by having to introduce and explain Helen and the feeling was so intense he would have leaped back aboard the train had it not been moving. But Logan was now coming toward them and, in the next moment, welcoming them and introducing his companion, Alan Campbell. Laughing, Logan told them that Tom's telegram had been garbled into "Will arrive Friday afternoon with one red hat," which accounted for their confusion.

Bundling them into a Buick convertible with its top down, Logan drove them off into the green Housatonic valley. Beside him, Campbell was having a fit over Helen, leaning over to tell Logan in a broad stage whisper, "She's a *dish*, she's a *dish*," and howling gleefully. In the back seat, Tom was feeling slow-witted and sure to disappoint these glib, sophisticated people.

Josh and Nedda Logan's house in South Brookfield was an old saltbox, painted barn red, and it overlooked a field threaded by a brook. Within it was a museum of their travels; paintings and bibelots from all over the world reflected Logan acquisitiveness and a curiosity and appetite for life. In the mementos and the photographs of famous people intimately inscribed lay a record of their remarkable theatrical accomplishment, and it was clear from Tom's first meeting with his deft hostess that she shared in it fully.

Tom recoiled from Campbell's airiness, but Helen liked him at once. She followed him around the living room while he unpacked two cases of apothecary jars the Logans had bought in the Paris flea market and arranged them skillfully. Admiring his worn-looking suit, she learned it had been made for him in London, that he had been married to Dorothy Parker and was, at present, estranged.

But Tom could not find his tongue and the more self-conscious he felt, the clumsier he became. The blush of his suffering, a great crimson splotch like a birthmark, appeared on his cheek and in trying to break his constraint, he studded the air with "shits" and "fucks" which got no rise at all in this company.

Josh and Nedda Logan tried hard to put him at ease with

praise of *Mister Roberts*, while Campbell paid him a private compliment about Helen asking, "Where did you find that gorgeous creature?" Over the drinks Campbell described *his* war experience of defying prebattle orders to dig a foxhole and instead building a vulnerable shelter complete with a window. Nor, he said, did the sneers of fellow soldiers inhibit him from making curtains for it. Tom laughed at Campbell's self-caricature and warmed to him.

Josh told of how, a few months earlier, he had gone to Cuba certain of the directorial assignment for Tennessee Williams's *Streetcar Named Desire*, and then learned it had gone to Elia Kazan. The result was a terrifying depression from which he emerged only through his infatuation with *Mister Roberts*. What touched him, he said, was its central theme, the sadness and dreariness and loneliness of war. He recognized its accuracy from his own Army experience in Europe. Capturing the essence of warfare in such magnificent prose was the work of a genius, he told Tom. "It knocked me out."

By the time Nedda led the party off to dinner, Tom was feeling at home. Late that same evening, Logan took him down to his workroom below the living quarters and told him what he had in mind.

He singled out Tom's scene in which Roberts makes his bargain with the captain, saying, "You see what happens to Roberts when the captain blackmails him into not requesting any more transfers? It lessens his prestige with the crew, turns the men against him, and thus a fulcrum."

It was the classic love story pattern, he explained, in this case between the hundred and seventy-three members of the *Reluctant's* crew and Mister Roberts—the misunderstanding, the growing apart, a revelation of the misunderstanding and, finally, a reconciliation. This was the scaffold of their play.

As Logan talked about the characters and what might be done with them on a stage, Tom was dazzled. He had never encountered such a protean sense of human emotions. It was not the theatrical expertise he had expected, although that was obviously abundant, but an exuberant curiosity and knowledge about life itself. After an hour with the man he knew his hand would assure a fine play and when Logan said, "Tom, why not stay here with us for the rest of the summer, and I'll help you write it," Tom could not believe his luck.

Before they could begin there were preparations to be made in New York. With an invitation to return whenever she chose, Helen resettled herself and the boys on 13th Street, while Nedda went in search of a secretary. She decided a male would be more adaptable to Tom's profanity, placed an ad in the *Times* and made ready to screen applicants at the Logan apartment in the Lombardy Hotel.

Tom went to break off his collaboration agreement with Max Shulman and was astonished to have him refuse. Max insisted that he had put in a lot of work and had the right to share in *Mister Roberts's* future. He wanted to be a party to future rewrites. Furious with him, Tom went back to Brookfield Center, where Josh serenely proposed he find a good lawyer and let him deal with it.

In mid-August Josh and Tom broke ground. Their working day began at four in the afternoon and its first phase, overcoming inertia, was a groaning agony. While Tom slumped in a corner of the sofa, withdrawn, lost in concentration, Logan paced the workroom, his seemingly boneless arms carving the air while he talked about character and emphasis and plot line. Occasionally Tom would break his sphinxlike trance with terse comment.

As the litter of cups, glasses and cigarette butts accumulated they would get a first reward in some moment of recognition and a laugh over it. They could feel momentum. They were underway, supplementing each other. Logan's strength was conceptual, seeing *Mister Roberts* in scene and narrative, while Tom's was in character and dialogue.

The secretary Nedda and Josh had chosen was Jim Awe, a stranger to stenography but a willing learner. He brought to these workroom conferences a collection of Bernard Shaw plays which he read with absorption while Josh and Tom did their sketchwork.

But Awe grew sensitive to their tones of voice, to that quality of their laughter which marked the moment of illumination and he knew the instant to lay aside his Shaw and take up Heggen and Logan. Here his fingers would thread a way across his keyboard with some bit of speech or action that was the play itself.

As the summer wore to its close, Helen visited regularly, sometimes bringing her boys. Nedda and Josh not only liked Helen but saw Tom's reliance on her and were soon active matchmakers. When they saw him being evasive about a wedding date they urged Helen to be firm with him. Josh took Helen aside to explain the practical advantage marriage would bring to her; he assured her the show would make Tom enough money to buy her that house in the Village.

But the effect of his advice was odd. She resisted the interference, telling him that neither things nor money were important to her and, in fact, she was no longer sure she *wanted* to marry Tom.

She was more explicit to Tom. While she admitted he had genuine interest in Tom's happiness, as she had grown to know Joshua Logan in this expectant summer, she had seen his possessiveness. He was a compulsive manipulator of those around him, and she found that infuriating. He revived unpleasant memories of huge Happy Felton and the overwhelming of slender Tom Parker. Just behind the Logan geniality she saw a bully.

"You're in awe of him," she told Tom. "He's not really giving you anything. It's all illusion. His talk is just nit-picking. He's a man to beware." Tom, of course, could hardly agree.

While Helen never lost her manners with him, Logan noticed that at times, while he was talking with Tom, a remarkable change came over her, as though she had swallowed a draught of Dr. Jekyll's elixir. Her ordinarily cheerful face would turn taut and white while her fiery hair seemed to rise from her head, making him think of Medusa.

Work went ahead meticulously. Two-thirty would find them in the workroom below, Jim Awe at his typewriter, reading, Logan peering through the French windows into the garden beyond as his thoughts began to focus. As Tom withdrew into the steamy quarters of the *Reluctant* he would take a long, long drag on his cigarette, slump deeper in the couch and go into a sort of trance, his body limp as a rag doll's and on his face a curiously steady, concentrated smile.

Logan was actor and director and on a good day the room became a corner of his stage and he moved about it, gesturing, saying a speech aloud, tentatively, trying it for stageworthiness. He was absorbed there, oblivious to Tom's murmurings until something he said came right, when he would look at him in surprise and gratitude, perhaps marveling at the violence or laughing at the vulgarity of what he had brought forth.

At such moments they could pass into a state of serene unity, one in which some third force took over and bowled them along, over and around yesterday's obstacles. It was uncanny, as though they had eluded gravity and reached a capability not only beyond Tom's but beyond his and Logan's combined.

Under this spell they said whatever came into their minds. They did not hesitate to propose the most outrageous ideas, sensing that even bad ones gave birth to good ones and that the exchange itself was stimulus. Here, on the ways of their combined imagination, they worked by boosting each other—not thinking alike, but bringing divergent ideas to merge. Their collaboration was becoming so complete they could rarely point to a scene or a line and say, "That's mine."

The joy of it was in getting some joint or fitting just right. When they did, they would laugh so uproariously at their inventiveness that Nedda, in some distant corner of the house, would fear for their reason.

At seven-thirty they would pause for drinks and dinner and then resume at ten, to work through until some small hour of the morning. When they were "hot," Jim Awe urged them on and so, with the help of a drink or two, they kept at it until three or four. Then, a jubilant Logan would bear the day's output up to the bedroom and wake Nedda for her reaction.

But in spite of their self-certainty there was endless fussing, a getting every line perfect before going on, that often seemed to Tom a losing of ground. October found them mired still in the first act's Navy exposition. It got them off to a slow, stubborn start and yet it seemed essential. They had been up against this problem so many times Tom was sure it was an impasse but Josh assured him it was no such thing and suggested they simply cut the Navy stuff. Great blocks of it fell away easily, and to their shared astonishment, it worked.

Nedda's decision on this last of the first act problems was a slow, judicious nod of approval. They were at the summit.

At this point in their progress, Logan realized his own participation had outgrown original intentions and he told Tom about it. In the midst of explaining an idea for the second act he said casually, "Look, Tom, I've just realized that I'm not behaving like the director of your play. I'm really your collaborator. Do you want me on that basis?"

Tom was caught by surprise. At first he thought it was a joke. When Logan insisted he was serious, Tom said he had no idea he would want to share in the writing credit. He had assumed all his devotion to *Mister Roberts* would be amply rewarded with a play to direct. It wasn't possible anyway. With Shulman still involved there would be three authors of the play. No, Tom said, he could not agree to it.

Logan argued that it was only fair. The play's structure would be a new one containing strengths the book lacked and he was providing the greater part of that. He was not asking to share equally in the royalties, only a third, and at the same time Tom would profit from the arrangement. With himself as coauthor they could make a more favorable deal with Hayward.

"Think about it," Logan told Tom finally. "If you don't want me as a collaborator, you go on and write the rest of the play by yourself. I can't go on like this."

Although Helen was in New York, Tom knew well enough what her reaction would be. "You see?" she would cry, all her warning vindicated. "Of course you're right to refuse. Your own draft is perfectly good. It needs no more than what any good director can give it. Tom, you've got to watch out. Don't let him take you."

But they had become a team, Josh and he. Without Joshua Logan, he was going to be lost. He imagined how it would be, trying to get on with it alone, perhaps returning, tail-between-legs, to Shulman. It was true that Josh had been supplying energies and knowledge he lacked. In that sense it was a fair demand. So, feeling empty, as though something vital had just been cut out of him, Tom went down the stairs to the workroom and found Logan quietly waiting.

"All right, Josh," he said. "It's a bargain."

XX

Tom Heggen would always look back on the long Indian summer of 1947 as the best time he ever had, and while Joshua Logan had enjoyed many good times in many places he would often agree with Tom, that it was the best.

In Logan's hill-bound principality, Tom would sleep until noon when some familiar sound, a delivery at the kitchen door or the clink of silver as John Tyndall, the Cuban cook, laid the breakfast table, woke him to another beginning. Like a true wizard with a commission from the sun itself, Josh would set the day's wheel turning. The morning's mail, with its news of the great and famous, might prompt his first joyous whoop over some promise the future held for them.

They would read the paper on the terrace and have a third cup of coffee, making ready, yet putting off for a few more minutes of exquisite agony, the getting down to work.

The amputation which their collaboration agreement had required was less painful, healing well, would probably leave a scarcely noticeable scar. There was plenty of balm for it. He could console himself in believing the agreement was just, that the play was part Josh and whatever reward he would have as director would not entirely square it between them. But above all, Tom could look along their road and see how it stretched from Brookfield Center to every height and pleasure he had imagined—the two of them in fruitful partnership. With Josh's guidance, he was capable of anything.

At three one morning, jubilant over their accomplishment, Tom and Josh decided to call Leland Hayward in Honolulu and read him all they had done. Although it was only midnight there, Hayward declined to be read to and urged them to put it in the mail. He would have it in two days, be able to read it and think about it. Besides, he was suspicious of their elation and Logan's assurance they would be ready for production this season.

But Josh brimmed with certainty. People hungered for a play that summed up the war. A competitor, William Wister Haines's *Command Decision*, was coming into New York now and in spite of disappointing reviews had a tremendous advance. Now was the time for *Mister Roberts*. No telling what the public would want next season. When Hayward pointed out they had no second act, Logan assured him there would be one, and in plenty of time.

Mid-October found Josh and Tom lingering over the opening of the second act, giving meticulous, loving care to the horseplay over the monumental liberty on Elysium. Deciding that Dolan's line in reporting aboard, "Howdy, Mr. Roberts. I'm drunk as a goat," might be followed by his dragging on a real goat, they collapsed in laughter.

Nedda was skeptical. One morning when they woke her to read a scrap of dialogue, the fruit of an entire night's work, she told the playwrights they had better face spending the winter here. Tom agreed, but Logan shook his head and smiled.

One day in early November Nedda announced she was going to New York for some shopping and a night's unbroken sleep, leaving them to their work. That evening, Tom came up with the device through which the crew could arrange secretly for Roberts's transfer, "the Captain's name-signing contest." But this left them stuck in the main "recognition scene," Logan's term for an episode in which a character learns something of such importance that his future is significantly altered.

They solved it together, foreseeing in the same instant that Doc would reveal the men's affection for Roberts in the line "This crew got you your transfer, Buster," and prompt his puzzled "How did you know?"

Tom supplied Doc's "I was a contestant," and they found that funny enough to break up over it. Then, as Awe typed, they said together, "And I was also a judge," and at that they howled, pointing at each other and hopping around the room, hysterical with their joy. When they pulled themselves together it seemed as though their characters had taken over the writing. Lines sprang from their mouths and Tom and Josh flew on, simply recording. In a few hours they had scene five, in which the crew awards Roberts its Order of the Palm and shyly bids him good-by. Then they hurried on to the final scene, that of Roberts's death, finishing the play at four that same morning.

It was a purging, elating moment. Logan broke out a fresh bottle of Scotch and they sat drinking it, delighted with themselves. The writing of Roberts's posthumous letter remained to be done, as did a certain amount of cutting, but the play was whole and they knew they done something fine together.

If certain subtle qualities in the book had been lost along the way, the play had many new strengths and virtues. They had succeeded in making Roberts talk. They had provided the unifying story. Most important, they deepened the emotional impact. They had been able to dramatize the poignant, and so often repressed, affection between men. They had done it simply, and without embarrassment. It was an accomplishment due in part to their having developed a similar admiration and affection between themselves.

They called Nedda in New York to sweep aside her sleepy protest that this was her night off, and to read her the end of the play. She was soon fully awake saying, "Oh yes, right. That's it, Josh. That's good, Tom," and sharing in their jubilation.

When dawn broke over the hills they were still too full of excitement to think of going to bed so Logan set up his projector, drew the shades against now broad daylight and showed Tom a film he had made. It was of a trip to Patagonia with his friend John Swope.

During the three months Tom had spent in Brookfield Center, he had progressed from awe of Joshua Logan to admiration and dependency. Most surely he had come to love him. At times he felt one with him, in taste, age, instinct and feeling. But for all the intimacy and affection, for all his recognizing Logan's brilliance as an enormous simplicity and self-reliance, he realized how bewilderingly complex the man was.

Logan's father had died when he was an infant, leaving him to grow up under the genteel, yet dynamic influence of his mother and of an equally devoted younger sister. It made for a family emotional situation similar to Tom's, just as their maturing found similar channels in college. At Princeton, Logan was head of the Triangle Club and spent his summers on Cape Cod with the University Players, a theater founded by another Princetonian, Bretaigne Windust, and Charles Leatherbee of the Harvard Dramatic Association.

The members of that company, all unknown at the time—Margaret Sullavan, Henry Fonda, James Stewart, Mildred Natwick, Myron McCormick, Norris Houghton, John Swope—were to be the nucleus of Logan's vast web of theatrical friendship.

At Leatherbee's invitation he quit Princeton for an apprenticeship to Constantin Stanislavsky, founder of the Moscow Art Theater, and he came back from Russia a proselyte, convinced the American theater was strangling in convention and artifice. He believed its salvation lay in massive infusions of subjective emotion. His new zeal found the New York theater in its worst Depression doldrums and he endured a parade of disappointments before his first success as a director, of Paul Osborne's *On Borrowed Time*. He consolidated it the same year, 1938, by directing three musicals, *I Married an Angel*, *Knickerbocker Holiday* and *Stars in Your Eyes*.

It was his own thirtieth year, one of such reassuring success that he made the trip to South America with John Swope and, at the end of it, took his spectacular psychological plunge.

Returning to direct Osborne's *Mornings at Seven*, he collapsed in its midst and went on to a pair of failures, *Two for the*

Show and *Higher and Higher*. In the midst of new self-doubts he married an alumna of the University Players, Barbara O'Neil. The marriage was shorter lived than Tom's.

The pace of Logan's mind accelerated so that he could absorb pages of dialogue and poetry at a glance. The energy that drove him was runaway. Night after night he did not close his eyes. Reluctantly acknowledging his "nervous breakdown" he entered a hospital but it was no refuge from irrational fears or his vertiginous seesaw of elation and depression.

He would drop out of sight for weeks, eluding friends and associates and the promises he had made them. Then Merrill Moore, a Boston psychiatrist whom he found sympathetic, started him toward recovery. At Dr. Moore's urging, Logan committed himself to a sanatorium and after a year and a half's absence from the theater he returned to direct the Rodgers musical *By Jupiter* in 1942. It was the first of his string of triumphs.

To Tom, even Logan's psychiatric adventures seemed enviable, the mark of his sensitivity and his compulsion to get to the truth of things. With him, he felt invincible. If the fall had been the best of times for them, the winter ahead would be even better. He was going to undertake a theatrical apprenticeship with this unerringly brilliant man with whom he had found so warm and mutually nourishing a kinship. It was more than a man had a right to expect.

In late November, when Tom came to New York, he took a room at the Lombardy, where the Logans kept their pied-à-terre. This was another wonder for Tom. Nedda's Christmas present to Josh, a 1914 Utrillo of a town square, hung in the bedroom and Dorothy Hammerstein had taken its blues to redecorate the apartment. It was an exquisite stronghold and when Tom turned up here, reporting for work, he found a new tension in its perfumed air. As hopes for *Mister Roberts* multiplied, scores of other people, strangers, appeared. When Logan wasn't talking or listening into it, the telephone was always ringing.

Logan's steam was up. Tom found him conferring with Jo Mielziner about the set, describing his needs for the principal playing area on the ship's deck. When he said that he wanted to lower eight passed-out sailors onto center stage by cargo net, Mielziner objected, "That's a half-ton of actors, Josh. A half-ton of actors requires a half-ton of counterweight and a steel beam to support it."

"How much?" Logan asked.

"Two thousand dollars," Mielziner replied without hesitation.

Nodding, Logan picked up the telephone and called Leland Hayward to report that they could have the cargo net for two thousand dollars.

"Will it bring two thousand dollars' worth of laughs?" Hayward asked.

"Yes," Logan assured him.

At the Leland Hayward office Logan busied himself with the logistics of out-of-town tryouts, the choice of a theater, making up the budget and the list of potential investors—matters so bewildering to Tom he felt underfoot. But between the calls and interviews, Logan assured him that a mountain of work on the script lay before him and it would commence with casting.

Meanwhile Tom fretted with inactivity. The summer's experience had left him in high gear. He was in a state of perpetual exhilaration much like the one Logan had undergone before the war, and the worst of it was he had so little to do. Strolling among the Christmas shoppers it seemed everyone else in New York was urgently busy. As he puzzled over how to fill these days he could not get over the suspicion that his real partnership with Logan had ended.

Before coming to town Tom had asked the law firm of Howard Reinheimer to untangle Max Shulman from his performance rights and now a meeting between them was called. Shulman, backed by his own lawyer, claimed to be no more than reasonable in insisting that he share in the proceeds of *Mister Roberts*. They had both signed the letter of agreement. He had put in a great deal of work on the strength of it and he was willing to put in more, but not to be shut out.

Tom found scarcely any logic and less decency in this argument. He saw only that his old scourge was demanding a free ride. *Ski-U-Mah* hairs, grown longer and meaner, stood out on his neck and an exchange of acrimonies between the two led the lawyers to do their talking for them.

When the lawyers had finished their maneuvering Shulman retained, for a limited time, 12.5 percent of *Mister Roberts's* dramatic rights and Tom retained a fury at him that would simmer permanently. Once when Logan was making haste toward a February opening Tom turned apathetic about it and explained, "It's Shulman. If we open in February it'll be before the cut-off date. He'll take part of my royalties."

Advised not to worry about it, that it was money that would only go in taxes, Tom grumbled, "It isn't the money. It's somebody using me. I'd rather have the money go to the government than to that bastard."

A fresh feeling of vulnerableness caused Tom to seek theatrical representation of his own and he chose Margot Johnson of the A. & S. Lyons agency. She promptly appealed to Houghton Mifflin to relinquish its 15 percent commission on performance rights. Paul Brooks, who had been hoping for news of a novel, felt this confirmed his fears, that Tom was lost to fiction. Reluctantly he consented to release the dramatic but not the motion picture or television rights. When the Reinheimer office objected, pointing out these rights were interdependent, Hardwick Moseley came down from Boston to talk to Tom.

Tom got on well with Moseley and brought Helen along to dinner with him, explaining they were about to get married. Moseley said that Houghton had no wish to poach on his play income, only to publish more Heggen books. While this openhandedness impressed Tom he was freshly schooled in the professional attitude and left the ethics to Margot Johnson. He did promise a new book as soon as he had *Mister Roberts* onto a stage and so out of his system.

Tom's fretfulness about the play brought him small comfort from Helen Parker. He would offer her the news from uptown, perhaps Logan's latest candidate for the role of Roberts, and, as a matter of course, she would challenge Logan's wisdom and his own courage to resist him. Helen and Tom would be arguing again.

Tom ended one such quarrel—it was over the fitness of Robert Montgomery to play Doug Roberts—by shutting her out of her living room to call Montgomery in California. He emerged an hour later to find her entertaining friends, Delmore Schwartz and Milton Klonsky among them, in the hallway outside her apartment. They were all furious with him but Helen was in a particularly steamy rage.

She was no longer tolerant of their unplanned future and continued to shop for a house. When she found a place she wanted him to see, he would refuse, saying it was too expensive or too inconvenient. Whereupon she would accuse him, justly enough, of not wanting a house at all.

"Not yet," he told her. "We've got to wait and see the notices."

"But what kind of life do you expect us to live?" Helen asked. "Like gypsies? How long will we be making love at my place? Or in the back of cars? How long will you be shutting my friends out of my living room so you can use the phone?"

Tom told her that first, before settling anywhere, he wanted to travel just as Josh and Nedda did between shows, storing up new ideas. He had seen nothing of the world. If *Mister Roberts* was the hit he expected they might begin with a look at Europe. If they found a place they liked, they could stay a while, long enough to do some writing.

"But I've got *children*," Helen cried. "What do you expect me to do with Tommy and Bruce?"

"You can put them in a school someplace," he said, "a school in Switzerland. Then you can see them when we're not traveling."

To Helen that sounded like a Logan idea and she made it the opportunity for one more assault on his yielding to him.

Sometimes Tom denied his deference to Logan. At others he admitted he admired him above all men and ticking off the evidences of his genius Tom confessed he could no more prevail over him than innocence could over knowing.

But Helen scoffed at Logan's expertise. That was all in Tom's mind, she said. He had become helplessly, perhaps pathologically dependent on him. She chipped away persistently trying to free Tom's half-conscious recognition that she was right, that he put up with indignities, deceived himself about them and wallowed in the pain of it all—like a patsy in love.

They would still be quarreling about it as they taxied uptown to join Josh and Nedda Logan at the Lombardy and take part in the regular evening exercise of interesting backers.

Although some big investors—Richard Rodgers, Oscar Hammerstein, Irving Berlin, Howard Cullman—were already in, *Mister Roberts* was still shy of its hundred-thousand-dollar nut and raising the balance was a primary urgency. Helen was becoming a liability to this effort. In her early visits to Brookfield Center she had saved her opinions for Tom's ear but now when Logan and Tom agreed about something they would notice her grimacing, clearly tormented by dissent. Logan was no longer amused and when prospects arrived, Nedda would often lead her off to the bedroom while he read the play aloud.

Helen was at large during the reading for the Howard Lindsays and when Logan finished Lindsay objected to the ending, saying you could not have a tragic ending to a comedy. There was a silence and then, as Logan cleared his throat, Helen burst out, "But you don't understand—that's the only *possible* happy ending," and for a moment all that could be heard was the drawing of the Lindsay pursestring.

Later, Helen and Tom would drift from one nightclub to another. After midnight they would quit the Stork and head downtown for one of the gay bars on MacDougal Street or a particularly bizarre transvestite cabaret off Second Avenue which appealed to Tom as the ultimate in depravity.

They made love rarely now and when they did it was joyless. This was due in part to the drink which had become a necessary anesthesia to him. Even a pair of Seconal capsules would not put him to sleep so he tended to drink his way to unconsciousness. But the chilling of their ardor had an additional source, in their changing relationship.

Although Helen was naturally pleasure-loving and permissive, Tom's obliviousness to the future awakened her cautionary instincts and she was inching from the role of playmate to that of guardian. There was a suspicion of the responsible, protective mother about Helen now which was just what Tom sought. But it was neither a stable nor a promising situation, tending as it did to lead Tom toward more infantile behavior and Helen toward disgust.

He had never punished his health so consistently. Even the abundant doses of whiskey brought him only a few hours of restless sleep from which he would struggle into the new day with a fierce headache and a queasy stomach. The medicine was a midday drink or two, enough to start the cycle again.

He had begun to shy from mirrors for a glimpse of himself often shocked him. He weighed only a hundred and twenty pounds and clothes hung loosely on his five-foot-eight-inch frame. The hollows in his face had deepened and the high cheekbones and square chin sharpened as though they might be painful against the pale skin.

His thoughts, which rarely strayed from *Mister Roberts*, see-sawed between a crest of pride and possessiveness, and a trough of fear that it was being abused, if not actually taken from him. Following Logan's example he could be objective about these anxieties, see them as abnormal and recognize it was time for the advice of a psychiatrist.

He chose a man with a particular interest in creative people. This was Leopold Bellak, a big, confident fellow with a glowing enthusiasm for *Mister Roberts*. Tom began seeing Dr. Bellak regularly, describing his trouble in sleeping, his professional problems that lay tangled in the relation with Logan and the personal one that focused on Helen Parker and their fitful marriage plans.

Dr. Bellak asked to see Helen and she came to him for several private sessions, which she claimed to enjoy since they gave her an opportunity to talk about herself at Tom's expense. But if Helen regarded the experience indifferently Tom took to his analysis with enthusiasm. Bellak's interest in the creative temperament made their sessions less therapy than literary conference and Tom enjoyed probing his past in such knowledgeable company. His visits to Dr. Bellak's Fifth Avenue office fed Tom's vanities and made him feel productive, as though he had put in a good hour at the typewriter, and they sustained him until the larger excitement of the *Mister Roberts* production began.

One afternoon in late November Logan asked Tom to come to his apartment to meet Henry Fonda and David Wayne, saying that although he was preparing to read Fonda the play, there was no hope of getting him. He had agreed to be on hand only because he hoped to get Logan to direct him in a film. It was Wayne whom Logan hoped to interest in playing Roberts. But on arriving he too seemed distracted, glancing at his watch and speaking of another appointment.

Then, as Logan began to read, losing himself in the characters, both Fonda and Wayne became transfixed, then helpless with laughter. When Logan finished the two actors lay back gasping and mopping their eyes. In regaining his voice, Fonda's first words were "I'm going to get Leland and Lou Wasserman to get me out of my commitments and I'm going to play Doug Roberts."

Whereupon David Wayne left hurriedly, without explanation. Thus, in the midst of congratulating himself on Fonda's decision and the solution of his main casting problem, Logan had misgivings over the offense to Wayne. When he reached him that evening he apologized, saying he had no idea Fonda would react this way, that it had all been an accident. Wayne cut him off, saying, "But I don't *want* to play Roberts. I want to play Pulver."

The remaining casting problems dissolved. Within two days they had decided on Robert Keith for Doc, Nedda's brother, William Harrigan, for the Captain, and announced an open call for the rest of the cast. New York teemed with young actors just out of service and eager for work and nine hundred of them turned up at the stage door of the Belasco.

Tom sat beside Logan in the orchestra watching them line up, forty at a time. Explaining they would be playing bare to the waist and there was no known way to fake chests and muscles, Logan asked them to take off their coats and shirts. Two hundred sightly torsos survived the cut and he asked these to read.

For the first time Tom heard *Mister Roberts* lines spoken on a stage and even in their clumsiness these boys, crowding each other, were becoming the characters he had drawn three years earlier. Sometimes the words sounded remote, no longer his, but at others they were more, an exhilarating multiplication of his mind, broken from a two- into a three-dimensional world.

Rehearsals began the day after Christmas and Tom came with all the anxiousness of a hopeful actor to take his seat in the second row beside Logan's. Josh himself seemed to be everywhere at once, on the stage explaining to Jo Mielziner, the set designer, that because of the rush to battle stations the ladders must be made of steel, then pacing the aisle with Hayward, studying the figures. Now he was sitting on the apron telling the cast that body make-up looks fake and in order that they glow with convincing Pacific tans he was installing a huge sunlamp in the dressing room. He wanted them under it at every opportunity.

In the theater, ready to bring the typescript to life, Logan was multiplying and dividing, extending himself into the infinite details of production. His energy was ever-replenishing. As the huge, irrepressible man bounded about the baleful theater it was as though every light in the house was creeping up to full brilliance.

At center stage he was describing the opening—the ship at dawn, the crew asleep belowdecks, then Chief Johnson's entrance, pantomiming a peep through the Captain's porthole, then a squirt of tobacco juice onto the palm tree—all his gestures bigger than life, yet precise, and real, giving glimpses of the magical things that were building in the corners of his mind.

Yet he did not impose on his actors. As he blocked out the action he would show them, and then let their own concept of the role emerge. He would try anything, even their most doubtful suggestions. Pausing at Tom's side, he explained that the moment of an actor's finding his characterization was his most vulnerable one, a time when he must be treated tenderly, as though in the crisis of some illness.

Within a few days Fonda found his Roberts. It was his natural role of soft-spoken authority, admired, followed by others unconsciously. The danger, Logan thought, lay in his overdoing it. Unlike most actors, Fonda tended to move and to face upstage, always understating, never making the normal, direct appeal to the audience.

Logan held every line, every cue and stage direction in his memory. If an actor faltered, he supplied him instantly. "Hank," he would say to Fonda, "you're not linking those thoughts. When Dowdy asks, 'You going over his head?' make the link in your mind. 'No, I'm going around his end, I hope. I'm going ashore.' " And Fonda would try it, tasting the words, and nod.

Surely, like some worshiped teacher among his students, Logan moved from actor to actor, giving each total attention, speaking of a gesture, an inflection, or an Equity ruling on rehearsal time, or a debatable extravagance as though each were at the forefront of his mind. Even Tom did not escape him entirely.

Sometimes he would look out into the orchestra for him and call for a new line, and Tom would improvise one. When Logan requested a first-scene speech to reveal Roberts's yearning for action, Tom promptly provided a passing task force with "Carriers so big they blacked-out half the sky! And battlewagons sliding along—dead quiet . . ." so that Logan marveled at his brilliant, short-order service.

In the battle-stations scene, Steve Hill gave the part of Stefanowski a characterization of his own, a quiet confusion in the midst of general hubbub, and Logan asked Tom's opinion. At Tom's nod, Logan said, "Okay, Steve. It's good. Play it that way," as though Tom were a partner to his decisions.

But such deference was rare and when Tom, suffering from neglect, put himself in Logan's path he was urged to work on the troublesome final scene, to find a way of giving Roberts's posthumous letter impact without going mawkish, and to plan on cuts, for they were running overtime. Alone, Tom found neither chore appealing and he waited, brooded, feeling useless and in the way.

Also he was feeling a sense of loss about the play now, something like the reaction of a mother whose child is taken from her to be reared scientifically by the state. Watching *Mister Roberts* take shape at Logan's urgings on the tongues and in the movements of the actors, he began to feel some resentment. Isolated as he was from the directorial act, he sensed a distortion, possibly a depreciation of his original intent. Logan, he decided, was aiming for belly laughs.

In spite of assurances that rehearsals would make them a team again, he found Logan increasingly elusive and in mid-January Tom quit his catbird seat for one in the rear of the orchestra. Here he sat alone sipping from a bottle of whiskey, an occasional disapproving glance from the director only adding an agreeable dimension to getting quietly potted. Moodily watching developments on stage he felt impotent, as though he were tied down and being grazed upon by a big, soft-nosed camel, gently, almost lovingly, nibbled away.

Helen Parker would find him here and slip into the adjoining seat with a reproachful glance at the bottle. Although out of habit she chided him for his passiveness she seemed resigned to it. She did not dispute his assurance that once this ordeal was over all would be well nor was she skeptical of his promise of a long, tropical vacation, what he described as "three weeks of blissful rest and sunshine."

Peter Cary was another visitor and as he watched a first run-through at Tom's side, he decided the play was nearly faultless. "I see what the play's about," he told Tom. "It's 'kicking-the-old-man.' That was only an episode in the book, but the play *is* that, a mutiny against paternal authority. And it's punished. The punishment is death."

Tom agreed, saying, "Nobody else has noticed that," but it was not entirely true, for Dr. Bellak had noticed. Even with so good a friend as Peter Cary, Tom could not admit to having a psychiatrist.

If Tom was spoiling for a clash with Joshua Logan, the lighting up of *Mister Roberts* intervened. In rehearsal the show was beginning to resemble Doc's description of war—overwhelming all the conflicting, individual moods and sweeping the whole company along in its own exuberant one.

The last rehearsal before going on the road was held on January 18, a Sunday, and some theater people were invited to watch. Surprisingly, half the orchestra filled and while the stage was bare and the cast performed under worklights, without costumes, this sophisticated audience laughed like children. The laughter, which was clocked at twenty minutes, constantly stopped the action and made the show run a full three hours without an intermission.

At its end the guests stood and clapped and whistled until the bewildered cast stumbled back and lined up on the stage. Fonda, caught as he was leaving the theater, was dragged on to take a bow protesting, "Are you crazy? This is a rehearsal," and to his astonishment looked out at a cheering, weeping audience.

The New York opening was set for the Alvin theater on the night of February 18, and before leaving for the New Haven tryout, Tom spent an afternoon drawing up a list of people he wanted there.

At the top of the list he put his mother and father as well as Ruth and Carmen and their husbands. Their presence would bring him the fullest pleasure. Realizing that opening night would join the childhood world of his wishing with this present one of accomplishment, he wondered how many others he dare include. Why not the stepping stones of the *Digest* and Houghton Mifflin? Why not Carol Lynn's earnest one as well? It was a time when most of the elements of his life could coincide, triumphantly.

While he guessed he could hardly bring Helen Parker in on his arm to meet his family, she could not be excluded. He depended on her volatile spirit more than he liked to admit to her or, for that matter, to himself.

As he tried to decide which other women to include, he was characteristically irresolute. No one girl seemed to supply his need.

They were forever withholding and disappointing him, sending him back to the others, as in a dance of ever-changing partners.

Deeply involved with Helen though he was, Tom could never exclude the possibility of other women. The nervy, bright-mouthed girls he spoke to in offices and bars always tempted him. Although he was not afraid to try, even on a few hours' acquaintance, his success with them was only moderate. They resented the machine-like determination with which he went about a conquest. He made it an exercise in which the girl surrendered more individuality than virtue and invariably she found it distasteful.

Also, Tom closed no door on the girls out of his past. He often thought of Carol Lynn, or Frenchy, wondering how they were and what they were doing. One morning he was awakened by a call from Frenchy—her voice warm and, as always, on the edge of laughter. She was in New York, had found a job at Franklin Spier, a book-publisher's advertising firm, and was sharing Marjorie Lundberg's apartment in Jackson Heights. A few hours later she came smiling into the basement bar of the Ritz on 46th Street to join him. She was plainer, more shapeless and utilitarian than he remembered but still radiantly ready to enjoy the story of his adventures with *Mister Roberts*.

Her own were not funny. Her husband, Bob Martin, had been killed in flight training but she spoke of it without self-pity. It was what she had come to expect of life. When they parted he had her telephone number and she his promise to call. Being with Frenchy was as enlivening as ever and Tom mourned that there was not more of him to go around. But it was always Frenchy's luck to be left out. Tom felt he could not add her to his party for the opening.

When Peter Cary told him that after some months at home in Okmulgee Carol Lynn had taken a job at *Coronet* in Chicago and just recently had been transferred to its New York office, Tom felt a powerful need to see her again. He tried her office number several times without reaching her and finally, just as he set out for New Haven, left her a message—that a ship named *Reluctant* had called.

Nor had Minnie Brill left his life. Adapting to her career as a radio and television actress, she had changed her first name to Holly and, when she announced she was going to change her last too, by marrying Charlie Irving, producer of the program "Search for Tomorrow," Tom felt she had forsaken him and was furious with her. That all his old girls had tenure in Tom's heart was tied to his wariness of commitment. Each, in her way, loved him and thus was an option he wanted to keep open, at least until February 18, when all evasiveness that went with having to prove himself would end.

The road tour began in New Haven on January 22 and the audience, drawn from the Yale community and thick with veterans, took to *Mister Roberts* like a long-lost buddy. The line that capped Pulver's sexual bragging, "Why don't you just get a job as a fountain in Radio City?" drew a roar that set the Shubert rocking on its foundations, and when the curtain fell there was no further doubt. *Mister Roberts* was a big, raucous hit.

The party which followed in Leland Hayward's suite at the Taft was a celebration and yet, ironically, it seemed that everyone had advice to offer on what was wrong with the play. There was a persistent complaint that the Captain was unbelievable.

While Logan listened patiently to the criticism he told Tom that everybody wants to play doctor when the patient is healthy; it was the sound of children at their games and he should ignore it. What *was* on his mind, he said, was the need for cuts. They had run forty minutes overtime.

Tom failed to see how they could take out more dialogue and said so. Every line served some necessary function. To this Logan replied, "It's equally painful for me, Tom, but we can't let the customers out after midnight." They must make new cuts, he said, based on the reaction of the New Haven audience. Now they knew where the big laughs were, the little ones would have to go.

Tom objected that the biggest laughs were often the Logan directorial touches such as the Captain's watering the palm tree. Did he propose cutting dialogue to save the horseplay? While he still could not openly disagree, Tom's Norwegian stubbornness was emerging and Logan sensed it. No, of course he did not propose any such heartlessness. He understood Tom's feelings and swore to protect the play. Deciding Tom had been spooked by the would-be playwrights around them he assured him there would be no important changes. They would not even listen to suggestions while here in New Haven and, turning to Leland Hayward, he included him in the pact.

But Logan's cutting went on so that at the end of the week, Tom spoke to Hayward about it, asking him to do what he could to alter Logan's determinedly farcical course. Hayward recalled his own promise not to offer advice but Tom argued that the play itself was at stake.

So, while they rode toward Philadelphia with Tom, Logan, Hayward and his wife, Nancy, gathered in the parlor car, the producer spoke up. "Josh," he asked, "when are you taking out the George Abbott touches?"

Logan appeared to be stunned. "What do you mean, Leland?"

"The sight gags," Hayward explained. "The Captain's entrance for one. Mannion's crepe-paper diaper for another."

"Don't listen," Logan said, putting his hands over Tom's ears. "Don't listen to him." Reminding Hayward of his promise, he asked him why he had said so divisive a thing—why in front of Tom?

While Logan did moderate the Captain's entrance, costuming him in a less garish bathrobe, Tom continued to feel he was bent on sacrificing the shades of meaning they had so painstakingly installed. Tom felt nothing more could be pared without draining the essence and when Logan asked further cuts his instinct was to cup his testicles. He could not get rid of the idea it was not just brevity Logan was after; that the shears were intended for him.

As the tour continued, Logan attracted new satellites, comrades of past campaigns, who stayed to scout a performance and offer gratuitous advice. The day after the Philadelphia opening Logan beckoned Tom over to meet one of these, a splendidly tailored fellow he took to be an actor.

It was Emlyn Williams, whose *Night Must Fall* he had admired a dozen years earlier. Esteem withered on Tom's tongue as he heard Logan explain that an overtenderness toward the *Mister Roberts* script was getting in the way of necessary surgery and, handing Williams a copy, he asked his advice.

Tom brooded over this development, believing it a maneuver of Logan's to have his own way with the play, and he was further stung to learn that Williams had found it "Too sentimental." When Tom protested that a man who disliked the play ought not to be tampering with it, Logan defended his friend as a brilliant technician and, incidentally, he had agreed that Tom was a talented writer.

The praise soothed Tom until Logan mischievously added that Williams found him shy and moody. "What," he had asked Josh Logan, "lies under that boy's dangling forelock? Do you suppose it's a birthmark? A scar? A mark of shame?"

Tom did not laugh at Williams's remark. He was hurt by the ridicule and determined to veto his suggestions but before he had the chance both Logan and Hayward declared that Emlyn had done the impossible, cut eleven minutes' running time from the show without doing it the least damage. For Tom the worst of it was they were right. He could find no fault with Williams's cuts.

As *Mister Roberts* bowled on toward Broadway, Emlyn Williams stayed with the show. His now-celebrated facility with the script, his high spirits and comradeship with Logan were such an invasion of Tom's territory that he grew sullen and irritable toward everyone.

In Baltimore, their last port of call before New York, Leland Hayward announced a cast party at the Oasis, a splendidly depraved place where, it was rumored, the girls stripped down to nothing. The indications were those of an obligatory evening but when it came time to go, Tom lingered alone in his room, drinking. Emlyn Williams's needling wit was threading down his own tongue and making him unfit for the hilarities getting underway.

In time, though just barely, the whiskey did its trick, opening his eyes to the sight of a grown man sprawled on a hotel bed playing a child's sullen game, and showing him the only way out of the room.

Reaching the Oasis he heard the noise of the party and made his way toward it. He searched among the faces until he found Williams's, then took the chair beside him and raised his forelock. On his skin Tom had printed with a penpoint, "I'se dot Negro blood."

Williams laughed, then Logan and Tom joined in. At that fine, hilarious moment it seemed to Tom that all his differences with Josh were insignificant, possibly even imaginary. They rolled away like smoke on the wind and he was ready for a real celebration.

Despite all encouragements the strippers disappointed their audience by clinging to their G-strings. One did pull hers down at David Wayne, who responded by unzipping his fly. When the intimidated girl backed off, Logan rose to make him the Royal Order of the Palm speech for valor in the face of the enemy. It seemed the funniest thing that had ever happened and the party thundered on to rival the crew's liberty on Elysium.

Back in New York Tom made last-minute arrangements, sending a blanket invitation to his *Digest* friends for the Tuesday night preview and persuading Helen Parker that with all the demands, his family's in particular, the opening would make on him, she should make up her own party with the Byfields.

He told her that immediately afterward they could begin a reasonable life together. The trip south was taking shape. They were to start in company with the Logans but leave them for a leisurely, premarital Caribbean honeymoon. Helen's suggestion of Haiti had been overruled by the Logans since there were no beaches there, but she agreed to Cuba, where the Logans had been previously. Helen was curiously yielding. All the fight had gone out of her.

Also, Tom reached Carol Lynn. Her voice was familiar and assuring yet guarded. She was reluctant to meet him but in the end agreed. They had been apart two years and now, coming to his table in a restaurant, she was shocked. With his eyes sunk deep in their sockets, cheeks hollowed, he might have been his own ghost. Anxiety and the liquor and barbiturates with which he contained it were written in his glassy eyes. Seeing her dismay, Tom admitted to being miserably tired, maybe even ill, from months of all-night work on the play. He scarcely slept at all, he told her, but the ordeal would be over on Wednesday night and he was going away for a long rest.

By contrast Carol Lynn was fresh and whole, clearly recovered from such damage as he had done her. At the same time he could feel she was still vulnerable to him and the desire and need for her, long packed away, burst forth. He told her what was the moment's truth, that nothing had changed his love for her, that no matter what happened it would be that way always.

While Carol Lynn clung to her own reserve, some small promise was made. After the play perhaps, after Tom was rested and could guess at the future, they would meet again. She agreed to come, with Vera Lawrence and the Hectors, to *Mister Roberts's* opening-night performance—though not to the party afterward.

On Tuesday night, watching the preview from the back of the house, Tom felt that the last fault had been hammered out leaving the play a dreadnaught. Nothing could stand in its turbulent way— and yet Tom had been detached. He felt as if he had wandered into a strange theater and beheld another man's work.

Afterward in the lobby old friends from the *Digest* clasped his hand to say that he had a great hit, that it would win the Pulitzer Prize and to see if he remembered them or if the anticipated swelling of his head had squeezed them out. *Something* had. Memory refused him names and his tongue would not budge beyond a "Thanks, glad you liked it." In his own ears he sounded like a recording.

Tom's worst fear of opening night was the threat it posed to a lifetime of juggling his worlds to prevent their collision. His Beard Avenue was going to intercept his New York and he believed that impossible. It defied some natural law and was bound to end in disaster.

Incredibly, on the day of February 18, the Heggen family did pass through the barrier to stand, life-size, in the lobby of the Lombardy. The effect on Tom was devastating. Mina was proud and expectant while T.O. was bewildered, awed by the deference of strangers and the anticipation of great events in the air.

But they were like children on a visit to a department store Santa Claus, eyes gleaming with the excitement of it all yet without a notion of what was real and what false about it. They had no understanding of the actual difficulty of his accomplishment and their failure to understand that was a measure of how far he had come. It was light-years.

He felt faint anguish, a remorse like homesickness that his parents were too innocent to understand how he had overreached them.

Backstage at the Alvin, Logan looked up from a conference at the switchboard, noticed Tom was toting a bottle and took him aside for some advice. He said it was likely Tom would be called out for a bow tonight and urged him to save his drinking until after that.

As the house filled Tom saw his family being seated, saw them recognize Helen Hayes nearby, whisper, stiffen with wonder. He found Carol Lynn and Vera Lawrence in the second row, then watched the actors getting ready, the lights going down. He stayed backstage until the first act was underway and the tide of laughter rising. Then he went to the rear of the house and watched the stateroom scene, long enough to sense it was in perfect timing. Then he walked out through the lobby into 52nd Street, where a cold, gritty wind blew bits of newspaper along the gutter. A surge of laughter pounded the closed doors at his back. On the opposite pavement a lone man clutched his coat at the neck and made his way toward the corner and Tom watched until he had disappeared into Eighth Avenue.

During the intermission he went down into the dressing room to share in the cast's buoyant sense of victory and there was persuaded to be made up for his bow. He was childishly delighted with the result. In the mirror he saw himself one with the actors, as well as the promise of a Caribbean rebirth. He wore his grease paint proudly into the wings to wait for the final curtain.

It came down to an outburst of applause. The din mounted and even after a score of curtain calls the audience refused to let *Mister Roberts* go. Finally Henry Fonda stepped through the drawn curtain and, as the house grew still he said simply, "This is all Tom and Josh wrote for us. If you want, we can start all over again."

This brought a new peak of applause and then the cry of "Author!," once, twice, then picked up in chorus.

Logan had come up beside him and Tom had intended to go out front now. He had even thought of a line to say but in this instant, stubbornness held his feet. He was not sure he had written all the play they were applauding but he was damned sure it was more than half, and he was not going out there as half a playwright. He looked up at the waiting Logan, recognized his eagerness for the acknowledgment and, catching the sweet scent of revenge, shook his head. Logan turned his back and walked away while Tom listened to the diminishing, gradually disappointed cries until they died.

As the theater cleared, friends in fur and Chesterfield overcoats invaded the wings in search of him. Tom clung to the *Reluctant's* deck while the audience dissolved and illusion collapsed all around. A group from Houghton Mifflin encircled him and he found himself explaining his make-up, how you looked washed out before the footlights if you didn't wear it. Max Shulman bobbed through, smiling congratulations, saying it was great, that he had been exactly wrong about the play and that what Tom and Logan had done was exactly right.

Later, as Tom stood with his mother and the rest of the family piling into a rented limousine, Carol Lynn and Vera Lawrence came up to say good-by but instead relented and came along to Leland Hayward's party.

The Lombardy's Jade Room swarmed with strange faces and Tom was relieved to have Joshua Logan's mother, Susan, gather up his relatives, settle them in a corner and begin identifying celebrities for them. She was ticking them off—Gertrude Lawrence, Elsa Maxwell, John Hersey, Jennifer Jones, Moss Hart—as he drifted toward the bar.

He acquired a full bottle and then looked around this celebration of his play for someone to talk to. Across the room Logan was surrounded. Tom recalled his midsummer anticipations of joining the aristocracy of the talented and successful. Bleakly he realized he was at its dead center and did not want to meet anyone or hear the compliments or endure the awkwardness of being polite to acquaintances. There was no possibility of conversation without a core of flattery and insincerity. What he felt most poignantly here was loneliness.

With all the elements of his past and present summoned, he did not seem to belong with any until he sighted the Carys. "We feel like city bumpkins tonight," Peter Cary said, making him laugh, as did Barbara, who was gazing at the Billy Roses and pointing out the enormous diamond necklace suspended over Eleanor Holm Rose's celebrated décolletage.

The Carys were fascinated but not awed and Tom felt no need to apologize to them for being drunk, which he soon was, nor to explain the bottle in his hand nor the make-up on his face. They would not ask what he was going to write next and he could tell them, knowing they would accept it as honesty, that he knew the show was a hit and was not worried about the reviews.

Helen came in with the Byfields. She wore a full-skirted dress of black slipper satin and lace which he had not seen before and he thought her as stunning as any of the celebrated beauties in the room. It pleased him to see heads turning and lips forming "Who's that?" as she passed. Joining her party, Tom said her dress was stealing the show.

"You haven't seen this before?" Helen laughed, then added with cheerful malice, "I guess you never take me anyplace swell enough for it. It's not new, you know. Ernie gave it to me last birthday."

With some help from Carol Lynn, Mina Heggen had identified the red-headed girl with her son. Similarly Helen had established the "Grant Woodsy" couple as Tom's mother and father and was intrigued to learn that the woman talking to them was Tom's ex-wife.

As he lingered at Helen's table Tom could feel the urgent glances of recall from his mother and in one headstrong moment it seemed both plausible and necessary that he close the gulf between them. In the next he and Helen were sauntering over to join his family and Carol Lynn.

Some of the actors were entertaining the Heggens with the story of Daisy the goat's glorious moment in Philadelphia. She had turned her back to a matinee audience and, with a pleasurable quiver of her tail, cleared her bowels. The laughter had been such that Henry Fonda sank to the hatch cover, head in hands, until he could be heard again. It brought a good laugh here as well.

Then Carol Lynn spoke earnestly of how the cast had become the characters of the book tonight. It was uncanny, she said, to be standing here talking to them. They seemed to have stepped right from *Mister Roberts*'s pages. What had moved her most was the realization they weren't acting, but *feeling* it. She had seen Henry Fonda weep during the Order of the Palm ceremony, and Dowdy too, when he learned of Roberts's death, had shed real tears. She had seen them splash on his shoes.

Even through the praise and through his alcoholic insulation Tom could feel the antagonism between these women of his. As his mother and his former wife smiled coolly at his scarlet woman little hairs bristled on every neck.

When she said good-night, Carol Lynn told Tom to get some rest and he said he would. "I'm going to sleep for three weeks now," he promised and urged her not to run off.

"I'd love to stay," Carol Lynn said with a saw-toothed glance for Helen, "but *I* have to work tomorrow."

Helen Parker was beside him when, just after one, the first of the reviews came in, a proof from the *Herald Tribune*. "A superior novel has been fashioned into a magnificent play," Howard Barnes had written, ". . . has heart, humor, profound meaning and an almost intolerable tension . . . a tumultuous and moving drama that no one who witnesses it will soon forget." Then some typed copy from the *Daily News* and a phone call from the *Times* confirmed it. *Mister Roberts* had been declared a huge, thumping hit.

When Tom looked around the room he found his family gone off to their rooms at the Madison and the party over. Upstairs, with the early editions scattered around the floor, the day's ironic disappointments and his protection against them were loosening, peeling off like sections of an old husk. If he was drunk he was also marvelously clear-headed and he could feel for the first time in weeks. He was hungry and thirsty and felt capable of a new book or a new play—and meantime he was fairly fulminating with desire.

As Helen rustled the magnificent, shining dress over her head he saw that what had floated its skirt was a pair of petticoats, tiers of starched, white material. They fascinated him and he put them on. Together they laughed at his reflection in the mirror until, at the height of their hysterics, they met in a passion as wild and hungry as that of their first night together.

XXI

Later that same day, February 19, Tom got around to the rest of the paper and found on the page following the *Mister Roberts* review a news story about Joshua Logan's future plans. He had proposed to Richard Rodgers and Oscar Hammerstein that they write the score, book and lyrics for a musical version of James Michener's *Tales of the South Pacific*. Leland Hayward was to produce and Logan would direct the play for presentation next season.

While Tom knew that Logan had been probing Michener's book, as he had *Mister Roberts*, for a dramatic line, he had no idea he was so far along with it, nor that he was to be so firmly excluded. This was especially painful since he believed Logan's interest in the Michener book owed much to *Mister Roberts*, that in Heggen's Elysium Logan had first seen the dramatic possibilities within the Northerner's dream of paradise.

Tom tortured himself rereading the article. Calta, the *Times*'s theater man, was equally surprised by the suddenness of Logan's decision, for the director had only just confided he had no immediate plans. Tom wondered if the announcement could be a reproof and public humiliation for him.

So a bleak sky encroached on his day of triumph. With every critic in town pillaging the dictionary for superlatives to bestow on his play, Tom was indifferent to their praise. Worse, with his masochistic nerve laid bare, last night's raves now seemed patronizing.

The reviewers seemed to agree that his own contribution was the lesser, a springboard for the Logan acrobatics. In the *Times*, Brooks Atkinson observed that the play had been cast with so much relish and directed so spontaneously that it gave the impression of not having been written at all, but improvised on the stage during rehearsals, "under Mr. Logan's idiomatic direction."

In the *News*, John Chapman wrote that since he was one of the very best directors in the American theater and knew just what sort of material a director needed, every line of the dramatization bore the "signature of Mr. Logan."

The *Time* magazine review was dominated by the photograph of a quizzical, wrinkle-browed Logan. It was framed by comment that as a story and a show, *Mister Roberts* was not much and was not meant to be, but as a human picture it was magnificent, due largely to coauthor Logan's brilliantly telling direction.

Time summed up the collaboration: "Author Heggen brought his successful short novel to Logan last August after deciding he didn't like his own stage version. For three months they hacked away at it together. Says Logan: 'Nothing could stop it. It got up on its two feet and walked by itself.' More accurately, 6 ft.-2 in., 200 lb. Josh Logan shoved the play into shape."

For six months Tom had been painting over the cracks in his relationship with Joshua Logan but there was no longer doubt of it—Helen's prophecy was fulfilled.

But even these melancholy thoughts could not survive the optimism which surrounded Tom. The advance sale of *Mister Roberts* stood at four hundred thousand dollars and the line at the Alvin box office swept out the door and halfway down the block. His phone jingled with good news. Fonda, backed by the cast, was on the cover of *Newsweek* while he, alone, was to be on the *Saturday Review's*.

Also he could make out beneath his injured feelings a larger truth, that any good writer is in the private, time-consuming business of mining and this could never keep up with Joshua Logan's headlong pace. The thought that he was capable of independent work comforted him. It did rouse a familiar anxiety over what he was going to do next, and it was Joshua Logan who offered him reassurances about that. When last in Cuba he had met a man named Kendrigan with a story about some American soldiers-of-fortune. Possibly there was an idea for a play in it, one with particular appeal to Tom.

This was one more lure for a Cuba already laden with them. He had come to believe in the South as though it were a sybaritic yet fully authenticated Lourdes. He was sure its warm sun and clear sea held rebirth for the emaciated roots and branches of his spirit. When Logan called to say he had reserved four seats on a flight to Miami for Wednesday, February 25, holiday promise overcame all resentment and Tom told him that he and Helen were ready to go.

However, over the weekend, Helen's boys came down with measles and feeling she must see them through the worst of it she agreed that Tom should go ahead with the Logans as planned and she would join them when she could.

Tom ordered her up some consolation, a huge basket of flowers from Irene Hayes, the six-foot palm tree which had been Hayward's opening-night gift to him and a model-airplane kit for the stricken boys. Helen responded with characteristic astringency. He must have forgotten that Tommy was only eight, she told him when he called to say good-by. The instructions were enough to tax a sixteen-year-old. It hardly mattered though since Tommy, as a measles patient, had to be kept in semidarkness. Well, it was the sentiment that counted she supposed. And the tropical foliage was fine. Surrounded by it as she was she felt already in Havana.

Flying south, toward Hemingway's island, Tom told the Logans of his admiration for that celebrated author and wondered about chances of meeting him. Logan explained that he had met him in 1940 while married to Barbara O'Neil. Her brother had boxed with Ernest in Paris. Just last year, with Nedda, he had visited Ernest and Mary at their Cuban place, Finca Vigia, and

Ernest had showed him three chapters of *For Whom the Bell Tolls.*

There was no assurance he was there but Logan promised to inquire through Hemingway's cronies. Two of the closest were Manuel Asper, who would be their host at the Ambos Mundos, and the Jim Kendrigan who conceivably would give some purpose to their holiday.

Arriving, Logan rejoiced to find his chauffeur of earlier visits. He was a wild-eyed fellow with a yellow grin who piled their luggage into his royal-blue touring car and drove them off to the old city and the Ambos Mundos.

A few hours later they were on the hotel's roof garden, a marvelous jungle of huge, potted geraniums, enjoying its magnificent view of the city when an old man wearing a peaked cap with built-in sunglasses appeared. Logan introduced Jim Kendrigan, the local *Time* stringer and coach of the Havana University football team. He was in his sixties, half-blind, his face netted with small wrinkles, and yet he was a powerful block of a man, instantly reminiscent of Hemingway.

Ernest, Kendrigan said, was not in Cuba although he was on his way from Sun Valley and would be arriving any day. Then, encouraged by Logan, he spoke of his own adventures. In a flat, down East voice punctuated by sly winks and a fishlike pouting of his mouth, he described the shooting down of his friend Manolo Castro in the street outside Havana University.

Castro had been a young Cuban with a determination to liberate the neighboring Dominicans from the oppressive rule of Trujillo. The assassination ended the conspiracy in which Kendrigan himself had played a part. For many months he had been host to some American mercenaries, former Flying Tigers, who were to fly arms to the Dominican insurgents. When delay made his charges restive, Kendrigan borrowed Horas Felicias, a fine house belonging to the *Reader's Digest* roving editor J. P. McEvoy, billeted the flyers there and supplied them with Havana's choicest rum and whores. The party ran more or less continuously until word reached Kendrigan that the McEvoys were returning, whereupon whores and Flying Tigers alike were turned out and a platoon of cleaning women summoned.

Tom's and Josh's eyes met in recognition. Here at the twitch of the Logan divining rod was a story for Tom's idea about veterans and their reluctance to come back from war. Flying the Hump had made modern buccaneers of these American boys, showed them how to live their childhood fantasies. Now this crack-brained plot was giving them a second shot at it, putting off the going home to dreary jobs in dreary towns. War love put them in sharp contrast with the Reluctant's crew, but then Roberts was a war-lover. Hell yes, he could write about the Tigers. When Tom said he thought there might be a play here, Kendrigan agreed to help and invited him to his apartment to talk about it.

On Saturday night when Tom and the Logans left a cool Havana bar to meet Helen Parker at Rancho Boyeros airport, they were feeling like natives. They spotted her from the balcony. She wore the harassed, February look of a New Yorker and they could hardly wait for her to share their enthusiasm for Cuba. Waving merrily, they shouted, "Hello Parker!"

While Josh spread pesos around, Nedda slipped past the immigration officials to expedite her release. Then, over protests about her winter clothes, they swept her into the blue touring car and off to see Horas Felicias, explaining it was the scene of a play Tom and Josh were going to do.

Although the McEvoys were not at home a houseboy showed them through the gaudy foliage of the central courtyard and then into the cantina, where he gave them drinks. This room opened through an arch of Spanish tiles onto a terrace and here he brought them steak sandwiches. In the sensuous Cuban evening Helen found the others' feeling of liberation contagious and, although she still complained of her clothing, allowed herself to be swept on to Sloppy Joe's.

It was after midnight when they arrived at the hotel and while Helen unpacked Tom explained she had only time to change since they were going on to see the performance of the famous Chrisantos.

Tom liked to rationalize his partiality for depravity as a blow against pretense and he explained that if Chrisantos's show was as described it must be the ultimate bare rejoinder to propriety. He supposed there was some catch though, a conning that would separate them from their pesos and leave them ridiculous. That was what a boyhood in the Midwest led you to expect.

Chrisantos performed in a once-fine mansion, now a Havana whorehouse. They were greeted at its door by a good-looking, red-headed girl, shown into a brightly lighted room at the front of the house and seated, a bit shame-faced with other tourists around a big bed. Helen admitted to a feeling of sorority with the redhead and wondered if she was to be a performer. As it turned out the girl who had the female lead was a different white girl chosen by the audience.

Chrisantos himself was black and, as superman, no disappointment at all. He appeared in a zooty white suit, disrobed to display his huge member and passed around the audience offering the ladies an opportunity to feel his awesome erection. Nor was there any fakery in his performance with his partner. In the midst of it Tom rose from his chair and went forward for a better view.

Filing from the steamy room he marveled, jabbered about Louis Mayer's advice to him in Hollywood and how Chrisantos pointed the way to untold wealth if only they could work out an agreement with the Hays office.

But Nedda and Helen seemed depressed by the experience and as they gathered around the table of a downtown bar Tom felt foolish about his enthusiasm. He ended by getting so thoroughly drunk that his next recollection was of an agonized midday awakening and the discovery that Helen had gone sightseeing by herself.

By afternoon he had revived enough to take her to meet Kendrigan. He lived on the Malecon in a *fin de siècle* apartment building recently crowned with a Bacardi sign and crumbling into pungent ruin. Kendrigan, white-stubbled, eyes red-edged, looked even scruffier here in his lair. The dark rooms were hung with photographs of his football and girls' softball teams, and he explained a pretty teen-ager, with a wink and his wheezing laugh, as his "protégé," a Panamanian whom he was teaching English and the piano. He had given up on history, he said, since she refused to accept that Panama had played so small a part in it.

When he got around to the Flying Tigers Kendrigan revealed that although the project had ended with Manolo Castro's death, some of the Tigers tried to revive it with impulsive schemes. One was to paint Dominican markings on their own planes and bomb Havana. Another called for conquest of the entire West Indies. Naturally they came to nothing. When Tom asked about the individual Tigers Kendrigan provided an enthusiastic but erratic recollection of the principal figures and how they got along with their Cuban counterparts.

Although Tom filled a dozen pages with notes he had very little to go on. Still, he felt the essence of character and situation for a play were in Kendrigan's grizzled head and only needed to be coaxed out. Kendrigan agreed to continue the talks as well as show them some Havana night life and meantime led them upstairs to meet a friend, a painter named Rene Portocarrero.

Portocarrero was a dark-skinned, bearlike fellow with mischievous black eyes and a beak of a nose and Helen was soon intrigued by his delicate, complex paintings. Then, by a chameleonlike reflection in her voice of his Spanish cadence and word, she revealed an equal enchantment with the man. When she insisted that Tom buy something, perhaps one of the abstracts, he grudgingly chose a gouache of flowers, the most representational of the canvases. Helen and the painter were disappointed but conceded that as the buyer the choice was his.

When he found that Helen was curious about voodoo Portocarrero assured her that Cuba was a special province of Satan and promised to take them to see one of his rites.

Helen's flirtation left Tom vengeful and when she encountered friends, a couple in Havana for a trade conference, he described Chrisantos's performance to them and, in spite of Helen's refusal to go along, dragged them off to see it. That evening, the

Ross, 1947, in a Houghton-Mifflin publicity photo.

UNIVERSITY OF DELAWARE
FOREIGN STUDY SECTION
ELEVENTH FRENCH GROUP
SEPT. 15, 1933

In September 1933, Ross left Bloomington to spend his junior year at the Sorbonne. It was the following spring that he had his first vision of a great American novel based on his mother's family in Indiana.

Opposite: Christmas 1933, Ross and Curt Lamorey, also at the Sorbonne, went to Italy for the holidays. This was taken as they crossed the Bay of Naples to Capri.

A picnic at "The Cove," in Rockport. Ross is seated in the center, Edith Hellman at the left, and Steve Tryon, the host, is standing at the right.

The barn in Pigeon Cove, Massachusetts, where Ross and his family stayed for two summers, 1943 and 1944, while Ross worked on his novel.

Ross, Vernice and the children at Indiana University in 1947. Ross had been teaching at Simmons College in Boston, Massachusetts, since 1941, but in 1945 he got his first advance for *Raintree County* and moved back to Indiana.

"Murmuring Maples," the Lockridge home in Bloomington from 1924–1937.

Frank Lockridge, Mary Jane Ward and Ross at a family get-together in 1947. Mary Jane Ward, Ross's cousin, had already published *The Snake Pit* with Random House. To Ross she was both colleague and competitor.

Ross and Vernice's home on South Stull Avenue in Bloomington. They bought this home in December 1947 after a long vacation in Southern California, where they'd gone in the hope of curing Ross's depression.

Ross at a publication-day autograph party (January 5, 1948) at L. S. /
an Indianapolis department store. This is the last known photograph of
before he committed suicide. It appeared in the local papers.

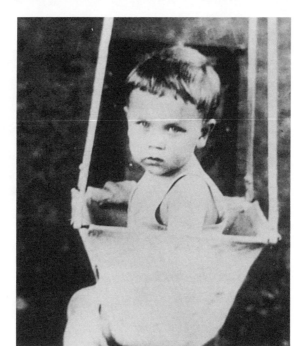

, age one, in Fort Dodge,
a.

lio photograph taken in
4 of Tom and his sisters.
men is three, Ruth eight
Tom five.

Tom, Ruth and Carmen at
their grandmother's farm in
Renwick, Iowa, in the summer of 1930.

Frances "Frenchy" Solem,
1940's. In 1939 Tom transferred to the University of
Minnesota, where he met her.

Tom in front of the Heggen home on Beard Avenue in Minneapolis.

Tom and a coworker at the copy desk of the Minnesota *Daily*, 1940. He worked there as an editor and columnist until he graduated.

In August 1942, a few days before going into the Navy, Tom married Carol Lynn Gilmer in Pleasantville, N.Y.

Tom with his mother, Mina, and sister Carmen before the fireplace on Beard Avenue, 1945.

In 1944 Carol Lynn joined the Red Cross, hoping to catch up with Tom in the Pacific.

U.S.S. Virgo, the last of four ships Tom sailed on in the Navy, and the model for the U.S.S. *Reluctant* in *Mr. Roberts*.

U.S. BUREAU OF SHIPS

Tom in uniform, 1945. This was Carol Lynn's favorite picture of him, and she always carried it with her.

Joshua Logan and Tom at Logan's home in Brookfield Center, Connecticut. As Logan talked about the characters and what could be done with them on a stage, Tom was dazzled. He had never encountered such a protean sense of human emotions.

Leland Hayward, producer of the play *Mr. Roberts*, and Tom in 1947, during rehearsals.

Henry Fonda, Tom, Leland Hayward and Joshua Logan discussing Mr. Roberts, 1948.

Tom, Herman Bernstein (in background), Henry Fonda, who played Doug Roberts, Jim Awe (in foreground) and Joshua Logan, during rehearsals for Mr. Roberts.

In July 1948, Tom sailed for Europe on the S.S. *Topa Topa*, a freighter. He hoped the trip would help him begin to write again.

Tom on the S.S. *Topa Topa*, 1948.

BOTH PHOTOS: GEORGE DANIELL

second of their "honeymoon," ended as drunkenly and separately as the first.

When he saw Josh and Nedda off to New York on Monday, Cuba reeled beneath Tom's feet and he promised both Logans that he and Helen would leave next day for the wholesome life of Varadero and the Kawama Club and that they would return rested, with an armful of notes and a start on the Flying Tigers play.

That afternoon Portocarrero came to the hotel and took them off to see a voodoo ceremony. On the way he explained that in Oriente province at the far end of the island the secret religion was practiced in earnest. The *nanego*, or priest, presided over ceremonies characterized by hypnotizing drums, drunkenness and sexual acts. Those present did enter a trancelike state in which their personalities changed; the weak became strong, the modest shameless. It was said that human sacrifices were still made. However, they would not see anything so dramatic today. Here in Havana the sacrifice was likely to be no more than a black rooster and the atmosphere that of a tourist trap. Nevertheless, Helen was fascinated.

Their journey took them across the bay by boat, then by bus and foot up a steep hill in Regla, where they entered a littered courtyard. All they found was a shed strewn with feathers, a makeshift altar at one end and at the other an ancient black man sleeping soundly. Clearly there was no matinee today.

This fizzling of Portocarrero's promise unmuzzled Tom's growling resentment. Helen had changed in Cuba. She was a different woman, pants-crazy and bent on provoking him, serving notice that his money no longer kept her, that she was fed up, that he had lost proprietorship. What was it all about? She was here, he reminded her, at his expense.

But they had no difficulty in laying their argument aside when they found Manuel Asper in the lobby of the Ambos Mundos. Tom asked about Hemingway and the manager proudly showed off the workroom where, in February 1939, Hemingway began *For Whom the Bell Tolls*. Yes, Ernest was back, Asper told them.

After a winter in Idaho, he and Mary had just returned to Finca Vigia, their house at San Francisco de Paula. The tower, with its writing room at the top, had been completed during the summer and Ernest was pleased with it, showing it off as the latest of his toys.

A visit? Well, it was not easy to say. His irascibility was well known. The feud with Dos Passos, who, incidentally, was staying at the hotel, still smoldered and now he had quarreled with Faulkner. No—one could not request an audience. Understandably Ernest did not wish to be among the historic sights. On the other hand he was often in town and dined regularly at the Floridita, a few doors down the street. Found there he was apt to be approachable.

Awaiting the elevator was John Dos Passos, and Tom spoke to him, reminding him of their ordeal in Boston. Dos Passos emerged from his characteristic shyness smiling, recalling the day in his gentle, nearly inaudible voice. As they talked Tom waited for him to speak of *Mister Roberts*, on which, two years previously, Dos had wished him good luck. But he did not mention it. His attention had turned to Helen. To Tom's annoyance, he flirted with her openly.

Tom wondered if Dos Passos had forgotten, if he lived in such self-absorption that he failed to connect, or was simply embarrassed at not having read the book. But as they parted he decided that Dos remembered perfectly but that there was some special agony reserved for celebrated young American writers—growing old —and it turned the most charitable of them misanthropic.

Tom felt uncharitable enough himself to accuse Helen of wanting to seduce Dos Passos, indeed any writer with a reputation. Her feeling of intellectual inferiority was pathological, he told her. She would never pick up literary distinction in bed.

In spite of his contentiousness Tom felt venturesome. As evening fell on the city and the rattle of ice in shakers drifted through the shutters, he suggested the Floridita for dinner. They had barely settled in the restaurant's bar when they heard the sonorous words of Spanish welcome at the door and Ernest Hemingway swept in shepherding his slight, gray-haired wife and tall son.

Half a drink later and prepared for a snub Tom and Helen walked to the Hemingway table and presented themselves. The Papa smile burst upon them like sudden sunshine. He introduced his wife, Mary, his son, Bumby. Chairs were brought, as were stemmed glasses, brimming with his own special, double frozen daiquiris.

Hemingway asked knowledgeably about *Mister Roberts*, Tom's Navy experience which led up to it and then the Pacific war as a whole. As he spoke of naval strategy and the crucial sea battles Tom grew silent, listened with the others to discourse about the stupidities of the military mind, the commonness of venality in man and finally his old adversary, the sea itself.

When Helen mentioned her book reviewing Hemingway said that Bumby was at work on a book about trout flies and thus all here were professional writers. So, with fraternity established there was no question but what they dine together. The captain was summoned to escort them and the *conjunto*, the strolling musicians, serenaded the party as it trooped into the dining room.

Hemingway seated Helen beside him and she basked in the triumph of her own big-game hunting. Drawing him out first about the Logans, then the kind of women he liked, she caught a shining Hemingway compliment. He didn't like those hard, businesslike girls, he told her. "It's good to be strong, but in a woman that's not enough. Now you're strong, but you're gentle too."

He went on expansively, focusing on Helen while Tom took little part and felt his hopes for this meeting, this scarcely conceivable fulfillment of youth's dreams, dissolve.

When Helen mentioned that they had met his friend Kendrigan and heard the story of the conspiracy, Ernest laughed. Of course he knew about it. In fact when the Havana police got wind that the American mercenaries who were to fly arms to the Dominican insurgents were billeted in the house of an American writer they assumed it was his place and raided Finca Vigia. He was away at the time and a Cuban lieutenant bore off his gun collection and scared Miss Mary half to death.

But of course the scheme was crack-brained and meaningless, not to be taken seriously. Jim Kendrigan was a dear old friend and he had no wish to speak ill of him but love for melodrama was driving him far from reality.

When Tom muttered his own interest in the Flying Tigers story he felt a change in the air, a chill breeze from across the table. There were no words of injunction but through the rummy mists Tom was drawing around himself he was sure he heard a pounding of the Hemingway hammer, posting his lands.

It was a painful irony, this meeting with Hemingway, for it ended in worse than disappointment. He wondered what he had expected of it—that they could meet as equals? Swap a few tricks? Despite Ernest's booming cordiality he felt patronized. The man was a crusher. He'd even gathered in his girl. Tom was left with a cold resentment toward Hemingway, more determined than ever to go ahead with the Tigers play.

The following evening, when Kendrigan came by the hotel to ask if they would enjoy some Cuban music and dancing, Tom said yes it sounded fine.

Kendrigan took them to Chori's Rumba Palace, a nightclub on the outskirts of Havana, to see the performance of some friends, a dance team called Alberto and Clara. Although Chori's was an ordinary sort of cabaret Helen was enchanted. The atmosphere recalled good times at the College Inn and travels with the Felton band. While Tom watched she made friends with the manager, his wife and the musicians.

As she snapped her fingers and swayed her hips to the gourdy rhythm, Tom sensed Helen was looking for trouble and he saw her discover it. Alberto had been one of Kendrigan's athletes, a skillful dancer, tall and sinister-looking. When he asked her to dance Helen immediately kicked off her shoes and went to him. With an exalted expression she danced with Alberto, round and round the floor. Tom, his own feet stubborn blocks, got drunk again and ended the evening in a jealous rage at her.

He awoke to the torture of his head and stomach, sure he had been poisoned. Beside him Helen breathed serenely. Although she had drunk nearly as much as he she was lost in child-sleep from which she would wake refreshed—and envy joined his torments.

When Helen awoke to his groaning she packed their bags and got them out of the hotel where Logan's driver was waiting to take them to Varadero. The trip was a long one, some ninety miles following the coast eastward through Matanzas, then along the spit of beach which reaches out from Cardenas toward Florida.

The Kawama Club, where Joshua Logan had spent both his honeymoons, was all he had promised. The guests were mostly Americans, prosperous, middle-aged couples from Greenwich and Shaker Heights, yet there was no need for them to fraternize. Isabel Silva, the hearty woman who ran the place, brought them to their cottage. It was set apart from the others and gave onto an immaculate white beach, shaded here and there by ceiba trees and leading to the clearest, bluest water they had ever seen.

For a day they lay under a benign sun, basting themselves with oil and dipping themselves in the sea. In the evening they were sparing with drink but had a good dinner. Back in their cottage Tom got out the notes he had made with Kendrigan and then drowsed into early sleep feeling he had taken a first step toward renewal.

One luminously mild evening they hired a jeep and drove into Varadero to stroll the main street. Tom pointed out a hand-embroidered blouse in a shop window and when Helen admitted she liked it he towed her inside. While she tried it on he asked the saleswoman if it was possible to have a matching skirt. It was. Driving back to their cottage along the sandy beach road, Helen clasped the package in her lap and it seemed they had gotten off on the honeymoon after all.

But their lease on paradise was a short one. At first it was just the weather. A parchment of clouds screened the sun and a wind that had roots in Minnesota rattled the palm fronds and whirled the sand in painful vectors. They scowled at the sky and put on sweaters.

Each morning's breakfast tray brought a copy of the English language *Havana Post* and on the fifth day of their stay Tom came across an account of Ross Lockridge's suicide. Although he had never met Lockridge, Tom reacted with a sense of crushing loss. Three months earlier Paul Brooks had sent him *Raintree County* and although he had objected to its effusiveness he had admired its humor and energy and the undeniable talent it reflected. He had seen the huge Houghton ads, read of Lockridge's financial success and suspected what it might be doing. Here was the terrifying proof that Lockridge had indeed been his brother.

His death had cheated them of meeting and of sharing their parallel experiences. He realized he had been putting off a letter to him, believing that chance would bring them together. He was certain Lockridge had had some secret for him, or vice versa, an insight which in the sharing could have helped them both.

Tom went to the barman as to a mother's outstretched arms and by noon he was drunk. He would not eat and took out his new torments on Helen, who could not understand what Lockridge's death meant to him nor why, when the weather turned fine again, he sat shivering in a sweater. He could no longer bear the smug, vacation sounds of tycoons nor the sight of their wives in funny straw hats and it annoyed him that Helen could lie for hours on the beach, make a feast of every meal and turn handsomer before him while he drank his way toward stupor.

A sleepless night ended in a predawn plea for Helen's attention. Then first light would single out the untouched notebook for his self-reproach. He could not look at it. Far from setting him on a path of his own, the Kendrigan business had made him more unsure of his judgment, more agonizingly in need of Logan's guidance than ever.

By midmorning his rancor took shape in some willfulness toward Helen. He would make the little cottage ring, blaming his cold on her insistence that a swim would sober him and restore his appetite.

His first drink was a necessity to lay the shame and confusion of their quarreling. He would while away the forenoon in the bar and at one, when the first twitterings could be heard in the dining room, he would stagger forth as guests silently snatched small children from his path.

Helen had his luncheon brought to the cottage but he was unwilling to eat or even look at it. He took to wearing her beach robe, because it irritated her and was a good way to spark a quarrel. But Helen stayed aloof. In the afternoon she went off for long walks along the beach to return more insulated than ever.

The steady drinking, an open appeal for Helen's help, was generally ended by his stomach. Late in the evening it would rebel, vomiting up the day's intake with as much pity-inducing retching and gagging as he could summon. Helen would sit by, thumbing a magazine.

At one such turning of his innards he left the pool of vomit at her feet. When she had cleaned it up she told him evenly that he was trying to show her she *had* to clean up his mess. She didn't. She was not bound to him. She was neither the mother nor nurse he required.

Early on their seventh day at Varadero, feeling helpless yet clear-headed, Tom admitted he was much worse. Instead of giving him back his health, Cuba had made off with more. "Helen," he pleaded, "take me back to New York and get me into a hospital." He needed to be an invalid for a while, he told her. He needed to be taken north and told what to do. Helen called for reservations and a car, and that same afternoon they flew back to New York together.

The Logans, who had gone to Europe with the Mielziners, had left Tom the key to their apartment at the Lombardy but once Helen had put him to bed there she was impatient to get away. When Tom protested he did not want to be left alone she said, "I have to go to Tommy and Bruce. You're always forgetting I have two boys."

"I'm not forgetting anything," he argued, "but they're not expecting you for another week."

She went angrily, slamming the door and leaving him to brood over their trip. As trial honeymoon it had failed most tauntingly.

She had been like a filly in heat, flirting compulsively. He thought that she would have gone off with any man who asked, that she had hung on to him only for the joy ride and the opportunity to meet other men.

While he could excuse her faithlessness on the animal level, he knew her obsessive attraction to literary reputation. It was such that he could read her dimming interest in him as a judgment. She was leaving him because he was washed up as a man and as a writer.

He knew reputation for the bubble it was but he had also learned its nourishment, how it fed the vain hungers and the deep ones too, quashing fears of rejection and threats of stronger men and giving promise to the need for love. You could hardly fail to cherish it, even though it was so liable at any moment to burst. Nor could you fail to defend it when threatened. Tom's only weapon was an equally wounding judgment of Helen—as literary nymphomaniac.

Next day, when she looked in on him, she brought along an invitation to a party Macmillan was giving for Arthur Koestler, just arrived from England. Tom said he didn't feel well enough to go. It was just the kind of contentious, alcoholic evening he had to avoid for a while, but she insisted. It sounded like fun and she wanted to meet Koestler. She would go, without him if necessary.

The mail had brought her another piece of cheerful news, she said. A year and a half earlier she had been in a taxi accident and at last there had been a settlement. While the lawyer had helped himself to half the sum, six hundred dollars remained and she had decided what to do with it. She was going to take herself and the boys out of the city for the summer. She knew of a barn for rent in Rockport, Massachusetts, and had already agreed to take it.

Tom's pent-up feeling of being forsaken burst forth. He told Helen that in putting her hands on two cents she could call her own she was quitting him and at a time when he needed her most. It was a vicious betrayal and clear indication she didn't care a damn about him.

"That's not true," Helen told him. "But, Tom, you don't

want a wife. You don't even want a mistress. You want a mother to look after you."

Tom shook his head. "Come on, Helen, say it. You don't think I can write anymore."

"That's not true either," she replied. "But I can't take the responsibility for it. I'm not cut out for a martyr. I resign." She picked up the pile of mail she had brought and walked to the door. Looking back for what was to be their last glimpse of one another she said, "There's nothing else I can do."

A farewell bubbled up from his own despair, words that Helen would never forget. "All right, you psychotic cunt," he said and turned away.

XXII

Tom learned that Helen had really left him. She had gone from the Lombardy to Jim Putnam's party for Koestler and not only met but enchanted the visiting novelist. They had left the party together and become as inseparable a pair as he and Helen had been.

Openly he made fun of her appetite for authors and cursed her for her perfidy. He learned that she had taken up with John Dos Passos too and that when Dos had brought her along to lunch with Edmund Wilson, the crusty critic had been furious at Helen's prattling interceptions of his own conversation. Tom could laugh at that and persuade himself he was well off without her.

Still, he missed her. He thought of her each time a phone rang or he caught a glimpse of a girl with red hair or, in the midst of a sleepless night, when it was clearest he had been cast off. She had that sense of timing, he realized, for getting on and off boats. It was a new experience for him—being dumped.

He had not made any lasting friendships in New York; for nearly a year he had lived within an acquaintance borrowed from the Logans and now he felt as disenfranchised and alienated from it as he did from the preparations for *South Pacific*.

Success had only intensified his plaguing insecurity. At literary and theatrical parties where new ideas, new girls swarmed around the buffet tables, he holed up in a corner and defied every effort to coax him out. With entrée everywhere he shied from new people and unfamiliar situations.

Not only had success failed to weave him into a new fabric of relationships it had cut him off from the old ones. Friends from home, even the relatively sophisticated ones from Pleasantville regarded him as changed, too rich and sought after to be counted the same fellow they had known. They suspected he wanted to hear flattery, which he did, and they supplied it and it sounded like hypocrisy, which it was, and trust became falsehood.

For all Tom's maverick behavior he lived within and depended on social structure. Like a pool-swimmer he needed that unyielding rim for the push-off. Beard Avenue with its hardscrabble budget, Sunday-school morality and belief in an honest day's work offered Tom the resistance for his daily act of mutiny and the generating of his special fuel.

Success thrust him into an environment without stricture. New York was a town where a fellow could drink and whore the night away, then sleep the clock around without raising a single eyebrow.

Still, he could not retreat; there was no way home again. In New York's bright, worldly light he could see old associations, his family in particular, as outgrown. They too expected the patronizing of a homecoming hero, and he obliged. He loved them. He needed them. At the same time, he found them simple as children and being home bored him stiff.

Mina Heggen rejoiced for Tom's victory, understood its material rewards and recognized it was carrying him into a world she could neither enter nor comprehend, but she could not see beyond *Mister Roberts*'s surface of comedy. She could not see it as an outburst of Tom's heart nor read its inner message. Instead of breaking down the emotional wall between Tom and his mother, *Mister Roberts* raised it.

Worse, *Mister Roberts* was making Tom a fortune. As the weekly paychecks for thousands of dollars accumulated they made a joke of T.O.'s warnings and his diligent, lifelong pursuit of financial security.

Success not only bore off Tom's primary need to struggle and admitted him to a vast landscape without traffic directions or even streets but it made him into a new, public person. He was beginning to feel that this recent Tom was an artifice, that he had left the real one, the solitary unknown, somewhere behind.

He knew that his work was bigger than he and that what gave him wholeness and inner direction was a viable relation with it, one immune to success or failure. Still the yearning for recognition was such a temptation and hazard. How easy it was to be jealous of others enjoying reputation and so admit that desire which was bound to strike at the circle of self-sufficiency. Now he could see plainly the act of the bitch-goddess as the severing of the relation between him and his blank page.

But Tom's block had a deep taproot in that he had succeeded all too well in demolishing his rival. The instrument, *Mister Roberts*, carried so clear an image of his resentment that Tom's principal reward was in guilt.

Awareness of his patricidal act paralyzed Tom. Starting to write was never easy for him. He had gone for months without producing a line but he had always been sustained by a sense of fertility, some stirring within. But now in the aftermath of *Mister Roberts* he was barren. He knew that he could not write without the stimulus of Joshua Logan.

It was the worst kind of block. It acknowledged that his gift, which he had taken as much for granted as youth and endurance, had been on temporary loan—flown because he had abused it. As he confided to Carol Lynn, "I don't know how I wrote *Mister Roberts*. It was spirit writing." His hope for a craft that would sustain him had collapsed.

Yet he knew that rescue lay in work, which was to say his imagination. That was the paradox. Survival in the physical world depended on his luck in the imaginative one, a place he had to keep the more intense and inviting.

It was neither. Its barrenness kept turning him backward to see where he had lost his certainty. Before he had gone far he would confront the galling reviews which attributed so much of the credit for the play to Logan. Tom could believe it, particularly since he continued to grieve over the Faustian pact he had made in Brookfield Center and to believe he had sold off an irreplaceable piece of integrity.

From such self-doubts he could squeeze the will to prove his was the mind and heart of *Mister Roberts,* promise himself to go deeper than he had and to make the most ambitious self-explorations in the hope of new discovery. Asking himself the ultimate questions of who and why he was showed him no way out of the labyrinth. His search always turned him out in the cul-de-sac of self-hatred, newly wasted and tormented by his dependence on Joshua Logan.

Logan's abandonment of him implicit in the launching of *South Pacific* left Tom without a collaborator and as bereft as any lover. But his despair over this act of desertion was infinitely deepened by its seeming to be a recurrence of the adolescent, disappearing father-figure experience, leading to the darkest tunnels of melancholy.

All Tom's thoughts reverted to Logan and the ambivalent feelings he had for him. At one moment he was despising himself for his dependence on the man, suspecting Josh had used him, squeezed the life juice from him and cast him off, while in the next he was anticipating Josh's return from Europe and the moment when they would sit down together and Josh would perform his magic, bringing the Flying Tigers play to life.

On good mornings, Tom resolved to have a scene ready to show him. When he thumbed his notes, looking for a place to start, Kendrigan seemed the likeliest, a cunning, licentious old rascal who becomes devoted to his impulsive flyers. But Kendrigan would take no recognizable shape out of Tom's earlier experience and the man stayed stubbornly silent.

Also he realized there was an irrationality, a madness all around the edges of the Tigers' conspiracy. There wasn't a reasonable man among them. It was going to be some job making the situation credible. It was too much Josh's conception to break into alone.

Just across town, Mister Roberts's besieged box office was taking in thirty-five thousand dollars a week, bettering by several thousand the receipts of its nearest rival, Tennessee Williams's A Streetcar Named Desire, yet the more it loomed, another Logan smash, the less it was Heggen's first play and Heggen's heart. At times he could not help wishing the thing bad luck.

He never went to a performance and only rarely, grudgingly agreed to the publicity man's requests. But when he learned that the cast was to judge a fashion show aboard a ship tied up in the Hudson River Tom's interest quickened. Joining the party of actors on its way to the pier he diverted it into a bar where he bought the drinks and proposed some ideas for the judging that were pure prewar Heggen.

As a result the jury from the Reluctant made its selections so ardently the models were terrified to appear and the event was declared a disaster. With curtain time approaching, the Mister Roberts cast rushed for taxis, bearing off one of the girls as hostage and as the caravan leapfrogged through midtown traffic toward the Alvin enough of her clothing was passed between taxi windows to make her subject to arrest.

With the last-minute arrival of this jubilant party and its captive safely transferred to a dressing room, the stage manager's anxiety was only partly relieved. He predicted disaster. Even though the performance was better than usual, he lectured Tom on the seriousness of what he had done, wanted him to know there was "a million bucks tied up in this show," and when Tom shrugged at the figure, banned him from the theater. Knowing that his subversiveness would be reported to Logan, Tom was satisfied with the afternoon's work.

When he turned up at the Logan office he would find Jim Awe at the telephone repeating the litany, "As soon as Josh gets back . . ." and it was clear that scores of others, people with more claim on his time than Tom, were waiting for Logan to return and

wind them up. It was this anticipation of being ignored, this vulnerableness that led him to pick a quarrel. He found the means in
a close look at the flowing proceeds from *Mister Roberts*.

The author's share amounted to thirty-five hundred dollars a
week but it was pared by the 12.5 percent to Shulman and 25
percent of the remainder, which went to Logan as coauthor, leaving Tom with a weekly check of twenty-three hundred dollars. If
he had known that Leland Hayward had given Logan a part, one-
sixth, of the producer's share, it had been a matter of indifference,
but seeing Logan's three salaries lined up, he felt fully victimized.
He told Awe that Logan had deceived him, that if he had known at
the time that Josh was getting a share as producer as well as his 6
percent as director, he would never have agreed to the coauthor-
ship. Recalling Logan's argument that it was "only fair," Tom
fumed, "Hell, it was only greed."

The very fact that he despised people who squabbled over
money made it worse. He told himself that just as with Max
Shulman, it was not the money itself. He had no need for money.
He was drowning in it. What he resented was being made a fool,
being shorn by someone so close, a man to whom he was so
vulnerable.

The idea festered so that in early May when Jim Awe called to
say the Logans were arriving and to ask Tom if he wanted to come
along and meet the boat, he refused. Admitting he was furious
with Logan he said he no longer wanted to see or to have anything
to do with him.

On landing, Logan received the news of Tom's sulk sympa-
thetically and set off at once to make his peace. He called at Tom's
room in the Lombardy and heard him out.

"What the hell is this?" Tom demanded. "You never told me
you were coproducer. I thought your only income was going to be
as director."

Logan seemed puzzled, as though he thought Tom a little
deranged, but then he proceeded warmly, patiently to explain,
"But, Tom, on every show I work on I'm *always* coproducer. I
thought you knew that. The only reason it isn't in the billing is

because Leland wants it that way. It's important to him to have full producing credit."

Soothing Tom's bruised spirit with assurances he was needed, that he wanted his help with *South Pacific*, that there would be time, of course there would be time, for long talks about the Tigers, Logan brought him around. Tom was soon listening attentively to an account of the Logans' European trip and how, while returning on the *Queen*, they had learned of a wonderful apartment at River House. Quentin Reynolds's wife, Ginny, had told them about it. If they took it, Josh promised, Tom would have a key.

Thus reconciled, Tom tagged along to the office, where the phones were ringing out a chorus of *Me, Me first*, and where Josh looked at the piled-up messages like a hungry man at last in sight of the feast.

Tom was getting over Helen Parker. In the streets, offices and restaurants New York teemed with pretty, laughing girls, all of them eager for loving. And when he tired of adventure there were old girls—Carol Lynn, Holly, Frenchy—with comfortable patterns of affection already built.

Frenchy Solem was especially appealing, not sexually, but because she had outdone him, thanks to her curious combination of recklessness, stoicism and bad luck, in a slide toward ruin.

On being dismissed for her irregular behavior by the Pan Am girls with whom she lived in Jackson Heights, Frenchy found an apartment in Greenwich Village, a fifth-floor walk-up at 4 East 10th Street. Here she did as she pleased, entertaining a colony of ex-Minnesota Scandinavians, each with some talent and some fatal vulnerableness which endeared them to her. Her circle included a male couple, painters, from a nearby loft, a promising composer who fed his drug habit with occasional work at the Post Office and Liz Wheeler, a big, dominant girl with lesbian designs on Frenchy which sometimes took shape as black-and-blue marks.

These friends of Frenchy's failed to stimulate Tom as such

bizarre groups once did. He would sit in their midst, withdrawn and unsmiling, and the others found it impossible to engage him in any way. He was interested only in Frenchy.

Once, when they were well along in a party, she told of how her husband, Bob Martin, had been killed. She described the instrument trainer, seat and control panel that swiveled in the top of a darkened silo. Then, from her closet, she produced Martin's uniform tunic and, putting it on, acted out his completing an exercise and, in the belief that the apparatus had docked, stepping out and cartwheeling to his death.

Frenchy was now an alcoholic and when the drinking was bad she could not produce her copy for the Spier agency. Sometimes she could not even get to the office. Tom could see in her wasted face that she had already done her vitals serious damage, and he groaned under his guilt, feeling that he alone had undermined poor Frenchy's life.

At times he considered marrying her but he also recognized that pity was no foundation for marriage, that together they would be more destructive than apart. Still he was drawn to her, as he had been in college, but with an important difference. Now it was her need that drew him, and he clung to that.

Life was yielding Tom every kind of second chance. When he was at loose ends he would drop in at the Carys' apartment on 75th Street and he felt safe enough with Barbara Cary to confess that he felt a literary fraud, and that he was so empty now he doubted he would ever write again.

Peter Cary reassured him, telling Tom not to worry about it. Why not, since he could afford it, take five years simply to restock his mind?

The Carys were convinced that hope lay in bringing Carol Lynn and Tom together again. Each had confided to Barbara that they were still in love and, so encouraged, she arranged an evening together. Tom took them all to "21" for dinner, where he earned the management's smiling indulgence as he waved away the Lucullan menu to order a hamburger and a glass of milk. Back at the

Carys' apartment, Tom was gently considerate of Carol Lynn, and so eagerly dependent on her judgments that hopes were raised all around for the Carys' scheming.

Yet Tom ended the evening with a guess that the future with Carol Lynn would be much like the past, a coming-together only for the tearing-apart, a reprise of the grim summer of 1942 when he was discovering no one could help him, that he must work the problem out by himself.

Late in the spring, Wallace and Mary Stegner saw the show and Wallace wrote Tom a long letter from Vermont with the welcome assessment that the book had more quality than the play, which, it seemed to him, had taken out too much Heggen and put in too much Logan. Tom received his mail at the new Logan apartment, where the letter was delivered, and where Logan opened the letter in error, read it, and was furious.

Tom on the other hand was delighted at this squaring-off between his two masters, even weighed Wallace's invitation to come up to Vermont, where, he was assured, the boredom of the simple life would soon drive him to work, but he knew that Vermont held no solution for his emotional problem and the chronic melancholy which was its manifestation.

He kept returning to the idea that Ross Lockridge's experience held some key for him. At a Greenwich Village party he told John Lawler, an acquaintance from his years on the *Daily*, that he was earning over two thousand dollars a week from the play. Without the least conceit he marveled at this, as though it were by chance. Then he went on to describe how rich Ross Lockridge had become from *Raintree County* and wondered if the sudden wealth had anything to do with his puzzling suicide. Tom told Lawler he was going out to Lockridge's home in Bloomington and find out.

While Tom never did go to Bloomington, he made regular trips to Minneapolis, trips he described to Barbara Cary as "going home to visit me old mither." His psychoanalysis was a biweekly reminder that his central anxiety was rooted in the past and that he must look there for deliverance. But after the first warm embraces and the exchange of news (he would soon be starting work on a

Cuban play with Logan, they were having the house repainted, deciding on a new car) there was a kind of awkwardness, as though a language barrier lay between them.

By long habit the Heggens did not reach beneath the surface of events and when Tom suggested that his miraculous hen on Broadway had laid him some difficulties, particularly of how to proceed from it, they could not understand. They took such pride in his accomplishment they could only measure it with their calipers—and marveling, saw nothing beyond its blessings.

While his achievement had gratified his parents' wishes, Mina's in particular, it had not satisfied them. Sometimes in the midst of their enthusiasm and flattery Tom would have a vestigial recollection of his mother calling him from the upstairs window, urging him to his feet. It was at such times he could feel a certain martyrdom to their childlike ambition and think of them, still tenderly, as "The Innocents."

Instead of permitting them to relax and enjoy him, to be indolent and silly with each other, the benefits of *Mister Roberts* seemed to have reinforced the old push. For them, life had presented a single problem, getting ahead, and they could not see how it was different for him. He was never prepared for that and warm expectations were repeatedly frostbitten. Each visit, undertaken with new hope, ended in old disappointment, old frustrations at the barriers of understanding, old anxieties of not being loved at all.

As he had since college days, he went out in search of someone to talk to. He found Bob Litman, who was back in Minneapolis, working at the Veteran's Hospital, and in the many evenings they spent together, Tom gave the impression of being on holiday between bouts of hard work in New York. While he never spoke of his writing and Litman was too careful of his friend to ask, Tom talked freely about his other concerns.

Over a glass at the Viking Room, Tom spoke of his course of analysis under Leopold Bellak. Indeed he was so enthusiastic that ultimately Bob Litman was persuaded to change his own specialty of neurology to psychology. Tom described his marriage with remorse, explaining that he had fallen out of love with his wife and no longer could give her "what a woman wants."

He did not mean sex alone, although that was part of it, but he was wary of women for their demands which always seemed to threaten his own strength and freedom. As a result he was conditioned to take from a woman without returning what she expected in understanding, affection, constancy—even loyalty.

Tom spoke with awe of Logan, described him as a genius, and told Litman of his admiration for Nedda too, adding that he wished he could find such a woman who would give him both freedom and devotion.

Tom, who had been using sedatives for sleep since Navy days, was now in constant need of barbiturates as a depressant. He was well into addiction, needing for composure twenty of the fast-acting capsules a day, and Litman wrote him prescriptions that would last him a week. On the pills alone Tom would appear so drunk, with slurred speech and unsteady balance, that bartenders refused to serve him.

But behind the motor sluggishness his mind was clear and thoughts of mischief restored his verve. Their sport was woman chasing and the game began in a swapping of such anecdotes as Tom's about the huge black he had seen lay a pretty redhead in Havana. They were often joined by other friends and the evening usually ended in the sharing, or trading, of girls.

"Ladar is what we need," Tom told Bob Litman and Doug Whipple while they sized up the girls at the Viking Room's nearby tables, "a beam that would sweep the joint and show up on a screen which girls are really ready." He had no sooner proposed this aid to courtship than the eavesdropping girls at the next table were laughing, moving to join them, and Tom, seeing the girls' interest in Doug Whipple, was devising ways to confound the predictable course of events.

Litman was at the critical phase in one seduction when Tom and Doug Whipple pounded on his door and set fire to it. On another night Tom and John Cotton turned up at Litman's house to announce they had a drunk and willing girl in the car outside and they amiably chatted with Litman's parents while he went out to take his turn. Rejoining them, Litman frightened Tom by announcing the girl was dead. While this was an exaggeration, Tom hustled her home and, when he couldn't get her through her front door, left her propped against it. Next day he coolly called her for another date.

On yet another night, Tom, Litman and a nurse from the V.A. hospital were careening along a narrow road, Litman steering a perilous course for Wynona, when Tom began to shout, "Faster, faster," all the while sprinkling the upholstery with whiskey. "So they'll know how it happened when they find us in the ditch," he explained.

When there was talk and laughter and the first flowing of the liquor, Tom could believe his ability to write was intact and all that was happening around him was important, fertile, sprouting with possibility. A novel, a Minneapolis story he could set in a local dive, was a tempting, even plausible idea.

But this elation invariably ended in hangover and dejection, all confidence collapsed. In the midst of one postspree depression he called Joshua Logan in New York to say that he had been thinking about Ross Lockridge again. He had thought about him all day with such a growing sense of identification that he had taken a room on the twelfth floor of the Radisson Hotel in downtown Minneapolis. He had called to say good-by. When he hung up he was going to the window and jump out.

Trading the telephone with Nedda, Josh talked to him for nearly an hour during which Tom confessed his depression was due in part to seeing his family. It revived old pains, he explained, and he was in such a deep depression he could find no reason for going on living. When Tom admitted he had had no food all day, Logan persuaded him to go downstairs, have something to eat and then come back to them in New York.

Tom did so eagerly, feeling as he always did when eastbound, that it was the only possible direction for renewal. Now his hopes of going back to work with Josh were reinforced by the belief he was making encouraging progress with Dr. Bellak—and the alternatives this indicated.

In the perspective of Dr. Bellak's Fifth Avenue office he could recognize the unhealthiness of his dependency on Logan, that if he were to write again effectively it must be independently of him. He knew he should abandon all thoughts of the theater and return to fiction. A novel, even a short story, something whole even if it was short, would be enough to free him and start his creative flow again.

When he caught sight of his former agent, Diarmuid Russell, in the grill room of the Ritz Carlton he made his way over to shake hands and say, "I never should have left you, Diarmuid. It was a mistake getting mixed up with all these depraved theater people." Laughing, Russell said he would welcome Tom back whenever he chose to come, and Tom agreed to, as soon as he had something to show him.

And, in fact, he was into something very encouraging. Probing his past for some mood, some state of mind in which to build, he had fastened onto the summer of 1940 between his junior and sophomore years and the bumming trip he had made that July. The family then lived at 5117 Portland Street in Southwest Minneapolis, a street of elms and small, white clapboard houses, each with its peaked doorway, in a row, alike as cornstalks, the very crossroads of homeliness, husbandry and penny-wisdom.

He had set out to find where the real, the whole life was. He had two indications—the persistent memory of an Oklahoma girl, unattained, still haunting after a year, and a dream of faraway, of a ship and some tropical, Spanish-speaking city.

Both quests ended in Oklahoma City with the discovery that Carol Lynn was away, at a girl scout camp, and in the loss of his skinny bankroll in a poker game with old friends from O.C.U. As he thought of it now, the collapse of those romantic, teen-age hopes in Oklahoma City, he began to see little glints of the larger truth in it, the loss of innocence and illusion, of the inescapability of fate. He began impressively:

I was rummaging in the attic of my memory, looking for a story to write. My stories never come to me unbidden, and they never come whole; there are always characters to be juxtaposed, incidents to be altered, the noncommittal chaos of experience to be arranged with luck into form and meaning. So I was trying to do that; I was looking for meaning, moving about the discarded furniture of the past, peering into the cobwebbed corners of remembrance, when I came upon this night in the year 1939, I looked at it, studied it; I backed away and studied it; and finally I knew that I had found not a fragment, not the unjoined corner of a story, but the whole thing; rounded, finished, and complete to a degree that I could never approach by artifice. I turned it over and over, and now the longer I look at it the lovelier it seems, and the more miraculous.

I remember a night in the late summer of 1939. I was sitting on my suitcase beside a lonely highway perhaps forty miles beyond Kansas City. It was midnight and better, and there was not a car on the road; not one. The night was one of those incredible arrangements of velvet, immobility and personal heavens that happen only in the middlewest. The skies are higher there, and they arch to a dome over your very head. There were the indigenous sounds of such a night; the rustling and breathing of growing crops and the ticktock shrillness of locusts, and they blended together into a silence more utter than soundlessness. Now and then I could hear the night-magnified noise of an automobile moving beyond the hills to the south. But none came my way.

And there he paused, thinking how to get into it, looking for the way he knew was there, but as he tried this and that trail, each turned false, led only deeper into the thicket. He could not find his way, could not write another word.

Seeking the cure for his barrenness he would look back to the time that was so productive, the six months from April to October 1945 aboard Virgo. He realized that the physical environment, the windowless, spartan stateroom, the confinement and boredom of endless days at sea, the rhythm of ship's motion a reminder that even this slow kind of time had an end had contributed to that remarkable output, a dozen well-made stories in half a year.

When he told a *Life* editor he was thinking of a long sea voyage on a merchantman, the slowest boat he could find, in hopes it would prime his writing pump, he was immediately commissioned to do an article on peacetime sailors, one that would draw a parallel with the crew of the *Reluctant*.

Tom chose S.S. *Topa Topa*, a freighter of the Waterman Line, which carried twelve passengers and made the voyage to Hamburg in ten days. George Daniell, a photographer, agreed to join him and take pictures. Then, with Joshua Logan's help, Tom planned a Logan-like tour of the Continent that would carry him through the Low Countries and France, along the Italian Riviera to Capri, then northward to Venice, Geneva and Paris.

He made further arrangements for company. Backstage at *Annie Get Your Gun*, Logan had introduced him to a dancer. She was short, Tom's size, and audacious, his sort, one of several theater creatures for whom he had ambitions. He persuaded her to fly over and join him in Italy.

Then, with the trip to look forward to, he relaxed and put off, until he was afloat, the daily agony of trying to write. He spent a weekend with Frenchy Solem Martin and some friends on Fire Island. At the beach he entertained with offshore naval exercises in a rubber raft and, as a famous sailor, convulsed his audience by shouts that he couldn't swim and, as he drifted to sea, a plaintive cry for help.

Tom was to sail for Europe on July 15 and Josh and Nedda gave him a bon voyage luncheon, to which he brought Frenchy. Alan Campbell, another member of the party, told of his great luck in finding an apartment, a duplex on 62nd Street. Explaining that he was away much of the time and the place was too expensive for him, he offered to share it with Tom, who accepted at once and agreed to move in when he returned from his trip.

As the farewell party trooped over *Topa Topa's* decks, the Logans were appalled at her austere accommodations and pungent smells, but for once Tom had the greater experience. He was at home here with the sounds of winches and the closing of hatches, far more than he would have been with the chimes and waltzes of a Cunarder's sailing, and he sowed assurances all around.

But from the moment *Topa Topa* slipped from her Brooklyn pier into the stream, it was clear that her officers and crew shared the merchant mariner's wariness of curious and meddlesome passengers. They were tight-lipped, making him feel a spy in their midst, and after a few blighted attempts at making friends he gave up, took to avoiding meals and stayed drunk for the voyage. The ship's company had made it clear there was to be no story for *Life*, nor was the act of going to sea again any tonic for his writing.

No seasick sailor ever regarded land more gratefully than Tom. He was the first ashore and the first to put some distance between him and *Topa Topa's* rusty sides.

Tom's chorus girl turned up as arranged and at first, just as in the early days of the Cuban trip, life seemed miraculously renewed. He was enchanted with the strange and lovely sound of Italian, spoken with such a proud articulation he felt that if he strained a little harder he could understand it, with the fine, ripe, fruity smells of streets and shops and then with the train, whistling shrilly as it raced along the Ligurian Coast, pausing only for tear-drenched scenes of parting and reunion played at every station.

It was strange, exotic and yet familiar, as though he had dreamed it before. It was a resigned, a pleasure-loving, yet satisfying place and he had the impression there was some secret here worthwhile learning. They stayed in Santa Margherita, sitting under a café awning to look out over the sea and watch the carriages drift by. In the morning they saw fishing boats come in with a catch and the old fishermen lay out their nets to dry. They took pictures of each other on the seawall to prove it was true and Tom wrote postcards home to Minneapolis, to Josh and Nedda, and to Jim Awe telling how grand it was.

Capri, towering from the sea, was even more a wonder. But the first surprise of Italy was wearing off. The terraces, the hotel rooms with shutters that made lattices of dancing sealight across the plaster, the bars and restaurants, seemed like the last ones. He began to wonder what he was doing here and soon he was asking more of travel than it had to give.

Feelings of not belonging, of being tolerated only until his money was spent brought on a boredom with spectacular views and famous ruins. He turned resentful of all the beauty for its failure to move him any more and suspicious that everything around him was some kind of dirty gyp. They were feelings that called for a drink and soon, in his disappointment, he no longer knew or cared in which ancient city he was neglecting the splendors.

The quarreling with his chorus girl gave him a terrifying sense of reprise in which he could believe that time had slipped back five months, delivering him to Varadaro, that it was Helen here with him and he had just read about Ross Lockridge in the *Havana Post*.

When the chorus girl had had enough of Tom she left for home and he went on alone, unwilling to accept, unable to admit that he couldn't even *travel*, for God's sake. He shortened the itinerary, lowered its aspirations and found at least one glimpse of the old world that would stick in his memory. It was of a nightclub where a girl calmly shed her clothes and danced naked on the table. At the end of August he flew back to New York.

XXIII

On the literary calendar, as on the academic one, September brought renewal and Tom felt optimistic about moving into the apartment at 8 East 62nd Street with Alan Campbell. It was just off Central Park and, for a pair of bachelors, it was certainly ample. Beyond the foyer a spacious living room led to a kitchen as well as a bedroom and bath, which were to be Alan's. Tom was to have the more secluded sleeping quarters on the floor above, reached by a flight of stairs.

What he liked best about the arrangement was Alan's swarming social life. After a dozen years of marriage, Dorothy Parker had accused Alan of a homosexual affair and divorced him. Their separation was to be a temporary one, but meanwhile he lived a busy, boozy, cosmopolitan life that was one part her uptown acquaintance and two parts a theatrical one of his own.

Although Alan was a handsome man with a swaggering presence, he was a mediocre actor. Nevertheless, as his ex-wife's collaborator he had become an able screenwriter. His talents were precisely suited to Hollywood's rhinestone standards and he loved the place. He adored stars and surrounded himself with all the glamour and pleasure he could contrive. He attracted people of all sorts and, so long as they were amusing, welcomed the spurious as well as the genuine. He moved from one party to another, carrying along an aura of gaiety and a retinue of admiring, good-looking women.

Alan Campbell knew *everyone* and he represented for Tom a New York that was the center of the artistic world and in which participation was, in itself, accomplishment. Mere survival here among the fangs and sharp teeth entitled a man to condescension toward the frogs of lesser puddles. Alan presided over a fraternity of cleverness and quasi-talent which offered reassurance to those in some doubt of their own identity and effectiveness.

While Alan's parties were drunken and in their final hours often revealed lingering guests as unpleasant enough to offend Tom, he was attracted to several of the girls. He liked Denise Razy, a handsome, vivacious French actress Alan had met in Paris. Denise dazzled Tom. Her tongue was agile as Alan's and when they joined in provoking each other's laughter, Tom's own bent for ridicule collapsed. When the three dined together, as they occasionally did, Tom was an oafish audience to their gossip and flights of worldly cleverness.

Outclassed, he consented to play butt of their jokes. They teased him about his searching for acceptable moods in his medicine chest and one night lined up his collection of pill bottles on the mantel, relabeling them Wit, Joy, Charm, Happiness—the states of mind that were forever eluding him. When he fumed about Logan they were moved by an especially devilish impulse. From the bookshelf they took down the original edition of *Mister Roberts* and, under Tom's name on the spine, gleefully added "and Joshua Logan."

Late in September, Alan introduced Tom to another actress he had known abroad. She was Leueen MacGrath, an alumna of the Royal Academy of Dramatic Art who had just come to New York to open in *Edward, My Son* with Robert Morley. She was a blithe, blond, coolly exquisite Irish girl with the spirit of a young animal. In his first moments with her, Tom liked her. She in turn thought him appealing, with a newly minted quality that set him apart from the others. Captivated, Tom spoke openly about himself, and soon got around to the unwelcome aspects of his success and his preoccupation with psychoanalysis.

Seeing her performance he was impressed by her plaintive articulateness and decided she was good. She not only had talent but her confidence in it gave her a pride and independence. He went backstage to find her, persuaded her to come along for a drink and, over it, decided he was falling in love.

He had another encouraging experience in that early fall of 1948. When he heard from Holly and Charlie Irving that they had bought Budd Schulberg's farm in Newtown, Pennsylvania, he asked them about the novelist, thinking that anyone who had written *What Makes Sammy Run*, and then been able to follow it up with another book, had something to tell him—if he would.

It was easily arranged and one Saturday afternoon the Irvings and a slender, ethereal-looking actress named Anna Marie Geyer, Charlie had brought along for him, collected Tom and set out for Pennsylvania. On the way, the idea of going to visit Schulberg as though he were an oracle ready with an utterance seemed ridiculous to Tom. His problems were, after all, personal, not writing ones, and he feared Schulberg would think him witless or gutless or both. Thus, when he came to face Schulberg, Tom could not bring himself to say why he had asked this audience.

Instead he kept up the hinky-pinky, the word game they had been playing in the car, and they drank a great deal. Even though Schulberg proved friendly and willing to talk about anything, Tom could not get around to his question. At one o'clock in the morning Schulberg pulled Tom into a corner and asked him what he wanted.

Pressed, Tom spoke at last, wondering if Schulberg had any idea of what he'd been through in recent months—strangers asking him to read their manuscripts or loan them money, new acquaintances behaving like old friends, and old friends becoming strangers. And he was drowning in money. He told Budd that he was now making, from all sources, eleven thousand dollars a week. The excess had become a symbol of what had happened to him, and of why he couldn't get started on a second book.

Schulberg knew so exactly that he filled in words, finished sentences where Tom hesitated, nodding as Tom talked. It was the gold-plated bear trap, Budd said, a product of the American love of success, success for its own sake. It had nothing to do with writing and it was important for a writer to understand that in order to avoid it.

Tom agreed but wanted to know "How do you go on?" He told Budd that he knew it was a matter of will and work and that he got up each morning—not early, because he had a hell of a time sleeping and generally stayed out late and drank too much trying to knock himself out—but still he got up each day and rolled a sheet of paper into his typewriter. But six, eight, maybe ten hours later it was still blank. Nothing, not a single goddam word.

Schulberg thought he should stop thinking of *Mister Roberts* as a big, successful book, that the fanfare itself was false and getting in his way. The book was no more than a modest start on a writing career and in any other country it would be accepted as that.

Tom said he knew that but still he tensed up, thinking that *Mister Roberts* was only a fluke, that he never could do that well again. This led Schulberg to argue from the opposite end to suppose that *Mister Roberts* was a great book, one he could never equal again, but nevertheless build from, as Maugham had done after *Of Human Bondage*, writing interesting, entertaining, although lesser books.

This led Budd to propose his theory of the writer's career, that it should be seen not as a flight of stairs, constantly ascending, but a mountain range. It goes up and down and levels off, then drops and even falls away, only to rise again. It is jagged and imperfect, but it thrusts up above sea level and, in the end, throws some sort of shadow against the sky.

Tom was stunned by this revelation. That was it, of course, he didn't have to top himself and he was so grateful he found the courage to ask a second question. "I've got another problem," he admitted, "one I've been ashamed to talk about with anyone but my psychiatrist. Working with Joshua Logan was so stimulating and satisfying that I've become creatively dependent on him. I don't feel whole without him."

Schulberg told Tom this was bunk too, that there was no comparison between the play and the book. The book was better, simpler, truer, and there was certainly more where it came from. But it was important he get out of the New York rat race, get away from the city's false values which seemed to be getting in his way. He proposed that if Tom could not go home to Fort Dodge or Minneapolis, he go home to himself—relax, take a long trip, make some notes on what interested him.

Tom and Budd Schulberg were still talking when the new day brightened over Bucks County and Tom was exuberant for he had what he came for. Miraculously, Budd had the answers—the mountain range, to get away, to go home to himself. Tom was clear-headed and sure in the beautiful, early morning light and as he and Schulberg embraced, he promised to return whenever he felt like it. He need only call, Schulberg told him in parting, and say he was on his way.

But he did not take up the invitation. When they met again it was a month later in a New York restaurant. Budd stopped at Tom's table to shake hands and Tom confessed he still had the blank-page trouble. As they talked Tom realized he had lost the gift Schulberg had given him in Newtown, that map of the way out.

He had put off going home to himself because he lacked the courage for the trip and dreaded he would find its destination uninhabitable. He clung to New York as a sanctuary offering hopes which depended less upon himself than others.

First there were the regular therapies of Dr. Bellak's couch. He had come to anticipate these as episodes in an unfolding narrative of self-discovery. Not only was he the story's main character, but all his hopes of writing again depended on his understanding it. And thus he rationalized a preoccupation with his analysis. It was neither illness, nor narcissism which made it so alluring—but business. It was a braiding of himself and his art into a single rope.

Then there were the town's infinite possibilities for love,

which for the present had focused on Leueen MacGrath. She was a departure from his recent girls in at least one respect. She was no easy quarry. When Tom confessed he was in love with her, Leueen took it lightly for granted—and refused to go to bed with him.

Leueen enjoyed Tom. After the theater she welcomed him to her side at Sardi's and, on nonmatinée afternoons took long walks with him in the park, listening to accounts of his analysis, laughing when he turned its techniques on her. She was so very youthful, he found it hard to believe she was six years older than he, had already been through two marriages in England. When she admitted that another playwright, George S. Kaufman, found her attractive and that she had gone out with him, she was surprised at the heat of his jealousy. It was not easy for Tom to accept that his rival was both an old man and an extremely successful one. At fifty-nine Kaufman was the author of thirty successful plays—two of them, *Of Thee I Sing* and *You Can't Take It With You*, Pulitzer Prize winners. Tom explained Kaufman as her father-image, and made fun of her for considering him a suitor. Still, when Tom proposed, she would not take him seriously. She maintained, jokingly and yet earnestly, that he didn't really mean it—that if she were to accept him, as lover or husband, he would lose interest. But if Tom saw an element of truth in what she said, it did not lessen his infatuation. Leueen was just the elusive woman to keep him interested.

But New York's principal attraction for him remained Joshua Logan. The big apartment in the River House with its airman's view of the East River had become a reality and one of the city's wonders. It was Josh's palace, a darkly gleaming place with the stuff he had gathered from all over the world on display. As soon as the paintings were hung and lighted, the windows and furniture swathed in thick silk and velvet, Logan handed Tom a key to the door and with it his assurance of full filial rights.

Nor was Tom backward about testing these daily. He made the place his mailing address and came by each afternoon to see what the postman had brought. When he remembered, he brought along his dirty shirts to go out with the Logan laundry and when he was alone at nights he would often head there, let himself in and stretch out on the huge, downy living-room sofa to wait for Josh and Nedda to come in. That sofa was the only place he was sure of sleep in all New York.

Logan, wholly immersed now in *South Pacific*, tried to interest Tom in it, persuaded him to read the script and offer suggestions. When he returned it, Tom pointed out a line, "Hey, fellah," and said it struck him as a sentimental and unlikely way for one sailor to hail another, and that ended it. Tom was not a part of *South Pacific* and he wanted none of its scraps. He never went to a rehearsal and just being around the *South Pacific* people was torture to him. At times he thought he would choke on his jealousy.

He could not help feeling that *South Pacific* was the bastard child of *Mister Roberts*, that the Pacific was *his* ocean and they had snatched it away without so much as a thank you.

Mister Roberts was still playing to standing room at the Alvin. There was a second company in Chicago and plans for a third in London. Noting that its anniversary was coming up on February 18, Logan said they must celebrate it with a fine luncheon. Tom looked forward to this, to bringing around a table in "21" the people and the excitement of the *Mister Roberts* preparations. He felt it would turn back time in a way that would be pleasurable and possibly even helpful to him.

Although the luncheon came off on schedule, Logan did not attend. Knowing that Josh had just begun rehearsals and aware of his single-mindedness about a show in production, Tom was not greatly surprised. He had even anticipated it, and hid his disappointment well.

Emlyn Williams, in town again and staying with the Logans, turned up as Josh's understudy, and Nedda came bringing a gift, a small, gold palm tree inscribed *Royal Order of the Palm—One Year* and signed with her and Nancy Hayward's names. Nor had Josh forgotten. Tom had a gift from him too, a gold penknife with the engraving *Thomas Heggen. Thanks J.L.*

When Emlyn and Nedda noticed his grogginess, Tom explained it wasn't the drink, but the pills he used for sleep and composure, and they chorused, "Oh, Tom, be careful with those pills or you'll kill yourself." Tom's consenting nod ended in a shrug that left neither Emlyn Williams nor Nedda Logan reassured.

A few days after the anniversary luncheon, Tom made an exciting discovery. He received in his mail the galleys of Tom Lea's novel *The Brave Bulls*, and while its publishers had hoped only for a favorable comment, Tom was hypnotized by the book and its hero, Luis Bello. He was a failing Mexican matador, deceived by his woman, preyed upon by friends and family, filled with self-doubt and a terrible need to re-prove himself to a remorseless public.

Here was a drama Tom recognized from life. Getting that onto a stage would be worth any amount of pain and labor and he hurried to Josh with it. Logan responded enthusiastically. He recognized the formidable problem of staging a bullfight in a Broadway theater but resourceful as ever came up with a solution. He thought they could screen the fight and proposed to Tom that as soon as *South Pacific* opened they could go to Spain and see some corridas. They could take a camera and make films themselves; bring them home, study them and figure out a way to do it.

Tom was elated. The only defect of the project lay in its involving another man's work. Still, he anticipated a principal role as conceiver and adapter and these prospects bubbled forth in some overdue correspondence. He wrote to Wallace Stegner and Alfred Jones telling them his new plans with enthusiasm, and then he did a rare thing. He went shopping—and bought some new clothes for the trip to Spain.

But *South Pacific* was becoming the biggest show of Logan's career—the huge cast was headed by Mary Martin and she was superb in her singing of Dick Rodgers's most elaborate score. Ezio Pinza, the Metropolitan's famous opera star, was beginning to look like a brilliant stroke of casting. The show was shaping into the triumph of his life.

As a result, throughout the month of March Tom scarcely saw him. And he found no opportunity to discuss the adaptation of *The Brave Bulls*, nor their Spanish research for it. Then at the month's end he learned that the Logans were planning their post-opening holiday with the Mielziners. The Logan station wagon was being fitted out with a Dictaphone so that Josh could get some writing done and he was going to mail the belts back to the River House office for transcribing. An elaborate itinerary was already drawn up, one that included visits with friends along the way, Spain and bullfights, but no mention of Tom as a member of the party.

It did not sound like his kind of junket anyway and with a mixture of disappointment and relief, Tom abandoned thoughts of going along. Although he continued to drop by the River House office and to chat with Jim Awe when he picked up his mail, Tom spurned Josh's offer of tickets for the *South Pacific* opening, and made no attempt to see him nor extract any promises for work on his return. When both the Pulitzer and the Critics Award went to *Streetcar* for the best play of the year—and in the post-mortems only Maxwell Anderson's *Anne of a Thousand Days* was mentioned as a contender, Tom had some last, spiteful things to say to Leland Hayward about Logan's farcical touches and then he was still. He accepted with equanimity that Josh was planning an adaptation of *The Cherry Orchard* for his next project. It was the end of the line for his hopes of working again with Joshua Logan.

The opening of *South Pacific* on April 7 was the triumphant success that knowledgeable New Yorkers had anticipated. It dwarfed the previous accomplishments of each of its celebrated artists. There was a new monument at the Majestic Theater taller, bigger than anything else in town, while at the Alvin the lobby was empty.

Simultaneous with *South Pacific*'s noisy welcome to Broadway and the Logans' departure for Europe Tom performed a number of retrospective acts, as though they might be final ones, ones he would be remembered by.

Over lunch at Christ Cella's, Peter Cary confided that the *Digest* was recalling him to the headquarters in Chappaqua, and Tom spoke gloomily of his own future. He could not write just any old book; it had to be one that topped *Mister Roberts*. He could not cut that stone from his neck, he said, and the consequence was these pills. He told of being so numbed with them recently that he had answered the telephone, begun speaking with a girl and simply drifted off to sleep, to wake an hour later with the receiver buzzing in his ear. Another time he had started down the stairs, pitched the whole length and was saved from breaking his bones only because he was so wholly relaxed. He knew he was doing himself irreversible damage.

And yet he brightened at the idea of the Carys' return to the country and he spent an afternoon with them looking at houses, none of which seemed quite right. That same night, sitting at their dinner table, he asked Barbara about a house she had liked but rejected because of its expense, saying, "Did you really like that house, Barbara? I mean is it the kind of place you can see yourself in?"

Realizing he was about to offer help, Barbara at first joked about it, pretending greed but then suddenly, sharply turned him down, making it clear they wanted no charity. When she had set him straight she smiled and asked, "What are you trying to do, get rid of all your money?" Tom nodded. Bequests were on his mind.

Old friends he had not seen in years now became important to him. When he heard from Vic Cohn that he would be in town for a night Tom looked forward to spending an evening with him. He picked Vic up at his hotel and took him off to 52nd Street for an evening of talk and listening to jazz. But it was disappointing. To Vic Tom looked wasted and sad while Tom found Vic preoccupied with his trip to London and the science convention he was to cover there for the *Star*. Time had got between them.

He called Chuck Roberts in Chicago to say he was trying to write but at present he was only typing lines and X-ing them out. He called Larry Myers, now teaching at the College of the Ozarks, "just to bull a little," he told him. But then he confessed he was having trouble with his writing and wished Larry was with him to talk about it. It was the middle of the spring semester, Larry explained, and much as he would like to, he could not come.

He wrote to Alfred Jones in Iowa to tell him that he was in

trouble with his writing, that he could not seem to find a subject that absorbed him and he worried he might never find the equal of the *Virgo*. He was also concerned that his money was going to slip away. Thus he was going to buy a motel in Minneapolis. He drew his old shipmate a sketch of it, a two-story affair, and explained that it would, with his family's help, keep the money rolling in even, Jones inferred, if his writing days were over.

Then, at the end of April, there was a noticeable brightening in Tom's disposition. Alan Campbell noticed it just before he left for California and he felt easier in his own mind about leaving Tom on his own. Leopold Bellak noticed it, felt that Tom had at last bottomed out of his despair and was making progress toward recovery. And Tom's family noticed it when, during the first week of May, Tom returned to Minneapolis for his mother's gall bladder operation.

It seemed to all those who were closest to Tom that he was getting better and only in retrospect does it seem likely that the change in his disposition was a recognizing that release from his torment lay in his own hands.

It was relatively easy. He had thought of self-destruction often as a conjecture, an exciting toy to play with when he was bored, as excuse for unconventional behavior and as a threat, an instrument to test the love of others, but, as he was finally convinced he could neither work without Logan, nor with him—it became a promise to himself. It was even possible to view it as a creative act—a sequel to *Mister Roberts* expressed in a medium purer than words. No facsimile—but life itself. Unassailable. An artistic act that was beyond collaborators and critics—contemptuous of them all.

Back in New York Tom went on doing familiar, habitual things. He put in his daily confrontation with the typewriter and, now the weather was getting warm, made plans for the summer ahead. The first Sunday after his return from Minneapolis he went down to Fire Island to look at a cottage. It was near Cherry Grove, just beyond the lighthouse, and the sign over its door read Camp Comfort. It stood in a row of similar ones with equally homely names.

He sat on the beach in front of it for several hours, enjoying the sun at work on his white skin. Then, although he was helpless about cooking and looking after himself and had no clear idea of how he would manage, he decided to rent Camp Comfort for the season.

He marveled at the ease with which he did things now. The decision to put an end to his life was a release and an elation. But he had not decided when, and that, he knew well enough, was an evasion like any other—like pretending to be a writer when you are not.

XXIV

Wednesday, May 18.

Tom awoke just before noon to grapple with a queasy stomach and a gluestuck head. Alan was still in California and Romona, who came twice a week, was not due until tomorrow. Thus he picked his way through a great untidiness—underclothing, half-emptied cups and glasses, butts and ashes, newspapers and magazines, strewn as by a gale—unoffended, to fix himself an eye-opener and put some water on to boil.

Outside, 62nd Street sparkled in the sun and people passed with a jauntiness in keeping with the spring weather. Thinking of what lay before him, Tom remembered that he had agreed to meet Leueen MacGrath this evening. Although *Edward, My Son* had closed, she had kept her role in the screen version and she had been to California in connection with that. She wanted to talk about something and he did not like the portents. Still, he looked forward to seeing her and to arguing her out of what he insisted was an unhealthy attachment to Kaufman, and into a willingness toward himself. Meantime, it was a fine day and wanted filling.

He also recalled that Leland Hayward had asked him to come along to Chicago next day in order to help him decide on replacements in the cast of the national company. He might do that. Now it was shopworn, he was feeling kindly and repossessive toward the play. And yet, as he thought about Leland's offer he suspected it was some kind of charity and that chilled him. He would have to call him later.

On the coffee table, facing the fireplace, stood his typewriter. It awaited him, cold and accusing as a woman unloved. The sight of it, with its reminder he must go to it now for another futile struggle, once the acutest of the day's sufferings, was now relatively painless.

He sat down and tried for nearly an hour to write something. Since coming back from Minneapolis he had been thinking about a Minnesota novel, not getting anywhere with it, but trying it, out of eight years' habit and the sourdough's hope that however disappointing the trail behind, the next turn will bring his strike.

In midafternoon he was interrupted by a telephone call from Mrs. Ed Solem. Frenchy's mother had come to New York at Tom's urging to look after her daughter and now she was calling to say he had not exaggerated. She had found Frances in grievous shape, her face puffy and colorless, her hands so tremulous she had difficulty in lighting a cigarette.

When Tom urged that she take her home to Minnesota, Mrs. Solem replied that Frances had refused to go, insisting she was not sick.

Tom told her this was not true. He had talked with her doctor, learned that she had cirrhosis and that if she did not stop drinking altogether, she would be dead in a matter of months. The doctor was prepared to say so tomorrow at an hour already agreed upon, and in both Frances's and her mother's presence. "Between the two of you," Tom told Mrs. Solem, "you ought to be able to get her on the train."

Mrs. Solem doubted it. She had been through all this with Frances, who felt she could be treated just as well here where her life was. She had said she would die of boredom in Fergus Falls and of the two, she preferred drink.

Tom then told Mrs. Solem about Frances's friend who turned up nightly with a fresh bottle. If it was only to free Frances from this corrosive influence she must get her out of New York.

Still Mrs. Solem despaired. Frances had even refused to go to the doctor's with her tomorrow. At this, Tom said he would see what he could do.

When he reached her at home, Frenchy was wary but as Tom joked with her she warmed, old, unbeatable spirit coming up. Then as he admitted he was in league with her mother and wanted to make sure she would be at the doctor's tomorrow, she turned silent, refused to answer until he said he would be there too, at two-thirty tomorrow. "If you're not," he threatened, "I'm coming to get you."

Frenchy laughed. "O.K.," she said.

When he hung up he realized he had decided against going to Chicago in the morning and he was about to call Leland Hayward and tell him so when the telephone rang.

It was Leueen MacGrath and she spoke with unusual gravity, brushing aside his banter to say that she had wanted very much to see him tonight as she had something to explain to him. It was a matter much better dealt with over a supper table than a telephone wire but that had just been made impossible by the arrival of Kaufman's sister. It was important to George that they be together tonight. Perhaps she could see him later in the week.

What she had to tell him, she now revealed, was that she was going to marry Kaufman. It would be announced tomorrow and she wanted him to know before reading it in the paper.

"It's all right," Tom said quietly. "I understand. Let me know when you're free."

His insouciance was thin camouflage for his disappointment. Even though Leueen had given him small encouragement and ample warning, even though he recognized the truth in Leueen's contention that he didn't want her to accept him, still it was a rejection, the more agonizing since in losing her he had been bested again by an old, yet vital, productive man.

Presently Tom went upstairs to his bathroom and took a nearly empty bottle of Seconal capsules from the medicine cabinet, shook several into his hand and swallowed them. Awaiting the soft, furry feeling they induced, the envelope of assurance that nothing really mattered, he was freshly aware of the danger involved in this generous midday dose and took extra pleasure from that.

Looking at the empty bottle he recalled that on Monday he had called the Sayer Drug shop on Madison Avenue for a new supply and he decided to walk over and pick up the prescription awaiting him there. But first he wandered around the apartment, settling at last before the desk in Alan Campbell's room. Here he collected Alan's bills, many of them overdue, and paid them. Then, gathering the envelopes, he went out to do his errands.

He ate a skimpy lunch at the drugstore counter and, on his way home, hesitated at the corner of 62nd Street. Thinking of a run to River House for his mail, he let several cabs go by and then decided he would telephone first.

Back in the apartment he called the Logan number and was surprised by an unfamiliar voice. "Is Jim Awe there?" he asked. "This is Tom Heggen."

"He's just left, Mr. Heggen. Jim's been breaking me in."

"Oh you're Joe Curtis, the new guy. How do you like it?"

"Fine. I'm getting to know the place a little."

"Have you heard from Josh and Nedda?"

"Yes, we had a letter this morning."

"They having fun?"

"Oh yes. They were in Bourgos, on their way to Madrid. They saw Dominguin."

"Any pictures? Is Josh taking pictures?"

Joe Curtis did not know about pictures for Logan had not mentioned any. But he went off to see about Tom's mail and from Curtis's description of it Tom said it did not sound interesting. He proposed to come by for it later in the week and at that time they have a drink together.

Next Tom called the Hayward office and while he waited for Leland, his secretary came on with a message. Bud Nye was in town from Minneapolis and anxious that Tom join him and Max Shulman for dinner tomorrow. There was a number to call.

Tom recognized this as some kind of peace feeler from Max, with Bud the go-between and instantly thought, all right, why not? Without his noticing, the fire of his anger at Shulman had gone out. He no longer cared and perhaps it would be good to see Max again.

When Leland Hayward came on the line Tom told him he had changed his mind about going to Chicago. There was someone in town he had to see.

"I think I know her," Leland said and they both laughed at that before Tom said good-by and wished him a good trip.

Then he called Bud Nye at his hotel and found his old admirer jubilant over some T.V. interest in his own novel, *Home Is Where You Find It*. Through it he saw the possibility of liberation from his bondage. He had been in St. Paul for the past several years, writing household hints for Brown and Bigelowe calendars. Although he said very little Tom was moved by Bud's expectations and caught in a double poignance—an envy for his new hopes and a sadness at their naïveté, something like an old courtesan's hearing an account of first love. At the end of it he agreed to meet Bud Nye and Max Shulman the following night at Cavanaugh's Restaurant on 23rd Street.

Just before six the doorbell rang and Tom opened his door on Holly Irving. She was dressed with expectations and her face fell at the sight of Tom in his rumpled shirt and khakis. "Oh, Tom, you forgot," she said. "You're coming to dinner with us—Charlie and Bob and me."

When Tom could not recall who Bob was, she explained, "My cousin, Bob Ravicz."

Yes, he had forgotten but he was glad she had come now. Although the drowsiness, the furriness of his tongue was controllable, he was encouraged by her concern to fall further into it, a weary man into a featherbed. While she moved about the living room, emptying ashtrays in the basket and glancing at her watch, Tom urged her to stay, at least for a drink, and talk to him.

Holly agreed to the drink and Tom sat down across from her.

Her expensive dress and hairdo, the busy life she led, made him realize she had fulfilled her dream of becoming an actress. If it was not in the way she had imagined, it was the feasible one.

Holly played Ellie Hughes, the neighbor, in a soap opera titled *Love of Life* and with a pride only slightly tinged with contempt, she told of how a woman had touched her and said, "You're Ellie Hughes, aren't you?" with such an exalted look in her eyes that Holly knew she could hardly wait to get home and tell—"Who do you think *I* saw today, right in the elevator at Altman's."

But as Holly began to explain that Charlie had made a reservation someplace, that Bob and Charlie were waiting at her apartment on 61st Street, Tom shook his head blearily and said he was in no mood for a restaurant, nor for sharing her. He wanted her to stay with him. With sodden helplessness he begged her not to leave him.

She couldn't, Holly said. Charlie would be along looking for her any moment, and she hurried on her way.

For the next few minutes Tom felt acutely depressed, first at having lost his round with Holly and then the more general, but no less intense sense of isolation that comes to those who are alone in New York's dusk.

Then, at eight-thirty, Tom had another unexpected caller. He opened his door to find Denise Razy, so chic and gay he had the feeling she had been sent in answer to his need. And in fact she had. Alan Campbell had suggested she look in on him.

"I saw your light," she said. "You're always here, poor dear. Don't you ever go out?"

"Only to see my analyst," Tom replied, and drawing her inside, insisted she stay and have a drink with him.

Denise walked around the room, at home, smiling at Tom, touching with her toe a piece of paper on the floor and, by her presence, cheering him.

In Alan's absence, Tom tried to amuse Denise in a style more Alan's than his own. He got off some viciousness about Joshua Logan, making her laugh at that and then, for the first time, talked frankly about himself. He explained his self-consciousness, the bumpkin role he accepted with her and Alan as the consequence of his blighted, middle-class origin. He spoke of his neighborhood in Minneapolis as a regular nursery of bigotry and hypocrisy. They invented it, he told her. He hated it back home. She could have no idea of the values and the stupidity of the people. He could never go back there to live again.

He was planning to write about it, however. He was getting around to a satirical novel with a Minneapolis background. But as he talked of this, his eyes strayed to the empty typewriter on the coffee table and his voice ran down like an old-fashioned Victrola in need of winding.

They made a supper from the refrigerator and began to talk of Alan. They were both loyal, praising his goodness and generosity, agreeing that the screen collaborations with Dorothy Parker had been mostly his work, yet getting around the edges of his dark side to the appalling drunkenness, his own dependence on pills, his homosexual friends, the certainty he had some homosexual affairs, his tender and yet vicious relationship with his divorced wife and, finally, his hopelessness with money. Alan, they agreed, would always be in debt.

Tom kept returning to Alan. While they talked about him, Tom appropriated Alan's vitality. When they stopped he had a feeling of encroaching darkness, of Denise drifting away. He could not dismiss that she was here because of Alan, only because he had asked her to look in.

It was late, Denise announced, and got up to go. Tom said he didn't want to be alone. Why didn't she spend the night? She could have Alan's room.

"I can't," Denise said. "I must go home and walk the dog." She kissed him lightly on the cheek and went to the door while he pleaded. "No, Tom. Really, I can't."

Next morning at ten-thirty, Tom's cleaning woman, Romona Cantero, let herself into the apartment with her key. When she found no one on the first floor, she climbed the stairs to Tom's bedroom on the second. It was empty. Then, entering the bathroom, she saw that the tub was three-quarters full of water and Tom's nude body was submerged in it.

When the police came they noted the many empty barbiturate bottles in the apartment. One, dated May 16, 1949, with eight capsules still remaining, stood on the sink's edge at the head of the tub. Beside it lay an open penknife engraved *Thomas Heggen*, with the word *Thanks* beneath it and the initials *J.L.* On the bottom of the tub, near Tom's chest, lay a Blue Star, double-edged razor blade.

The autopsy was performed the following day by Dr. Thomas Gonzales, Chief Medical Examiner, who found the cause of Tom's death to be "Submersion in fresh water in bathtub. Probable suicide. Contributory cause, overdose of barbiturates; 3.5 mgms. in 100 grams liver, 4.0 mgms. in 100 grams brain, 210 mgms. in ½ stomach content (seconal & amytal)."

XXV

Jim Billings came for Tom. At the city morgue he confirmed the body was that of his brother-in-law, Thomas Orlo Heggen, age twenty-nine years, four months, twenty-six days, and took it home to Minneapolis.

Mina Heggen wanted Wallace beside her and he came to Beard Avenue bringing the comfort of his manly calm. He was surprised to find that Tom's death had made for such a swarming of Heggens. There were relatives he had never seen. Nearly a hundred, family and quasi-family, gathered at the Werness Brothers funeral parlor. Many were red-headed and most, down from Minnesota and Wisconsin farms, still had the flavor of Norwegian in their speech.

Family filled one side of the chapel, leaving the other to Tom's friends. The Logans were still in Europe and no one had come from New York, but old comrades from the *Daily* were here. Bob Litman, John Cotton, Vic Cohn, Doug Whipple, George Pritchard and Bud Nye were pallbearers and they were stunned at the sight of Tom in his coffin. Mummified, cosmeticized, he might have been anyone, except Tom Heggen.

Behind were the reporters, the copywriters, all the wistful young people in town who hoped to write a book someday. Some had scarcely known him, and yet they claimed him as part of their

431

own dream and they were here to mourn that part of themselves they were burying today.

The family pastor, Dr. E. S. Hjortland of Central Lutheran Church, had not met him but his records told that Tom had been confirmed and he chose that as preface for his eulogy. Only last night he had introduced himself to *Mister Roberts*, but he did not boggle at a judgment. The novel, he told Tom's mourners, was marred by bawdiness. However, he saw indications in the young author's work that, had he lived, he would have written something worthwhile.

This brought mutterings and groans from the friends' side and word was whispered from one to another that the real wake would begin as soon as this fake one was over.

It took place at the Club Bar and it was an appropriately Tom kind of memorial service. It was drunken and sometimes boisterous with outbursts of laughter, but it was also unbearably sad.

Epilogue

Tom Heggen and Ross Lockridge were individual writers with special conflicts that brought them to the end of their lives. If it is unwise to generalize from these particulars, certain things can be understood from them.

Success itself, even when we know it to be fantasy, holds out such promise to us all—fame, money, power and love. They are reasonable promises to the soundest minds, and the compulsion to succeed can become an obsession over which no one has control.

Yet in fulfillment, success can act on a man like a hallucinogen, parting him from reality. I think of Ross at Manistee, pounding out those howling, outraged letters to Boston. He could not accept that his publishers had any business but *Raintree County*, nor that their enthusiasm for it inevitably fell short of his own.

But far more corrosive than the runaway high is the downside that follows it, releasing one by one the destructive forces a man carries at his.chest—envy, guilt, self-doubt. In Tom's compromise at South Brookfield, agreeing to the collaboration in exchange for an assurance of triumph, he became dependent on Joshua Logan. What followed was his desperate attempt to repossess his talent in the Flying Tigers play, and his final admission that he no longer believed he had written *Mr. Roberts*, that it had been "spirit writing."

In the midst of these private certainties of his lost gift, he had to confront his public image, the Tom Heggen praised for his fresh genius and drowning in the money that accrued to it. Ross's self-constructed "hell" was of a different kind and I wonder whether, if Tom and Ross had met, one would have recognized his own demons in the other.

Some of the questions about them still haunt me. But if the search for answers has yielded no specific conclusions, I have found some compensating rewards: an insight into the individual, psychological structures of the two men, the influences of family and childhood converging and being exposed in a tremendous public success that in the end claimed both Ross and Tom as a sacrifice, and finally, an understanding of human experience and the fellowship which that offers.

Afterword to the Da Capo Edition

A quarter century has passed since I wrote *Ross & Tom*, but the story still seems the essence of ambition's tragedy. Ross and Tom were such ordinary, American guys, but they were burdened with a credulity about their talent and a lamentable lack of grit. It was these qualities that combined to bring about their suicides.

In the half century since their deaths fame has become one of our liveliest growth industries, and nowhere more dramatically than in the world of books. From my perspective as an editor, writer, and teacher, what has changed in the writing/publishing world is the grace and good nature of it. What was once a calling, a virtuous occupation in which one renounced material riches, has, it seems, become as competitive as the auto business. The bookish community, readers not the least, is ever more in thrall of the powerful forces that create public attention.

Vernice Lockbridge's charge that the publisher's promotion of *Raintree County* brought about her husband's death seemed altogether wacky at the time, and yet Ross and Tom's experience, that of fledgling writers emerging under the light of the media, can be seen as a prototypical crisis of celebrity. The publicity surrounding a book's publication tends to inflate the author's balloon of belief in his own genius—and then leave it to collapse. For a tender ego, the effect is devastating.

435

In 1906, William James identified "the bitch goddess, SUCCESS," and blamed her for "our national disease." Her charms are no less enticing today. Pursuit of famousness is no longer shameful, but taken for granted.

The passage of the years has brought me a further insight to Ross and Tom's foreshortened careers. Living out one's destiny is likely to be downhill, painful, humiliating, but it's the courageous way. How else does one find out?

On my bedroom wall hangs the Japanese artist Yoshitoshi's wood-block print of Chikako, daughter of a nineteenth century ship-builder, as she leaps to her death in the snow-shrouded Asano River. Anxious-faced, hands together prayerfully, legs flailing, bright kimono flying, she soars to her end as gracefully as the two white cranes escaping her intrusion of their airspace.

Chikako's celebrated suicide was a sacrifice intended to free her once-wealthy and honored father from a debtor's jail. To us at least, it is a bewildering demonstration of filial loyalty.

The explicit, common thread is liberation from a human situation that seemed unendurable. In Chikako's case, it was a father's dishonor; in Ross and Tom's, it was a muse's estrangement. But whatever grace they found in this voluntary exit, for us it is elusive, as phantasmal as the grounds of their despair.

J. L.
April 2000

Index

437

About the Author

John Leggett was born in New York City in 1917 and is a graduate of Andover and Yale University. During World War II he was a naval officer and served in the Pacific Fleet.

Mr. Leggett was an editor at Houghton Mifflin for six years before his first novel, *Wilder Stone*, was published in 1960. In the same year the author became a senior editor at Harper's Publishers, which also published his second novel, *The Gloucester Branch*, in 1964. In the fall of 1967 Mr. Leggett left publishing to devote full time to writing and his third novel, *Who Took the Gold Away*, was published in 1969. His short stories and articles have appeared in *Esquire, The New Republic, The New York Times, Ladies' Home Journal, Mademoiselle* and *Harper's*. He has been a Regents' Lecturer at the University of California, Irvine. Mr. Leggett is now the head of the Writers' Workshop at the University of Iowa. When not residing in Iowa he lives in Manchester, Massachusetts. Mr. Leggett is at work on a new novel.